THE RULE OF LAW AFTER COMMUNISM

The Rule of Law after Communism

Problems and Prospects in East-Central Europe

Edited by
MARTIN KRYGIER
Professor of Law, University of New South Wales

ADAM CZARNOTA
Senior Lecturer in Law, Macquarie University

Routledge
Taylor & Francis Group

LONDON AND NEW YORK

First published 1999 by Ashgate Publishing

2 Park Square, Milton Park, Abingdon, Oxon OX14 4RN
711 Third Avenue, New York, NY 10017, USA

Routledge is an imprint of the Taylor & Francis Group, an informa business

Copyright © 1999 Martin Krygier and Adam Czarnota

British Library Cataloguing in Publication Data
The rule of law after communism : problems and prospects in
    east-central Europe. - (Socio-legal studies)
    1. Rule of law - Europe, Eastern 2. Post-communism - Europe,
    Eastern 3. Political questions and judicial power - Europe,
    Eastern 4. Europe, Eastern - Politics and government - 1989-
    I. Krygier, Martin II. Czarnota, Adam W.
    340.1'1

Library of Congress Cataloging-in-Publication Data
The rule of law after communism : problems and prospects in east
    -central Europe / edited by Martin Krygier and Adam Czarnota.
        p. cm.

    1. Rule of law--Europe, Eastern. I. Krygier, Martin.
II. Czarnota, Adam W.
KJC4426.R85 1998
340'.11--dc21   98-42336
                                                    CIP

Transfered to Digital Printing in 2013

ISBN 978-1-84014-005-7 (hbk)
ISBN 978-1-138-25468-8 (pbk)

Contents

List of Contributors

Adam Czarnota is Senior Lecturer in Law, Macquarie University, Australia.

Dencho Georgiev is Senior Research Fellow, Institute of Legal Studies of the Bulgarian Academy of Sciences, Associate Professor at the University of National and World Economy, Sofia, and Representative of the Republic of Bulgaria to the World Trade Organization.

Piotr Hofmański is a judge of the Polish Supreme Court, Criminal Law Division, and Professor of Criminal Law, University of Białystok, Poland.

Andrzej Kaniowski is Professor in the Department of Philosophy, University of Łódz, Poland.

Susanne Karstedt is a researcher in sociology, University of Bielefeld, Germany.

Martin Krygier is Professor of Law, University of New South Wales, Australia.

Maria Łoś is Professor of Criminology, University of Ottawa, Canada.

Lech Morawski is Professor of Legal Theory, Nicholas Copernicus University, Toruń, Poland.

Antal Örkény is Professor of Sociology, Eötvös Lórand University, Hungary.

Péter Paczolay is Chief Counsellor in the Hungarian Constitutional Court and Head of the Department of Political Science, Faculty of Law, József Attila University, Szeged, Hungary.

Wojciech Sadurski is Professor of Jurisprudence, University of Sydney, Australia.

Kim Lane Scheppele is Professor of Law, Political Science and Sociology, University of Pennsylvania, U.S.A.

Philip Selznick is Emeritus Professor of Sociology and of Law, and founder of the Jurisprudence and Social Policy Program, University of California, Berkeley, U.S.A.

Grażyna Skąpska is Professor of Sociology, and Associate Director of the Institute of Sociology, Jagiellonian University, Cracow, Poland. She is also an associate of the International Centre for the Development of Democracy, Cracow.

Vilmos Sós is Professor of Philosophy, Hungarian Academy of Sciences.

Jiřina Šiklová is Professor of Social Work, Charles University, Czech Republic.

Andrzej Zybertowicz is Associate Professor and Director of the Institute of Sociology, Nicholas Copernicus University, Toruń, Poland.

The Rule of Law after Communism: An Introduction

MARTIN KRYGIER and ADAM CZARNOTA

It has often been remarked that law counted for little in communist states. At first sight this observation might appear puzzling. After all these were not legal deserts. They were abundantly supplied with laws, lawyers, courts, judges, prosecutors, prisons, and police. Lots of police. Nor were these simply hollow façades. Many of the laws were about the sorts of things one would anywhere expect to have laws about, and they were applied. Some people went to gaol on the basis of convictions in courts for offences against the law; others were acquitted. People sued and were sued. And if not everything happened in accordance with the written law, where is it otherwise?

Still, some things were indeed special about law under communism. In the early phases, typically called Stalinist, much political rule was of the sort prescribed and accurately characterized by Lenin - "rule that is unrestricted by any laws" (Lenin, 1951: 41). Even after regimes were stabilized, extra-legal political rule was pervasive and insidious. For not only were communist states despotic - hardly a novelty in human affairs - but they were despotisms of distinctive character. Central to that distinctiveness was the overwhelming presence and significance of the Communist Party and apparatus in virtually every sphere of life. Above the law, in fact and often explicitly encoded in the law itself, the Party ruled. Party decrees, secret instructions, "telephone law", all represented ways in which the Communist Party, though it might happily *use* law was ultimately not subordinate to it. And the Party was everywhere. These really were societies in which, to an extent rarely matched in human history, the personal (and everything else) was potentially political.

This did not mean that whatever the Party wanted it got. On the contrary - as the subsequent collapse of communism, and the disarray it left, revealed

1

- a great deal that happened in communist states was outside the control and against the wishes of Party leaders. It was also often outside the law. For this represented a deeper truth than any caricature of an omnipotent Party can. The Party sought to rule *through* law, among other devices. And many people conceded as little legitimacy to law as they did to those other devices. Among all the sources of constraint and possibility available in everyday social life, law in communist polities typically had far less normative significance than many other things, and than in many other polities. As an ingredient in or restraint upon what people did and thought they should do, and on what they thought others could and would do, it was not prominent or salient. In the Bulgarian simile, it was like a door in the middle of an open field. Of course, you could go through the door, but why bother? One consequence was that in communist societies, the balance between, on the one hand law, and on the other "access", connections, influence, and fellowships of "dirty togetherness" (Podgórecki, 1994: 51, 115, 131-32) heavily favoured the latter. Of course, this can be said of many other regimes, and these differences between the social significance of law in different places might often be ones of degree rather than of kind. But of communist regimes it could be said systematically, and such differences of degree were radical.

Communism is now finished, institutionally throughout the former Soviet Union and its empire and ideologically virtually everywhere. Though these are accomplished facts they are not simple ones, and their residues and implications are hard to discern and to estimate. Even more difficult to estimate is the character of what will replace the former system. That is generally true, and it is particularly true with relation to law.

Central among the slogans of opponents of that system were "the rule of law", "legality", "the subordination of politics to law". Among the first wave of post-communist constitutional amendments throughout the region was the declaration that the state was "law-governed". But, as has now become plain, the transition from slogans to successes is slow, uneven and fundamentally uncertain. The rule of law is a complex achievement. Its character is contested, its necessary conditions difficult to spell out, sufficient ones even more so. Even those elements we understand and agree upon are difficult deliberately to implement, partly because they are not simply matters of legal-institutional "hardware" but of legal-and-broader cultural "software" as well. They involve social expectations, incentives, and opportunities. They require infrastructure, money, capacity of legal enforcement, but they involve will as well.

Laws can fail to curb power for many reasons. They might not be intended to do so; they might not have the support of institutions able to do so; such institutions as exist might have no money, power, political support; their incumbents might lack the will to enforce them - particularly against strong opposition. Moreover for the rule of law to be instantiated in everyday life, it is not just officials that matter. Conviction in the legitimacy, clout and relevance of the law to life must be widespread. That cannot simply be decreed. And even if it could be, we would be torn between different things to decree. For if it is generally true that not everything one wants is compatible with everything else one wants, this is particularly evident at times of rapid social, economic, political and overall systemic transformation.

All the more so when the transformations take as their starting point what remains of the uniquely state-centric social, political and economic order that was communism. For one central paradox of post-communist transformations is that, for the time being at least, the state is necessarily a major actor in implementing changes - both in its own nature, character and province and also in society at large. For the purposes of freeing space for markets and the rule of law, for example, it is called upon to divest itself of its erstwhile functions, and many of its functionaries. At the same time it is constantly called upon to initiate and implement changes that no other actor is in a position to, and ones which go well beyond, and often are in tension with, many classical conceptions of the rule of law. How to ensure that the state is as strong and effective as it must be to do what it must do, while inducing it to be as restrained as it must be so as not to do what it must not?

In the post-communist region, denunciations are common of *instrumental* uses of law, while demands are equally common that the state transform existing reality, most commonly by laws specially designed for the purpose. Demands occur for strict allegiance to positive law, in states where there are also strong demands for settling scores with the past. Many of these scores involve real or alleged wrongs which are condemned today, and rightly so, but which often had legal authorization or broke no existing positive laws when committed. Among the potential casualties of applying law to them today are what are often said to be central elements of the rule of law: that the law not be retroactive, that there be no punishment without a legally defined crime, no crime without a pre-existing law. Many people wish for a clear, stable and reliable legal framework, at the same time as many (not always different) people want the state to change many and complex sets of legal and institutional arrangements. And so it goes, on and on.

The variety, difficulty and inconsistency of many of these pressures means that, just as war cannot be left to generals, so, too, the rule of law cannot be left to lawyers. Too many spheres of life, too many values, too many hopes and fears, are implicated. The rule of law is not just a legal problem, maybe not even primarily a legal problem. To understand its nature, conditions, complexities, consequences, one needs to range far. And so this book has tried to do.

The book makes no claim to comprehensiveness or even to coherence of approach. That is not due to oversight or lack of stamina, but to conviction that today is not the time nor the post-communist world the place for such ambitions. Instead the book includes a variety of approaches, questions and answers, all of which focus on law and the rule of law but which touch on and draw upon a variety of other disciplines, considerations, and problems as well.

The book begins with general considerations and moves its focus inward to consider more particular problems. Part I involves exploration of the concept of the rule of law itself; Part II considers its most explicitly developed application: constitutionalism. Part III looks into some of the vast range of moral dilemmas that are opened up when one grapples to adapt law to confront an often distasteful past - not all traces of which *have* passed. Part IV deals with the intriguing and distinctive problems, perhaps unprecedented though not unparalleled, of crime in post-communist societies. Part V deals with some international implications and ambitions stimulated by the collapse of communism and its aftermath.

The over-arching ideal that governs these discussions is the rule of law, and the first thing to appreciate about this ideal is its complexity. Too often, discussion of the rule of law takes the form of simple recipes for institutions: punish only prospectively, not retrospectively, on the basis of clear, public, stable rules, interpreted by an independent judiciary, enforced by non-corrupt bureaucrats and police. And so on. But the rule of law is not simple and it is not a recipe. It is a cluster of values which have to do with the functions of law and the purposes of good laws. How they may best be made good, through what institutions, with what consequences, at what cost, are all variable matters.

The values at the heart of the ideal of the rule of law are teased out in Philip Selznick's subtle and nuanced introduction to the idea. The rule of law represents, as Selznick puts it, a "practical ideal" of great importance, but one which is unevenly and always incompletely attained, whose specific content is contested and whose institutional manifestations vary considerably.

A key distinction on which Selznick insists is that between what he calls negative and affirmative conceptions of the rule of law. This parallels his later distinction between social and political *baselines* which must be secured, and conditions for *flourishing*, for which we might then aim. The negative conception of the rule of law focusses upon the minimum conditions necessary for law to restrict arbitrariness in the exercise of power. It is primarily conceived as a curb on power, a shackle on the state. We have other values, of course, but they are different from the rule of law. Broader versions of this negative conception stress that, as a curb on power, it is a restraint on *everyone's* potential to act arbitrarily, not just on the state's, and stress also the benefits of such restraints for all citizens, who can gain - through knowledge of what is legally permitted and prohibited - knowledge of what others are likely to do, even though they are otherwise unknown others. But narrow or broad, the negative conception begins and ends with restraint.

Selznick has great respect for this negative conception, as he does for the baseline security that it aims to secure. No "higher" values should be allowed to serve as grounds for denigrating the often painfully sought and only sometimes won virtues of the rule of law, thus negatively conceived. However, Selznick also insists that while the negative conception is crucial, it does not exhaust what is of value in the rule of law ideal, for that extends to "values that can be *realized,* not merely protected, within a legal process. These include respect for the dignity, integrity, and moral equality of persons and groups. Thus understood, the rule of law enlarges horizons even as it conveys a message of restraint".

There is a tendency among devotees of the rule of law, particularly and understandably in countries where it has so long been ignored and abused, to favour the negative conception and be suspicious of any larger ambitions for law. They have experienced such ambitions "on their skins", in the Polish phrase, and they are allergic to them. In particular they are suspicious of what is often called "instrumentalism" in the law, and they take it to be subversive of the rule of law. Selznick's sensitive demonstration that one can value legal protection while also valuing substantive improvement through the law, and that these are both ambitions compatible with the rule of law, is one of crucial importance in post-communist states, where these are often presented as zero-sum choices. Not every claim to what he calls "a higher form of instrumentalism ... fidelity to legitimate purposes" need be rejected as a rejection of the rule of law. Some such claims might indeed further it.

Lech Morawski's chapter, focussing on some of the jurisprudential assumptions of post-communist polities, complements Selznick's neatly.

Like Selznick, Morawski stresses without embarrassment that the concept of the rule of law is inherently value-laden. It is characteristic of liberal democratic societies. Like Selznick, too, Morawski discerns quite different "conceptions" of this concept, to borrow the distinction made originally by John Rawls (Rawls, 1972: 5). Selznick observes that what he calls the negative conception of the rule of law is closely connected to the "model of rules" of legal positivism, where law *stricto sensu* is conceived of as limited to authoritatively posited rules of a legally autonomous system of rules. The affirmative conception, on the other hand, corresponds to an alternative conception "which subordinates rules to principles and purposes, that is, to the reasons that justify the rules". Morawski argues that the positivist conception reigns in post-Communist Poland, and he argues against it.

There is an important difference of nuance and emphasis between the two chapters, however, which reflects the differences in the societies and legal orders with which they are primarily concerned. Though Selznick writes about the rule of law generally, he does so from within a country with a strong and strongly institutionalized legal order and tradition; Morawski does not. Selznick seeks to show how such an established and secure order can be called upon to excel, to thrive, how it can legitimately be *infused* with good. Morawski seeks to show how a weak legal order with a sorry history can legitimately be *purged* of evil. Both consider a positivistically conceived rule of law inadequate to the tasks they consider important, and both argue that law can properly incorporate considerations of value. Selznick wishes to institutionalize the doing of good. Morawski does, too, of course, and his discussion of the *inefficacy* of positivist rule of law in modern interventionist polities points in a comparable direction to Selznick's. But Morawski has a more basic concern - how not to perpetuate evil - and debates about that issue, and the many circumstances in which it is a live one, resonate strongly throughout this book and throughout the post-communist region.

Selznick's chapter makes clear that one needs to know much more than legal dogmatics to understand the place of law in any society. And so too the rule of law in a civil society. The rule of law *contributes* to a particular sort of society and it *depends* upon "a culture of lawfulness, that is, of routine respect, self-restraint, and deference". Moreover, this is a complicated business, for "[a]s a distinctive legal culture the rule of law must affect conduct and consciousness at many levels". What Selznick observes generally is illuminated in persuasive detail by Antal Örkény and Kim Scheppele. They add what might be called an ethnographic dimension to our understanding of the rule of law after communism and they make plain that we cannot understand the role(s) that law plays in a society if we ignore this dimension.

Örkény and Scheppele distinguish between three levels at which law operates and at which the rule of law might be found to be more or less salient: the constitutional level, the level of state-citizen relations and the third level of relations among citizens. Lawyers are most easily impressed by the first two levels, and Örkény and Scheppele show that at the first level the rule of law has remarkable bite in Hungary. The Constitutional Court has more prestige and its judgments more legitimacy than virtually any other institution, or than comparable institutions have in virtually any other country. At the level of state-citizen relationships, however, the picture is very different, and at the third level - which is of course where most lives are mostly lived - the law is a bit player, crowded out by informal but often deep relationships among friends and quasi-friends. To understand this particular configuration, one must go beyond legal dogmatics, or even legal sociology of a general sort, to an understanding of the particular nature and history of particular societies and types of societies. In Hungary, as in most post-communist societies, public institutions are rarely trusted. They are to be kept at bay. And without trustworthy impersonal institutions, strangers are kept at more than arm's length as well. But *friendship* is a multi-purpose institution, which does a lot of work - but only among friends. As Örkény and Scheppele explain, distinctive and enduring aspects of state-socialist regimes were the interlinked phenomona of an omnivorous and distrusted public power and an underdeveloped civil society. In their place:

> Well-developed friendship networks substituted for many relationships that might otherwise have been carried out at this level of civil society organizations. As a result, friendships under state socialism were not just mutual solidarity pacts providing emotional support; they were also economic agreements and elaborate exchange relationships. Friends could get you what you needed to get on the (all-pervasive) black or grey markets. Friends could find you (off the books) jobs. Friends could find you good doctors, or wonderful pálinka, or rare flats, or scarce periodicals. Friends provided advice, services, protection from an intrusive government. And besides, they were your friends.

Charming though these deep relationships might often be, they have their pathological sides too. One in particular is that the distance between insiders and outsiders is destructively great and often impassable. Law and strangers are on the outside, and outsiders stay outside. For routine and productive relationships to occur among strangers, public institutions must be able to undergird and secure such needs, and lubricate social relationships, in ways that people trust. That is a major job of the rule of law, and it is not an easy one to get done where it has not historically been done.

One question which flows from the sociological dimension introduced by Örkény and Scheppele, is whether the rule of law depends for its effectiveness more on sound institutions or on congenial social and cultural underpinnings. To the extent such underpinnings are thought to matter, a second practical question is what can one do if they are weak or hostile. Perhaps the rule of law just needs the right institutions. Perhaps, on the contrary, it cannot exist without a welcoming constitutionalist culture. Model constitutions and institutions are readily available, often free of charge. Cultures are harder to win, or to lose.

Martin Krygier distinguishes between two very different sorts of assumptions and biases which underlie much thought and writing about what is possible in the domain of institutional reform, and many other sorts of reform as well. The first is a bias common among optimistic reformers. Its natural object is institutions. The second is found among sadder, but they might say wiser, pessimists. Its orientation is cultural. So Krygier explores institutional optimism, on the one hand, and cultural pessimism on the other. Both are prevalent in the post-communist world, and in pure form they have directly contradictory implications. Few people avow either of them in pure form, but many approaches betray their often unconscious, subterranean, influence.

The first tendency focusses on institutional design. Typically it draws upon theoretical models or foreign comparisons. Often it ignores, or does not know what to make of, cultural particularity. The second emphasizes such particularity. In extreme forms it encourages scepticism about the potential for successful grafts of imported institutions, ideas, and values. Krygier seeks to establish the insights and limitations of both tendencies. He supports the view that institutional designs need to be culturally grounded, but rejects a variety of common forms of cultural pessimism. All of these, rather than encouraging sensible caution about problems that might be confronted and pitfalls to avoid, tend to rule out transformative possibilities in principle. Krygier finds no intellectual, and therefore no moral, ground for supporting such tendencies. He also seeks to convey some of the complexity of relationships between culture and agency in the processes of generating constitutionalism. He concludes, on a note of resolute - indeed heroic - indecisiveness, that while there is no overwhelming reason to believe that constitutionalism and the rule of law will be successfully established in post-communist Europe, there is equally no reason to believe that they will not.

The second Part of this book deals with a specific way in which the ideal of the rule of law is today approached, by way of constitutionalism. This is an ideal closely related to the rule of law, but more specific in focus. Its primary tools in the modern world are written constitutions, constitutional courts, and thereby explicit and enforceable limits on state power. People who value the rule of law often have constitutions in mind.

Whatever the possibilities that should and/or might occur in the field of constitutional design, much that *actually* happens will be shaped by what already has happened in the countries concerned. The powers of inertia, continuity, and tradition, are strong, whether or not we imagine them to be modifiable. They are generally so and they are too within political and legal institutions - even those which emerge from political revolutions. Péter Paczolay offers a useful and well-informed survey of what is old and what is new, what exists because someone wants it to and what exists because it already did, in the constitutional structures of "transitional" polities. He stresses the extent to which formal notions of legal continuity fail to encompass the reality of the revolutions which have taken place in the region, but equally he denies that any sense can be made of many abiding themes and institutional structures in the region if we imagine that everything has changed. His chapter is largely descriptive, but it has a clear normative bias: in favour of constitutionalism and the restraint of power by law and against any ventures, however substantively appealing, that might endanger "the delicate structure of a young democracy". The potential tension between his stress on formal legality and Selznick's and Morawski's receptiveness to substantive concerns is a microcosm of the tension which attends all efforts to establish the rule of law in the midst of so many competing values and priorities that contend in the post-communist world.

Such tensions pervade constitutions and their interpretation too. In his combination of philosophical reflections on the point of constitutionalism, and his close analysis of several important and contentious cases, Vilmos Sós shows the manifold ways in which constitutional law and ordinary politics are interwoven in Hungary's recent constitutional development. On the one hand, the reigning post-communist political paradigm was that of constitutionalism: "the very conviction of a political community that modern democracies require a constitutional system: constitutionalism and democracy are interrelated, constitutionalism best serves the needs of the operation of a democratic society". On the other hand, like all post-communist constitutions, the Hungarian constitution of which Sós writes, is in no way aloof, above, or the "unmoved mover" of the political system; it is involved in daily politics in many and close ways. Political issues are often framed as constitutional ones, and the Hungarian Constitutional Court is required to judge upon them, even though their strictly *constitutional* significance is dubious. And the Court has been adventurous too: purporting to decipher the "invisible constitution" of Hungary, when the "visible" one is judged silent or inadequate. Those who support the values which emerge as this constitution is rendered visible, generally support the court; those who do not, do not. What is at risk, however, according to Sós, is the *constitutionality* of its pronouncements, the notion that the constitution is the frame, the ring, within which everyday political struggles occur, not merely another element in those struggles. Sós clearly respects the Court and many of its judgments. He does remind us, however, that "this body, however respectable, is not the embodiment of national sovereignty".

The court is one institution, parliament another. And though unlike the former the latter is elected, neither is a simple microcosm of "the people". This is true in every polity, but it is dramatically so in post-communist societies, where the gulf between ordinary lifeworlds and elite institutions is particularly large. Indeed, though she offers no populist panacea, Grażyna Skąpska thinks that in post-communist arrangements - particularly in Poland but elsewhere in the region as well - ordinary people have had so marginal a role that this threatens the "jurisgenerative" (law-engendering) force of the liberating events of 1989. And this is a key issue, since, as she emphasizes and as this book demonstrates in a variety of ways and contexts, "to debate the prospects of liberal constitutionalism in East Central Europe, one must reach 'beyond the heads of lawyers' into the political process on the one side, and life-worlds of society on the other".

There are many ways of seeking to institutionalize constitutionalism. The typical politician's and lawyer's way is to start at the top, to consult experts, draft documents, broker elite agreements. Skąpska questions the value of such approaches, at least on their own and at least as they have come to pass in the context of post-communism. The *constitutional moment* of liberal enthusiasm has passed and has lost its legitimizing and compromise-inducing potential in Poland and elsewhere, and "[w]hat we are observing is the loss of that special time which results in a loss of authority by the political elites. This is accompanied by exhaustion of the unifying, anti-communist principle which dominated social minds before the collapse of the old regime".

In Poland, the end of communism was negotiated, in the famous "round table talks", between governing and opposition elites. Subsequent discussions, which ultimately if circuitously led to the present constitution, were dominated by parliamentary representatives - excluding the significant proportion of right wing parties which had failed to enter parliament in 1993 - and their partisan considerations. Skąpska is sceptical of "the chances that the formally binding document will be transformed into a 'social constitution', a result of society's judgment and self-reflection." She cautiously introduces the notion of "grass roots constitutionalism": "a process of slow formation of constitutional principles 'from below', in the everyday experience of citizens participating in local governments, non-governmental organizations, associations, and ethics commissions whose members participate in the decision-making processes or in conflict resolution, and construct their by-laws". She is well aware of the difficulties involved in such a process, particularly in the light of the "anti-legalistic" character of post-communist social culture, and she offers no happy endings. But then, she would insist, neither do the processes, which have dominated hitherto, of ignoring popular involvement in elite processes.

The processes that Skąpska critically discusses culminated in the April 1997 Polish Constitution. Wojciech Sadurski focusses on a central aspect of that constitution, specifically on its protection of rights and freedoms. He discerns in this result of parliamentary debates and compromises an uneasy mix of divergent, and often contradictory, influences and elements. In particular he stresses the role of three intellectual traditions which often point in different directions: socialist, Christian/nationalist, and liberal. His own view, at least in relation to a *constitution*, is liberal, that is to say, he views the specific function of constitutions - as distinct from statutes and other sorts of laws - as being "to define and restrict, in a fashion that cannot be easily changed, the scope and rationales for legislative and executive actions. Constitutional rights impose limits upon majoritarian decisions in the political process". From this point of view, the new Polish constitution, and the philosophical conceptions which inform it, leave a lot to be desired.

Sadurski commends the Constitution's list of rights for several virtues: its extensiveness, the robustness of the constitutional mechanisms for rights-protection, and the opportunities it provides in places for "liberty-enhancing, anti-restrictive interpretation(s)". Nevertheless he condemns the freedom it allows the legislature to restrict constitutional rights, the combination in the constitution of citizens' rights with their purported duties, and its conflation of "rights in a strong constitutional sense with the declarations of goals which impose no determinate limit on state power, and which cannot serve as tests of the constitutionality of state actions". His discussion goes to the heart of what constitutions are or should be for. It also raises the basic issue of whether provisions that might be harmless in some constitutions in some states might nevertheless carry dangers elsewhere. Thus in relation to the familiar debate over whether the combination of unenforceable guidelines with purportedly enforceable rights will devalue the latter, Sadurski concedes that it may not always do so. In particular, such provisions might well cohabit harmlessly "in systems where the values of constitutionalism, rule of law, and the protection of rights are securely established". The situation is different, however, "in a system where a nihilist tradition of treating a constitution as a purely decorative instrument is strongly embedded, and where the fundamental notions of constitutionalism and rule of law have a weak place in the collective consciousness". For better or worse, as we have seen, most post-communist legal orders are of this second sort.

And it is precisely such orders that most acutely raise the vexed and complex issues surrounding contemporary attempts to come to terms with an unsavoury national or at least political past. That is the concern of the third Part of this book. These issues surface in a variety of ways and speak to a range of concerns: those of justice, of social order, and of the publicly expressed narratives in which societies understand themselves, and citizens understand each other. The best known problems are those associated with vetting former operatives of communist states, and these issues are taken up in the chapters by Andrzej Kaniowski and Jiřina Šiklová. However, the past is present or made present in many other contexts as well.

An intriguing and little known such context is that dealt with in the chapter by Adam Czarnota and Piotr Hofmański. The focus of this chapter is a Polish statute of 1991, "on the invalidation of judgments against people repressed for activity in aid of the independent existence of the Polish State". The aim is clear and laudable, the victims of such judicial evils were many, and the unjustifiable suffering which they were forced to endure is undeniable. But when a court is charged with establishing whether applicants had been convicted *for activity in aid of Polish independence*, the sheer complexity and difficulty of its task is enormous. What was the applicant actually doing and why? How, fifty years later, can a court tell? When was a robbery or assault committed in aid of independence and when was it simply robbery or assault? When did a peasant who resisted forcible acquisition of his produce do so for Polish independence and when because he just did not want to part with his produce? When was a joke about Stalin or Bierut an element in the fight for Polish independence, and when was it just a joke? What are the limitations on our ability to make amends for yesterday's wrongs, and how much should these limitations affect our plans to do right today? What unintended consequences might flow from our endeavours and when do they nullify the good we do, or try to do? None of the answers to these questions is obvious and none is easily essayed without a detailed practical knowledge of the sorts of cases which come before the courts charged with decision in these matters, and the dilemmas these institutions are required to face. Hofmański's experience as a judge affords distinctive and invaluable insights into these questions, which inextricably and simultaneously raise issues both of the most general principle and the most highly particular practice. Readers are likely to disagree about whether law is "a good means for easing the wounds of the past", but it is not easy, in the light of the experience discussed in this chapter, to dismiss the issue.

Even less easy to dismiss, for more pervasive in public debate, are questions about what to do about the participation in public life of those suspected of being among the thousands of operatives, spies, informers, and other shady operators working - usually in secret - for the former communist state. Understandably this raises issues which are not merely pragmatic but engage the deepest passions of people who were victimized, excluded from positions, tortured or otherwise maimed by the previous regimes. Should those in some way connected with those regimes now be excluded from positions of responsibility? Should their earlier activities be brought to public attention? Should they be tried? If what they did then was legal though evil, should it now be the subject of investigation which, though well intended, might still stretch the rule of law? Here the considerations are complex and often painful, and the partisans of different positions are often not those one would have expected. Thus some of the bravest dissidents, such as Adam Michnik in Poland or Jiřina Šiklová in Czechoslovakia, object to "lustration" or screening of those alleged to have collaborated with the former regime (at times to the direct and painful cost of their present protectors), while others insist that their countries will suffer under a permanent moral stain unless something is done about the evildoers in their midst. In this book, too, some contributors, notably Kaniowski and Šiklová, oppose lustration, while others, including Łoś, Zybertowicz and Morawski, believe it is necessary.

Kaniowski seeks to expose the axiologies, the moral substrata, which underlie the competing positions of participants in the Polish debate over proposals for what he calls "moral lustration": the attempt to settle moral "accounts with the post-war Polish past" by revelation of the data contained in secret service archives. Similar axiological positions can be found throughout the post-communist world. Kaniowski believes that these substrata are far more significant in accounting for what people argue in this matter than the pragmatic or utilitarian terms in which arguments are often clothed. He also believes that Polish debate is caught between two starkly opposed ethical approaches. Supporters of lustration, he alleges, assume a far-reaching moral identity between the institutions which were responsible for evil deeds - particularly the secret services, the legal and political apparatus, and various professional groups dominated by the Party - and the individuals who were employed in these institutions or were members of these groups. On this reasoning, since the former are rightly to be condemned, so too their operatives equally, and therefore deserve condemnation. Lustration is for people of this view a "form of settling accounts with the previous system and its institutions through evaluation of the individuals".

Many opponents of lustration, Kaniowski argues, start from a similarly hostile evaluation of the institutions reviled by lustrators, but they refuse automatically to carry their judgment of these institutions through to a judgment of individuals who worked for them. Individuals should, they say, be judged on the basis of what they actually did and didn't do, taking account of the concrete circumstances in which they were and the options available to them, not on the basis of their closeness or distance from institutions which were devoted to evil ends. These anti-lustrators eschew dichotomous moral evaluations, emphasize complexity and differences of degree and have a "distaste for sharp and unambiguous line-drawing". Kaniowski is clearly on their side. His essay serves not only as a close delineation of the ethical foundations of two opposing positions in this passionate public debate, but a powerful argument for one of them.

Kaniowski's subtle and deep discussion ranges widely over the moral complexities of life in communist system and the complexity appropriate to judging the actions of those who lived in them. His support for those who "make the very *subjects* of moral actions the central point of moral evaluations, ranking the institutions and organizations as secondary", stems from his belief both that this is the ethically superior position to adopt and also that it is the only one consistent with respect for the rule of law. It is, he claims, the opponents of lustration who insist on "[a] clear commitment to the principle of legality and (b) the tendency to separate clearly 'legality' from 'morality'". This involves a determination to put limits on the scope of legal responsibility, to cover acts not attitudes, and only acts *of individuals, covered by law.* None of these limitations, Kaniowski argues, is respected by moral lustrators, and to that extent neither is the rule of law. Here one might compare Kaniowski's conception of the rule of law with the more morally-infused conception of Morawski. The differences between these views might remind outsiders viewing the debates occurring in post-communist Europe, that as important as the positions to which different protagonists arrive is the fact that strong arguments are available for many of them.

Jiřina Šiklová concludes this Part with a passionate, and also powerful, critique of the course of lustration in Czechoslovakia, now the Czech and Slovak Republics. Here too, there are no illusions about the evil of the communist system, against which Šiklová was an active dissident for over twenty years. But Šiklová is witheringly sceptical about the motives of lustrators; the perhaps unintended but often tragic effects of accusations of collaboration on those innocents whose names come to appear, for one reason or another, in secret police files; and the paradoxical but easily explained facts that many of the great sharks of the communist system swim freely in the lustrated post-communist Czech Republic and Slovakia, while minnows are gathered up and publicly humiliated in the indiscriminate fishing expeditions of the lustrators.

Of course, on these issues there is an enormous range of legitimate disagreement, as is evident in the next chapter, by Maria Łoś and Andrzej Zybertowicz. Their chapter, and the subsequent one in this fourth Part, by Susanne Karstedt, deal with the nature and explanation of crime under post-communism. Łoś and Zybertowicz focus specifically on "state crime" and attribute many of its most disturbing characteristics to the presence of legacies, and influential members, of the communist past in the post-communist present. On their view, post-communist state crime has unique aspects attributable to the lingering power and pervasive influence of people and practices who had gained strategic positions in the previous era. In particular they stress the importance of pre-collapse intelligence and counter-intelligence networks, which were usefully traded in or traded upon in the elite arrangements which paved the way for the peaceful demise of communist regimes and in the political and economic formations which have subsequently crystallized. Their point is both empirical and methodological, for they believe that the phenomena they stress are overlooked not only because they are hidden, but because many researchers fail to look for them. Indeed, according to Łoś and Zybertowicz, "all those who have tried to analyse the 'evolution' and eventual self-destruction of the communist system in straight, 'above-ground' terms of traditional sociology or economics miss a vital part of the reality concerned; an oversight that renders impossible a congruent and meaningful explanation of those developments". By contrast, Łoś and Zybertowicz bring forth a great deal of evidence to show the existence of arrangements which they consider fundamental though - indeed because - subterranean. As a result of such arrangements, they claim, "old networks, partly legitimated and shielded by the new establishment, have become a vital infrastructure for new forms of organized/state crime". These networks are those of the *nomenklatura* generally and of the secret services more specifically. They had enormous political resources under communism which, Łoś and Zybertowicz argue, they have managed to parlay and convert into economic and also politically strategic positions, after the systemic changes which purportedly overthrew them. Their "parachutes" were well prepared, and their safe landing was, the authors allege, not blocked. They entered the end of communism, as they exited it, "well prepared for the shift towards capitalism and determined to capitalize on their privileged position and connections. Moreover, they had been socialized to regard legal constraints as not applicable to themselves."

Apart from their challenging diagnosis of the sources of state crime, Łoś and Zybertowicz advocate a number of anti-"state crime" measures which they believe have been largely ignored, or underemphasized, in post-communist Poland. Many of them have to do with cancelling advantages of those who entered post-communism from elite positions in the old regime. More generally, they recommend these measures as "logical responses to the normative vacuum created by the collapse of the old order". On the existence of that vacuum, if not on everything else, Susanne Karstedt's chapter - dealing both with "crimes in the suites" and with "crimes in the streets" - is in accord with Łoś and Zybertowicz.

However, if Łoś and Zybertowicz stress the *exceptionality* of the transition from communism, owing to the specific nature of the preceding regime, Karstedt stresses parallels between this "great transformation" and that earlier one which ushered in industrial society, and which gave the title and theme to Karl Polanyi's great book (Polanyi, 1957). According to Karstedt, one specific aspect of that book, which Polanyi stressed but has been otherwise neglected, is that it was an account of the death of one mode of regulation and the far-from-instantaneous birth of a new mode. In that earlier transformation, "[t]his process of deregulation and re-regulation obviously was related to social disorganization and especially to deviant behaviour and crime. It induced a pauperization of the population ... and a wave of crime, in the streets as well as in the emerging markets of capital and commodities and in business administration". Karstedt's essay illuminates the many ways in which the present transformation echoes that past one. These include three types of regulatory crisis - of "inconsistency ... enforcement ... imbalance" - which were manifest on both occasions, and the "anomic" consequences - both in the "suites" and in the "streets" - of deregulation and re-regulation. Whether the parallels Karstedt demonstrates throw doubts on the significance of the exceptionality on which Łoś and Zybertowicz insist, or whether they simply speak at different, but not necessarily inconsistent, levels of abstraction, are matters of fruitful conjecture and debate.

The final Part and chapter of the book take the post-communist experience where it is rarely taken: into the domain of international law. Dencho Georgiev notes that, even before the changes of the 1980s and early 1990s, "[o]ne of the most important aspects of the idea of rule of law in Eastern Europe ... was that of its *external* or its *international* dimension. Society, it was felt, had to be based on the idea of law - not any law, but one conforming to certain principles, requirements and standards, which existed *outside* that particular society in the international sphere, in countries perceived as 'normal', as models of the *Rechtsstaat*". This was related to a wish not merely to be *like* "normal" countries, but to *join* the international community of such nations, nations which shared, among other things, the rule of law. One result of that sense that standards of democracy and rule of law were "external" to totalitarian societies but common to "normal" ones, Georgiev claims, was that "the most natural place to look for them was, of course, international law". In consequence, many post-communist legal reformers seek to give special emphasis to these standards in their domestic law.

And they do so, Georgiev argues, for a second reason. Subjects of communism were familiar with polities which routinely put political power above law. They wanted a different sort, one in which law could override power, one where there were, in one sense or another, "higher laws". Binding constitutions were an example of such laws. More tentatively, these ambitions were essayed in international law. Georgiev seeks to take these ideals, which sought inspiration from international to domestic law, and turn them around, to vindicate an international rule of law. He does so, conscious of the opposition by legal positivists, Marxist-Leninists and international realists to the notion that there can be anything realistic, worthwhile or attainable in the notion of an international rule of law. He, by contrast, in a sophisticated and subtle discussion, seeks to suggest that "it could paradoxically turn out that Eastern Europe has started its changes referring to 'international' models, only to become itself a model for international change", where in both cases the aspiration emerges for deliverance from a rule of power through increased reliance on the power of rules.

* * *

The discussions in this book cover a lot of ground. However, though they range widely, the chapters in this book neither exhaust the topics they explore, nor the topics that could be explored, in reflections on the rule of law after communism. But they do enough, we believe, to suggest the crucial, and inescapable, importance of such reflections. If all they did were to encourage more and better thinking on these matters, in and about the post-communist region and elsewhere, we would be well pleased. For the matters are precious. The Marxist historian, E.P. Thompson, once incurred the wrath of some erstwhile allies when he called the rule of law a "cultural achievement of universal significance" (Thompson, 1977: 265) and indeed he might have exaggerated a bit. But he did not exaggerate much, or in a bad cause.

Bibliography

Lenin, V.I. (1951), *Selected Works,* vol.2, Moscow, Foreign Languages Publishing House.

Podgórecki, A. (1994), *Polish Society*, Westport, Praeger, 1994.

Polanyi, K. (1957), *The Great Transformation. The Political and Economic Origins of our Time,* Boston, Beacon.

Rawls, J. (1972), *A Theory of Justice,* Oxford, Oxford University Press.

Thompson, E.P. (1977), *Whigs and Hunters,* Harmondsworth, Penguin.

Part I

The Rule of Law

.

1 Legal Cultures and the Rule of Law

PHILIP SELZNICK[1]

The rule of law is a quintessentially jurisprudential topic. It cannot be studied, however, without taking into account historical, cultural, and sociological contingencies. Especially important is the study of legal cultures, such as the common law tradition, the civil law tradition, and non-Western traditions. Furthermore, many jurisprudential debates, such as positivism versus natural law, are best understood as alternative visions of legal culture, that is, of appropriate sources of authority and appropriate styles of thought.

Nevertheless, despite attention to contingency and variation, we must remain sensitive to perennial issues of law and justice, such as the interplay of rule and principle, will and reason, form and substance. In examining the rule of law, there is no question of dismissing or ignoring the great questions that have preoccupied legal thought and practice.

In what follows I treat the rule of law as a practical ideal, that is, as one that takes account of enabling conditions, contingent circumstances, and necessary trades. We know, for example, that legal cases can never be *completely* alike because to some extent they must be forced into categories that make sense for purposes of legal judgment. Yet the standard is practical insofar as it can function effectively as a guide to decision and institutional design. Thus we begin with the understanding that the rule of law, like all practical ideals, is at best incompletely and variably effective.[2]

A Flexible Standard

Our conventional understanding of the rule of law is deceptively simple and straightforward. There should be, we say, a government of laws and

21

not of men. Of course this maxim is not meant to be taken literally, as if the passions and interests of human beings, their choices and strategies, could be eliminated from the legal process. Rather, the decisions made by legal actors - legislators, judges, and other officials - should be governed by certain ideals and standards. Two norms have been considered especially important. First, no official, however mighty, is above the law and beyond its reach. When President Harry Truman tried to avert a major strike in 1952 by seizing the steel industry, his attempt failed because the Supreme Court called his action unconstitutional. Second, no one should be punished, as Dicey put it, "except for a distinct breach of law established in the ordinary legal manner before the ordinary courts of the land" (Dicey, 1956: 188). More generally, he said, "the rule of law is contrasted with every system of government based on the exercise by persons in authority of wide, arbitrary, or discretionary powers of constraint". These are familiar principles, but their precise meaning remains controversial and is open to change.[3]

Most people would agree with Dicey that, wherever it is effective, the rule of law restrains arbitrary power, especially by limiting discretion in systematic ways. Hence the counterposition of "laws" and "men". But how limited must discretion be? by what means are those limits to be set? what constitutes arbitrariness, and how is it to be remedied? These are subjects we continue to analyse and dispute. How these and related issues are resolved, when theory meets practice, has much to do with the kind of law - the legal culture - that will emerge.

There is, of course, no single model. Within and among rule-of-law communities, there is much debate as to whether specific practices, rules, and institutions further the ideal, or undermine it. Although we may take certain baselines for granted, such as an independent judiciary and respect for precedent, these norms are subject to variation in how they are understood or implemented. Is judicial independence necessarily compromised by the election of judges? It is not easy to say which practices and institutions are *best*, from the standpoint of the rule of law.

Consider the idea of due process. Some general principles are fairly easy to identify. A person accused should be able to test the legitimacy of authority, present proofs and arguments, and be judged without prejudice or caprice. These premises may be widely shared, but they do not specify particular institutions or procedures. They do not necessarily require an adversary rather than an inquisitorial process, nor do they necessarily bar self-incrimination. The premise of truth-finding may imply a right to be heard in one's cause, but the nature of the hearing is not fixed. Trial by jury may or may not have a central place in the legal process, including criminal proceedings.

In part these are differences in judgment as to what the rule of law requires. More important for legal culture are variations that stem from distinctive histories. Within the rule-of-law world a pluralist sensibility prevails. There is no lively argument about the relative worth of the civil law and common law traditions. For the most part they are taken to be roughly equal alternatives, each successful and deficient in different ways. Similarly, within the common law world we recognize important differences in British, Canadian, and American jurisprudence. We do not suppose that the counter-majoritarian role of the US Supreme Court is seriously open to debate and revision, however difficult it may be to defend judicial review of legislation on democratic principles. Thus within the Western tradition there is room to accommodate different histories as well as different judgments.

We cannot understand the rule of law if we do not first distinguish "law" from "the rule of law". The law of a community includes a great variety of authoritative norms, including enactments, judgments, and precedents. To be recognized as law some threshold criterion must be met. There must be rules for determining which norms are authoritative. However the law thus recognized may be very rudimentary. It may allow for largely unhindered official discretion; and there may be, for most people, very limited opportunity to assert claims of right or to test and criticize authority. The rule of law calls for a higher standard. It says legal institutions should do more than meet the threshold of legitimacy; they should have a certain *competence*, at least that of effectively restraining arbitrary discretion and, as a condition of lawful punishment, providing notice of what conduct is unlawful and will be punished.

Hence we must confront the ambiguities of both "rule" and "law". The rule of law must be in some sense a regime of rules, but not any sort of rule will do. The rules must have a certain character if rule-of-law standards are to be met. For example, they should not be so vague as to make it difficult to know the precise obligations of officials and citizens. Therefore we shrink from translating the expression "rule of law" into German as "Herrschaft des Gesetzes". "Herrschaft des Rechts" is more accurate because that phrase preserves the connection, however problematic, between positive law and underlying principles of justice and morality.

If we properly insist on a *distinction* between "law" and "the rule of law", it does not follow that they have no *connection*, whether as concepts or states of affairs. On the contrary, the ideal takes its departure from what is latent in legal experience. As Lon Fuller and others have argued, it is difficult to govern peacefully and effectively, with secure authority, if laws are ad hoc, unstable, secret, obscure, impossible to perform, or experienced as radically unfair (Fuller, 1969: ch.2). These conditions produce demands - from above as well as from below - for laws that resonate with the rule of law. Therefore the ideal is not alien to the social reality of law, if we include in that reality, as we must, the energies and expectations it generates. Of course, it may require considerable effort and struggle to turn those expectations into secure and workable institutions. Even a Whig history is a history of progress mediated by conflict.

When we discuss "legalization", as a social phenomenon, we may or may not be talking about the rule of law. Legalization may be understood, with negative connotations, as a process which extends the reach of legal authority by multiplying regulations and by intruding into hitherto autonomous, self-regulating spheres of life. More positively, "legalization" may refer to the extension of rule-of-law ideals and norms to new arenas, such as managerial authority in industry. We then look to the distinctive contributions law can make to fairness, legitimacy, and the vindication of rights. This process may well have costs and limits, but they are the special costs of instituting a *kind* of authority and *kinds of law*.

Negative and Affirmative Conceptions

Once we reach this threshold understanding - that the rule of law means "law plus standards" - we can discern two very different perspectives. The first is a negative, limited, low-risk understanding of the rule of law; the other offers a more affirmative, more expansive, more high-risk conception of what the ideal contains. Narrowly conceived, the rule of law is a set of negative safeguards against the abuse of power. Officials are to be chained down by constitutional constraints, procedural rules, including rules of evidence, and institutional arrangements, such as a hierarchy of courts. The negative conception has great appeal. It concentrates attention on the most serious and manifest wrongs officials can do, such as gaoling critics or seizing their property. Furthermore, such a conception is clearly supported by specific historical achievements and widely recognized principles of justice. For these and other reasons there is a strong sociological basis for accepting the idea, expressed by Joseph Raz, that "the rule of law is essentially a negative value...merely designed to minimize the harms to freedom and dignity which the law may cause in its pursuit of its goals however laudable these may be" (Raz, 1979: 228).

This negative, restraint-centred conception captures the spirit of what we may call the "modern" or "classical" conception of the rule of law. This is the legal culture of "autonomous law", distinguished from "repressive law" and "responsive law" (see Nonet and Selznick, 1978). In autonomous law legitimacy is the lodestar of the legal order; protecting legitimacy is the central concern of legal institutions, practices, and beliefs. Having won great authority to hold rulers accountable, the judges (and the legal profession) must do all they can to sustain respect and encourage obedience. Driven by those concerns, the judges limit their own authority to deviate from rules and precedents; and the legal system treasures its autonomy. Autonomous law demands the separation of law and politics; insists on a corollary distinction between lawmaking and adjudication; and accepts the principle that the rule of law is a "law of rules" - rules that sharply limit judicial discretion.

As this legal culture developed it transcended national differences, such as the important contrast between parliamentary sovereignty in Britain and the American constitutional experience, which limits the power of the national and state legislatures. But these and many other variations did not change the basic character of the *Rechtsstaat* or rule-of-law state. Despite significant divergences in pattern and in origin, there emerged what could properly be called a Western legal tradition.

The rule of law is often identified with that legal culture, and especially with the institutions of autonomous law. Yet that is by no means a unanimous view. Among contemporary students of jurisprudence, I discern a reluctance to give up the larger promise of the rule of law (see Shapiro, 1994). That promise can be summed up in some general formula, such as the one I have preferred - the progressive reduction of arbitrariness in positive law and its administration - or, for example, Ronald Dworkin's more focussed (and perhaps more controversial) notion that "the rule of law...is the ideal of rule by an accurate public conception of individual rights" (Dworkin, 1985: 11f).

This alternative vision is plausible because we cannot really separate the negative and positive aspects of the rule of law. Indeed it would be highly unsociological to try to do so, for we would then miss the moral and institutional dynamics which create demands for justice, and which induce rulers to accept accountability. Even a negative conception of what the rule of law entails must be able to distinguish genuine respect for a legal process, even one that is fairly rudimentary, from cynical manipulation of it. If abuse of power is the evil to be remedied, we must have some idea of what abuse means and how it is experienced, and this raises issues of fairness and equality. If the rule of law vindicates rights, we must know what rights are appropriate for the context at hand, how they are determined, and how difficult or easy it is to invoke them. If accountability is the animating principle, then a rule-of-law culture gains texture and depth as the rational foundations of accountability are strengthened, as norms of accountability are extended, and as opportunities are enlarged for appeal from practice to rule and from rule to principle. For these reasons, we should not reduce the rule of law to its most rudimentary forms.[4]

In contemporary discussions of the rule of law we find much that goes beyond the negative virtue of restraining official misconduct. The rule of law, it is said, and not only very recently, is a regime that protects the weak against the strong, provides for the peaceful settlement of disputes, facilitates economic transactions, and creates a framework within which private enterprise can go forward. This thicker, more positive vision speaks to more than abuse of power. It responds to values that can be *realized*, not merely protected, within a legal process. These include respect for the dignity, integrity, and moral equality of persons and groups. Thus understood, the rule of law enlarges horizons even as it conveys a message of restraint.

The negative conception is closely connected to what Dworkin called the "model of rules" (Dworkin, 1978: ch. 2). In the model of rules the discretion of officials, especially judges, is limited by norms of clear content and definite scope rather than by more general, more indeterminate standards or principles. This commitment to rule-centred decision became, in the heyday of autonomous law, a centrepiece of legal culture. The result, as in any cultural configuration, was a set of characteristic attitudes and practices, such as where one should look for legal change and what opportunities there should be for access to justice. Thus understood, a rule-centred legal culture is something more than "a government of laws rather than men". It gives that notion a special spin and a distinctive content. The paradigm of law becomes a definite rule, and applying rules is, ideally, something like a mechanical process.

The alternative is a legal culture which subordinates rules to principles and purposes, that is, to the reasons that justify the rules. This is not a rejection of rules. Rules can still have, and must have, an indispensable role in routine decision-making. Nevertheless, a transition away from rule-*centredness* occurs when principles move from weak to strong authority, from a dimly perceived background to a more prominent foreground of the legal culture.

In such a culture rules become derivative, contingent, and problematic. Principles can be appealed to as legitimate bases for criticizing rules, and for changing them. Furthermore, when principles have strong legal authority, decision-makers can take better account of particularity and concreteness. When we know the principles or policies a rule is meant to serve - when we know the reason behind the rule - we can make rational adjustments and exceptions. That is, we can devise rules that are more finely tuned, more closely adapted to specific problems or situations. Principles are more abstract, to be sure, but abstraction has the paradoxical effect of easing the transition from form to substance, and therefore from law to justice.

On this view, a principle-centred legal culture is not alien to the rule of law. Rather, it is an alternative vision of that ideal. It is captured by the idea that legal actors should attend to the "spirit" as well as to the "letter" of the law. And the spirit of law is found in the substantive as well as procedural values that underlie and animate it. The expansive view builds upon rule-of-law principles, especially rationality, consistency, and the rejection of arbitrariness. But it finds arbitrariness, and a want of rationality, in rules that are inflexible, insensitive, or justified *only* by history or precedent.

Furthermore, such a conception is open to what we may call a higher form of instrumentalism. The use of law as a means to political ends is ordinarily and often properly understood as subversive of the rule of law. It is an affront when the values we associate with legal decision-making, which protect the integrity of the process, are subverted in the interests of some external purpose, whether benign or evil. But fidelity to law may also include fidelity to legitimate purposes, such as public safety or environmental protection. When these purposes are domesticated - controlled and channelled - by procedures that successfully integrate means and ends, the instrumental authority of purpose can be accepted as legitimate.

In a rule-centred legal culture the appeal to history can be blunt and crude. A supposedly determinate *history* can serve as a surrogate for an enacted or otherwise determinate *rule*. Yet the history of a community has many strands, which are often diverse and conflicting. Which strands are to be recognized as authoritative, and therefore as defining the legal culture, may be strenuously contested.

Consider, for example, the very different conceptions of history and community that have influenced constitutional interpretation in the United

States. These are starkly revealed in the famous case of *Bowers v Hardwick*, decided in 1986. In that case the Supreme Court upheld the constitutionality of a Georgia statute which made sodomy a criminal offence punishable by imprisonment. The Court's majority said the Constitution did not protect homosexual sodomy if a state legislature wished to prohibit it. As the then Chief Justice said, "To hold that the act of homosexual sodomy is somehow protected as a fundamental right would be to cast aside millennia of moral teaching". A vigorous dissent denied that customary morality is self-justifying. "I cannot agree", wrote Justice Harry Blackmun, "that either the length of time a majority has held its convictions or the passions with which it defends them can withdraw legislation from this Court's scrutiny" (*Bowers v Hardwick*, 478 US 186, 210 (1986)).

In this opinion the majority gives great weight to customary morality as a source of law. For these justices, in this context, past practice matters more than abstract principle. The dissenting justices have a very different view. They do not reject tradition, however. They do reinvent it. For them the relevant tradition is the American constitutional order. This is tradition of a special sort. It allows for change, growth, criticism, and reconstruction; and it consists of premises and values, not of particular rules and practices. To identify such a tradition is to locate implicit principles and guiding purposes. In this perspective the moral order is not constituted by particularities of belief, observance, or connectedness; nor is the authoritative community, the safeguarder of the moral environment, necessarily or preferably local rather than national. Rather, the community is defined by more general ideals, such as democracy, equality, and the rule of law and these ideals may be best upheld by national or even supra-national authority.

This experience suggests that the analyst of legal culture should study the interplay of historicity and principle. Each is a potential source of legitimacy; each has costs as well as benefits. A blunt appeal to history is likely to lead, as in the Hardwick case, to a cramped, ungenerous view of legal rights. Such an appeal validates the claims of entrenched elites and presumes the persistence of homogeneous communities. It slights the claims of new interests and changing conceptions of law and morality. Indeed the majority opinion in *Hardwick* made no contribution to thoughtful and responsive elaboration of fundamental law.

On the other hand, a preoccupation with constitutive principles has its own costs and problems. Justice Blackmun claimed that the Constitution protects "the fundamental interest all individuals have in controlling the nature of their intimate associations with others". Like similar formulations of abstract principle, this one suffers from rhetorical overreaching. Surely not every intimate association is defensible; many that are defensible are proper subjects for regulation; and not every intimate association is a sufficiently fundamental interest to merit constitutional protection. Moreover, in stressing the rights of individuals, the claims of community, and of countervailing values, are ignored or neglected.

In the *Hardwick* case we see important differences in styles of legal reasoning. We know that legal reasoning always demands some combination of legitimacy and cognition (see Selznick, 1992: 452). But what combination? To safeguard legitimacy the law insists on received premises, and the liberal minority in *Hardwick* attempted to articulate such premises. At the same time, legal reasoning must deal, in some cognitive way, with facts pertinent to the case at hand, including the *contemporary* authority of an historically accepted rule or principle. These differences in jurisprudential perspective are not innocently academic or theoretical. They guide the claims of litigants, the decisions of judges, and the policies of administrative officials. As patterns of practice and policy emerge, distinctive legal cultures are formed.

Challenges and Prospects

Let us take a look backward and then consider some of the challenges and prospects of a post-modern or pragmatist conception of the rule of law.[5] In this updated version the rule of law is defined by ideals of rationality, equality, fairness, and integrity. As a result, the meaning of arbitrariness is enlarged. What is arbitrary is determined by more subtle understandings of rule, principle, context, and obligation. Officials of all kinds, in many different settings, find to their dismay that hitherto accepted practices now constitute abuse of power. Similarly, the meaning of accountability is transformed when officials no longer find full justification - and bureaucratic protection - in close adherence to prescribed rules. As the authority of purpose moves to the foreground of the legal culture, accountability is measured by fidelity to ends and values, not rules alone, and to pragmatic criteria of problem-solving and achievement.

Thus a post-modern legal culture promises more, and more is asked of it. The promise includes extension of rule-of-law values to all social spheres in which power is exercised and may be abused. This enlargement of depth and scope - of meaning and application - has dangers and downsides as well as benefits. The greatest danger is overreaching. When principles and goals are stated abstractly it becomes very easy to promise too much; or to find, in a single principle, a sure guide to policy; or to suppose that specific, contextual parameters for evaluation and decision are irrelevant or unneeded. In short, the post-modern conception runs the risk of dissolving itself into a cloud of abstractions, thereby joining the roster of failed utopias. We should keep that risk in mind, but we should not allow it to frustrate inquiry, or to sound retreat to a rule-of-law model that has its own great failings and limits.

In the new conception a major step is the willingness to transcend, and the competence to transcend, the limits of formal justice. This occurs because experience shows that formal justice can lead to arbitrary, impoverished, self-defeating decision-making. Formal justice equalizes parties and favours strict adherence to rules, precedents, and received classifications. These virtues serve genuine needs of legal process, especially clarity, certainty, and institutional autonomy. If unchecked, however, they encourage the decay of legality into legalism.

Properly understood, "legality" refers to norms of legitimacy, regularity, and fairness. It is a close synonym for "the rule of law". Legalism, on the other hand, is a pathological state marked by adherence to rules and procedures without regard for purpose or effects. Moreover, formal justice looks backward, not forward. Just because it is committed to legitimacy and certainty, formal justice tends to serve the status quo. Therefore it is experienced as arbitrary by those whose interests are ignored or only dimly perceived. A "legalistic" legal culture loses touch with social reality and has few resources for dealing with social change.

The most important outcome of this move from formal to substantive justice is a broadened meaning of legal equality. The classic rule-of-law model is comfortable with the idea that all who are governed in a political community are entitled to equal protection of the laws. However, this standard, narrowly interpreted, requires no more than treating like cases alike by consistent application of established categories. The categories themselves need not be examined. Thus there can be general rules, applied with impeccable regularity, whose function is to institutionalize perceived differences in the moral worth of persons and groups. On this view, a caste principle, and even chattel slavery, can be made compatible with the rule of law.

In the decades following the Civil War, the US Supreme Court was called on to interpret the Equal Protection Clause of the Fourteenth Amendment, which was a constitutional confirmation of the Union victory in the Civil War. For a time the Court held to a constrained, formalist, low-risk interpretation. In 1886, for example, the justices upheld a law forbidding sexual intercourse and marriage between blacks and whites, on the ground that the law applied equally to both races and to all members of each race. Ten years later it was decided that "separate but equal" facilities for blacks in public transportation met the standard of equal protection.

By the middle of the twentieth century this conception of equal protection was radically revised. Propelled by a deepened concern for civil rights, the Supreme Court justices revisited their understanding of legal equality, and did so in a spirit of reconstruction and refreshment. They rejected as unconstitutional legislation whose premise it was that, due to race, sex, or ethnicity, some people are intrinsically more worthy than others. They laid the groundwork for a more subtle - and more realistic - understanding of legal equality, one that refused to identify equal treatment, regardless of circumstances, with respect for personal integrity and dignity. As it expanded the meaning of "equal protection", the new jurisprudence created a new legal culture, one that greatly encourages the erasure of stigma and the acceptance of cultural diversity. A sense of mission emerged - a mission to make good the constitutional promise of moral equality. This sense of mission was wholly alien to the spirit of formal justice.

Yet even in its generalized, expanded, pragmatic form the rule-of-law ideal seems wedded to the project of liberal universalism and even liberal individualism. These doctrines are unsympathetic - even downright hostile - to the claims of legal and cultural particularism. They are attracted to (and have done much to legitimate) an abstract, impersonal, universalist morality. The rule of law, it is thought, upholds standards that transcend parochial beliefs and interests. In that universalist perspective, localism breeds narrow-minded bigotry, and tradition is suspect as a source of legal authority. This is shown in the contrast I referred to above between the majority and minority opinions in the *Hardwick* case, where the majority invoked the blunt claims of history and the minority formulated more abstract principles of critical morality.

It is easy to understand the appeal of universalism, and of its presumed corollary, the impersonal standpoint in moral judgment. Universalism is quest for community that looks outward rather than inward. Its paradigm experience is the embrace of strangers. Furthermore, universalism is an indispensable part of critical or reflective morality. To assess a practice, or a received morality, we must envision alternatives. Therefore we look beyond specific historical experiences; and justice everywhere requires some detachment from personal and parochial perspectives.

But the Western mind has too often identified critical morality with universalist conceptions of rationality, freedom, democracy, and justice. Enshrined in a Declaration of Human Rights, these ideals peel away custom and set special identities aside. The message is that people need the protection of universal norms to offset the limited perspectives of local and even national communities. That message is basically sound. Although the human-rights project has suffered from overreaching, its main conclusions are confirmed by the long and widespread experience of suffering caused by indifference to human rights.

Does critical or reflective morality necessarily presume an ethos of universalism? By no means. What we learn about morality from experience and reflection must take into account another side of human nature and a different dimension of social life. Our best understanding of critical morality includes the truth that human well-being is most likely to be achieved within *particular* forms of association and culture. Abstract principles are only pale reflections of human feeling and perception, only weak indicators of the texture of social life. In fact people live and thrive in and through the concreteness of social participation. This generalization is recognized when we include, among human rights, rights to cultural membership and cultural distinctiveness. Such rights reflect a widespread need, or at least a yearning, for authenticity and rootedness. A corollary is respect for cultural differences, including a variety of legal and constitutional perspectives. As I have argued elsewhere, we can appreciate and respect diversity without embracing a radical relativism (Selznick, 1992: ch. 4).

A related question is: Can the rule of law accommodate virtues of reconciliation and cooperation? Can it disenthrall itself from the imagery of the abstract individual? Does legal integrity necessarily require top-down authority or adversary confrontation? Need it disparage personal virtues, or fail to inculcate them? Is the preference for settling disputes by mediation and compromise - a preference shown by many students of law and society - a challenge to rule-of-law values and institutions? Are those institutions necessarily threatened by attempts to make a legal system more person-centred, more responsive to human needs, more aware of its own often negative impact on the continuities of social life?

What about rights? The rule of law is often associated with the protection of rights, and this makes sense because a major preoccupation of judges and legislators is to discover and establish legal rights and duties. However, we should be careful to distinguish rights-*centredness* from other, less single-minded ways of affirming rights. Among non-Western legal cultures - cultures no one could possibly characterize as rights-centred -

many personal and group rights are routinely claimed and as routinely recognized. These include rights of property, inheritance, honour, disputation, and much else. Indeed, no society can function without recognizing claims to preferential if not exclusive rights of possession and distribution. Rights-centredness is something more: uncontrolled proliferation and over-eager assertion of rights; a tendency to absolutize rights or make them increasingly definite and exclusive. Rights-centredness creates a distinctive legal culture. It is, however, only one way of taking rights seriously.

Instead of being locked into historically contingent practices and beliefs, a pragmatic conception of the rule of law is prepared to reinvent itself. It does so by enlarging the range of relevant values and by paying close attention to contexts. The rule of law need not be, and should not be, best exemplified by an impersonal machine grinding out decisions in accordance with what Max Weber liked to call "calculable rules". Nor need it lead to what my colleague Robert Kagan calls "adversary legalism". The weapons and strategies of adversary confrontation are more appropriate in contexts where no continuing relationship is contemplated than in others which call for healing, cooperation, and a focus on the future.

There is an instructive parallel in the theory of bureaucracy. Recent experience and much study have brought into question the Weberian model, which identified bureaucracy with defined jurisdictions ("spheres of competence") and with rule-governed decision. This was, Weber thought, the most rational form of organization. But as in the case of the classic rule-of-law model, Weberian bureaucracy turns out to be an historically contingent form of rationality, to be sure more rational in important ways than its predecessors, but not necessarily the last word. A post-bureaucratic model is more fully purposive, more flexible, more congenial to initiative, more accepting of leadership. In this organizational culture, where it exists, authority is diffuse and communication is not rigidly channelled. Consultation, participation, fluidity, and openness, are prized, not discouraged.

Is this a rejection of rational organization, or even of bureaucracy? Surely not. The aim is greater rationality and a different kind of bureaucracy. Although the organizational culture (which is also a legal culture) becomes less authoritarian, there is no question of abandoning authority. To reconstruct authority is not the same as doing without it altogether; delegation of authority continues, and with it the creation of spheres of competence; rules remain indispensable. If there is a post-bureaucratic world, it will not be one in which bureaucracy is eliminated.

Rather, bureaucracy is reinvented by moving flexibility and purpose to the foreground of the system and its culture.

Much the same may be said of the transition from a classical or modern to a post-modern or pragmatic rule of law. Two fundamental ideas are carried over from the limited, more negative model, to the more expansive, more affirmative conception: the constraint of will, especially official will, by principles that protect the security and autonomy of persons and groups; and a corollary commitment to core values of accountability, liberty, regularity, and social peace. At the same time, in a post-modern spirit, these commitments are not fixed and limited, not wedded to particular forms or practices. Instead, they are treated as potentially subject to elaboration and enrichment in response to the imperatives and opportunities of history.

In this process there is or should be a dual focus on *baselines* and *flourishings*. We hold fast to the vital minimum even as we reach for the more subtle, more elaborated, more problematic ideal. Without protection of baseline values and procedures, the rule of law loses focus, obscured in a utopian plea for a world untainted by power or authority. This is the danger in radical criticisms of "liberal legalism". The criticisms are useful in so far as they show how the classical rule-of-law model undermines solidarity and delivers a cramped, impoverished justice. Such criticisms are misplaced, however, in so far as they lose purchase on the need for elementary constraints on the abuse of power.

There is nothing strange or exotic about the dual concern I recommend. It follows a familiar logic. In parenting and education, for example, we cannot act responsibly if we fail to address foundational needs for nurture, stimulation, and discipline, as well as elementary expectations with regard to learning and character. But we would fail as parents and educators if we did not encourage and support more complex virtues and higher competencies.

* * *

The view I have put forward offers a strategy for reconciling the Western legal tradition with its non-Western critics, and indeed with criticism from within. If we generalize the rule of law, and assimilate it to social and political theory, we can reach beyond Western mind-sets, especially individualism, contractualism, and rights-centredness; and beyond Western practices, especially legal practices that encourage divisiveness or undermine personal and social responsibility.

We can and should uphold what is valuable in the Western tradition. This includes, especially, what we have learned about bringing power to account and about moving law closer to justice. But the more important lessons are general, not specific. They are open to adaptation and revision in the light of other experiences and more comprehensive interests. The rule of law is not the "legalism" with which Confucianism contended in ancient China; nor need it be indifferent to the potential contribution of law to justice and morality. The rule of law is not the heavy hand of the state; nor is morality cabined by the claims of custom.

In Eastern Europe or China today, the Western legal culture, even with its limitations, has a poignant relevance. To disparage it in such contexts can be, in its own way, insensitive and irresponsible. Nevertheless, we see much evidence of the need to reconstruct and go beyond the negative conception of the rule of law. This appears most clearly, perhaps, in the confrontation between rule-of-law ideals and the welfare state. The welfare state is a manifestation of positive government in quest of social justice. Among contemporary American conservatives such a regime is perceived as incompatible with the rule of law because it is mainly substantive, not procedural; because it is an engine of redistribution, not a neutral enabler of private choices. On the other hand, contemporary Germany has written into its Basic Law a union of the *Rechtsstaat* and the *Sozialstaat*. The latter is more likely to be the face of the future, the former a rearguard action which can only limit but not destroy activist government.

Assuming that is so, much remains to be understood about how rule-of-law values can be made compatible with the regulatory state. To advance that understanding I believe sociologists of law will have to be more deeply involved in the study of bureaucracy. There has always been a close analytical and historical connection between sociology of law and sociology of organizations. This connection is made more urgent by the ever-increasing demand to make regulation more flexible, more facilitative, and, at the same time, a more effective instrument of public purpose.

* * *

I close with a brief coda on the uneasy integration of law and society as it bears on the rule of law. It is an unspoken premise of legal sociology that the line between legal and non-legal institutions is blurred in reality and should be blurred in policy. In some important sense, not fully understood, an integration of law and society is both recognized and espoused. This is what Lon Fuller had in mind when he recoiled from the phrase "law *and* society". He did not consider that an appropriate name for what we were about when we in Berkeley founded the Centre for the Study of Law and

Society. He preferred the phrase "law *in* society". This sensitivity may also explain why some people baulked when I said, years ago, that in legal sociology we must maintain our grasp on the "distinctively legal", that we should not allow law to be dissolved conceptually into the broader idea of social control. I was making an analytical point, but the response, I believe, was to a perceived symbolism, one that contained the apparent suggestion that law has a special dignity and that non-legal elements of the normative order are of lesser value and importance. Whatever the merits of that controversy, the implicit theory of socio-legal integration is not far to seek.

That theory is normative as well as descriptive. A tacit assumption is that the integrity and effectiveness of *both law and social life* will be retained and even enhanced by their mutual integration. The quest is for law that fits into and strengthens the continuities of social life; and for the kind of society and culture that will permit law to perform its special functions and realize its potential moral worth. The integration of law and society does not contemplate unravelling the social fabric in the name of law; nor is law to be made impotent or irrelevant.

This topic has been a prominent, almost fully explicit theme in the postcommunist countries of Eastern Europe. As we know, there has been a great revival of interest in "civil society", and in the related idea of "normality". Totalitarian communism had tried to establish complete control over social life, and in the attempt did much to destroy the institutions and spirit of civil society. There are echoes here of Hegelian and Marxist thought. In those doctrines civil society is roughly equivalent to modern economic life, driven by self-interest, sustained by rights in property, advanced by corporate organization. Nowadays the idea is extended to include other autonomous or semi-autonomous spheres of social life. In a flourishing civil society private life - life not sustained or controlled by government - is the chief source of order and well-being. Furthermore, civil society is a reservoir of reserved rights, which limit the authority of government. Thus civil society is distinct from government, and a brake on government, yet there is a paradox, because civil society is sustained by law and is even, in some respects, constituted by law.

Since the seventeenth century we have known that the containment of despotism requires a counterposition of state and society. This was already implicit in the English common law tradition. When common-law judges invoked social experience and necessity, especially the security of transactions and of property interests, they implicitly postulated rights against the state. The common law was taken to be continuous with the community's traditions and institutions. Nevertheless, the law is part of government. Therefore the counterposition of state and society cannot be absolute. Hence the idea of civil society, which includes the rule of law, or something like it, points to the *continuity* of state and society. In that conception, and in social reality as well, the rule of law mediates the relation between state and society. Therefore sociologists should not accept an easy identification of law and the state. In important ways civil society *detaches* law from the state.

Finally we may ask: who owes fidelity to law? On a narrow view of the rule of law, this is a virtue we look to in *officials*. But the model cannot really be confined in that way. As a distinctive legal culture the rule of law must affect conduct and consciousness at many levels. A community committed to the rule of law will be marked by respect for legitimate authority, and it will accept obedience to law as a moral obligation. That obligation is limited, to be sure, yet it must be accepted as a prima facie guide to conduct.

Thus the rule of law requires a culture of lawfulness, that is, of routine respect, self-restraint, and deference. Such a culture is undercut by widespread alienation or deep division. Furthermore, the rule of law requires public confidence in its premises as well as in its virtues. The premises include a dim but powerful understanding that positive law is always subject to correction by standards of truth and justice. In a rule-of-law culture, positive law does not have the last word.

Notes

1   This chapter is a slightly revised version of a lecture presented at the international conference of the Research Committee for Sociology of Law, Tokyo, 1 August 1995.

2   One sociologist has expressed the view that the rule of law is an impossible dream because "the central finding of legal sociology" is that "discrimination is ubiquitous", and this conclusion "devastates any claim that the rule of law prevails, that like cases can be treated in like fashion" (Black, 1989: 96 f). This conclusion ignores significant differences in amounts and significance of discrimination, that is, in the effectiveness of rules and the possibility of fairness. It seems the system is deemed *attainted* by the ubiquity of discrimination. Hence there is no point in studying different levels of achievement in the administration of justice. On this view, only utterly mechanical decision-making can count as fulfilling the rule-of-law ideal; since that is not possible the ideal must fail.

3   For example, Dicey's formula is consistent with the existence of common law crimes, which are now subject to much scepticism from the standpoint of rule-of-law standards.

4   A reductionist strategy would miss the special connection between Western modernity and the rule of law. To understand the costs and benefits of that configuration, as it affects non-Western communities, we must know what attitudes and institutions the rule of law encourages, and which it rejects. How else can we know to what extent and in what ways even an expansive view of the rule of law may become, for other traditions, a burden and a stumbling block?

5   On post-modernism and pragmatism see Selznick, 1992: 12 ff. There I note that "post-modern" need not be identified with ideas that emphasize the prevalence of incoherence and the virtues of deconstruction. "Post-modern" can also refer to views that accept openness, fluidity, and plurality as necessary and welcome features of modern life; that reject untempered individualism in favour of more person-centred, more collaborative forms of life; and do so in a spirit of optimistic commitment to personal growth and collective intelligence.

Bibliography

Black, D. (1989), *Sociological Justice*, Oxford University Press, New York.
Dicey, A.V. (1956), *Introduction to the Study of the Law of the Constitution*, Macmillan, London.
Dworkin, R. (1978), *Taking Rights Seriously*, Harvard University Press, Cambridge.
_____ (1985), *A Matter of Principle*, Harvard University Press, Cambridge.
Fuller, L. (1969), *The Morality of Law*, Yale University Press, New Haven.
Nonet, P. and Selznick, P. (1978), *Law and Society in Transition: Toward Responsive Law*, Harper Colophon, New York.
Raz, J. (1979), *The Authority of Law*, Clarendon Press, Oxford.
Selznick, P. (1992), *The Moral Commonwealth: Social Theory and the Promise of Community*, University of California Press, Berkeley.
Shapiro, I. (ed.), (1994) *The Rule of Law: NOMOS XXXVI*, University Press, New York.

2 Positivist or Non-Positivist Rule of Law?

Polish Experience of a General Dilemma

LECH MORAWSKI

I

The principle of the rule of law is a complex one. We may distinguish at least two components: a substantial one, that is the level of institutions and rights which a legal order must provide in order to guarantee the implementation of the rule of law; and a procedural one, that is the level of those norms which determine how the substantial institutions and rights operate or function in a legal system. If we say that the rule of law presupposes, for instance, the separation of powers, majority rule, freedom of speech or the right to a fair trial, we undoubtedly consider problems relating to the substantial component of the rule of law. Of course, there are many controversies with respect to details but in general agreement prevails at least as to the most basic elements of the substantial part of the rule of law.

Thus, if we grasp a society as a composite of three different but closely interrelated subsystems - political, social and economic - we may distinguish the following substantial elements of the rule of law:

(a) the right of the members of each society to choose the political system under which they live, the legal admissibility of the existence of opposing groups and parties and the possibility of peaceful exchange of ruling groups as the basis of political order;

(b) freedom of speech and expression, right of assembly and association as the basis of social order;

(c) the right to private property and a free market as the foundation of the economic system (Morawski, 1995).

Let us notice that this is really a very general and abstract characterization. On the one hand, it is so abstract in order not to exclude the possibility of different forms of society with divergent institutions and rights, schemes of organization and patterns of behaviour. On the other hand, it does not even include all characteristic substantive features of the rule of law. In this sense it aims only at pointing out which forms of society the rule of law is connected with and which ones it firmly excludes. The answer to these questions is relatively simple. The rule of law is a characteristic value of democratic and liberal societies and in this sense it would be a contradiction in terms to speak about a "totalitarian *Rechtsstaat*" (Marsh, 1961; Stelmach, 1992: 22).

Someone could raise the objection that this is a purely conceptual decision which arbitrarily expresses preferences in favour of western civilizations and against other forms of political and social order. A Marxist would say that the mere fact that the society does not tolerate private property does not have to mean that people in such a society must feel oppressed, not to mention other (historical and contemporary) civilizations for which western institutions and rights may be completely exotic.

This kind of critique is indeed justified to a certain degree. Firstly, the rule of law really expresses preferences as to some forms of social organization, in the sense that it favours democratic and liberal values. However, let us notice that from the historical perspective the rule of law has always been connected with these values and I do not see any reason not to take this fact into account. It is simply a historical fact that the notion of the rule of law is value-oriented like many other juridical categories, say parliamentary democracy, tolerance, etc. Otherwise, it would be very difficult to explain why it plays so important a role in ideological and political debates. However, I would agree that the mere fact that the rule of law is not respected in a given society should not automatically lead to moral disapproval of that society. This certainly would be unjustified, not only in relation to many historical societies but even to some contemporary ones (especially so-called "primitive societies"). In any case, bearing in mind that the rule of law is only a historical concept and should be handled with awareness of that fact, we should also not forget that in relation to our civilization it is interlinked with such highly respectable values that every case of its violation is strongly disapproved and condemned.

Secondly, if someone further insists that jurisprudence should not manifest human preferences, especially political and ideological ones, and thus follow the Weberian postulate of *Wertfreiheit,* we propose to distinguish the rule of law from the mere principle of legality (Morawski,

1995). As opposed to the former, the latter does not refer to any special set of substantive values but solely to whether the law is observed by public authorities or not. Thus, we may easily imagine a state (eg, a totalitarian one) which rigorously observes the law but does not respect the rule of law since, for example, this law violates some basic human rights.

II

Now I want to focus attention on procedural problems. As I said above, the procedural background of the rule of law determines how legal norms operate and function in a legal system. This relates primarily to three basic questions:

(a) what is considered to be a source of law;
(b) how legal norms may be repealed;
(c) how the legal order treats the duty to obey the law.

If we take into consideration these three elements we may contrast two opposing concepts of the rule of law which I propose to call the positivistic and the non-positivistic rule of law (Morawski, 1993, 1994. See also Alexy, 1992).

The positivistic rule of law may be explicated in terms of the following three theses:

1. only norms embodied in official legal texts - statutes, acts passed with the authorization of statutes (civil law countries) and judicial precedents (common law countries) - may be considered sources of law;

2. legal norms may be repealed exclusively by other legal norms (statutes, precedents) or by use of so-called collision rules (*lex superior ...*, *lex posterior ...* and so on);

3. a duty to obey a law may be annulled or suspended solely by legal norms (say in self-defence).

Putting the positivistic conception negatively, so to speak, we might say that according to this conception, principles and rules which are not embodied in legal texts - eg, rules of justice or rationality principles (I propose to call them extra-textual norms) - are not sources of law, so our legal rights and duties may not be derived solely from them. (Obviously this does not exclude the possibility that extra-textual rules may play a very important role as supportive materials which in conjunction with statutes justify judicial decisions.) Further, the extra-textual norms may not override legal norms or justify any departures from them. This is just the point of difference from the non-positivistic rule of law. According to the latter:

1. the source of law and thus of our legal rights and duties may be not only norms embodied in official legal texts but, in exceptional situations, also extra-textual norms;

2. legal norms may be repealed not only by statutes or precedents but may also lose validity if they violate extra-textual rules in extreme and intolerable ways;

3. in exceptional situations extra-textual norms may justify departures from legal norms (acts of civil disobedience are admissible or at least tolerable in certain circumstances).

I call the first conception positivistic because it was created in its most mature and comprehensive form by Legal Positivism in the nineteenth century. Legal Positivism broke with the old Roman tradition according to which rules of justice are intrinsic and immanent components of every legal order, even if a legislator did not explicitly refer to them. It was German Positivism that reduced the notion of law to statutes and all normative acts authorized by them (*das Recht = das Gesetz*) (David, Grassmann, 1988: 156). Common law practice differs from this conception only in that it accepts a more extended concept of the sources of law, including also judicial precedents which in Continental countries - due to the Justinian principle (*non exempli sed legibus judicandum est*) - do not belong to the formal sources of law.

It is unquestionable that from the nineteenth century up to now, both in civil law and in common law countries, the positivistic interpretation of the rule of law has dominated political and legal theory and practice. However, after the Second World War the experiences with totalitarian regimes (Fascism and Communism) gave rise to a severe critique of Legal Positivism. In practice this attitude has found its most spectacular manifestation in the position of German courts which did not hesitate to violate even the *nullum crimen sine lege* principle if they found that Nazi legislation had led to extremely unjust and intolerable results (see Alexy, 1992). In theory the same attitude is represented for instance in writings of Gustav Radbruch (1956: 347), Robert Alexy (1992), Lon Fuller (1969) and Ronald Dworkin (1971, 1986: 11). All these scholars take the position that law and legal texts are not the same, that a legal system must include not only statutes and precedents but also some other rules (eg, rules of justice, rationality principles or rules of political morality) even though they are not embodied in any legal text.

Undoubtedly, the mainstream of criticism of positivistic thought flows from natural law schools and concerns the question of how positivism resolves conflicts between law and morality. This is, of course, a very important kind of criticism. However it would be a mistake to say that the positivistic rule of law may be questioned only from a moral point of view and/or on natural law assumptions. In my opinion one can accept some version of non-positivism and yet not accept any version of natural law. In this context I would like to recall the kind of critique which refers to the fact that the positivistic rule of law does not meet rationality requirements of modern interventionist states and the ideology of the welfare state. In particular it may stand in deep conflict with instrumental values on which the effective functioning of the modern interventionist state, especially its economy and administration, is based. Thus, one may raise against the positivistic rule of law not only an argument from morality but an argument from efficacy, based on empirical and sociological data, as well.[1]

III

Before I consider the problem of the rule of law in Poland after the collapse of Communism, I should briefly characterize the use of this concept in the communist period. Certainly, Poland and other communist states rejected all basic substantial elements of the rule of law. They never accepted the institutions of parliamentary democracy and the most fundamental political freedoms and rights. The communist states practically replaced market economy by central planning, reducing the right to private ownership in many important aspects. These are commonly known facts, so there is no need to say more about them.

It is, of course, not surprising that Poland like all other communist states rejected the most substantial components of the rule of law. This is simply because these components obviously reveal strong commitment to western values and political preferences and as such they are incompatible with communist ideology.

However, it may be surprising that Poland, and probably other communist states as well, did not accept the procedural background of the rule of law both in its positivistic and non-positivistic versions, even though in this case there appears to be no such commitment to western values. The communist states rejected the positivistic interpretation of the rule of law since they did not accept the hierarchy of formal sources of law typical of positivism. Though they declared in theory the superiority of statutes over governmental and administrative acts, in practice the communist states performed practically all important tasks and functions just by means of administrative acts. In many cases statutes were reduced to ideological declarations devoid of any practical significance. This was manifestly evident with respect to the Polish Constitution. Whole chapters of the Constitution were never applied (eg, provisions about free elections or political rights). There were neither administrative courts nor a Constitutional Tribunal. Ordinary courts had no right to control legislative acts from the viewpoint of their constitutionality or even legality. In this way there was no possibility of preserving the formal hierarchy of sources of law declared in the Constitution. It is also commonly known that in crisis (and not only crisis) situations the communist rulers did not hesitate to replace legal acts by political directives and instructions directly addressed to administrative agencies and other public authorities. In this way the Communist Party in fact exercised legislative functions, though they had no legal authorization to issue any binding acts for state organs and public authorities. This practice was widely applied, particularly in social, economic, administrative and, of course, political matters (see Rzepliński, 1989).

The communist rulers rejected the non-positivistic interpretation of the rule of law as well. They never permitted the use of any extra-legal norms unless the legal text itself made reference to them. As to this, the Polish Supreme Court stated that the law must be observed, even if it is unjust, as long as it is not repealed by the legislator.[2] In this context it is worth mentioning that, by moral rules or rules of justice to which reference in legal texts was made, frequently what was meant was not rules shared and accepted in society but rules proclaimed by communist ideology. The institution of civil disobedience was unknown and departures from legal norms could not be justified by reference to rules of justice. These considerations seem to demonstrate the thesis that the procedural background of the rule of law is only apparently value-neutral and in fact it is based on some ethical assumptions. In the case of positivism it is a conviction that the law-making processes must be legitimized by special procedures and special authorities so that not everybody may legitimately create the law. In the case of non-positivism it is an assumption that the law must be in principle consistent with socially approved values and norms. Both assumptions strongly hampered the rule of the Communists. Besides, they were inconsistent with the instrumental approach to the law that was so characteristic of the communist state and just for this reason they had to be rejected.

The foregoing considerations give rise to the conclusion that the concept of the rule of law declared in all socialist constitutions had only a declaratory character and it had nothing to do with its counterpart in western democracies. Moreover, not only did socialist states not accept the rule of law but it is even doubtful whether they accepted the principle of legality, understood as a duty of public authorities to regulate and arrange social matters on the basis of legal precepts. As I said, in communist practice the law was conceived as a purely instrumental value. Hence, the answer to the question whether to follow legal provisions or not, depended on a broadly understood calculus of profits and losses. Because of this attitude, if the observance of legal precepts was profitable for the rulers they strongly insisted that legal norms be followed; if not, the public authorities did not hesitate to disobey them. This kind of instrumentalism - contrary to the instrumentalism characteristic of the interventionist states in western democracies - we may call unrestrained or wicked instrumentalism, because it did not acknowledge any legal restraints (say, human rights) on political power.

IV

After the 1989 collapse of communism in Poland, a process of deep reforms (some of which had started already in the 1980s) was initiated, aiming at far-reaching transformations of the political and legal system. One of them was the amendment of the Polish Constitution. A statute of 29 November 1989 introduced a new clause into the old Stalinist Constitution of 1952. The clause stated that "the Polish Republic is a democratic state, governed by law and implementing rules of social justice". This clause referred to the old German concept of the *Rechtsstaat* which in Continental Europe may be conceived as the counterpart of the Anglo-Saxon idea of the rule of law. In consequence of the transformations, all the typical institutions of parliamentary democracy have been introduced in Poland, with free elections, legal opposition and a multi-party system. The political system is based on the principle of separation of powers. All basic political freedoms and rights have been revived. The Constitutional Tribunal, the system of administrative courts and the institution of the Ombudsman have been set up. The judiciary has received real autonomy and independence from political decision-makers. At the same time deep economic changes have been carried out. Free market mechanisms have gradually replaced central planning. The direct management of economic activities by the state has been partly limited. Several, sometimes very heavy, restrictions of property rights have been abolished. Obviously these processes have not always gone smoothly, without disturbances or obstacles (for example, former owners of nationalized property are still waiting for restitution or at least compensation). Yet one must admit that these reforms have evidently contributed to the establishment of all the basic substantial elements of the rule of law.

V

Now I wish to come to the next subject of our considerations, namely the problem of the procedural component of the rule of law. After 1989 the Polish legislature and judiciary stood before a serious dilemma over which interpretation of the rule of law to choose. It was a grave and controversial problem because every choice had to take a position on at least three questions:

(a) the breakdown of communism and the rise of a new political and legal system;

(b) the necessity of far-reaching reforms; and

(c) (maybe the most controversial question), how the present law should deal with the past and the communist law.

The answers to these questions make abundantly clear that the Polish legislators and judiciary have unequivocally taken the side of the positivistic position. Likewise, the majority of Polish jurisprudence has declared itself in support of the same position.[3] Thus the positivistic credo is clearly manifested in decisions of the Polish Constitutional Tribunal. Firstly, the Tribunal has restricted the concept of sources of law exclusively to what we have called the official legal texts, which include the constitution, statutes and acts passed with the authorization of statute. They do not include any rules of justice and/or any other extra-textual norms. Naturally, Polish courts refer frequently to divergent rules of morality and other extra-textual rules, but they are only allowed to do this provided that the legal text itself authorizes such references or the extra-textual rules only support conclusions derived from statutes. The clause on the rules of social justice from Article 1 of the Polish Constitution should be understood in just this way. In other words, according to the Constitutional Tribunal, extra-textual rules may not be considered an autonomous source of law, independent in relation to statutes, and consequently a source of our legal rights and duties. Secondly, extra-legal rules cannot override legal norms. Therefore the Constitutional Tribunal argues that legal norms cannot lose their validity only on the ground that they violate rules of justice or rationality principles. Thirdly, the Constitutional Tribunal maintains that rules of justice cannot justify any deviation from legal norms.

It seems to me that there are two possible explanations for this choice: firstly, commitment to the tradition of civil law countries and, secondly, political reasons. It is commonly known that, on the one hand, the Communists firmly rejected Western democracy and parliamentarism and, on the other, they constantly emphasized resemblances and connections with the legal culture of civil law countries which is strongly influenced by Legal Positivism. However, these connections seem to have been only apparent. In reality, the Communists not only rejected the political institutions of civil law countries, developing a quite peculiar concept of the legal system, but they rejected the positivistic ideology as well. In this context it is worth mentioning that in Germany, where Legal Positivism was far more influential than in Poland, the courts did not hesitate to reject the positivistic concept of sources of law when, after the Second World War, it appeared necessary to call Nazi officials to account.

Thus, it seems to me that not tradition but rather political reasons have contributed to the choice of the positivistic interpretation of the rule of law. In order to understand the situation in Poland, one should take into account the fact that after the fall of communism only the most discredited functionaries of the Communist Party lost their jobs, whereas the great majority of judges, administrative officials and other public authorities have preserved their positions. These people form a considerable political force in today's Poland and naturally they want to preserve the sort of legal order which guarantees them at least security and impunity. It is easy to demonstrate that it is precisely the positivistic rule of law which conforms most to these expectations. In my opinion this is because the positivistic conception presupposes the so-called thesis of separation of law and morality (Hart, 1958: 71) and in this way it accepts dogmatically the priority of legal norms over moral rules in every situation; giving, thus, the practically unrestricted possibility of legalizing all kinds of atrocities. The separation thesis implies several important consequences referring both to the content and to the criteria of validity of legal norms. Let me mention some of them:

1. legal norms are valid even if they are extremely unjust or inconsistent with some other extra-textual rules;
2. legal norms must be obeyed even if they are extremely unjust or inconsistent with some other extra-textual rules and nobody can be prosecuted because he had followed such norms,
3. "the law can have any content".

The last formula is tantamount to the famous Kelsenian thesis which follows from the fact that, according to Legal Positivism, the criteria of legal validity are strictly formal (simplifying the matter: in order to be valid it suffices that the legal norm is correctly enacted and not repealed) and they do not refer to the content of legal precepts. In the past, the Communist rulers made great use of the separation thesis and all its consequences, both passing inhuman laws and forcing unconditioned obedience to them. Nowadays they attempt to employ the separation thesis in order to protect themselves from any legal responsibility (Morawski, 1995; Moś, 1995). To attain this goal they resort to various devices and "holy" principles of the positivistic credo. To the most characteristic belong:

1.   The *Nullum Crimen Sine Lege* Principle

The Communists argue that even if the Communist law was inhuman it was law and it was their duty to follow it. Nobody can be prosecuted because he followed the law (the same argument was used by Nazi offenders before the Nuremberg Tribunal and German courts). Moreover we should notice that at that time in many cases certain deeds, evidently illegal from the viewpoint of international standards (divergent forms of oppression against political opponents), were not prohibited by the Communist law at all and due to the *nullum crimen sine lege* principle they cannot be prosecuted at present.

2.   *Amnesty, Abolition and other Forms of Legalization*

As one of the Justices of the Polish Supreme Court said, the worst thing was that the Communists had committed crimes and later they released themselves from any responsibility (Dybowski, 1992: 125). Amnesty and abolition-devices or other forms of legalization of all sorts of atrocities[4] were frequently used in critical situations when the Communists felt endangered (after the death of Stalin; shortly before the fall of Communism). Of course, one could argue that the present parliament may repeal the controversial acts of amnesty and punish the offenders but then it would infringe the *nullum crimen sine lege* principle.

3.   *Procedural Tricks*

The competence of the Constitutional Tribunal is restricted by statute to acts passed after 1982. Thus, the Tribunal cannot question, for instance, the legality of acts issued during the martial law period.

Many years ago, Gustav Radbruch accused Legal Positivism of making German jurists helpless against the crimes of Nazism (Radbruch, 1956). The case of Poland demonstrates that the positivistic interpretation of the rule of law has at least helped the Communists to avoid responsibility. Saying this I do not suggest that there is a necessary connection between positivism and totalitarianism. Quite to the contrary, in the course of history Legal Positivism has usually accompanied liberal and democratic systems. However the case of totalitarian states demonstrates that in extreme situations the most noble principles of the positivistic rule of law may be easily misused. In this way the *nullum crimen sine lege* principle, instead of protecting against the arbitrariness of the governors, in today's Poland guarantees impunity to people who, on normal rules of decency, should be punished. In my opinion we may avoid or at least reduce this possibility by calling in question the dogma concealed beneath the positivistic rule of law: that law is a complete, closed and self-correcting system and therefore it never requires any support from external rules.

One could raise the objection that some inconveniences, or even injustices, which follow from the positivistic rule of law are a price which must be paid by societies willing to transform their political and economic systems. According to this view, in spite of some defects the positivistic rule of law is a more reliable and effective instrument of reforms, ensuring certainty, stability and predictability of legal decisions and that is why it should be preferred. I do not share this opinion. As I said before, against the positivistic rule of law may be raised not only an argument from morality but an argument from efficacy as well.

VI

The advocates of the positivistic rule of law do not take into account at least two facts which seem to impair the positivistic rule of law: namely, the deep changes both in the functions of law and in the structure of contemporary societies that have taken place since the nineteenth century when the concept of the rule of law was developed (Morawski, 1994: 289). As we know, the primary purpose of liberal law was to protect public order and basic social institutions (eg, democracy, property, human rights) and the positivistic rule of law was adapted to the fulfilment of these tasks. Contemporary law, inspired by the ideology of interventionism and the welfare state, operates not only as an instrument of protection but as an instrument of social guidance and public policy, as a medium of pursuing social tasks and programmes. In my opinion, just to the extent to which law functions as a medium of social guidance, it becomes incompatible with the old positivistic rule of law. The clash of the positivistic rule of law with interventionism produces various phenomena which undermine the very essence of this principle. Let us mention only some of them.

In the first place, there is the growing exercise of discretion which should facilitate the adjustment of legal regulations to constantly changing circumstances but which very often leads to arbitrariness and results in unpredictability and uncertainty of legal decisions. These effects, inconsistent with the rule of law, also produce the selectivity of interventionist law. In this context Renate Mayntz rightly points out that interventionist law operates mainly through the mechanisms of purposive selection (Mayntz, 1985: 54). It stimulates the development of the less advanced branches, regions and social groups, establishes preferences and attempts to distribute burdens and profits justly. In consequence the positivistic ideal of law, understood as a set of maximally general and abstract rules, is being gradually replaced by a collection of different laws for different branches, regions and social groups. These transformations result in the growing instrumentalization of interventionist law (Morawski, 1993). Likewise contrary to the positivistic rule of law is the fact that numerous specialized activities are taken out of the reach of legislation and subjected to administrative agencies, because legislation, with its time-consuming and rigid procedures, is evidently inappropriate and inefficient as an instrument of social guidance.

At the same time, significant transformations of social structures occur. Systems theory rightly argues that increasing differentiation and complexity is the most characteristic feature of modern societies (eg, Wilke,

1986). Contemporary societies are not homogeneous entities any more but a multitude of highly complex and specialized subsystems (eg, economy, administration, military, education) with divergent organizational structures and patterns of activity. This fact makes it not only impossible to regulate social processes in accordance with the positivistic paradigm, that is by means of the most abstract and general rules, but it induces the rapidly growing fallibility of decision-making structures. No matter how carefully the legislator or administrator might act, no matter what mechanisms of correction of mistaken decisions a legal system might provide, we do not escape the possibility of error or failure. It seems to me that this fact contributes most of all to the crisis of the positivistic rule of law, simply because it is impossible to reconcile the positivistic claim for absolute observance of all legal provisions with the fact that these provisions may produce disastrous or harmful consequences. The positivistic rule of law becomes plainly unreasonable if it is applied to law that operates as an instrument of effective social guidance but in given circumstances produces extremely harmful results.

Let us illustrate this thesis by just one example. Some years ago the Polish Constitutional Tribunal stood before the following dilemma: due to statutory provisions, the salaries in the sphere of public administration and in other branches financed by the budget should have been raised, but such a decision would inevitably lead to the collapse of public finances. Commenting on this fact, the Tribunal clearly stated that the drastic break-down of the budget may justify the refusal of administrative bodies to implement the statutory provisions about a rise in salaries.[5] Now we may ask the Positivist: should the Tribunal bring the Polish economy to ruin in the name of fidelity to law (*fiat iustitia pereat mundus!*). Naturally, the Positivist would attempt to escape this dilemma, probably saying that it was the task of parliament to repeal a mistaken statute. But it did not, and we all know that for this or that reason such situations appear quite frequently and will appear more frequently in the future, simply because of the constantly growing fallibility of our decisions. It is unquestionable that the courts and other decision-makers must also take decisions in such circumstances when legislative errors and failures lead to disastrous consequences but they cannot be corrected by parliaments in appropriate time. We may ask once again why we should tolerate these consequences if they can be corrected by courts or other decision-makers in easy and simple ways. In particular, why should ordinary citizens bear the costs of legislative failures? I do not know any positivist who has given a serious answer to this question, apart from fairy tales about certainty, predictability and so on. These are indeed only fairy tales because law which makes disorder, produces extremely harmful consequences, and hence induces the resistance at least of reasonable people, so this cannot make a stable basis for predictable and certain decisions. The reality of contemporary states clearly shows that the positivistic dogma, that law and order are inseparable, is mistaken. Unfortunately, law makes disorder as well (sometimes very expensive and harmful disorder) and for this reason alone the positivistic claim that law must always be observed regardless of consequences, should be modified. Certainly the need for this modification is most urgent in transitional regimes. Here legal systems are not only most incoherent because they encompass "old" and "new" rules which very often contradict each other, but also law penetrates social reality most deeply, and in consequence of that it may produce particularly unpredictable and dangerous effects.

VII

Elsewhere I have carried out a detailed analysis of objections against the non-positivistic rule of law (Morawski, 1995) but to avoid misunderstandings some remarks are necessary here. The non-positivistic rule of law does not aim - as is sometimes argued - at a replacement of positive law by a more or less indeterminate collection of extra-legal principles. I merely assert that reference to extra-legal rules is admissible only in extreme cases, when law is intolerably unjust or unreasonable and a legislator has no possibility or opportunity to react in appropriate time. In other words, it is admissible only if observance of legal norms brings evidently more harms and costs (social, economic, moral) than disobeying them (the principle of lesser evil). Thus the recourse to extra-textual rules should only compensate for the most intense inadequacies of legal regulation. Certainly the notion of extra-textual rules (especially rules of justice and rationality principles) needs explanations and this is the task of courts and jurisprudence. However we should not exaggerate this problem. For centuries law has worked with evaluative terms and general clauses which are no less indeterminate than our extra-textual rules. Naturally it would be simple-minded to say that the mere modification of the rule of law delivers us from all defects and failures which law, particularly (but not only) law inspired by an ideology of interventionism, produces. Yet in my opinion such modification would be profitable and in the case of transitional regimes - as the Polish experience demonstrates - it is simply necessary.

Notes

1   See for instance Friedmann, W. (1971). This idea is called sometimes the "Hayek theorem" and was formulated in 1944. On this subject see also: Jones, H. (1963).

2   Orz SN from 13 06 1959, OSPiKA 1960/45.

3   Morawski, L. (1992). However, to be just I must admit that there are some (very weak) efforts made by the legislature and judiciary to oppose the positivistic interpretation of the rule of law (eg, The Polish Supreme Court declared that it would be contrary to the rules of justice to acknowledge that the membership of an organization which fought against communist terror was a crime even if it was a crime according to the communist statutes (Orz SN from 27 02 1991, OSNKW 4-6/1991/poz 21).

4   A similar strategy was used by the Nazis in Germany - see Golding, 1995: 283.

5   Dec. CT from 29. 01 1992, K 15/91.

Bibliography

Alexy, R. (1992), "Zur Verteidigung eines nichtpositivistischen Rechtsbegriffs", in *Öffentliche oder private Moral?*, (ed.) W. Krawietz and G. von Wright, Berlin.

David, R. and Grassmann, G. (1988), *Einführung in die grossen Rechtssysteme der Gegenwart*, Muenchen.

Dworkin, R. (1986), *A Matter of Principle*, Oxford 1986.

————(1971), "Philosophy and the Critique of Law", in *The Rule of Law*, (ed) R. Wolff, New York.

Dybowski, T. (1992), *Sądownictwo a obowiujący system prawny* (Judicature and the Law), Materials of a Conference organized by the Polish Supreme Court, Warszawa (in Polish).

Friedmann, W. (1971), *The State and the Rule of Law in a Mixed Economy*, London.

Fuller, L. (1969), *The Morality of Law* (in Polish, Warsaw).

Golding, M.P., "Transitional Regimes and the Rule of Law", in *Challenges to Law at the End of the 20th Century*, 17th IVR World Congress, vol. IV, Bologna 1995.

Hart, H.L.A. (1958), "Positivism and the Separation of Law and Morality", 71, *Harvard Law Review*.

Hayek (1994), *The Road to Serfdom*, London.

Jones, H. (1963), "The Rule of Law and the Welfare State", in *Essays on Jurisprudence from the Columbia Law Review*, New York and London.

Marsh, R. (1961), "The Rule of Law as Supra-National Concept", *Oxford Essays in Jurisprudence*, (ed.) A. Guest, Oxford University Press.

Mayntz, R. (1985), *Soziologie der öffentlichen Verwaltung*, Heidelberg.

Morawski, L. (1995), *Zasada państwa prawnego-próba reinterpretacji* (The Rule of Law - In Quest of a New Interpretation), Zeszyty Naukowe, UMK IUS (in Polish).

————(1994), "The Rule of Law in the Welfare State", in *Challenges to Law at the End of the 20th Century*, 17th IVR World Congress, vol. IV, Bologna 1995, 289, and "Spór o pojęcie państwa prawnego" (The Debate about the Rule of Law), 4 *Państwo i Prawo* 5.

————(1993), "Instrumentalizacja prawa" (Legal Instrumentalization), 6, *Państwo i Prawo* (in Polish).

Moś, U. (1995), "The Rule of Law or the Fear of it. A Case of Polish Transition", in *Challenges to Law*.

Radbruch, G. (1956), *Rechtsphilosophie*, Stuttgart.

Rzepliński, A. (1989), *Sądownictwo w Polsce Ludowej* (Courts in Socialist Poland), Warsaw (in Polish).

Stelmach, J. (1992), "Filozoficzne aspekty dyskusji o państwie prawnym" (Philosophical Aspects of Debates about the Rule of Law) in G. Skąpska (ed.) *Prawo w zmieniającym się społeczeństwie*, Cracow: Jagiellonian University, 222.

Wilke, H. (1986), "Three Types of Legal Structure", in Guenther Teubner (ed.), *Dilemmas of Law in the Welfare State*, Berlin and New York.

3 Rules of Law: The Complexity of Legality in Hungary

ANTAL ÖRKÉNY and KIM LANE SCHEPPELE[1]

When the subject of the rule of law is raised in conjunction with newly democratizing polities, it is generally spoken of in the singular as *the* rule of law. In this chapter, we want to problematize this familiar idea by pluralizing the idea of the rule of law, creating in effect "rules of law" that may be unevenly followed across a complex and changing society. Rule of law ideologies may be present in some social contexts, with some sorts of partners and in some situations but not others. Whether a country is operating under "the" rule of law is a judgment about the way that assessments of legal legitimacy and legal efficacy fit together across different parts of the society, about whether *on balance* laws function in the world roughly as they were intended to by law-makers and about whether the law-makers themselves are meaningfully bound by the laws they make. In short, the idea of the rule of law is a shorthand for a complex situation on the ground, nowhere more so than in societies that are newly committed at an official level to bringing about such a state of affairs.

We take Hungary as our example because we know it. But also, Hungary is interesting for theoretical reasons. Probably more than any other country in the post-soviet world, legalism has maintained a strong presence over a long period of time here, even in regimes that were not committed to human rights. Hungary is often referred to as a "country of lawyers". Before it was brought into the Soviet empire, Hungary had a long tradition of an independent and highly respected bar, even in the fascist period (Kovács 1994). It also had a working practice of legalistic administrative management going back more than a century to the Compromise of 1867 creating the Dual Monarchy. This agreement was, after all, constitution-like. In considering Hungary's heritage of legalism, some episodes stand out because they represent the triumph of legalism against long odds. Between

1920 and 1958, for example, successive parliaments failed to agree on a new civil code and so technically Hungary had no civil law at all. But the Hungarian courts went on operating, having adopted through internal rules a precedent system and a practice of published decisions to guide their operation so that they created a clear positive law on the model of England. Even when Hungary was governed by regimes that had little respect for human rights, a sort of legalistic culture persisted. For example, during the Second World War, many Jewish families whose property was confiscated were given formal certificates issued by courts that named the property to be seized and gave reasons for the seizures in a pure example of legalism without rights. (This practice later stopped as the seizures speeded up and the property was simply taken.) Under the Kádár regime in the mid-1960s, a decade after the forcible nationalization of property, a plan was announced to allow people whose property had been taken into government control to get some compensation through the courts. Court records from that period show that the claims to restitution were handled in a professional and legalistic manner with respect to proof of ownership and the evaluation of claims (though the actual amounts given out in restitution were very small). Even in this highly politically charged area at an inauspicious time, legalism was able to establish a toehold. In addition, throughout the 1970s and 1980s, one of the most popular television shows in Hungary featured dramatic re-enactments of minor civil disputes that would give rise to lawsuits, followed by an expert commentary by a popular judge who explained the legal arguments that would be used in such a case.[2] Hungary is an interesting country to examine with respect to the rule of law in the post-soviet period because it already had a strong tradition of legalism, even if that tradition was not always paired with respect for rights.

Since the changes of 1989, public opinion polls show very strong support for legalistic ideology. In a 1991 Szonda Ipsos survey of 1000 residents of Hungary, respondents were asked whether they could ever imagine themselves breaking the law. Fully 65% said that such a thing "could never happen", 19% said that there was only a low probability of such an occurrence, 14% said it might happen, but only 2% said it could happen easily. And this was despite the fact that people were given choices of reasons why they might break the law including, for example, self-defence (21% of those who could imagine breaking the law said that this would be a reason they might do it), because of poverty (20%) and with merely a traffic violation (16%). Perhaps this is because people do not generally believe that they will become victims, for in that same survey, fully 37% reported that they thought that they would never be the victim of a violent crime while 23% said that they would never be the victim of a property crime. Another 45% said that there was some probability of being the victim of a violent crime, while 17% said that there was a high probability of such an occurrence, while on the property crime side, 51% said that there was some possibility of such a crime happening to them and 26% said that there was a high probability. The general public in 1991 did not want to treat law-breakers leniently. In this 1991 survey, people were asked whether they would punish someone who stole from a supermarket. Fully 81% said they absolutely would, while only 12% said it would depend on circumstances and 6% said that they would not. All of this shows a strong commitment to a belief that the law should be followed, will in general be followed and should be greeted with unswerving enforcement if it is not.

Even in Hungary, however, we believe that the success of the rule of law across some of the levels of society is only partial. (But we believe also that success of the rule of law is always partial, even in democratic regimes with longer histories.) It is interesting to see, however, just how commitment to rules of law is distributed across the society. At this point, we can only suggest the general shape of such a distribution. What we present below is an analysis pieced together from available sources and the experiences we have both had doing research on related topics in Hungary.[3] We present our ideas as a framework for thinking about rule of law questions rather than an actual map of final results because such a map would need more comprehensive data with which to draw it.

We also want to suggest that understanding the distribution of rules of law is an important component in making sense of the presence and persistence of informal law. Sometimes informal law may fill in gaps left by formal law, since no code - no matter how much it pretends to completeness - can cover every problem that might emerge. But sometimes informal law *substitutes* for formal law if people believe that the formal law is too complicated, irrelevant or unjust. Informal law always exists alongside and in some tension with formal law, and so it helps in understanding informal law if one examines the places where the formal law is vulnerable. This is what we are trying to do in this article. Since the rule of law is an ideal that in every society is realized only in partial form, it is crucial to understand variation in adherence to a rule of law model across a society in order to understand the opportunity for and limits on informal law.

Layers of Legalism

We believe that it is important to distinguish at least three levels of formal legal commitment in a society: the constitutional level, the state-citizen level and the citizen-citizen level. Even within these levels it may be important to distinguish further, but for now, we are going to paint with a broad brush. The rule of law commitment is not the same at each of these levels in Hungary, and we suspect that Hungary is not alone in this pattern, though Hungary has a distinctive historical context.

Constitutionalism and the Rule of Law

At the constitutional level, the rule of law implies that at a minimum the institutions of the state are themselves routinely operating in accordance with formal law. At this level, a well-functioning rule of law regime means that the constitution must be given a position above the state institutions themselves and must be referred to when disputes among them arise. It cannot be altered merely for strategic purposes of the institutions that have the capacity to alter it. The various branches of state power must stay within their constitutionally allocated powers; they must defer to the other branches in their areas of authority; decisions made by the specially empowered constitutional court with respect to the powers of the various institutions must be followed; within each state body, internal rules of governance must be publicly established and maintained. In short, the rule of law at the constitutional level implies that all state institutions must themselves follow the law of the constitution.

In Hungary, the rule of law has been astonishingly well established at this level. In fact, Hungary probably has a better track record on this question than most democracies with longer pedigrees.[4] Hungary was the first country among the post-soviet states to adopt a substantially new constitution. In fact, a new constitution had been suggested by the Hungarian Socialist Workers' Party government at the start of 1989 in what later turned out to be its last days. So constitutional change was already on the agenda when the Roundtable talks were held in the summer of 1989. One of the products of those talks was a substantially revised constitution in which about 80% of the clauses were amended from the Stalinist constitution of 1949. This 1989 set of amendments (and re-amendments by the elected parliament of 1990) established a republic with both a pluralistic parliamentary system and commitments to a sweeping set of human rights. Hungary is, as we write, in the throes of a public debate about adopting a new constitution which will almost certainly make only minor changes from the existing text, but which would have the added legitimacy of being voted on as a whole text by a democratically elected parliament. From the time of the change of system in 1989, Hungary has been governed continuously by a working constitution that was itself adopted in accordance with the procedures established in the old constitution. In his influential parallel opinion in the death penalty case, Constitutional Court President László Sólyom provocatively described Hungary's transition as a "rule of law revolution"[5] precisely because there was never a moment of legal rupture.[6]

The Hungarian Constitution establishes a very strong Constitutional Court, which has taken advantage of its broad powers of review to become the most powerful high court in the world. This has created a sort of public constitutional discourse that marks the Hungarian "transition" as unusual. Starting a full five months before the first elections, the Constitutional Court began by striking down a whole series of existing laws, including the death penalty, the use of a universal personal identification number, the abortion law and the tax on mortgage payments that the state-party government had attempted to impose to cover the budget deficits that haemorrhaged as state socialism was collapsing. Holding only a tenuous grip on power, the last Hungarian Socialist Worker's Party government obeyed all the decisions of the Constitutional Court, with the exception of the absentee ballot decision. This decision required the government to come up with a workable strategy for allowing Hungarian citizens absent from the state on the day of the election to vote while they were abroad. With the election fast approaching, the Parliament voted to amend the constitution to limit voting rights to those physically present in the state at the time of the election rather than delay the election to establish new procedures. But this is the only time in the first six years of the Court's history that a Parliament has ever changed the Constitution rather than change the contested law to comply with the Court's decision.

Since that time, the Court has struck down more than 200 new laws as unconstitutional - about one law in three passed by the Parliament in two different elected governments. Almost all of the major "transition" laws have been found to be unconstitutional, at least in part. And no matter how firm the parliamentary support was for the initial law, the Parliament has always obeyed the Court, going back and adopting a new law to comply with the Court's interpretation of the Constitution. The media law took the longest to revise, because it was impossible to get the required two-thirds parliamentary majority for nearly five years after the Court's decisions finding the existing law unconstitutional. But even topics one would expect to be politically controversial - like the requirement that gay and lesbian couples be given the same rights in civil law as heterosexual couples - passed the Parliament with only minor dissent, because the Court had required it.

Other evidence of constitutional compliance can be found in the several occasions when the President of the Republic has sought from the Court opinions about the constitutionality of a law before he has signed it - and when the President even asked the Court questions about his own competency. The Supreme Court in 1995 established the practice of seeking interpretive advice from the Constitutional Court on legal questions in concrete cases that have constitutional implications. Following the major decisions in spring 1995 that important parts of the government's IMF-mandated austerity programme were unconstitutional, the Prime Minister actually came to the Court for a meeting with the judges to ask how the programme might be changed to be constitutionally sound. Clearly in all the major centres of state power, respect has been very high for constitutionalism and for the Constitutional Court which has set itself up as the guardian of that value.

Interviews with public officials also suggest that constitutionalism is a high priority issue.[7] When asked why they followed decisions of the Court and did not rely on their own interpretations of the Constitution, members of Parliament as well as current and former ministers responded similarly by saying that such a thing was unthinkable in a "jogállam", a constitutional rule of law state. Their conduct shows a respect for constitutionalism as well. When, after the second election, the new government decided that it was time to formalize the constitutional changes by establishing a constitutional drafting committee to propose a new text, the coalition did not use the 72% of the seats it controlled to ram through its preferred draft, even though a two-thirds vote would have been sufficient to amend the current constitution. Instead, the governing coalition proposed a series of complex changes in the house rules of the Parliament to require *both* the agreement of five parties out of six in the parliament to any change from the existing text *and* a two-thirds vote in the parliament before a new constitution could be adopted. Believing that the creation of a constitution needed to be a politically consensual process, the governing coalition actually gave up some of its own power voluntarily in defence of that principle.

It is not just in the Constitutional Court and constitutional drafting committee that the value attached to constitutionalism can be seen. The constitutional committee is the most important committee of the Parliament, with the power to review any law at any stage of drafting to see whether it complies with the Constitution. At the request of only a single member of Parliament, the constitutional committee must convene to ensure that constitutional requirements are not violated by proposed laws. (The high rate of laws that are found unconstitutional by the Constitutional Court even though these laws have made it through this process in the Parliament suggests that this system is not perfect.[8] But this is due in part to the fact that the Parliament has passed a huge number of very complex laws very quickly and the committee does not have a large enough staff of trained constitutional lawyers[9] to review all the new laws thoroughly.)

The rule of law as a matter of state obligation is supported strongly not just within the institutions of state, but also among the general public. This is true even though the Hungarian rule of law revolution was very much a top-down affair with political elites leading the way. In a 1994 Szonda Ipsos survey that asked a random sample of Hungarians what were the most important political goals with which the state should be concerned, constitutionalism came in second only to social security. Other state goals like education of the poor, freedom of speech, the problems of ethnic Hungarians abroad, retroactive justice, and other important issues on the Hungarian political scene all scored lower than constitutionalism as a state goal in this general survey.

And this support for constitutionalism carries over to support for the Constitutional Court, which presents itself as the guardian of the Constitution against the political branches of government. In repeated surveys that have been taken since the early days of political transition, the Constitutional Court is the most popular institution of the government, with the exception of the President of the Republic. Figures 2, 3 and 4 show the ratings for 1991 (where courts in general and not the Constitutional Court specifically were inquired about), as well as for 1993 and 1994, where the President and the Court have more than a full point lead on a five-point scale of trust in the various public institutions ahead of the government and the Parliament. Among public institutions that are evaluated *as institutions* the Constitutional Court is the most highly respected state body. (We believe that the ratings of the President are not ratings for the office as such, but instead for President Árpád Göncz in particular. Göncz is a former dissident writer who has taken on the role of national grandfather and who has little concrete power in what is basically a strong parliamentary system. His personal approval ratings are almost identical to the ratings for the office.)

Figure 1: Priorities in State Goals for the Hungarian Government, 1994
(The survey was carried out in Hungary in 1994)

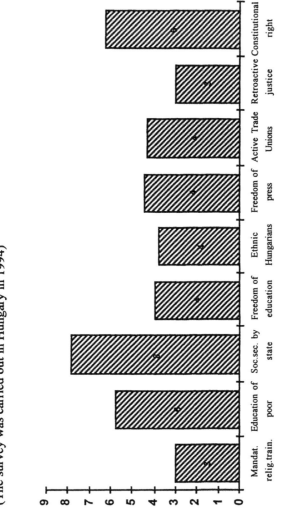

Figure 2: Trust in Public Institutions 1991
(The survey was carried out in Hungary in 1994)

(scores indicate mean trust levels, with positive numbers indicating positive levels
of trust and negative numbers indicating negative levels of trust)

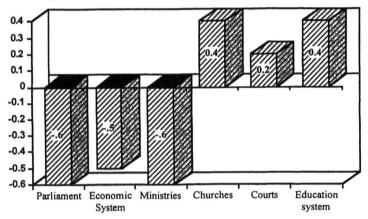

Figure 3: Trust in Public Institutions 1993
(The survey was carried out in Hungary in 1993)

(scores indicate mean levels of trust with positive numbers indicating positive
levels of trust and negative numbers indicating negative levels of trust)

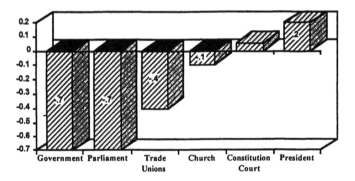

Figure 4: Trust in Public Institutions 1994
(The survey was carried out in Hungary in 1994)

(scores indicate mean levels of trust with positive scores indicating positive levels
of trust and negative scores indicating negative levels of trust)

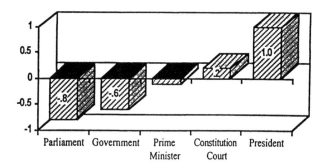

When asked how well these government institutions serve the people,
the Hungarian public rates the Constitutional Court far above the
Parliament and the government, and the Court's positive evaluations have
increased over time. No matter where the government and the parliament
stand in the ratings, the court is always at least 20% ahead of them in
popularity. (See Figure 5 - Nészabadsdg, 26 February 1996.) After its June
1995 decision striking down the government's fiscal austerity programme,
public approval for the Court soared to nearly 90% while support for the
government dropped to nearly 20% .

Figure 5: Support for Hungarian Public Institutions Over Time

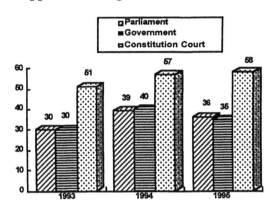

At the constitutional level, then, the rule of law is strong in Hungary.

State-Citizen Interactions and the Rule of Law

The rule of law as it pertains to state-citizen interactions is a completely different story, however. At this level, the rule of law implies that the state must act pursuant to laws and in a procedurally accountable manner with its citizens. This implies that there are regular procedures in place that allow citizens to know how the state will treat them and that provide clear channels for challenging decisions made about them. The state must also respect the constitutionally and legally guaranteed rights of its citizens and must not act in an arbitrary or discriminatory manner. Citizens, in turn, must fulfil their legitimate obligations to the state in a timely and correct fashion and must do their best to follow the legitimate and reasonable laws.

At this level, so far as we have been able to observe, the rule of law has a very loose grip on practices in Hungary, though there is still a great deal of publicly expressed support for a rule of law ideology here as well. In that 1991 Szonda Ipsos poll that tapped Hungarian attitudes toward legality, people were asked whether they believed that minor tax cheating or applying for welfare benefits by filing a false report were acceptable behaviours. On the tax cheating question, 23% said it was very improper; 48% said it was improper; 24% said that it was only slightly improper but only 5% said it was not at all improper. Fraudulently applying for welfare benefits was even more harshly judged: fully 55% said that such behaviour would be very improper and 39% said it was improper. Only 4% said that such reporting would be only a little improper and a mere 2% said that it would be not at all improper.

In practice, however, the state-citizen relationships fall short of realizing this rule of law ideology. Though the highest level of the Hungarian state has a strong devotion to such beliefs, the administrative levels of the state that deal with individual citizens do not routinely yet have this sort of commitment. Part of this is due to the way in which constitutionalism is constructed in Hungary. While the Constitutional Court has the power to review all statutes and legal regulations in Hungary, it does not have the power to review decisions in concrete cases, either from other courts or from administrative practices. That means that if an individual feels that her constitutionally protected rights are violated either by a state official or through a court judgment, she has no appeal to the Constitutional Court if the law under which her case was decided is constitutionally correct. In other words, there is no review of the constitutionality of concrete decisions, only of concrete laws. Parts of Hungary's administrative apparatus still have little effective independent review process and even when administrative decisions can be reviewed in the ordinary courts, constitutional principles are not always used effectively by judges who have had little training in constitutional thinking.

This leads to some serious problems. For example, groups in Hungary must register with a local court to get status as an official organization. Being denied this certification means that the group cannot exist as a legal entity. The law on associations has already been reviewed by the Constitutional Court and has been found constitutionally unproblematic. But in 1995, two groups were denied certifications by ordinary county courts, and these certification denials were upheld on appeal by the Supreme Court even though in both cases the judges used criteria for denial that were nowhere in the associations law. (In one case, a judge denied a gay rights group its certification in part on the grounds that its name, Melegek - The Warms - was an unconventional use of the Hungarian language. In the other case, a judge denied certification to a humorous political party - the Páto Pál Párt - on the grounds that it promoted a political programme that was not serious.) Once the groups exhausted their appeals through the regular courts and lost at every level, there was no way for them to raise the constitutional question of whether the *interpretation* of the law violated their constitutionally guaranteed right of freedom of association. The negative newspaper articles that greeted these cases eventually embarrassed the Supreme Court into making an agreement with the Constitutional Court to the effect that the Supreme Court would seek advice on questions like this to prevent this from happening again. But the discretion to take the case to the Constitutional Court rests with the Supreme Court under this new agreement and not with the aggrieved parties. The agreement is too new to see just what effect this has on the constitutional practices of the ordinary courts.[10]

It is also constitutionally unclear what happens to the outcomes in civil cases that were decided under laws that later were judged unconstitutional. For example, in one petition to the Constitutional Court, a man complained that his social security benefits had been unconstitutionally withheld. At the time of his retirement, the pension law in force refused to count any years of work that were performed before 1949 in figuring out how large a pension he was entitled to. That law was later declared unconstitutional by the Constitutional Court on the grounds that it arbitrarily discriminated against people who started their working lives before the start of the state socialist regime. But the man's pension happened to have been calculated during the short window when the statute was in force and his benefits continued at the level that such calculations dictated. In his petition, he said that justice now required his pension to be recalculated on the basis of the new, now constitutional, rules. But because this was a concrete case and the current law was not a problem, the Court could not hear it, and the man had already exhausted his appeals within the social security system. There was nothing more that could be done, even though it was clear that the result should not have been allowed. There is now a law in effect that fixes this problem for criminal cases. All criminal sentences have to be reviewed when the criminal law under which someone was convicted is later declared unconstitutional, but in civil cases like this one, there is no guarantee of review.

Apart from these constitutional blind spots, there are other problems with citizen-state interactions. Examples of bribery are all too common, where state officials agree to be bought off to look the other way when someone is doing something illegal. One Hungarian friend of ours who now lives in America, for example, was caught in Budapest without his car registration on a routine traffic inspection by the police. Instead of being given a ticket (which it was pretty clear he would not pay since he was leaving the country the next day), he was asked "how much it would cost in the US?" for this sort of violation. Left implied in this exchange was that if the police officer was paid that amount, then our friend could go free.

Which was just what occurred. Such examples are not unique to Hungary (and in fact, have been common in other parts of the world which have longstanding commitments to the rule of law), but they do show a general problem with rule of law values.

Bribery has a different function in former state-party systems than it has in functioning capitalist systems. In capitalist systems, on average, people working in the public sector can expect a living wage from their state employment. But if such were ever the case in Hungary, it is the case no more, and so state sector employees must often revert to bribe-taking just to survive. We can see that bribes in former state-party systems are not just examples of individual corruption, as they would be if they occurred in the "West", but they are corrections of a malfunctioning system of prices for public services.

For example, in the state-financed medical system that is technically supposed to be free for patients (and for which citizens pay very high taxes), it is well understood that everyone pays the doctor out of her own pocket for any medical care. There are even fixed amounts that these "tips" are supposed to be. For example, in present-day Hungary, one consultation with a doctor costs between 3,000 and 5,000 Hungarian forints, about $20-35 in American dollars. Paying for a doctor to preside over a woman giving birth used to be done in payments of bottles of liquor or a painting or sculpture. Now such payments are done by general agreement exclusively in cash - about 20,000-30,000 forints. A filling from a dentist costs between 2,000 and 3,000 forints. (In fairness to the doctors, these tips constitute a substantial part of their income because they are radically underpaid by the state.) None of these "prices" are posted, but everyone knows what they are. And if these "tips" are not paid, service would still be given by right, but the patient would always feel at risk that the doctor would not be as careful in her case. Families that have a sudden hospitalization for which they have not been able to save find themselves borrowing money from friends to pay these required "tips". This is another thing that is not supposed to happen, but it happens routinely and everyone knows it.

In some ways, these bribes may be seen as simply correcting failures in a non-market system, at least in the old days. These sorts of bribes were completely common at that time, and while they were illegal, everyone knew about the system and participated. It was a sort of secret public agreement in which everyone collaborated in a set of minor illegalities. But things have gotten more complicated in the post-soviet days. Now these bribes that were formerly taken for granted are still technically illegal, but in addition to this common bribe-taking, there is a rise in more serious forms of criminality.

How do citizens distinguish between serious criminality and garden-variety bribes? The answer to this question is uncertain, leaving citizens who were once sure of the rules (even though they were not legal rules) at a loss to say where the boundary between illegal-but-common and "really" illegal conduct is.

For their part, citizens mostly respond in kind to this lack of a rule of law guarantee from public officials and state-run institutions. Citizens take out their anger against these administrative abuses through strategic refusals and evasions in the tax system. People treat the tax system like a sort of strategic game, in which they try to gain whatever they can from the system. The tax system in Hungary has truly punitive rates, and so tax evasion abounds. For example, in the private sector, there is a 48% social security tax on all personal income that must be paid by workers on their gross salaries. (The equivalent tax for state workers is only 10%.) But there is an additional tax of 58% for private employers (42.5% in the state sector) on the gross salaries employers pay to workers as well. So, if a worker is paid $100 in gross salary in the private sector, then the state gets $58 from the employer and $48 from the worker. This means that the employer pays $158 in salary, from which the employee takes home $52. The state gets $106. In the state sector, an employer would pay $142.50 for a gross salary of $100 of which the worker takes home $90. With tax rates like these, it is no wonder that workers and employers collaborate to declare to state officials only parts of what workers are getting paid. Or the worker is simply not on the official books at all. This creates a system in which a person may have one "official" job in which she is declared as a regular employee and all taxes are paid on that salary - but that same person may have three or four unofficial jobs, all off the books.[11] In a system where salaries are routinely paid in cash, income is easy to hide and the practice of tax evasion is widespread (despite public opinion which strongly disapproves of the practice). The state is now trying to crack down on this, but such tightening of the enforcement rules is widely resented.

Or take the tax on rental properties. Currently, flat owners who rent their property are supposed to pay to the state roughly one half of what they take in as rent. Some flat owners renting to wealthier foreigners can ask for double what they need to get from the property and actually get that amount legally, but such doubled rents are absolutely unaffordable for Hungarians who do not own their own flats. So deals are made - the property is technically not being rented, but just "borrowed" for free; any money that changes hands is paid in cash and there are no receipts. This creates a certain sort of solidarity among friends (about which, more later) but it does not follow the letter or spirit of the law.

Tax dodging is always a temptation in any regime, but it is irresistible in a system where there is little rule of law ideology visible in practice in administrative or bureaucratic interactions and where the tax rates are ridiculous. Rather than behave on principle, saying that it is one's civic responsibility to follow the law, people behave strategically, doing whatever they think they can get away with. The tax system does not seem like a general contribution to the public good or the general quality of life in Hungary, but instead is like a punishment. The tax collection system is also so centralized that people feel it is unresponsive and distant. All of these things of course produce the disastrous effect that the tax system doesn't collect anywhere near what it is supposed to, and the government has responded by raising rates, which only makes the problem worse. Crackdowns on tax evaders are greeted by the public like an illegitimate intrusion on privacy and decency because the system has little legitimacy at this level.

And this is the very same system that has such admirable constitutionalism at the top.

Citizen-Citizen Interactions

At this level, the rule of law looks yet again very different. A rule of law ideology at this level would imply that citizens treat each other with respect, that agreements are kept and that strangers, while not treated with the same intimacy as friends, nonetheless can count on being treated according to well-understood rules that may, if necessary, be enforced through courts. It also implies that there is a back-up system in the judiciary for intimate relationships that break down, so that in the event of divorce or a friendship that goes badly wrong, individuals can turn to the courts for a fair resolution of the grievances. A rule of law ideology at this level does not imply that people are always going to court; it implies instead that most people will internalize the legal rules, act according to them and use the court system to back up serious violations of expectations which should, in a rule of law society, be relatively rare.

In Hungary, once one leaves the state sector (which still covers a great deal of daily life in former state-socialist systems generally and in Hungary in particular), then the rule of law has a different feel. In probably every society, rules that operate among citizens, particularly among friends, are less likely to be formalized than rules at other levels of the social order. And in probably every society, there will be a strong differentiation between the rules of law that exists among friends and family on one hand and those that exist among strangers on the other. But the legacy of state socialism leaves its mark even here because friendships and family relationships have a different set of purposes and expectations than in societies with more differentiated social institutions.

Rules that exist among friends in Hungary have the character more of moral guidelines than of formal rules. At this level, the effects of the larger political and economic transformations, so obvious at the constitutional and administrative levels, are barely felt. Life goes on now in Hungary at this intimate level very much as it did before the political changes of 1989. In some ways, this should not be surprising because intimate life was less directly implicated in the macro-political regime than either state sector or state-citizen interactions.

What was distinctive in state-socialist regimes, however, was the underdevelopment of civil society. Formal organizations to protect interests, engage in economic activity and provide routinized problem-solving were not legally allowed. Even social clubs, impersonal associations and spontaneous meetings were limited. Well-developed friendship networks substituted for many relationships that might otherwise have been carried out at this level of civil society organizations. As a result, friendships under state socialism were not just mutual solidarity pacts providing emotional support; they were also economic agreements and elaborate exchange relationships. Friends could get you what you needed to get on the (all-pervasive) black or grey markets. Friends could find you (off the books) jobs. Friends could find you good doctors, or wonderful pálinka, or rare flats, or scarce periodicals. Friends provided advice, services, protection from an intrusive government. And besides, they were your friends. Even now, government statistics estimate that roughly 40% of the economy operates through black or grey market exchanges though surveys report people as getting relatively small percentages of goods through these mechanisms. The actual instances of friendships substituting for regulated (and therefore taxed) markets must be very high.

Since the changes, civil society has still not organized to the extent that it is organized in the West. Friendships, and particularly family relationships, are very strong and carry out multiple functions that in a more socially differentiated society would have been carried out by other impersonally organized formal organizations. In the absence of trustworthy impersonal institutions that might mediate between state and society, friendships and family relationships provide a setting within which trust and security are possible. The broader community does not provide security because, as we will see, rules among strangers are not very well established.

Disputes among friends are, unfortunately, inevitable, but such disputes are rarely solved in Hungary (or in most places for that matter) by turning to formal law. Instead, in Hungary, the parties are nudged by other friends to work something out. Since a dispute between two people is generally thought to be the equal fault of both, no one can sit on a high horse and refuse to participate in the reconstruction of the friendship after a dispute. Pressures come from one's circle of friends to make amends, aided by a little back-channel communication that conveys the points on which compromise may be possible. Sundered friendships are serious matters, for they affect whole social circles, exchange relationships and systems of connections. So they are not just a private matter between the two parties; there is a sort of social pressure to make up. One of the most important cleavages in Hungarian politics, for example, can be explained by reference to a long-standing feud between former friends who after their break formed separate political parties that might otherwise have been united in a common cause. While there are some people who remain on good terms with both of the now feuding former friends, most people felt compelled to take sides. This was an extreme case of a breakdown of a dispute resolution mechanism. Usually, however, friends patch things up. The informal enforcement mechanism of becoming known as a person who causes trouble or who is an unreliable friend is usually enough to get people back on track. Courts are almost never used for the purposes of remedying breaks in friendships or other close relationships.[12]

Among strangers, however, this code of honour does not apply, but nonetheless it is still rare to use formal dispute resolution mechanisms. There is very little solidarity at the level of the community and few formal or informal mechanisms that can bring strangers into line with reasonable expectations. "Shark" taxis charge exorbitant rates; people sell poisoned paprika in the markets;[13] car theft is rising; landlords throw stranger-tenants out of their apartments with inadequate notice. Sometimes these sorts of things wind up in court; more often the loser just absorbs the loss because the court system is overburdened relative to its scarce resources and the public expectation is that it will take years for cases to come to resolution. This causes people to preserve the view that strangers can't be trusted, so they remain wary and strategic in their own attitudes. Strangers are trusted as little as possible. Instead, people prefer when possible to deal with their friends where the informal methods of dispute resolution work best.

Conclusions

Our survey of the levels of legality in Hungary is certainly painted with a broad brush and there is more detail that needs to be filled in with better evidence. But there is something important in our framework, we believe, for theoretical thinking about the rule of law. In any social system, the rule of law is a variable achievement, and a country that is very good at one level may be very weak at another. People who value the rule of law when they are acting as MPs or judges may themselves have different values when acting among strangers in a market; the very people who are wonderful as friends may be the bureaucrats that alienate others in the state sector. The rule of law - the formal values that an ideal of legality contains - may itself be sufficiently different at different social levels that one might consistently believe, for example, that one should behave honourably with one's friends and not with any public administrator because there is nothing that the latter has done to earn one's trust. All of these things are a matter of legal culture, which is as variable within a particular locale as it is between locales.

But it is important to think about the *relations among* the levels as themselves defining what sort of rule of law regime a particular society has. Though the three levels we have described are bound to come apart in all societies to some extent (hence the persistent gap between formal and informal law in all societies), there also has to be some correspondence among the levels if the society is not to be totally anarchic and unintegrated.

In a well-balanced society, the three levels should all have rules that are not only predictable but also integrated with each other. It is possible, of course, to have different norms regulating state-citizen and citizen-citizen interactions without contradiction. For example, norms of procedural regularity are likely to be more important among bureaucrats than among friends. But broadly speaking, there will have to be some overlapping principles that carry across the multiple levels for a society to be normatively integrated. The principles that binding agreements must be kept or that people may only be bound to behave in certain ways with their consent (or with representatives of their perspectives involved in the process of commitment) are likely candidates for such integrating principles. While the presence of some integrating principles may be derived from theoretical considerations, however, only empirical investigation can show what principles are in fact operating at the different levels.

A period of rapid social, political and economic change - like the one that Hungary and other post-soviet states are going through - is likely to create imbalances and difficulties adjusting norms across these levels. As long as the period of disequilibrium is temporary, serious problems may be avoided. But the challenge in countries like Hungary now is the challenge of the middle level. While the constitutional level of politics is quite clearly operating according to the rule of law, and while the friendship/family relationships that sustained people under state socialism by and large remain intact, it is the state-citizen and civil-society organizational level that must fill in the moral gap between these levels. Here, we see encroachment of normative regularity from both sides - from the constitutional level down as various forms of review of the administrative apparatus are instituted and from the friendship level up as new civil society organizations emerge and establish themselves as trustworthy. This latter process is occurring mostly through friendship networks "going public" and attracting new stranger-supporters. The political parties in Hungary, for example, mostly started as friendship networks that became general membership organizations, attracting strangers and thereby distributing the benefits of the solidarity of friendship to these new associates. Splits and fights within the political parties (most recently the Democratic Forum split again and created another splinter party on the centre-right) show the limits to this sort of strategy. But generally, filling this middle level will not be easy and there are bound to be many experiments that fail or have problematic results along the way.

The general lesson to be learned from our inquiry here, however, is that the rule of law needs to be considered not only as a political concept, but as a social one as well. Rules of law may be plural and variable even within a single society. Rapidly changing societies may be the best place to disentangle the layers, which may be changing at different speeds. Such investigations will no doubt show that considering a society as operating under *the* rule of law may be entirely too simple an idea for sociologists to use without knowing more.

Notes

1   Another version of this article has appeared in Örkény and Scheppele (Winter 1996-97).
2   For those familiar with American television, this show can be compared in its folksy yet legalistic quality to a show like the "People's Court" which also features cases that show the relevance of law to daily life explained by a friendly judge father-figure.
3   Örkény has long experience with survey data in Hungary and knows public attitudes well; Scheppele has been working for two years at the Hungarian Constitutional Court reading petitions from ordinary citizens who complain about constitutional violations. Our evidence is cobbled together from various sources as well as our personal observations and could, of course, be improved upon by more systematic data.
4   In the US, for example, imperial Presidents often threaten the authority of the Supreme Court. Roosevelt wanted to change the law to pack the court with judges sympathetic to him; Nixon said that he was not sure he'd follow a ruling of the Supreme Court on the Watergate tapes; Reagan's attorney general announced that the executive branch was a "coequal" interpreter of the Constitution and that the Supreme Court's views were merely one of many on the matter. In Germany, the recent Constitutional Court decision that prohibits the mandatory display of crosses in Bavarian schools has been met with widespread civil disobedience in that state and in France, the regime of "cohabitation" under Mitterand would be hard to square with the constitutional text. All of these things would be unthinkable in Hungary at the present moment for reasons that we detail below.
5   Decision 23/1990 (X 31) AB. Death of Penalty Case.
6   See János Kis, "Between Reform and Revolution", manuscript, for an analysis of the Hungarian transition, arguing that while legal continuity was preserved, there was a fundamental break in the sources of legitimacy of the pre- and post-1989 constitutions and so the 1989 events can be properly considered a revolution.
7   Scheppele has been interviewing current and former ministers as well as members of parliament whose favourite laws were declared unconstitutional by the Constitutional Court.
8   One member of Parliament who is also a member of the constitutional committee suggested in an interview with Scheppele that the Parliament had a hard time guessing what the Court would do because the Court sometimes invokes the idea of an "invisible constitution". The problem with an invisible constitution, this MP suggested, was that it was like a car driving around at night without its lights on. It is not so easy to avoid an accident when you can't see it coming, he said.
9   This training problem exists in part because constitutional law did not exist as a case-law field until six years ago and any lawyer who attended law school before that time would not have had even the basic grounding in how to think about such a system.

10   In fairness to the ordinary court judges, applying constitutional principles in the course of interpreting provisions of the civil or criminal code is not anything they've been trained to do. So it's not surprising that they don't do it very well in general. In other legal systems, like Ireland or Germany, or more recently Spain, where written constitutions were grafted onto existing legal systems, it took at least a generation or more of judicial education before such constitutional principles were routinely applied in the ordinary courts. In Hungary, there is now the beginning of such education. Scheppele was involved in a project with counsellors at the Hungarian Constitutional Court who have just prepared the first casebook of Hungarian constitutional law. This book will be used in the coming years in judicial training sessions around Hungary. Before now, there were no materials that could be used in such training sessions, but the results of the first session, held in 1995 in Eger, were extremely promising. The judges at that session were very eager to learn constitutional law and only needed some assistance in getting oriented in the more than 1,200 decisions that the Constitutional Court published in its first six years of operation.

11   This is one important reason why the official income and standard of living figures cannot be trusted for Hungary!

12   But see Inga Markovits (1995), for evidence that this may not have been true in the former GDR. There, under state socialism, about 60% of the disputes handled by the local courts were between former friends, current relatives and other cohabitants.

13   In the summer of 1994, paprika sales were stopped by the government after it was discovered that a substantial fraction of the paprika tested contained dangerous levels of lead oxide.

Bibliography

Kovács M. (1994), *Liberal Professions and Illiberal Politics: Hungary from the Hapsburgs to the Holocaust,* Oxford: Oxford University Press.

Markovits, I. (1995), *Imperfect Justice: an East-West German Diary,* Oxford: Clarendon Press.

Örkény, A. and Scheppele, K.L., (Winter 1996-97), "Rules of Law. The Complexity of Legality in Hungary", 26, 4, *International Journal of Sociology,* Issue on Constitutionalism in Eastern Europe, edited by Irena Gross, 76-94.

4 Institutional Optimism, Cultural Pessimism and the Rule of Law

MARTIN KRYGIER[1]

What are the prospects for constitutionalism and the rule of law after communism? What would one need to know to hazard a guess? In the state of the world and the state of the art, our answers to these and similar questions must necessarily be tentative, incomplete and controversial. One reason for that is simple ignorance. There is so much to know, and so much that we don't know and are unlikely to, until some time after it has happened. That, as it turned out, is how we learnt about the prospects of communism. And after the collapse of that unifying imposition, things are even more complex.

Among the twenty-seven post-communist countries, and their four-hundred million inhabitants, there is not one prospect but many. The post-communist world is very varied. In some areas, such as parts of former Yugoslavia, talk of the rule of law is fantasy - inspiring and perhaps fruitful fantasy but fantasy nonetheless. In other areas, law has some hold on the options open to political and other actors and on the imagination of a wider public. This is true, to an extent, of Poland and Hungary. Everywhere there are constitutions and legal institutions, but in many places it is clear that the law is not really on any one's mind; even less is it in anyone's heart. Albania and Byelorussia appear to be such countries and so, in the main, does Russia. In Hungary, on the other hand, the Constitutional Court is arguably the most powerful such court in the world, some would say too powerful (Sajó, 1996: 31-41), and its judgments on the law are authoritative and almost always heeded. Even here, however, in many areas of life the taste for legality is not at all strong and is slow to be acquired (Örkény, Scheppele, 1998).

And if the present is variable, the future is likely to be even more so. As Stephen Holmes has observed, "[a]ll we know for sure is that the multiple processes underway are unscripted and unsteered, and that there is no guarantee of a happy end" (Holmes, 1995: 1). Given this variety there are many different prospects and many stories to tell.

But the variety of these stories stems not only from the many ways in which we are ignorant. It flows equally from the different things we believe we know, which may not be so. Perceptions and predictions reflect underlying, often unconscious, assumptions and biases which observers bring to the materials. And such presuppositions - about matters of fact, possibility and value - even where they are unconscious, influence what is seen, what is done and what will be tried. Unless they are aired they will tend to do their work unnoticed. Even if this is good work, no devotee of the rule of law can be happy that things so important go undeclared.

What people regard as significant in and for post-communism often tells us as much about who they are or, as the phrase goes, where they are coming from, as it does about what they are purporting to discuss. It tends to betray as much about their intellectual, or even just personal, biography as it instructs us about the matters with which they deal.

Historians, for example, are prone to insist upon ancient legacies which allegedly govern present realities and thwart or determine the fate of present actions. Political scientists and economists tend to have shorter memories. Many of them discuss matters of institutional design as though they were drawing on slates which are virginal, or very easily wiped clean. They are far more concerned with what to draw on the slates than what to draw from them. Local intellectuals view with scorn and distaste the *hubris* of imported "experts" who keep telling them, often with mock humility and real insensitivity, what they must do to get from where they are to where they should be. Cultural pessimists - both from home and abroad, and not always more sensitive - imply that they needn't bother because they won't get far, starting where they do and carrying the cultural baggage that they do.

Such differences of viewpoint reflect the variety of assumptions and biases which underlie, often too deeply to be noticed, much thought and writing about what does, can and should go on in the region. I want to bring two such biases to the surface and examine them. Both are prevalent, and in pure form they have directly contradictory implications. The first is common among optimistic reformers, and its natural object is institutions. The second is found among - usually sadder but they might say wiser - pessimists. Its orientation is cultural. So first I will speak of institutional optimism, and second of cultural pessimism.

Those with an institutional bias spend a great deal of time discussing the best form that laws, constitutions and institutions should take. Typically such forms are modelled on others considered to have worked well somewhere else or are advocated on theoretical grounds: constitutions, parliamentary arrangements, presidents, privatization, rules of property, bills of rights, and so on. Those of a more cultural turn of mind are often sceptical of such institutional experimentation, at least when the institutions are new or foreign. If institutions are alien to the cultures onto which they are grafted, this approach suggests, the grafts are unlikely to take. In post-communist societies, moreover, institutions of the rule of law *are* typically alien, and, so culturalists often assume, many of the existing political and legal cultures are not likely to be receptive to solutions of the first, institutional, kind. Uncongenial national traditions and/or the experience of communism are often pointed to here.

Few people avow either of these options explicitly, at least in pure form, but many approaches betray their often unconscious, subterranean, influence. One rough indication of where anyone stands on these questions is their reaction to failure of institutional reforms. Institutional optimists will blame contingent characteristics of the institutions in place, or the particular ways in which the reforms have been - or not been - instituted. They will advocate improvements and, often, greater zeal and purity of motive. Everyone in the region knows an economist of this sort. Cultural pessimists, by contrast, will knowingly shrug their shoulders, and mutter the particular regional equivalent of "it was ever thus". Russia and the Balkans produce especially many such melancholic types, but they are everywhere. I wish to show that, though neither alternative is baseless, both can be seriously misleading and neither is an adequate guide to the chances of developing either constitutionalism or the rule of law. I will take each approach in turn.

Institutional Optimism

Thinking about institutions, it is tempting to think about law. Indeed lawyers find the temptation irresistible. And so, legal and constitutional measures - to constitutionalize the polity, to protect rights, to facilitate legitimate business activities and proscribe illegitimate ones, and much else - are plentiful, in post-communist Europe and elsewhere, and the literature on them is not small. That in itself is not a bad thing. But it is not clear how good a thing it is. In what circumstances do constitutions and other measures have any bite; in what circumstances are they worthless? What is it about the instruments and institutions themselves that makes for good consequences, what for bad? What beyond these instruments and institutions is necessary for a written constitution to be a working one? Are such conditions sufficient, and if so, is there any need for constitutions? Perhaps they will be unnecessary where social and political conditions are propitious and useless where they are absent. We don't have rich answers to these questions, but in post-communist Europe we have plenty of legal and social experiments which bear on them.

Some post-communist actors - both among elites and in sections of the society - hope that law will come to have a particular role and significance in their societies; a role and significance that it did not have under communism nor - in many countries in the region - before communism either. They hope that it might take root as a relatively impersonal, independent and institutionalized practice and medium for the exercise and restraint of power; one which might contribute to channelling, but also to setting limits on the power of citizens and states, including powerful citizens and powerful states. That is how things work, they believe, in "normal" countries.

These people hope, in other words, that not just law but the *rule of law* might be introduced, in societies which have long lacked it or never had it. That was implicit in the peaceful, and legal, way in which most of the "refolutions"[2] that ended communism occurred, and such hopes lie behind the rewriting of constitutions, the establishment and development of new institutions, such as constitutional courts, and a great deal of legalistic rhetoric from political and other leaders. In some countries, such as Poland and Hungary, moreover, there appears to be widespread popular endorsement of such ambitions (Kolarska-Bobińska, 1994) and at least strong rhetorical endorsement by most of the political class (Arato, 1994: 180-246; Krygier, 1994: 104-20). What should be done to promote these ambitions and what chances do they have?

A lot of attention has been devoted to the drafting and passing of rights-bearing constitutions. Many people think this is central and devote much attention to theoretical and practical arguments in favour of, or against, particular constitutional arrangements. Yet some countries do well with unsightly constitutions, while others seem to get nowhere with works of high constitutional art. Hungary has the most influential body of constitutional law in the region, though its constitution is a hastily scrambled together set of amendments to the original communist constitution; with neither the amendments - still less the original - being of great legal distinction. Poland has only just (in 1997) managed to get the new constitution which has been the subject of discussion since 1989. In the meantime it made do with an amended Stalinist constitution. Conversely, most of the former member states of the USSR have new, even sparkling, constitutions, but human rights of every sort are immeasurably less protected than in Hungary and Poland. Sometimes this is because the constitution is poor, as with the Estonian, which one author commends as "impressive for its voluptuous and baroque fairytale articles". As he goes on to observe, "it would be an exaggeration to say that such abundant constitution-drafting is helpful for a judge or for others who have to apply this norm" (Blankenagel, 1996: 61). On the other hand, it is obvious that even a perfectly designed constitution can never be either self-interpreting or self-enforcing. It needs institutions and it needs something far less palpable but just as important - what might be called a spirit of constitutionalism - and we have no recipes for producing that. More broadly, we lack recipes for the effective protection of human rights wherever they have long gone unprotected. But we don't lack chefs.

Institutionalist menus primarily feature laws and institutions, rather than societies and cultures. They are particularly congenial to lawyers. It is natural for them to think that law and lawyers are of great importance, particularly when it is their own laws which so many people seem to wish to emulate these days. And there is no shortage of legal "experts" who have been enlisted as advisers by post-communist governments. If, say, the criminal code of Atlanta Georgia seems to work well, why not hire an Atlanta lawyer to write a code for Tbilisi Georgia. Stranger things have happened.

At their worst, such performances manage exquisitely to combine arrogance with ignorance.[3] They are often well-motivated, though. The foreign expert knows something which the indigenous neophyte is keen to know. The former can see at a glance the lack in benighted post-communist societies of what is routine and effective at home. Why not recommend it? Particularly when home is a high-prestige country, such as America, and its laws are high-prestige laws, and when many people regard their own values *and* the institutions that secure them as universally applicable. More particularly, when it is so much easier than learning about the other Georgia. Indeed, in order to be fully equipped one needs to learn nothing new.

Locals, and international funding agencies, often welcome such experts. It is not irrelevant that the money always travels in the same direction as the experts: from west to east. But that is not the only reason.

Emerging from a horrendous political, social and economic order, and living in considerable chaos and uncertainty, citizens in post-communist societies often have an exaggerated form of what Australians call "cultural cringe", in relation to experts from "normal" countries. They feel that they have so much to learn, that elsewhere is already known. And with respect to many institutions, practices, and ways of behaving, this attitude is at least preferable to its opposite - which, unfortunately, can also be found. One does not, after all, have to be a victim of cultural cringe to appreciate that many achievements of "normal" countries had no parallel in the communist world, to regret this, and to wish that it might now change.

As practised by lawyers, the simple universalism of this first approach is often fairly unreflective. Laws are often treated as kinds of technical equipment, social machinery, which can be transported and plugged in wherever the need for them arises. That laws "in action" might also be - and depend upon - complex cultural accretions lies outside most lawyers' expertise (and, often, their range of interest). But there can also be sophisticated reasons to ignore local peculiarities. Economists assume rational economic actors, not Russians or communists - *homo economicus,* not *homo sovieticus.* This is not necessarily because economists are parochial or ignorant, but because their manner of theorizing does not start from empirical particulars. Asking what any rational actor would do in the circumstances, they focus on clearing the space and designing incentive structures to enable such actors to do what one thinks they should do. Overall, and if circumstances allow, ordinary people are expected to do likewise. Many theorists of constitutionalism and public choice are accustomed to think similarly. Their underlying social theory is individualist, their mode of procedure is rationalist, and their ambitions are literally unbounded. To do this sort of work well, it certainly helps to be clever, and many of those who do it certainly are. It is not necessary, however, to know very much about the societies on which you bestow your advice, and many don't.

The fruits of such approaches are mixed. At their best, they can allow richly informed theoretical discussion, of practices and institutions of real and demonstrated value, to be brought to bear on important problems. They can also aid in the transplantation of institutions, values, and traditions of thought which are worthy, highly valued, and might stimulate thoughtfulness in difficult conditions. Since a key problem of communist societies was intellectual isolation, this is all to the good.

More prosaically perhaps, good legal craftsmanship is more than likely indispensable both for effective laws and for the development of a culture of legality. It is intrinsically a useful thing to propagate in societies where it is thinly spread around. There are technically preferable ways of dealing with many problems which have occurred in non-communist societies and may well occur in post-communist societies. Well-constructed laws might help provide them. Some countries have rich traditions of thought about constitutional law and constitutional interpretation; others - among them all post-communist countries - have few such traditions at all. And legality is not possible without adequate legal infrastructure. This includes independent and adequately trained lawyers, satisfying career paths, an independent and adequately paid judiciary, a police force trained in some ways and not others, open to some incentives and not others, and so on. There has been a lot of serious thought about such matters in liberal democratic societies, and it would be silly not to draw on it.

And some transplants work. Think of the extraordinarily successful institution of the ombudsman in Poland: copied from Scandinavian models by Polish lawyers, with no local or regional precedent; installed by unsympathetic but usefully uncomprehending Communists in the 1980s; and - to the surprise of everyone including the first incumbent, who made it so - fast to become the best known official defender of citizens' rights in post-war and now post-communist Poland, one of its most popular institutions, and the home of, successively, two of its most respected public figures. Similar remarks might be made about the more cautious but increasingly significant Polish Constitutional Court, or the younger, bolder and much more powerful Hungarian Constitutional Court. Why, then, reinvent the wheel or insist that Polish or Hungarian wheelwrights have nothing to learn from foreign ones?

Yet, as every sociologist of law - though not every lawyer - knows, the effectiveness even of particular, special-purpose laws depends on a lot besides the laws themselves. Even more so, constitutionalism and the rule of law. Although more thought has been given to the export of specific laws and institutions than to what might be necessary to make them count, if no one is listening it doesn't matter too much what the law is saying. And if one is concerned with why people listen and why laws count, then - as Marc Galanter has observed of a quite different question - "[t]he answer will not yield to the most painstaking study of the law, for the deep fountains of change are outside it" (Galanter, 1992: 24). Since, moreover, there are differences both within and between societies in this regard, one might need to learn not just about people or societies in general, but about particular features of particular societies.

Some institutionalists do know the societies about which they speak. They emphasize institutions, not because that is all they understand, or because of simple economistic assumptions, but because of theoretically informed observation of post-communist societies themselves. Some, like Stephen Holmes, are well aware of culturalist pessimism, but they find it unpersuasive. Holmes argues powerfully that many such explanations suffer from severe methodological and empirical weaknesses, that culturalists have not made the case for the decisive importance of cultural legacies in current behaviour and that, at least in relation to the post-communist region, cultural pessimists frequently overlook a simpler and methodologically more adequate explanation of institutional failure. For, Holmes insists, the real problem for legality and rights in post-communist societies is not that cultures are hostile but that public institutions are pitifully weak; "[l]iberalization cannot succeed under conditions of state collapse, for the democratization of state authority is pointless if no state authority exists" (Holmes, 1995: 29). And the real lesson of post-communism for anyone interested in rights is:

> not that state power endangers liberal rights, but *exactly the contrary*, that liberal rights are wholly unrealizable without effective extractive, administrative, regulative, and adjudicative authorities. Rights protection and enforcement depend on state capacities. Statelessness, therefore, means rightlessness....Rights, quite obviously, are an enforced uniformity. Equality before the law cannot be secured over a vast territory without a relatively effective, honest, centralized bureaucratic organization. (Holmes, 1995: 356)

Thus the simple (though it is rarely simple) institutionalization of public power is a necessity, logically prior to any particular form of that institutionalization: crudely put, to have a nice state you must first have an effective state. Such institutionalization depends upon complex capacities, social, political and financial resources, and intellectual craftsmanship and design. In this sense it is certainly true, as Holmes puts it, that "the Hobbesian problem has to be solved before the Lockean solution looks attractive" (Holmes, 1995: 38). And given the complexity and changefulness of contemporary societies, it is no small matter to solve the Hobbesian problem. Nor the Lockean one either. A major question central to the proper understanding of constitutionalism and the rule of law is: what sorts of state strength are indispensable for the attainment of these values, and how might they be institutionalized? The understandable preoccupation with avoiding those sorts of strength which *destroy* these liberal values should not delude us into regarding a weak state as a positive achievement.

However, even if one is persuaded that strong public institutions are crucial to the defence of rights, as I am (Krygier, October 1996: 26-32; Winter 1997), this does not dispose of the problem of culture. For there is, first of all, a general methodological difficulty which afflicts every attempt to explain sources of disappointment in post-communist societies: there are so many potential candidates, and many of them point in similar directions. So, is it hostile political culture, state weakness, poverty or bad weather which explains the weakness of the rule of law in, say, Russia? Sad to say, Russia has them all, and not much of the rule of law. How to choose? Even if we eliminate the weather, since Norway and Iceland appear to have overcome it, the answer to our question still seems over-determined. Worse still, it is not clear that these potential explanatory factors are unrelated or exclusive alternatives. In the conditions of post-communism, they seem so entangled and mutually reinforcing that it is extremely hard to know how to distinguish between them. There are, for example, many reasons why rights-friendly institutions are weak in post-communist conditions, and inhospitable cultural legacies may be significant among them.

For what Holmes terms a "crisis of governability" (Holmes, 1995: 31) is not a causal primitive, but rather a complex *result*, which is likely to have many causes. Such a crisis might go on to have many important effects, but in such circumstances it is hard to pit "state collapse" *against* other putative causes, which themselves might augment the effects of state weakness, and, more important, might contribute to that very weakness. And "effective and accountable instruments of government",[4] too, which can uncorruptly and enforceably administer clear and socially useful laws which people are used to obey, are the product of many things - institutions, personnel, traditions, resources, ways of behaving and being expected to behave. Culturalists might plausibly insist that many of these elements have cultural sources, and are not merely a matter of "institutional architecture and resource allocation" (Holmes, 1995: 38). So a strong state explanation might not be an *alternative* to a cultural legacy or weak civil society explanation, but a result of factors that such explanations pick up. Markets and the effective defence of rights do have political preconditions, and Holmes is right to emphasize them. Yet these preconditions, in turn, might plausibly be argued to have non-political preconditions too. Russia might have all sorts of problems because it lacks an effective, infrastructure-providing state, and it might lack such a state, *inter alia*, because it has inhospitable cultural and other legacies. You can't just buy one and plug it in; even if it is splendidly designed and even if - as is rarely the case in the region - you could afford to buy one at all.

Cultural Pessimism

So, in any event, say partisans of the second approach mentioned above. Post-communist societies, it is often said, *lack* important cultural prerequisites possessed by societies which their leaders seek to emulate, and *possess* cultural legacies incompatible with such ambitions. In particular this approach emphasizes aspects of social and political culture, purportedly necessary for liberal achievements, and missing from the history of the region.

It has become increasingly evident that not every value advocated for the region is valued in the region, even when - as with "rights", for example - the label is widely used (Krygier and Czarnota, 1996: 101-38). "Human rights", so we are often told, "are historically and ideologically the property of the liberal democracies of the west...they enshrine values which are universal neither in time nor in place. They are in essence the Enlightenment's values of possessive individualism" (Sedley, 1995: 386; see also Gray, 1993: 26-50). Moreover, means of institutionalizing such values allegedly travel even less well than the values themselves. All sorts of "hard facts" (di Palma, 1990)[5] can be assembled to show, for example, why post-communist soil is particularly inhospitable to grafts of constitutionalism, democracy, or whatever else it is from the West that seems desirable in, but absent from, the East.

Very often these hard facts amount simply to the absence of aspects of Western culture which are taken to have contributed to what the West has. Thus, by comparison with western Europe and its offshoots, many post-communist countries lack traditions of legality, democracy, tolerance. Middle classes were rarely well developed. So too capitalism (and Protestantism). They are poor, and in relation to the great centres and engines of modernity, they have always been peripheral. The political orders of many, for long periods, were despotic or at least non-democratic. The eastern countries among them belong not to Latin Christendom and the law-centred civilization that it spawned but rather to Orthodox and - to a lesser extent - Islamic civilizations, where law and the rule of law played less prominent roles. To the extent that law counted, it did so primarily as an instrument of central command, and less - if at all - as a medium of communication and defence among citizens and between citizens and the state. And whatever the countries of the region might once have been, for the forty to seventy years preceding the collapse of communism, they experienced communism. That experience and the "bloc culture"[6] it generated, many allege, is good for nothing, certainly nothing so liberal as the rule of law. And I have not even mentioned that "tangled tragedy of mass rape and barbaric slaughter" which allegedly is "[t]he history of all the southern Slavs in the Balkans" (Whitney quoted in Salecl, 1994: 90-91), peopled for centuries by "irreconcilable warring tribes" (Gelb, quoted in Salecl, 1994: 91).

Such lines of thought are reinforced by the increasing modishness of cultural and "civilizational" explanations of social behaviour, which is becoming evident in many disciplinary contexts. Samuel Huntington finds the world divided into seven or eight civilizational blocs, most of them millennia old, and only one of them - the West - hospitable to the rule of law (Huntington, 1996). Apart from what he says about post-communism, which will be discussed below, he endorses the now widespread talk of "Asian values", which, it appears, are very old, good for business but bad for liberal democracy. And even if one wanted to adopt them (as some Australian politicians appear to), they - like other civilizational characteristics - are not for sale.

Robert Putnam (1993) distinguishes between those regions of Italy which possess "civic" culture and many good things that flow from that, and those which don't, and suffer. The sad lesson for reformers is that he finds these differences going back about a thousand years. He doesn't rule out the possibility of useful institutional reform, but he does emphasize the time it takes, and he does rather take the edge off it. As he extrapolates for the post-communist region:

> Many of the formerly Communist societies had weak civic traditions before the advent of Communism, and totalitarian rule abused even that limited stock of social capital. Without norms of reciprocity and networks of civic engagement, the Hobbesian outcome of the Mezzogiorno - amoral familism, clientelism, lawlessness, ineffective government, and economic stagnation - seems likelier than successful democratization and economic development. Palermo may represent the future of Moscow.
>
> The civic community has deep historical roots. This is a depressing observation for those who view institutional reform as a strategy for political change. (Putnam, 1993: 183)

What are constitutionalists to make of all this? There is no doubt that cultural inheritances often do reproduce themselves and mould the frames of thought and action of their heirs. This issue has been addressed in a variety of ways and with a variety of concepts. Wittgenstein spoke of *Lebensformen* presupposed in all of our social activities and thoughts. Heidegger of *Dasein*. Michael Polanyi stressed the role of "tacit knowledge" in even the most advanced and innovative forms of thought. Bourdieu coins the concept *habitus*. Gadamer, Shils, and the early Oakeshott speak of tradition. All of them explore phenomena pointed to by Wittgenstein's description of language, as:

> an ancient city: a maze of little streets and squares, of old and new houses, and of houses with additions from various periods; and this surrounded by a multitude of new boroughs with straight, regular streets and uniform houses. (Wittgensten, 1967: 8)

Most of this city existed before any of us was born, some of it will be renovated in our lifetime, much of it will not. Some we will come to dislike, much will seem to us obviously, even naturally, right and appropriate. In any event, we cannot even think without it. Moreover, unlike a city and like language, our cultural context is not merely inhabited, but it inhabits, shapes and moulds those brought up in it. After all, cities can be razed to the ground and rebuilt from scratch, though it is a rare and abnormal practice and post-war Warsaw is not a good advertisement for it. In complex cultural traditions such as language, myths, national legends or indeed law, however, it is far harder to liquidate the presence and authority of the cultural past; Warsaw again is exemplary here. In culture, unlike architecture, after all, one is not simply an inhabitant and manipulator of existing structures, though one might be that as well. One's thoughts, values, symbols, are enveloped and to a large extent constituted by the given. Such cultural traditions are not mere instruments which can be taken up or put aside at will; the existence of such traditions and one's participation in them is a precondition for the renovation of elements of them and for the invention and construction of others. No one starts from scratch.

Like ordinary language, cultural traditions shape and to a considerable extent constitute what succeeding participants in the traditions believe, imagine, practise; indeed what they find it possible to believe, imagine, practise. We do manipulate cultural traditions, to be sure, and successful manipulations often enter and alter the traditions that we contribute in passing on. But before we manipulate, we inherit, inhabit, and participate in traditions which began earlier and last longer than we: this constrains our power. Not only does the pre-existence of cultural tradition constrain what individuals can do or think to do, it influences the continuing fate of what they come to do. And our successful manipulations often survive us to become part of the present of our successors. This constrains their power. It would be senseless to deny the importance of these aspects of life. In such a context novelties continually occur, but they do so "within an already existing idiom of activity" (Oakeshott, 1991: 121). Like those much discussed boat-repairers at sea, participants in most complex traditions are deeply constrained by their environments. In both cases, not everything one does is determined by the environment. On the other hand, it is difficult to walk away.

This is generally true and it is true of the rule of law. Where institutions and rules of restraint are strong, a large part of that strength typically flows - not directly or solely from the institutions and rules themselves - but from the traditions in which they were formed and from the culture which they themselves generated and which grows around and encrusts them, coming to form and shape the routine expectations of participants and observers. As Philip Selznick has remarked:

> The starting mechanism [of institutionalization] is often a formal act, such as the adoption of a rule or statute. To be effective, however, the enactment must build upon pre-existing resources of regularity and legitimacy and must lead to a new history of consistent conduct and supportive belief. Institutions are established, not by decree alone, but as a result of being bound into the fabric of social life. Even so weighty an enactment as the United States Constitution cannot be understood apart from the legal and political history that preceded it, the interpretive gloss given it by the courts, and the role it has played in American history and consciousness. The formal acts of adoption and ratification were only part of a more complex, more open-ended process of institution-building. (Selznick, 1992: 232)

Moreover, the wider social efficacy of official law requires, not merely that elites observe and seek to enforce it, but also that it enter into the normative structures which nourish, guide, inform, and co-ordinate the actions of ordinary people; people who do not merely comply resentfully when they feel they might otherwise be punished, but who comply happily (enough) even when they are confident they will not be. And for the rule of law to *count*, rather than simply to be announced or decreed, people must *care* about what the law says - the rules themselves must be taken seriously, and the institutions must come to matter. They must enter into the psychological economy of everyday life - to bear both on calculations of likely official responses *and* on those many circumstances in which one's actions are very unlikely to come to any official's attention at all. They must mesh with, rather than contradict or be irrelevant to the "intuitive law" of which Leon Petrażycki wrote, in terms of which people think about and organize their everyday lives. None of this can be simply decreed.

If institutions are to endure and take on strength, then, they owe their solidity to things deeper than the bare existence of appropriate rules, to understandings and expectations - many of them borne by and grounded in cultural traditions, within which the rules take on meaning and significance. These understandings, expectations and traditions, in turn, gain strength from their often invisible pervasiveness. Where thickly institutionalized constraints *do* exist - indeed typically where they do their best work - they are often not noticed, for they are internalized by both the powerful and those with less power, as the normal ways to behave. Limits are not tested because people cannot *imagine* that they should be. Without all this, all the more when a state's and society's traditions are *hostile* to restraint of power by law, one lacks a great deal. These are hard facts indeed.

However, cultural sensitivity is not the same thing as cultural determinism. The former might encourage "piecemeal social engineering"[7] which - in the face of some institutionalist enthusiasms - would be salutary. The latter is likelier merely to encourage despair. And when, as often in recent debates, culture is invoked as a kind of prime "unmoved mover" of the social world, there are reasons to share Hermann Goering's reaction to the term, though they are not his reasons. Not to evade the cultural point, but perhaps to sharpen it, certain distinctions should be kept in mind.

First of all, it pays to distinguish different sorts of cultural explanations from each other, since they emphasize different things and often point in different directions. Such explanations are not necessarily logically inconsistent with each other, but each tends to focus on different cultural *layers* in a society's past which allegedly form its present. The main candidates appear to be: aspects of culture common to the *civilization* to which a society belongs, those which stem from *national* traditions, and those which flow from the communist regimes which dominated in the area until very recently.

The currently most-discussed representative of the first alternative is Samuel Huntington's recent work, *The Clash of Civilizations and the Remaking of World Order.* Huntington emphasizes *civilizational* differences which allegedly are the primary sources of allegiance and division in the globe, which are rooted most deeply in religion and are millennia old. While he is primarily concerned with international relations, his comments about civilization and culture suggest that they go all the way down. Among the "central characteristics of the West, those which distinguish it from other civilizations", is the rule of law: "The tradition of the rule of law laid the basis for constitutionalism and the protection of human rights, including property rights, against the exercise of arbitrary power. In most other civilizations law was a much less important factor in shaping thought and behaviour" (Huntington, 1996: 69-70). On this basis, it appears that one can ignore the pre-communist authoritarian regimes that ruled for much of the history of Poland and Hungary, and that distinguished them from interwar Czechoslovakia. One need not worry too much that all three suffered under forty years of communist rule either, since all three belong to Western Christian civilization. They should therefore be able to manage constitutionalism and the rule of law, though neither is a feature of their recent experience. Whether one of these countries might do better than another does not appear from this approach, nor is it clear why either should do better than Croatia. All three countries, however, must be presumed to have more chance than Romania and Serbia (Orthodox) and Bosnia (Islamic) which, given their civilizational disqualifications, presumably needn't even try.

Some culturalists, more modest in their ambitions, deal merely with central and eastern Europe rather than the planet. Even here, however, their analyses diverge dramatically. The two most popular candidates in cultural explanations of regional affairs are old national or regional traditions, on the one hand, and the cultural consequences of communism, on the other. Of course, there almost certainly are significant residues from both, and the latter might have reinforced the former, but their implications differ. If analyses of the first sort are correct, then discussion of these countries as "post-communist" misses the deeper cultural point.

Thus, writers on Yugoslavia often portray communism as little more than a giant glacier enveloping the seething tribes within. It managed to keep them frozen still for a time, but on melting down exposed them in all their ancient vileness, tragically alive and refreshed once more. Writing of less apocalyptic matters, Jerzy Jedlicki reminds us, in a brief but nuanced discussion of "The Unbearable Burden of History" (Jedlicki, 1990: 39-45) in Eastern Europe, that this is not the first time that many East Europeans have sought to "return to Europe". He seems to suggest that they were never really there in the first place, but since the eighteenth century have nonetheless repeatedly indulged in dreams of "return". He suggests that many of the reasons for their backwardness continue to weigh on the countries of the region. Prospects that the most recent attempts to "return" might succeed, while not closed, are not enormously promising: "There is no linear development in East European history, but rather a Sisyphus-like labour of ups and downs, of building and wrecking, where little depends on one's own ingenuity and perseverance" (Jedlicki, 1990: 40).

Sacrificing nuance for rhetorical power, John Gray explains that:

> in throwing off the universalist institutions that supposedly nurtured Homo Sovieticus, the post-Soviet peoples have not thereby adopted the Western liberal self-image of universal rights-bearers, or buyers and sellers in a global market. Instead, they have returned to their pre-Soviet particularisms, ethnic and religious - to specific cultural traditions that, except in Bohemia, are hardly those of Western liberal democracy...not, manifestly, an ending of history, but rather its resumption on decidedly traditionalist lines - of ethnic and religious conflicts, irredentist claims, strategic calculations, and secret diplomacies. This return to the historical realities of European political life will remain incomprehensible, so long as those realities are viewed through the spectacles of ephemeral Enlightenment ideologies. We will not, for example, understand current developments in Poland if our model for them is the transitory nightmare of Marxian Communism; we will gain insight into them if we grasp them as further variations on historical themes...that are millennial. (Gray, 1993: 27)

So much for all those Poles who treated the label "post-communist" seriously, and imagined that forty years of communism had made some mark on their country. According to Gray, that is simple Enlightenment folly. With this revelation come both bad and good news. The bad news appears to be that it was all a ghastly mistake, worse still a Western mistake (though it came to Poland from the East). The good news is that it will have no enduring effects, since it was just a "transitory nightmare" dreamt up in the West, and therefore not Polish at all. That will be particularly welcome news to those in the third group of culturalists, such as Sztompka, who atttribute much of Polish and other post-communist "civilizational incompetence" to the "bloc culture" which all communist countries shared and which stemmed directly from the imposed communist political order and the social adjustments it generated.

Subjects of communism, Sztompka argues, developed a number of civilizationally incompetent cultural traits, which he elaborates in terms of a series of dichotomies that he takes to be exaggerated in post-bloc societies, and the first pole of which, so to speak, is characteristically favoured there: "(a) private vs public, (b) past vs future; (c) fate vs human agency; (d) negative vs. positive freedom; (e) mythology vs realism, (f) West vs East, (g) usefulness vs truth" (Sztompka, 1991: 295-311; see also Sztompka, 1995). Sztompka argues that the culture of civilizational competence is indispensable for the workings of civilized institutions, and post-communist societies are not rich in it. Though he does not argue that nothing can be done or that culture is unalterable, he insists that it lies far deeper than institutions, is rarely the product of design, and takes far longer than institutional structures to change. Similar views about "post-communist" cultural residues are widespread in the region and among scholars of it.

Thus, according to many scholars seeking to decipher the phenomenon of post-Communism, there was a distinctive and deep pattern to and legacy of the social impact of Leninist regimes. It was most apparent in the lack of a routinely and normatively regulated public sphere. As Jowitt argues, what was common to societies under Leninist regimes and what often pre-dated them was:

> a worldview in which political life is suspect, distasteful, and possibly dangerous; to be kept at bay by dissimulation, made tolerable by private intimacy, and transcended by private virtues or charismatic ethics...the Leninist legacy, understood as the impact of Party organization, practice, and ethos *and* the initial charismatic ethical opposition to it favour an authoritarian, not a liberal democratic capitalist, way of life; the obstacles to which are not simply how to privatize and marketize the economy, or organize an electoral campaign, but rather how to institutionalize public virtues (Jowitt, 1992: 293). (For similar characterizations, see Clark and Wildavsky, 1990; Podgórecki, 1994; Sztompka, 1991.)

The consequences of this were clear in regard to law. Law existed, at times in bulk, but primarily, and professedly, as a subordinate - indeed servile - branch of political, administrative, and at times quasi-theocratic power.[8] The role of law was conceived of in almost exclusively instrumental terms, sometimes as a repressive instrument of social control, sometimes as an executive instrument of centrally determined goals, values and decisions; never as an independent check on governmental power. Communist rulers saw the law as a flexible statement of subjects' duties rather than of their rights, still less of duties with which state institutions themselves should comply. In any event, whatever the law said, the Party might decree otherwise and the law would bend. Citizens also did not expect the law to vindicate their rights or to restrain state officials; still less party officials. Nor were they often persuaded that their own legal duties amounted to moral ones. Thus, in surreal parody of the classical debates of jurisprudence, Communist rulers maintained a "higher law" which was not law at all, and subjects were strict legal positivists, for whom law and morals had no necessary connection. Indeed it was often assumed that each was inversely related to the other.

In eastern Europe, one to two generations have lived in constant negotiation and manipulation of, and subordination to, this vast and pervasive growth, of what Zygmunt Bauman calls the communist "patronage state" (Bauman, 1993). In the ex-Soviet Union almost no one living knows any other way to live. The problem bequeathed by these states is - as the London *Economist* observed - "not so much Eastern Europe's underdevelopment as its misdevelopment" (16 May, 1992: 59). As the *Economist* also notes, such problems are "in some ways trickier to sort out; westerners had experience of modernizing backward countries, but not of redirecting wayward ones suffering from sophisticated socialism".

To the extent that such bloc-wide problems and a post-communist culture exist, then even Huntington's Western Christian post-communists and Gray's Bohemians will be afflicted with them, and it is hard to see immediately what can differentiate post-communist Poland from post-communist Serbia. More surprisingly still, if one were to concentrate on bloc culture above all, perhaps the Czech Republic - which had a heavy dose of it - should be expected to do worse than the former Yugoslavia, where it lay less heavily on the ground. But that is not how it looks at the moment.

Apart from the fact that each of these cultural perspectives - civilizational, national-historical, post-communist - differs from the others in the depth of archaeological excavation that is encouraged, there are two similarities between them all, and two differences also worth noting. The first similarity is that they all are congenitally prone to a methodological fallacy that Holmes has identified among many students of Russia:

> *they confused analogy with causality.* Their thesis was, put crudely, that the world is the way it is because it reminds us of the way it used to be. ...Formulated diagnostically, they mistook the false pleasure of pattern recognition for the genuine pleasure of causal explanation. The past is such a wonderful predictor of the future, in truth, because the past is almost infinitely rich. Genetic stories with a determinist hue usually result from an unspoken sifting of the evidence. If you examine the past closely, you can find foreshadowings of just about anything that comes to pass. (Holmes, 1995: 6)

Secondly, and partly because history makes so many stories available, cultural explanations have a seductive promiscuity about them. Thus, at this *fin de siecle* moment, the analogies that most authors favour serve to confirm disappointed expectations, since there are many such expectations about. But when - not so long ago - expectations were overwhelmed with equally unexpected, but apparently triumphant developments, culture was equally available to help out. Neal Ascherson well exemplifies this uplifting usefulness of culture:

> In 1944, we thought, the tree of Polish history had been sawn down for good, and a new house had been built over the stump. In 1968, some holes had appeared in the floor of the house, and certain uninviting parts of the stump could be seen through them. But in the mid-1970s, as the floor began to disintegrate, the truth of what was taking place could no longer be ignored: the tree was growing again, shoving its huge, amputated head up through all the concrete laid on top of it. All of Poland's political and spiritual tradition was reviving...Each successive shock - 1970, 1976, and finally 1980 - broke away more pieces of the house that Gomulka had founded a generation before. And each time, more of this buried but ominously authentic Polish consciousness emerged into light. (Ascherson, 1981: 96)

Unfortunately, it is hard to know in advance what that "buried but ominously authentic Polish consciousness" will dictate. Worse still, it appears often to change its mind. At the moment that Solidarity came to power, it was common to observe that Polish *politics* were distinctively promising, because they had a large and experienced counter-elite, unlike the rest of the post-communist region. Polish *economics* was far less happy, not only because it was in a particularly bad way at the time but also because Poles had no real traditions of economic activity. Over the last eight years, however, the counter-elite has more often than not been in disarray, and the economy is one of the - if not *the* - strongest in the region.

Notwithstanding these overarching similarities, it is important to attend to the particular layers of culture that are invoked. Different forms of cultural explanation generate quite significant differences in analysis and predictions about particular countries in the region. Is a country's present a recycling of the immediate communist past, the mediate national past, or the civilizational framework which has shaped the land since time immemorial? Though it might be all three, it makes a very great difference what one emphasizes.

Moreover, devotees of the rule of law might draw significantly differing levels of cheer and gloom from the variety of cultural determinisms currently on offer. Poles and Czechs will be happy enough with Huntington, for he emphasizes their civilizational, and apparently ineradicable, Europeanness. They will, however, draw apart on Gray's advice that Poles (and virtually everyone else in the region), lacking Bohemia's democratic experience, should try something else. This may not even please those

Czechs persuaded by Gray's form of cultural archaeology, since their experience - twenty-one years between two world wars - might be adjudged too recent and brief to count for much. But if it *does* count for anything, that might suggest the following question: if the Czechs could do it then, why can no one else do it now? The answer might come from Sztompka's emphasis on common bloc culture, which puts Czechs back in the same listing boat with the whole region. Worse still, since Czechoslovakia suffered an altogether harsher imposition of that culture than, say, Poland, the tables might be turned. Who lies deeper, then, and who is more present in his effects: Masaryk or Husak? Hard to say.

On the other hand, if there is any abiding feature of their societies that central and east Europeans dislike, chances are that, on Huntington's and Gray's love for the *longue durée*, they are stuck with it. But not on Sztompka's analysis. It is hard to see what you can do about the civilization or millennial national tradition to which you belong. On the other hand, if Sztompka is right, there is still room to move. Bloc culture is usually characterized as formidable and inescapable by those who describe it, and yet, *in principle* - though rarely in design - theirs is a more optimistic variant than its other culturalist competitors. After all, communism was new once too. If so much can be effected by forty to seventy years of communism, and if many of these effects were apparent well before its collapse (as it appears they were), then perhaps post-communism will generate its own culture with its own institutions and without the insuperable difficulties that inhospitable cultures are often thought to present.

These remarks suggest a broader set of reflections on cultural explanation, wherever it occurs. A nation's presently significant cultural *traditions* are not the same as its cultural *history*. In part, they are made up of residues of that history, but not all and not only. They are not *all* of that history, since much that happened left no trace, and much of which we have traces has no *present* resonance or significance for anyone except historians. It is part of a nation's past, not its present; a past that is truly "a foreign country. They do things differently there" (Hartley, 1963: 9). It is a major and underexplored question about traditions of every sort: what is it that distinguishes those residues of the past which mould successive presents, whether recognized or not, and those which sink without presently effective traces.

One reason that the question is so hard to answer is that presently effective culture and cultural templates are not *only* historical residues. Often they are retrospective reconfigurations or even creations rather than the deep unalterable patterns and codes that they might seem to be. We have plenty of examples of the identification, reappropriation, and idealization of "pasts" - what has been described as the "invention of tradition" (Hobsbawm and Ranger, 1983) - which are in fact present redescriptions or inventions, drawing strength and legitimacy from their alleged antiquity. When they are taken up and talked up, they can be drawn upon to make plausible the claim that "we have always done it this way", even when we haven't. Even if we haven't, that we *believe* we have is a social fact of contemporary significance.

It is, however, a fact of a different sort than it is often taken to be. Its present significance depends on how it is taken up, not merely or even necessarily primarily on how, or even whether, it was once laid down. Rather than being an ineradicable cultural template to which later generations must passively conform, it may be a late invention or an oft-repeated cliché which - among other things - might serve to dissuade people from trying what they otherwise might, and what they might quite enjoy. Is the past of which a tradition speaks really inherited from the past, and particularly the past it alleges, or is it a more or less retrospectively imagined and selected, perhaps invented "past"? Has it seeped into social context without entering consciousness, its authority made manifest rather than acknowledged, or is it dependent on the existence of particular reflective contemporary attachments and evaluative commitments? Is it really transmitted from when it says by whom it says, or is it merely believed to be? If it is so transmitted, why should that matter more than a good story - whether or not it is true - that many people believe? Until we have confident answers to questions such as these, we should be a bit discriminating in attributing too much to culture or civilization or tradition, *tout court*.

A related point can be made. Cultural pessimism, and more broadly cultural and civilizational determinism, tend to slight the patently *dialectical* nature of participation in culture. It is the *interweaving* of inheritance and present response that makes cultural traditions as tangled and absorbing as they are. Inheritance is not sovereign, responses are not autonomous. The one - like language - provides contexts and resources for action and thought - often as important as they are unseen; the other - like speech - embroiders, improvises and innovates within these contexts, with these resources, often in unprecedented ways. Cultural traditions are ambiguous in their implications, open to interpretation and reinterpretation, there are many of them, and they often conflict. They condition, but they do not necessarily determine, and they in any case never can rule out novelty (Krygier, 1994:

45-67). Versions of the past are continually being refashioned for present purposes. In all complex and enduring traditions, there is constant interplay between inherited layers which pervade and - often unrecognized - mould the present, and the constant renewals and reshapings of the purported past in which authorized interpreters and guardians of the tradition indulge, and must indulge. This is all fairly obvious, but alertness to present response rather than solely to past inheritance can change our view of options available to contemporary actors. The Polish historian of social thought, Jerzy Szacki, has made a similar point in emphasizing the contrast between what he describes as "objective" and "subjective" conceptions of tradition:

> Working with a subjective conception of tradition, we move away from apprehending it in categories of 'pressure', 'weight', 'nightmares', etc, in categories of the 'rule of the past over the present'...With a subjective understanding of tradition the direction of interest is reversed: not the rule of the dead over the living, but of the living over the dead is the real subject of research on tradition. A conception of tradition as something simply given, which can only be accepted or rejected according to a traditionalist or utopian scheme, is thus overcome. There appears instead a complicated problematic of 'continuation and transformation', changing values, selections; currents, thanks to which islands of tradition crop up and disappear in the stream of inheritance. (Szacki, 1971: 149-50)

It is an obvious mistake, then, to think of participation in culture as a purely subjective matter, since it rarely begins with single individuals and, as culture, can never *end* with them. However, it is a less obvious, but often just as egregious, error to assume *in advance* that novelty is foreclosed by uncongenial inheritance. A dialectical understanding of culture and tradition gives *more* significance, not less, to the ingenuity, skill, craftsmanship, virtuosity of current actors. It does not render these talents pointless.

Moreover, even assuming that cultural scripts are unambiguous and their boundaries clear - which is a heroic assumption in present, perhaps any, times - current interpretations of a culture's past are often influenced by other things - some of them cultural too - which are drawn from outside the particular culture in which an interpreter is thought to stand. But then, if such interpretations are influential, the culture can come to accommodate much that is external, and might seem alien, to its origins. In the contemporary world, many of us are hybrids, and many cultures are too. So are legal and political orders. This is not to say that every graft will take. Much will depend on its prestige, the skill, energy and power of its promoters (and opponents), its intrinsic character, its adaptability to the interests of important social groups, as well as on the degree of clash between it and endogenously developed cultural values. But cultural syncretism is not new in the history of civilizations, and it has often spawned cultural and institutional novelties which nothing in the host culture allowed one to predict. New things, after all, do happen, some grafts take, and people learn. Poland, for example, never had an ombudsman; nor Hungary a Constitutional Court. They do now and both are effective institutions. Perhaps the first capitalists really did need to be Protestants. Later generations, it appears, can be Confucian. Indeed, today it almost appears that to be successful they *have to be* Confucian.

Cultural explanations often rely on metaphors of depth and shallowness, to distinguish between phenomena of greater and lesser significance. Such metaphors, and the distinctions they suggest, should be treated with respect but also with caution. In particular, we should be cautious about eliding depth with age and shallowness with youth. On the one hand, such metaphors clearly point to important differences. We are all aware of aspects of cultures and social structures which seem characteristic and durable over long periods, and which change slowly; and others which are ephemeral and change or vanish fast. It makes sense to speak of the former as deeply embedded and the latter as shallowly planted. But there are dangers in reifying such helpful metaphors. If not all of cultural history is presently effective, then it must follow that old is not necessarily deep, or at least that it might as well be "deeply buried" and presently ineffectual as "deeply embedded" and ineradicable in its effects. Nor is new necessarily superficial: capitalism is new in South Korea and Taiwan, but its effects appear deep enough. It is hard to imagine them being quickly washed away. A written constitution was new in the United States, and the world, in 1787, but it stayed around, becoming a deeply significant aspect of American, and not only American, political and legal culture. But if that is the case, what do we learn when we are told that despotism is old in eastern Europe and the attempt to foster the rule of law is new? If that is all we know, then not a lot.

Cultural determinisms are liable to be embarrassed by novelty, not only in practice as we all are, but in principle. Just as such explanations often surface when rationalist optimists are disappointed, so they tend to generate an intellectually overreaching *theoretical* pessimism, where that is rarely warranted. This is the burden of di Palma's polemic against theoretical pessimism about the possibility of democracy in hard times and places, and it might be applied to constitutionalism and the rule of law as well. Such pessimism, in the face of cultural and structural "hard facts", is the product of "a dismal science of politics (or the science of a dismal politics) that passively entrusts political change to exogenous and distant social transformations. Applied to the future of democracy [and, one might add, constitutionalism], such a science translates instinctively the structurally improbable (the hard facts) into the politically impossible" (di Palma, 1990: 4). It accounted for social scientists' failure to anticipate the collapse of despotisms in Spain, Portugal, Latin America and communist Europe. In each case, as in many cases where pessimism is plausible, there were many reasons for it but not enough to foreclose more optimistic possibilities. In each case, however, many observers took such pessimism as sufficient reason to rule out such possibilities and discourage those who strove for them. As I write, Hong Kong democrats are being deluged with similarly unhelpful advice. But as di Palma has brilliantly demonstrated, "[h]ard facts do not mean necessity" (di Palma, 1990: 8). And as he goes on to demonstrate in rich and arresting detail, "[w]hatever the historical trends, whatever the hard facts, the importance of human action in a difficult transition should not be underestimated" (di Palma, 1990: 9).

Finally, and at the very least, this *Babel* of explanations suggests that, even if at what might be called the ontological level cultural explanation is onto something important, we have no adequate theoretical basis to dissuade anyone from trying something new, at least not merely on the ground that it *is* new. Here our problem is as much epistemological as metaphysical. It is undoubtedly true that many aspects of culture often lie deep within and some do not, and that some are sticky and relatively resistant to change, and others less so. It is less obvious that, at present, anyone has any clear way of telling which is which and how much. Retrospective cultural explanations are often illuminating, but not in telling us what to do next.

For even if one is aware of cultural obstacles, what should one do about them? Hard facts are even less clear as guides to action than they are as explanations of conditions of action. It is one - important - thing to point out that everything that happens in societies is significantly "path dependent" (Stark, 1992: 17): what a society is, has, and does depends crucially on what it was, had and did. It is something else simply to repeat the proverbial Irish answer to a request for directions: "I wouldn't start from here."

Should one infer from hard facts that nothing is worth trying? Or that one should try harder? It is a hard choice and it makes a difference. One might, of course, be persuaded to try something else, and that is always worth considering. But such consideration must be grounded in local knowledge, and it must go beyond both "can-do" optimism and what might be called "can't do" pessimism. It needs to be informed by real and particularized understanding of what remains significantly present from the past, and thought about what can be done in the light of it, rather than by generalized clichés about what allegedly happened at some time or times in that past.[9]

Conclusion

Along with its many other problems, the post-communist world seems fated to rehearse all the familiar arguments between universalism and particularism. The difficulty is that, in the present stage of social experimentation in the region, these arguments are not merely academic. To what extent are the societies that experienced communism merely specimens of *human* societies, not fundamentally different - as a result of communism, culture, or anything else - from such societies wherever they are found? To what extent did they remain Polish, Hungarian, Bulgarian, etc, societies that merely endured communist states? To what extent did they become "communist societies"? What if all of the above are true, at different levels of analysis? Will the paths of these societies diverge, now that the unifying force and similarities of communist political *apparats* have crumbled? To what extent will those divergences be determined by old and varied traditions, present conjunctures, or new initiatives?

A good deal hangs on the answers to these questions. It is a brand of pessimism which can slide into racism, peremptorily to rule out families of nations from participation in valuable institutional and cultural possibilities, on the grounds that they are not used to them. Condescension and marginalization are softer forms of the same phenomenon. On the other hand, only if culture and communism count for nothing will it be easy to understand what might be done in Poland, say, without understanding Poland. Or simply by understanding America. Yet many of the universalist assumptions and ambitions of post-communist institutional transformers are built on explicit or, more usually, implicit denials of the possibility that there are *fundamental* social and cultural particularities anywhere. Such denials might be justified, but they are hardly self-evident. For if communism produced societies that were truly *sui generis*, as some writers have alleged,[10] then the fact that this is the first post-communist transition in history is a deep fact. If, however, pre-existing historical particularities and traditions have reasserted themselves on the rubble of communism, then those who would seek to understand the present and future will need to know something about these particulars from the past.

We still lack a persuasive theoretical paradigm within which all these variables can plausibly be fitted; and so we guess. Perhaps that is all we ever do. In any event, whatever *we* say, citizens in the region must decide what to *do*. Theoretical analysis can be of some use here, if only to clear away misconceptions, but its constructive helpfulness remains modest, particularly when it is in the disarray I have described. Actors will still have to choose, and analysts will only later sort out what has happened. Perhaps, as Hegel thought, this is always the case.

At various times, dissidents under communism described the situation in their countries as hopeless and serious, hopeless but not serious, and sometimes - when dizzy with success - wonderful but not hopeless. There are contemporary, post-communist parallels to each of these tragi-comic diagnoses. For what it is worth, my own guess about the matters I have been discussing is: serious but not hopeless, and certainly not hopeless in principle. For while there is no overwhelming reason to believe that constitutionalism and the rule of law will be successfully established in the region, it needs to be stressed that there is equally no overwhelming reason to believe that they will not.

Notes

1   The present article has appeared as Krygier, Winter 1996-97.
2   The term is Timothy Garton Ash's, and conveys the sense in which the dramatic events of 1989 were both more than reform and less than classical revolutions. See Ash, 14.
3   Or so a Polish colleague muttered, while together we endured a conference of such performances.
4   (Holmes, 1995: 40). At the end of his article, Holmes does ask, "But why not see state weakness itself as itself a cultural legacy?" (at 50), but the question goes unanswered.
5   Di Palma's first chapter, "Rethinking Some Hard Facts" discusses many of the reasons adduced for pessimism about the possibility of democratic transitions in post-dictatorial states. The rest of his book is a brilliant demonstration that hard facts should not necessarily be assumed to be insuperable facts.
6   I borrow the term from Piotr Sztompka, 1993.
7   The phrase, of course, is Karl Popper's. He contrasts it with "Utopian social engineering".

8   I have sought to place this conception of law within a more general frame in Krygier, 1992.
9   Such clichés have played no small part in western diplomacy in the war in Bosnia-Herzegovina. As a result, specific aims of particular actors have been glossed over on the basis of half-understood clichés about "ancient ethnic hatreds" for which, it appears, no one alive is responsible and about which, conveniently for some, nothing can now be done. See Malcolm, 1995.
10 Cf. Marody (1993); Mokrzycki (1991: 211; 1992). This is also the position of Jowitt, though he sees intensification of tendencies in preceding societies, rather than discontinuities. See also Sztompka (1984) and Zinoviev (1985).

Bibliography

Arato, A. (1994), "Revolution, Restoration, and Legitimization: Ideological Problems of the Transition from State Socialism", in Michael D. Kennedy (ed.), *Envisioning Eastern Europe*, Ann Arbor, University of Michigan Press.

Ascherson, N. (1981), *The Polish August. The Self-Limiting Revolution*, London, Allen Lane.

Ash, Timothy G. (1986), *We The People*, London, Granta.

Bauman, Z. (1993), "Dismantling the Patronage State", in J. Frentzel-Zagórska, (ed.), *From a One-Party State to Democracy: Transitions in Eastern Europe*, Amsterdam-Atlanta GA, Editions Rodopi.

Blankenagel, A. (1996), "New Rights and Old Rights, New Symbols and Old Meanings: Re-Designing Liberties and Freedoms in Post-Socialist and Post-Soviet Constitutions", in Andras Sajó (ed.), *Western Rights? Post-Communist Application*, The Hague, Kluwer Law International.

Clark, J. and Wildavsky, A. (1990), *The Moral Collapse of Communism. Poland as a Cautionary Tale*, San Francisco, Institute of Contemporary Studies.

di Palma, G. (1990), *To Craft Democracies. An Essay on Democratic Transitions*, Berkeley, University of California Press.

Galanter, M. (1992), "Law Abounding: Legislation around the North Atlantic", 55, *Modern Law Review*.

Gray, J. (1993), "From Post-Communism to Civil Society: The Re-emergence of the Western Model", 10, 2, *Social Philosophy and Policy*.

———(1995), *Enlightenment's Wake*, London, Routledge.

Hartley, L.P. (1963), *The Go-Between*, London, Heinemann.

Hobsbawm, E. and Ranger, T. (eds) (1983), *The Invention of Tradition*, Cambridge, Cambridge University Press.

Holmes, S. (1995), "Cultural Legacies or State Collapse? Probing the Postcommunist Dilemma," Collegium Budapest/Institute for Advanced Study, Public Lecture No 13.

Huntington, S.P. (1996), *The Clash of Civilizations and the Remaking of World Order*, New York, Simon & Schuster.

Jedlicki, J. (July-August 1990), "The Revolution of 1989: The Unbearable Burden of History", 39, *Problems of Communism*.

Jowitt, K. (1992), *New World Disorder. The Leninist Extinction*, Berkeley, University of California Press.

Kolarska-Bobińska, L., "A jednak warto było!" ["And yet it was worthwhile!"], *Wiadomośći Polskie*, (25 April 1994), Sydney. Centrum Badania Opinii Spolecznej, *Czy Potrzebna Jest Nowa Konstytucja?* [Center for Research on Public Opinion, *Is a New Constitution Necessary?*] Warsaw, February, 1994.

Krygier, M. (1992), "Legal Traditions and their Virtue", in Skąpska, G. (ed.), *Prawo w zmieniającym się społeczeństwie*, [Law in a Changing Society] 243, Cracow: Jagiellonian University.

————(1994), "Dialektyczna natura tradycji",11, *Socjologia Wychowania, Acta Universitatis Nicolai Copernici.*

————(Winter 1996-97), "Is there Constitutionalism after Communism? Institutional Optimism, Cultural Pessimism and the Rule of Law" 26, 4, *International Journal of Sociology*, Issue on Constitutionalism in Eastern Europe, edited by Irena Grudzińska Gross, 17-47.

————(October 1996), "The Sources of Civil Society. Part 1", *Quadrant.*

————(November 1996), "The Sources of Civil Society. Part 2", *Quadrant.*

————(Winter 1997), "Virtuous Circles. Antipodean Reflections on Power, Institutions and Civil Society" , 11, 1, *East European Politics and Societies.*

Krygier, M. and Czarnota, A. (1996), "Rights, Civil Society, and Post-communist Society", in Andras Sajó (ed), *Western Rights? Post-Communist Application*, Amsterdam, Kluwer Law International.

Malcolm, N. (Spring 1995), "Bosnia and the West. A Study in Failure," 39, *The National Interest.*

Marody, M. (1993), "State and Society in Poland", in Jacques Coenen-Huther and Brunon Synak, (eds), *Post-Communist Poland: From Totalitarianism to Democracy?*, New York, Nova Science Publishers.

Mokrzycki, E. (1992), "The Legacy of Real Socialism, Group Interests, and the Search for a New Utopia," in W. Connor and P. Płoszajski (eds), *Escape from Socialism: The Polish Route*, Warsaw, IFiS.

————(1991), "The Legacy of 'Real Socialism' and Western Democracy", 2, *Studies in Comparative Communism.*

————(1991), "Społeczne ograniczenia reform wschodnioeuropejskich," (The Social Limits of East European Economic Reforms", 3, *Krytyka.*

Oakeshott, M. (1991), "Rational conduct", in *Rationalism in Politics and other essays*, new and expanded edition, Indianapolis, Liberty Press.

Örkény, A. and Scheppele, K. (1998), "Rules of Law: The Complexity of Legality in Hungary", chapter 3 *supra.*

Podgórecki, A. (1994), *Polish Society*, Westport, Ct., Praeger.

Popper, K. (1996), *The Open Society and its Enemies*, fifth revised edition, London, Routledge and Kegan Paul.

Putnam, R. (1993), *Making Democracy Work. Civic Traditions in Modern Italy*, Princeton, NJ, Princeton University Press.

Sajó, A. (1996), "How the Rule of Law Killed Hungarian Welfare Reform", 5(1), *East European Constitutional Review.*

Salecl, Renate, (1995) "The Ideology of the Mother Nation in the Yugoslav Conflict", in Michael D. Kennedy (ed.), *Envisioning Eastern Europe. Postcommunist Cultural Studies*, Ann Arbor, University of Michigan Press.

Sedley, The Hon Sir S. (1995), "Human Rights: a Twenty-First Century Agenda", *Public Law*.

Selznick, P. (1992), *The Moral Commonwealth*, Berkeley, University of California Press.

Stark, D. (Winter 1992), "Path Dependence and Privatization Strategies in East Central Europe", 6, 1, *East European Politics and Societies*.

Szacki, J. (1971), *Tradycja. Przegląd problematyki*, Warsaw, PWN.

Sztompka, P. (1991), "The Intangibles and Imponderables of the Transition to Democracy", 24, 3, *Studies in Comparative Communism*.

————(April 1993) "Civilizational Incompetence: The Trap of Post-Communist Societies", 22, 2, *Zeitschrift fur Soziologie*, 85.

————(August 1995), "Looking Back: the Year 1989 as a Cultural and Civilizational Break", paper presented at the annual conference of the European Sociological Association (ESA), Budapest.

Wittgenstein, L. (1967), *Philosophical Investigations*, 3rd ed, Oxford, Oxford University Press.

Zinoviev, A. (1984), *The Reality of Communism*, London: Victor Gollancz.

———— (1985), *Homo Sovieticus*, London: Victor Gollancz.

Part II

Constitutionalism

5 Traditional Elements in the Constitutions of Central and East European Democracies

PÉTER PACZOLAY[1]

The most general characterization of the changes that occurred after 1989/90 in the Central and East European region is the turn of these countries from authoritarian or dictatorial form of government to the Rule of Law. What does this general and abstract statement really mean? I approach this question first by some general remarks and considerations, secondly, from a more practical point of view by examining the traditional elements in the constitutions of the Central and East European democracies. Here the main focus is on how the traditional patterns of constitutionalism (eg, state structure, form of government, basic rights, etc) have been changed. My analysis is broader than a constitutional scholar's general approach since it also includes the political scientist's point of view.

The Complexity of Challenges Faced by Post-Communist Countries

Social theory has to elaborate different strategies that would be able to facilitate the transition of former socialist countries into a *Rechtsstaat*. The countries of the region have to face the following difficulties simultaneously:

1. The first task relates to the realization of the principle of the Rule of Law. That task in Western countries has been resolved mainly in a gradual and organic development. By contrast, the establishment of rule of law in post-Communist countries has generated a fast and radical transformation and abandonment of bureaucratic socialism, a definitive breach with an institutional order that has taken root through forty years.

2.   In the meantime a second task has to be faced that involves the problems arising from the complexity of modern society: for example regulatory crisis, environmental, technological and informational problems, and so on.

3.   The countries of the region are also in the process of transition to market democracy: a transition that cannot be so easily modelled as the transition to constitutional democracy, and the costs of which are very high.

4.   Furthermore, societies regaining their freedom devoted a lot of energy, and mostly in vain, to facing the past: to compensate for property losses and other violations suffered during the previous regime, to identify secret agents and those who committed political crimes, and so on. Instead of helping citizens to come to terms with the past, these procedures generated sharp debates, clashes and conflicts.

5.   Several countries of the region have to face an even more difficult task: to build a new state (former Soviet Union, Yugoslavia, and Czechoslovakia).[2]

So there is no other choice but to attempt at the same time to institutionalize the principle of rule of law, and to answer to the regulatory crisis of modern societies; and deal somehow with the other difficulties, too.

A specific though essential aspect of the breakdown of communism was the replacement of the former authoritarian legal system with a new, democratic one. With respect to the East European transition, under the notion of a "democratic legal system" I understand basically the following:

- from a formal (institutional-procedural) point of view, the fulfilment of the criteria of *rule of law* and *constitutionalism*;

- substantially, the realization of some basic *democratic* values such as liberty and equality.

Victory of law over power in most East and Central European countries is now both a fact and an ideal. It includes:

- the safeguarding of human rights by legal means,

- the limitation by law of government and all other factors of political life,

- the exclusion of the use of force from political life,

- the regulation by law of all political processes,

- the proscription of *ex post facto* application of rules governing the resolution and arbitration of conflicts of interests.

Nevertheless, threats to constitutionalism are permanently present in the region. After the collapse of communism, former socialist countries sing *una voce* the song of Rule of Law, and unanimously confess themselves constitutional States. But the ideal of Rule of Law must be more than rhetorical. It has to be guaranteed by institutional and legal safeguards, and it must fulfil standards commonly respected by Western democracies. The phenomena that mostly jeopardize constitutionalism throughout the Central-East European area are nationalist hostilities and the violations of ethnic minority rights that lead to armed conflicts in countries of the former Soviet Union and Yugoslavia. But one must not disregard other serious challenges to constitutionalism.

Tradition and Constitution-Making

Before examining how the traditional elements of constitutions (state machinery, individual rights, etc.) have been replaced by a new sense and content, I feel it necessary to outline theoretically the connection between time, tradition, continuity, and constitution-making. Continuity and discontinuity are legal problems of general concern to the cultural tradition of society.

An essential feature of society is tradition - the handing-on of formed ways of acting, a formed way of living, to those beginning or developing their social membership (Pocock, 1973: 233-234).

Tradition is closely associated with continuity. Oakeshott warns us of the important characteristics of tradition. Paradoxically, tradition - despite its seemingly timeless and eternal character - reflects the fact that *everything is temporary*. But temporariness does not mean arbitrariness. Therefore, the crucial point remains: the claimed rationality of the communist social revolution meant an arbitrary intervention into the life of society, thus trying to violently eliminate the previous tradition. The stable element in continuous change is the principle of *continuity*:

> authority is diffused between past, present, and future; between the old, the new, and what is to come. It is steady because, though it moves, it is never wholly in motion, and though it is tranquil, it is never wholly at rest. (Oakeshott, 1991: 61)

In socialist societies, tradition was replaced by artificially invented mythologies of the working-class movement that could not play the important function of transmitting values, ways of life etc, to the members of society. Transmission of past traditions was replaced by following the model of the Soviet Union. Hence, this break with the past and with previous traditions resulted in societies described by anthropologists as "timeless" societies. The hubristic view of the future, the invented past, the stagnation of the society, and the rejection of all changes and reforms, are factors that led socialist countries to an extremely aberrant concept of time.

To a certain extent this derives from the tradition of the Enlightenment and the French Revolution that created an artificial contradiction between tradition as obscurity and modernity as rationality. The viewpoint that rational modernity can be overcome only after the defeat of traditionalism has had its day, and both ideologists and politicians try to balance the two concepts. Revolutionists are "by profession" anti-traditionalists, so in that sense the anti-traditionalist propaganda of communist ideology was far from surprising.

(i)   Legal and Constitutional Tradition

Legal tradition undeniably forms an important part of the entire set that makes up the tradition of a country or people. Its close relation to the political system makes it more sensitive to political changes, and a degree of its legal tradition is surrendered to the fate of the political regime. Therefore it is not surprising that basic changes in the political system (eg, a revolution) undermine the existence of the legal tradition. But legal tradition, essentially because of the autonomy of law, will survive those changes. Revolutions tried to exchange the old legal system for a new one, but a deeper investigation of these attempts verifies that either a complete and fundamental replacement failed (as in the Russian and socialist revolutions) or surprisingly the new rules, norms and institutions inherited a lot from the previously existing tradition (eg, the legislation of the French revolution and the Napoleonic era which enacted former customary law).

How can legal tradition be defined? A widespread definition of legal tradition emphasizes the following features:

- historical development - and a set of deeply rooted, historically conditioned attitudes about the following subjects:

- the nature of law;

- law and the political process (role of the law in the society and the polity);

- organization and operation of a legal system;

- legal profession (role and place of lawyers in society);

- law-making;

- law-application and enforcement;

- legal education;

- relation to the law in the cultural system (Merryman and Clark, 1978: 3).

The denial and refutation of the existing legal tradition requires the employment and transplantation of different models. Consequently, the Soviet legal system presented these models to various socialist countries. As a result the adaptation of this model led to an irrational uniformity of more than a dozen legal systems with very different traditions.

Political factors also contributed to the initial uniformity of socialist laws. The creation of the people's democratic legal systems was preceded by the existence of a powerful socialist State which had 30 years to test, new to the world, a number of entirely original solutions. Obviously, in the beginning the new socialist States simply adopted many of these formulae. Having these ready, they did not have to be invented (Eorsi, 1979: 386).

It is also obvious that these "people's democracies" did not choose the Soviet solutions because they were ready-made. Rather they were forced to do that by the Soviet Union. This uniformity was so strong that the great Western expert on communist law, Professor John Hazard, could identify a distinctive legal family of socialist countries (Hazard, 1969). This arbitrary uniformity can be easily confirmed with examples pertaining to the constitutional history of these countries. The seizure of power by the communists was followed by an introduction of new constitutional systems without regard to the constitutional traditions of the country. For example, despite its stormy history, Poland has a respected constitutional tradition dating back to the late Middle Ages. In fact, the first written constitution in Europe was enacted by Poland on May 3, 1791 (Ludwikowski, 1991: 94). After World War I the reborn state of Poland promulgated in 1921 a new so-called "March Constitution" which was later amended repeatedly in order to enlarge the powers of the President. However, the victory of socialism in Poland made it necessary to enact a new, socialist constitution. After a nationwide discussion the Constituent Assembly adopted the final text of the constitution on July 22, 1952. This constitution was modelled after the Soviet constitution of 1936 (Blaustein and Flanz, 1973: 14).

The same incident took place in Czechoslovakia. Between the two world wars, this new country attempted to build a democratic constitutional order, however the communists successfully erased the national traditions. Though the constitution of 1948 meant a clear break with the traditions of the Western-modelled "bourgeois" constitution of 1920, the constitution of 1960 moved the Czechoslovakian political system still closer to the Soviet model, and also proudly declared Czechoslovakia a "socialist republic" (Skilling, 1976: 12).

It seems superfluous to mention that Hungary had to face the same break with the past in order to mechanically follow the example of the Soviet constitution. Constitutionalism in Hungary has an interesting history. In fact, for many centuries the basic conditions of constitutional order were regulated by a series of fundamental - so-called "cardinal" - laws stemming from various historical periods beginning with the thirteenth century onward. In 1222 the "Golden Bull", a royal edict named after its appended gold seal, assured a series of liberties similar to the Magna Carta of England, and the right of armed resistance against the king, should he break his pledges. On August 18, 1949 the first written constitution in the history of the land (Law XX of 1949) was adopted by a parliament in which at that time there was only one political party (the MDP or Hungarian Workers' Party), with 71 per cent of the seats in parliament (all the other representatives were elected as candidates of the Hungarian Independence-Popular Front (Magyar Függetlenségi Népfront) led by the single party. The constitution came into effect on 20 August 1949, thus giving a new meaning as "constitution day" to a traditional Hungarian national holiday in honour of Saint Stephen, the first king of Hungarians. This "socialist" Basic Law was strongly influenced by the Soviet constitution of 1936. The draft of the constitution was prepared by a commission that thoroughly studied the

Soviet constitution and visited Moscow in order to draw inspiration there. As a result, the provisions of the Soviet constitution were literally translated.[3]

The upheavals against the communist regimes were aimed at restoring the traditional values of these countries, hence the return of the West European connection in the case of the Hungarian revolution (Rakowska-Harmstone, 1985: 220).

Although the legal nature of revolution has been widely discussed in the philosophy of law, a persuasive result or consensus has not yet been achieved. Kelsen, who developed the classical legal theory of discontinuity, is, as usual, very clear on this question. For him, a revolution in the most general sense occurs whenever the legal order of a community is nullified and replaced by a new order in an illegitimate way, that is in a way not prescribed by the first order itself (Kelsen, 1945: 117).

Kelsen stresses the importance of the so-called rules of succession: the rules that regulate the legitimate mode of succession or change in the regime. In accordance with international law, if territory and population remain identical then no new State will come into existence. On the one hand, a revolution in a broad sense establishes a new government. However, on the other hand, a new government established by a revolution with the violation of the existing constitution and the rule of succession, thus creates a new legal order. International law recognizes the continuity of legal order even in the case of revolutions. But if we ignore or go beyond the interpretation of international law, then we have to acknowledge the break in the legal system created by a revolution. Kelsen develops a peculiar test for continuity: if the constitution is changed according to its own provisions then the state and its legal order remain the same. It does not matter how fundamental these changes in the contents of the legal norms are. If they are performed in conformity with the provisions of the constitution, the continuity of the legal system will not be interrupted (Kelsen, 1945: 219).

Contrary to the formal approach of Kelsen, Alf Ross emphasized the necessary discontinuity of a new constitutional order. According to Ross, the new constitution is brought into effect by a political ideology. During the final change of competencies there exits an authority not enacted by another authority, but which is simply presupposed (Ross, 1958: 81). Unlike Kelsen, whose purely legal explanation pertains to the nature of changes, Ross's argument reveals how the legitimacy of a constitutional order goes beyond the legal system.

(ii)   Legal Change and Continuity (A Continuous Legitimacy)

In accordance with the purely formalistic approach presented by Hans Kelsen, it is unquestionable that the transitions in most East and Central European countries were only constitutional amendments, and the State and its legal order remained the same. Usually Round Table Talks between Communists and the opposition were followed by a quick implementation of the agreements by the Communists parliaments. Constitutions were adopted either by these bodies (as in Hungary) or by freely elected post-Communist parliaments (as in Bulgaria, Czechoslovakia, Poland, Slovenia, ...). Only Romania went through a violent transition, and a constituent assembly was elected in May 1990. In other words, the old legal order remains valid within the framework of the amended constitution while its legitimacy rests upon the old constitution as well as the old legal order! This creates a serious problem, because if the legitimacy of the new order is founded upon the previous constitution then this means the acknowledgment of the legitimacy and legality of the former constitutional system and its legal order. This implies that the constitutionality of the legal rules issued before 1989 can only be adjudicated in relation to the old constitution which would justify a lot of legal acts within the communist regime, including expropriations or dictatorship of the proletariat etc, which were in conformity with the 1949 constitution. This juristic and formalistic background weakens the entire transition, which claims to build a completely new legal system. A juristic and constitutional foundation for the break is created when aspects of discontinuity with the communist past are stressed. Nevertheless, this specific case reveals the discrepancy inherent in the form and substance of a legal order. Therefore some theorists argue that a constitution, or at least an ultimate rule of succession of rules, cannot be wholly replaced in accordance with its own stipulations; purported replacements are really "legal camouflage" for a "peaceful revolution" in which the replacement is a *break* with the past (Finnis, 1973: 53).

The Hungarian experiences in transition undermine Kelsen's formalistic approach, thus laying bare the sociological reality that displays fundamental changes and obvious divisions. These changes were determined to be constitutionally protected since the actual circumstances of the transition involved a fundamental compromise with the former regime. A peaceful transition, which undeniably is a supreme value compared to violent revolts, was very desirable. Perhaps the future will guarantee that all changes will remain within the framework of the constitution, even when it is challenged by certain political groups attempting to accelerate the transition. The transition from communism to constitutionalism is often compared to the lessons learned from the breakdown of national socialism and of other totalitarian regimes. However, there is a great difference from the point of view of the continuity of law: totalitarian regimes in Nazi Germany, Fascist Italy, and Francoist Spain never tried basically to change property relations, social stratification, nor the entire body of law. These governments did not attempt a conscious discontinuity of the legal system. On the contrary, they exploited the existing, inherited body of law and judicial system for their own purposes (Kirchheimer, 1961: 300-302). During the special and completely peaceful Hungarian transition perhaps too much importance was placed on continuity. Nevertheless, the revised and amended constitution required the transformation of the legal system, therefore it was necessary for the political changes to be followed by comprehensive legal changes. The gradual changes at a certain point arrive at what we can call a revolutionary change in the sense of revolution as fundamental social change. This stage of the transition results in an inevitable transformation of the entire legal system.

In terms of continuity and discontinuity, the new regime is challenged in two ways. First, it has to define its sources as legitimate to the legal order. Then, if the scope of the new order is to construct a new legal system, it has to compare the degree of discontinuity with the former system, including such issues as political justice.

The Traditional Elements of the Constitutions Examined

Constitutional documents regulate quite different issues, but they necessarily covered - even in their "fictive" socialist form - the following issues:

- The definition of the State, the form of government (sovereignty, republicanism, independence, etc). As the substantial determination of the State was usually radically changed, I do not examine this question here.

- The structure of the State, or the machinery of government. The Parliament, the government in the continental sense, the judiciary, and other State organs were necessarily also regulated by Socialist constitutions. Here we can follow how the substance of these provisions was fundamentally changed in the new or amended constitutions.

- Socialist constitutions comprehensively listed citizens' rights, and also guaranteed them formally, but in reality they did not matter and were curtailed by legislation. Here again, we can examine the substantial change in interpreting the fundamental rights. Nevertheless, special guarantees of safeguarding human rights, such as judicial review, were alien to Socialist constitutions, thus safeguards of human rights are not discussed here. (Only Yugoslavia and its member-states had Constitutional Courts operating since the sixties, and Poland a Constitutional Tribunal since 1982.)

(i)   The Main Branches of Power

Separation of powers was theoretically denied by Marxism-Leninism, and practically the Socialist constitutions realized a concentrated and unified power structure, where the constitutional design served the unconstrained rule of the Communist parties. Parliaments had - under the constitutions - immense powers, but mainly two features illustrated the authoritarian character of these regimes: firstly, elections were not free, and the formation of political parties was banned; secondly, the broad powers of Parliaments, including legislation, were usually exercised not by the assembly itself but were transferred to a body entitled to substitute for it. These Presidiums, Presidential Councils or State Councils replaced the elected assemblies, and exercised executive powers as well (execution of the laws, international relations, nominations, etc) (Bartole, 1993: 84-86). These organs symbolically concentrated the powers of the executive, the Head of State, and the legislature.

The transition abolished all of these organs as symbols of concentrated and unified power. Two basic changes occurred in this respect: the political system turned into a pluralist and democratic one where political parties can be freely formed, elections are fair and free; and in the constitutional design, the principles of separation of powers and checks and balances are implemented. Several new constitutions expressly state that the State structure is based on the separation of powers; some others implement the principle without mentioning it separately. Article 11 of the Constitution of the Russian Federation declares that State power in the Russian Federation shall be exercised by the President, the Federal Assembly, the Government, and the courts. Article 2 of the Czech Constitution mentions that state power is exercised by means of legislative, executive and judicial bodies. Article 8 of the Bulgarian Constitution clearly divides the legislative, executive and judicial powers. Other constitutions are not so expressed. The Hungarian Constitution does not declare the principle of separation of powers, but the provisions pertaining to the power branches realize the separation of powers. The Slovakian and Romanian constitutions also avoid clearly stating the principle of separation of powers.

One important question that needs to be studied, is how the new or amended constitutions understand and implement the principle of separation of powers. Only a few preliminary remarks are offered here:

1.   Does there exist a coherent theory of division and separation of powers in post-Communist countries?

2.   What is the reason for avoiding the declaration of separation of powers in several constitutions?

3.   Could the provisions regulating the powers of the different branches dissolve the concentrated power system inherited from Communism? Do they provide effective guarantees for the independence of the different branches, or do they remain only declarations (eg, the independence of the judiciary)?

4.   Do the new constitutions take into consideration the fact mentioned earlier, namely that the meaning and substance of separation of powers has immensely changed at the end of our century?

As a hypothesis I would suggest that ideas about the separation of powers circulate in the new democracies, which both are old fashioned and rarely or never realized in the continental European political system. This can be proved not so much by the actual texts of the constitutions, but rather by scholarly interpretations and Constitutional Court decisions.

Another strange characteristic of the new constitutions is the uncertainty regarding the actual design of the main branches. In most constitutions each of the branches is - often without a rational reason - doubled: the legislative, by introduction of the bicameral system; the executive, between government and the president; and the judicial power, between the ordinary judiciary and Constitutional Courts.

Especially obscure is the philosophy behind the bicameral system. Second chambers may play different roles:

(a) Quite simply doubling of the lower chamber. The Czech Republic has a Senate whose members are elected by a majority system (while representatives of the lower chamber are chosen on a proportional system). The Senate may if it wants discuss a draft law, and even return it to the Chamber of Deputies. In that case the lower house can approve the law by an absolute majority. The function of the second chamber is no more than to slow down the legislation. The situation in the Romanian State structure is similar. In Poland the upper house, the Senate, has more substantial powers, but its basic function is still to control the legislative process. Unlike in the Czech Republic, a two-thirds majority of the Sejm is required to overrule the Senate's veto.

(b) Second chamber in a federal state. In the case of the Russian Federation the existence of a second chamber - the Federation Council - consisting of two representatives of each constituent entity of the Russian Federation (Art 95) is obvious and logical. Its jurisdiction (Art 102) is also peculiar, for example approval of border changes within the Federation, impeachment of the President, appointments, etc.

(c) Corporate second chambers. For example the National Council of Slovenia is composed of members representing employers, employees, farmers, small business people, independent professionals, non-profit organizations and councillors representing local interests.

The evaluation of the bicameral system in new democracies shows that countries chose very different solutions and only a very few of them - federations - do really need the bicameral system. Otherwise, the second chamber serves the more articulate representation of interests, especially in the case of the corporate solutions, or tries to improve the quality, and not the efficiency of the legislative process. Nevertheless, in these latter cases I doubt the real function of the second chambers.

The problem of the dual executive needs to be discussed in detail below, while the problem of the division of the judiciary pertains to judicial review, a question that belongs to the new features of East European constitutions.

(ii)   Parliaments

Socialist ideology and constitutional law considered the parliament the supreme organ of the State which had the monopoly of power. The principle of the supremacy of Parliament prevailed only in regard to the State organization, and did not affect the leading role of the ruling Communist party. Otherwise the socialist State organisation was based on the principle of the indivisibility and unity of power, expressed mainly in the "class substance" of the power. This principle was realized in the primacy of the supreme representative body, which could exercise its power without any control. There existed no State organ that could counterbalance the power of the supreme representative body.

Naturally, this supreme body served to guarantee the leading role of the Marxist-Leninist party that in some countries was expressedly declared also by the Constitution. Beside the principle of the unity of power, the other basic principle of the socialist State organisation was that of popular sovereignty. Both principles supported the supremacy of the Parliament, giving the Parliament the double character of being at the same time the supreme body of State power and that of popular representation. All these theoretical considerations were put into practice by the text of the Constitution.

Parliaments went through fundamental changes during the transition. First of all, the political system does not any more serve the unlimited rule of a single party, but is a pluralistic multi-party system with all its consequences. Secondly, the system is based on the principle of separation of powers. For example, according to the original text from 1949 of the Constitution of Hungary the Parliament exercises all the rights deriving from popular sovereignty. The new 1989 text of the Constitution refers to the Parliament as one of the organs exercising the rights deriving from popular sovereignty. This reflects basic conceptual changes in the philosophy of the Constitution, according to which the constitutional order of the Republic of Hungary is based on the principle of the separation of powers. This principle naturally deprives the Parliament of its - theoretically - absolute power. The constitutional meaning of popular sovereignty has also been basically changed:

> In the Republic of Hungary all power shall belong to the people exercising its sovereignty through its elected representatives as well as directly. [Art 2, sec 1]

This formulation emphasizes that the new Constitution relies also, beside the organs of representative democracy, on procedures of direct democracy such as popular referendum or popular initiative.

Nevertheless, parliaments in East Central European countries somehow resemble the heritage of their Socialist past. Constitutional power of the Parliaments is concentrated on three main areas: legislation, the determination of the basic orientation of governmental policy, and the election of top state officials. These three competences invest the Parliament with great power. All important powers are concentrated in the hands of the Parliament, although the will of the parliamentary majority can be restricted by several means: (a) qualified majority requirements for the enactment of the most important laws and the election of high state officials; (b) constitutional control by the president of the Republic over some aspects of the legislative work; and (c) judicial review by the Constitutional Court.

To sum up, the powers of the Parliament, despite the implementation of the separation-of-powers principle, are great, and the new constitutional system has preserved many features of the former system, which was based on the supremacy of Parliament. This is reflected also in the fact that the Parliament has a wide range of exclusive legislative competences, while no subject is excluded from its competence. However, the new constitution has severely restricted the "archdemocratic" pattern of the omnipotence of the popularly elected assembly, which in the Communist countries conformed perfectly with single-party rule. This historical experience in East European countries discredited the idea of parliamentary omnipotence.

In some constitutions the competences of the legislature and the executive are not clearly distinguished. The Hungarian parliament inherited special competences from the old text of the Constitution. The National Assembly is declared to be the highest organ of the State that, "exercising its rights deriving from popular sovereignty, shall guarantee the constitutional order of society and shall determine the structure, orientation and conditions of government" [Art 19, sec 2]. Its exclusive competences include determining the socio-economic plan of the country; determining the balance of state finances; dissolving local government bodies whose activity is contrary to the Constitution. While in the case of Hungary and Poland the vestiges of the old constitutions influence the respective regulations, surprisingly some of the new constitutions also vaguely formulate the relations of the legislative and executive powers, as in the Bulgarian constitution that invests the parliament with the rights to appoint and dismiss ministers or the Head of the National Bank. In this respect the

Romanian Constitution is the most consequential, separating clearly and definitely the branches of power (Bartole, 1993: 106-07).

In addition to the inherited powers, parliaments gained new sources of authority during the transition. As a recent analysis of East Central European parliaments observes: "In the initial post-communist period parliaments served as both symbols of, and the institutional expression of political change... In all East Central European states, parliaments rapidly became identified as the quintessential institutions of democracy" (Judge, 1994: 25). Parliaments, and political parties within them, became the centre of democratic consolidation during the transition. But this process is in several aspects unbalanced, and this is leading to a dramatic decline in respect for parliaments. Parliamentary elites cannot in the long run replace the necessary forms of the activity of civil societies.

(iii) Parliamentary or Presidential System and the Problem of the Dual Executive

There is an ongoing discussion among constitutional scholars and political scientists regarding the respective advantages and perils of the parliamentary and the presidential system (Linz, 1992; Lijphart, 1992). The classical debate between parliamentarism and presidentialism has emerged also in East and Central European countries. They have difficulty deciding this dilemma. Generally speaking, East Central European countries decided in favour of parliamentarianism, and the introduction of the presidential institution - with the exception of Czechoslovakia and Romania - was a novelty. In the meantime presidents in virtually all parliamentary systems of the region tried to reverse the original situation in favour of presidential powers. Some scholars note that many East Central European states have come to occupy a position somewhere between classical parliamentary and presidential systems, namely "semi-presidential" government (Elster, 1993: 196). I would not go so far, but would rather emphasize the ambition of presidents themselves to enlarge their power.

The following, often contradictory, factors can be counted as determining the choices of the individual countries:

- traditions of a presidential institution (especially in Romania and former Czechoslovakia), or the lack of such traditions in most countries;

- need expressed by the society for a strong leader or a patriarchal authority;

- the contrary fear of the rule of one man. All these and other factors have led to a wide variety in the power configuration. The two factors that determine whether a presidency is strong or weak are the manner of electing the president (by direct popular elections or indirectly by the Parliament), and the range of powers attributed to the President in the following fields;

- national defence and foreign policy;

- appointment and removal of government;

- exercise of legislative initiative or veto;

- dissolution of parliament;

- appointment of state officials without the counter-signature of government;

- emergency powers (Elster, 1993: 196).

The regulation of presidential powers is not only varied but often vague. Therefore the characterization of single solutions is not easy. The Russian presidency is definitely strong, some commentators speaking of "super-presidentialism". There are two ex-Yugoslav republics that established presidential systems in their new constitutions: Serbia and Croatia (in 1990 and 1991, respectively), thus concentrating enormous powers in the hands of the presidents (Varady and Dimitrijevic, 1994: 79). The directly elected Romanian and Polish presidents also have strong powers. The Polish president has especially broad powers in government formation, over legislation (a two-thirds majority is needed to override his veto), and he has the right to dissolve the parliament when the president and the parliament cannot agree on the budget. The Romanian constitution is premier-presidential, similar to the French. Bulgaria and Slovenia adopted parliamentary systems combined surprisingly with the direct election of the head of state (Shugart, 1993: 30-32). The Czech Republic, Slovakia, and Hungary are purely parliamentary systems, although the vague and inconsistent formulation of presidential powers make it possible for presidents to claim stronger competences.

The inconsistencies and gaps regarding presidential powers in the present text of the Hungarian Constitution led to a long constitutional dispute between the president and the prime minister. The conflict of competences between the President and Government had arisen on different issues: who should represent Hungary in foreign affairs; what are the powers of the president as commander-in-chief of the army; and what are the rights of the president in appointing the presidents of the public radio and television? The last two issues came to the Constitutional Court. After the Constitutional Court's decisions the conflict did not come to an end at all (Paczolay, 1993: 39-43).

Constitutional systems of the region could not make clear choices on the manner of election of the President, and its relation to presidential powers. Continuous conflicts emerge in most countries between Parliament and president, or between the two poles of the executive power. It seems that hybrid presidential/parliamentary system or semi-presidentialism, and a dual executive is gaining territory and support in East European democracies. This can result in advantages as well, especially in the case of a popular president who can represent national unity, enjoy far more respect from the society than other political actors, and counterbalance other power branches. But all in all, presidential roles and powers are very flexible and uncertain in most countries, and one can observe a growing gap between the formal and informal powers of the presidents. I suppose that this peculiar part of the institutional arrangement has the most chance to undergo changes in the future.[4]

(iv) Executive Power

Interestingly, executive powers attract definitely less interest among scholars than questions concerning the parliament or the president. This is surprising because a country, after all, is run by the government. The explanation may be that during the transitions parliaments became the central organs of the new political systems, while presidents fulfil a much more popular role than prime ministers, and, in addition, theoretically it is more challenging to find a place for the president in the constitutional system than to deal with the executive. The prevalence of the representative-legislative assemblies goes so far as to sacrifice the stability of the executive, either by weakening the government or by uncertainly dividing the executive power between the government and the president. As a matter of fact, the lifetime of governments depends more on the stability of their underlying majority, than on the constitutional arrangements. Fragmented parliaments result in delicate solutions. Only one government in the region - the Hungarian - has survived for four years, despite the tragic death of prime minister Antall. It is true that in Hungary the constructive vote of non-confidence also strengthens the government. Similarly, the Bulgarian Constitution provides for a stable government. But the main point is the stability of the majority.

(v) Fundamental Rights

All countries in the region have reformulated their Bills of Rights. In the case of human rights the hypocrisy of the socialist constitutions was quite shocking. They enumerated a long list of different rights, without giving them any real guarantees. Therefore the main concern in case of fundamental rights is not the actual wording of those rights, but their safeguarding. As already mentioned, this is one of the really new elements in the post-Communist systems, therefore I will not go into details. Questions of human rights serve as the real test for the new constitutions: are they really relevant and do they realize the Rule of Law, or are they simply written declarations, absolutely irrelevant for protecting human rights, and just serving to cover by lip-service and propaganda the crude reality of power structures? This is a delicate question. Sometimes it is very difficult to adjudicate how this or that country respects human rights. Despite the continuous internationalization of human rights, countries can differ greatly in protecting and respecting human rights. It can lead to hypocrisy again to watch the human rights situation in other countries, and in the meantime not ratify the basic international human rights documents. Countries that are undoubtedly regarded as constitutional democracies differ dramatically in the level of protection for certain human rights. So one has to be very cautious in formulating judgments about another country's human rights protection. But this modest caution cannot prevent us from honestly revealing when a state uses, or more precisely abuses, whatever solemn declaration of human rights it has, just to hide the real situation. What socialism really taught us is that words in themselves are not enough any more; you can call an authoritarian regime democracy, constitutions can list countless human rights, though none of them is observed, and one can speak of the Rule of Law, and still exercise the most arbitrary power. All our scholarly and practical efforts to establish constitutionalism become meaningless if we allow the abuse of words, and we buy all self-definitions at face value.

As for the list of human rights the following questions can be considered:

(a) Among the main characteristics of the new bill of rights, a fundamental conceptual change has to be emphasised. While socialist constitutions acknowledged only the category of "citizens' rights", the new ones reflect the idea of inviolable and inalienable "human rights". Socialist ideology has rejected classifications such as "innate" or "inalienable" rights. This conceptual change is reflected in provisions such as that of the Hungarian Constitution, which says: "the Republic of Hungary recognises the inviolable and inalienable fundamental human rights" (Art 8, sec 1).

(b) Restrictions of rights are relevant to judging the extent to which human rights are protected. It was the well-functioning practice of Socialist states to constrain citizens' rights guaranteed on paper, by legislation or mostly lower level decrees. No doubt, international human rights covenants for the sake of compromise adopt the same techniques, and rights can be limited by public interest. But the use of language in the new post-communist constitutions resembles the old-type limitations. Especially the Romanian and Bulgarian Constitutions allow limitations on the basis of legitimate interests of others, national security, public order, public health and morals. The Hungarian Constitution as amended in 1990, contains a general clause, according to which statutes shall not limit the essential content of fundamental rights. (Art 8, sec 2)

(c) Finally, we have to decide to what extent the social rights are the vestiges of socialist constitutions or necessary elements of the rule of law in general?

Conclusions: Democracy and Constitutionalism

There is a large consensus in Central European societies and polities regarding the acceptance of democracy and constitutionalism, despite serious challenges. But these two normative theories may also conflict, and frequently we play off one theory against the other, eg, stressing the values of democracy (government by people, right to say something in all matters, equal distribution of wealth, etc, according to different concepts of democracy) against the formalism and legalism of constitutional decision-making procedures. It is, of course, a delicate question to decide between the two sets of values in cases of sharp conflict, and people's attitudes are conditioned by political culture, traditions, etc.

Poland and Hungary for example chose the peaceful and constitutionally controlled way of demolition of Communism, and establishment of a democratic order. This choice - if considered seriously and consistently - means that the constitutional framework of the transition must be inviolable even when a conflict between democratic claims and the formalism of constitutional procedures is raised. In the name of democracy, one can criticize the Parliament, the government, the Constitutional Court, and other constitutional institutions. This approach to democracy stresses the importance of effective representation and the recognition of all kinds of interests. It calls for the coordination of all interests in the decision-making procedures and often praises the advantages of direct democracy. This loud appeal to democracy and to "people in general" can easily lead not only to criticism of constitutional institutions but also to the denial of their legitimacy. Such defiance of the constitutional framework is unacceptable, even when it is formulated in the name of the will of the (hypothetical) majority. It is not to be questioned that there are remarkable arguments in favour of the practice of direct democracy and against the shortcomings of the formal procedures of representative democracy, but the delicate structure of a young democracy must not be endangered by populist demagogy, nationalistic propaganda, violent actions, unlawful blockades, and other infringements of people's rights.

The political system of modern Western democracies is built upon three principles: first, the majority principle limited by the protection of minority rights; second, the legitimization of the power structure by free elections; third, the delegation of the right of decision-making on most basic matters to the representative assembly.

Most contemporary theories of democracy are not satisfied with a concept of political democracy that guarantees for the individual only formal equality in politics and before the law. These theories of substantive democracy idealize a fuller, deeper and more substantial concept of social, industrial, and economic democracy. But do not forget one of the sad and severe lessons of the past decades: those demands and social experiments that tried to realize these other ideals of democracy not *within* the framework of political democracy but *instead of* it, have led not to democracy but to dictatorship. It seems to me that East European societies, including Hungary, despite their hatred of the socialist regime, identify a just social system - including that of democracy - as one which results in the almost equal distribution of material wealth and burdens.

Political democracy is an indispensable condition for all other types of democracy. Processes and methods of political democracy must precede our substantial requirements of democracy. This and nothing more is the reason why we must safeguard the formal-procedural principles of political democracy and not compromise them even for reasonable and widely supported social interests. In this sense I define a democratic society as a free society where the rule by the people is combined with a great degree of self-control.

There are great discrepancies in defining what a just and fair society is in the new-born East European democracies. As a consequence of the difficulties outlined above, it will be a very great task to restore the essential characteristics of the legal system: generality, rationality, certainty, non-retroactivity, and consistency. A democracy dedicated to realizing the Rule of Law must not yield on these requirements, even if two revolutionary transitions within forty-five years are too much for a legal system which is built on the continuity of thousand-year-old institutions and principles. In multiparty democracies, law-making should be a difficult technical process demanding great skill. Let me conclude by returning to the idea that the superiority of Law over Power guarantees the constitutionality of the transitions. If the legal system collapses, forces like those that have often emerged in Eastern Europe's past will again gain power.

Notes

1   This paper was presented at the *Law & Society* Conference in Glasgow, Scotland, on 12 July 1996.
2   The last three difficulties are discussed by Elster, J. (1993: 170).
3   For the political circumstances at the time of adapting the constitution, see Hoensch, J.K. (1988), 187-194.
4   *East European Constitutional Review* devoted its Fall 1993/Winter 1994 issue to the question of the postcommunist presidency, including a comprehensive table of presidential powers in Eastern Europe.

Bibliography

Bartole, S. (1993), *Riforme costituzionali nell'Europa Centro-Orientale*, Bologna, Il Mulino.
Blaustein A.P. and G.H. Flanz (eds) (1973), *Constitutions of the Countries of the World*, vol. VIII, Oceana Publications, Dobbs Ferry, New York and Poland.
Elster, J. (1993), "Constitution-Making in Eastern Europe: Rebuilding the Boat in the Open Sea", 71, *Public Administration*.

Eorsi, G. (1979), *Comparative Civil (Private) Law,* Budapest, Akademia Kiado.

Finnis, J.M. (1973), "Revolutions and Continuity of Law", in *Oxford Essays in Jurisprudence* (Second Series), Clarendon Press, Oxford.

Hazard, J. (1969), *Communists and Their Law; A Search For The Common Core of the Legal Systems of the Marxian Socialist States,* Chicago, University of Chicago Press.

Hoensch, J.K. (1988), *A History of Modern Hungary,* Longman, London and New York.

Judge, D. (1994), "East Central European Parliaments: The First Steps", in *The Emergence of East Central European Parliaments: The First Steps,* Budapest, Hungarian Centre of Democracy Studies.

Kelsen, H. (1945), *General Theory of Law and State,* Harvard University Press, Cambridge, Mass.

Kirchheimer, O. (1961), *Political Justice. The Use of Law for Political Ends,* Princeton University Press, Princeton, New Jersey.

Lijphart, Arend (1992), *Parliamentary versus Presidential Government,* Oxford University Press, Oxford.

Linz, J. (1992), *The Failure of Presidentialism,* Baltimore, Johns Hopkins University Press, and Lijphart, A. (ed.) (1994), *Parliamentary versus Presidential Government,* Oxford, Oxford University Press.

Ludwikowski, R.R. (1991), "Searching for a New Constitutional Model for East-Central Europe", 17, *Syracuse Journal of International Law and Commerce.*

Merryman, J.H. and Clark, D.S. (1978), *Comparative Law: Western European and Latin American Legal System,* Indianapolis, Bobbs Merrill.

Oakeshott, M. (1991), *Rationalism in Politics and Other Essays,* Liberty Press, Indianapolis (new and expanded edition).

Paczolay, P. (1993), "The New Hungarian Constitutional State: Challenges and Perspectives", in A. E. Dick Howard (ed.), *Constitution Making in Eastern Europe,* Washington DC, Woodrow Wilson Center Press.

Pocock, J.G.A. (1973), *Politics, Language, and Time,* New York, Atheneum.

Rakowska-Harmstone, T. (1985), "Communist Constitutions and Constitutional Change", in Keith G. Banting and Richard Simeon, *Redesigning the State. The Politics of Constitutional Change,* University of Toronto Press, Toronto and Buffalo.

Ross, A. (1958), *On Law and Justice,* University of California Press, Berkeley-Los Angeles.

Shugart, M.S. (Winter 1993), "Of Presidents and Parliaments", *East European Constitutional Review.*

Skilling, Gordon, H. (1976), *Czechoslovakia's Interrupted Revolution,* Princeton University Press, Princeton, New Jersey.

Varady, T. and Dimitrijevic, N. "On Ex-Yugoslavia", (Fall 1993/Winter 1994) *East European Constitutional Review.*

6 The Paradigm of Constitutionalism

The Hungarian Experience

VILMOS SÓS

Since the appearance of Thomas Kuhn's *The Structure of Scientific Revolution* (Kuhn, 1962) more than thirty years ago, the term "paradigm" has been used to express the specific patterns, scopes and conceptual ranges of the history and theory of science, that, in a given period, have a dominant, or even exclusive control over a given science. Within a paradigm, the community of scholars builds on those prior scholarly results that have promising future prospects, thus laying the foundations for further scientific research. The concept of paradigm-based theoretical work implies that justifiable and relevant problems of scientific research, as well as the accepted heuristic and verificatory methods of solving them, are established within the scope of that paradigm.

In order that a theory may function as a paradigm, two conditions have to be met: (i) it has to be novel and successful enough to attract more scholars who remain committed to this specific theory than to any rival theories, and (ii) it has to be open enough that, within the scope of the theory, it presents a significant number of problems and tasks for generations of scholars to come.

Such an understanding of the notion of paradigm in the philosophy of science is applicable primarily to the natural sciences. In the humanities however - and economics, a "hard core" social science, is no exception either - no theory has gained such dominant control as occurs in the case of natural sciences. With respect to the philosophy of law or jurisprudence, we have seen co-existing theories and notions in competition and constant debate with one another. Nevertheless, these theories have certain paradigmatic features. The term paradigm denotes a social attitude, conviction and commitment, namely that a circle of experts on a given issue, a community of scholars, is in possession of methods and means for solving problems within their competence.

Such an attitude holds true for those involved with the theory or philosophy of law. There is, however, one peculiarity that limits and, at the same time, also widens the validity of the legal philosophical paradigm. It is limited inasmuch as commitment to a specific paradigm will not become a generally accepted norm in society, not even in the philosophical or legal community. However rational or widespread a certain legal concept might be, there is nothing to indicate that at a given time and place one can become successful only on that basis. This limitation is derived from another, complementary, attribute of the legal paradigm. A natural science paradigm tells us how to achieve what we want; it can tell us nothing about what to want and achieve. The desired goals and values, whether moral or efficiency values, are divergent, and, quite often, conflicting. Within the political community, however, a tradition has taken shape that regards constitutionalism as a basic norm, capable of harmonizing desired values and goals with their efficient realization. The paradigm of constitutionalism is the very conviction of a political community that modern democracies require a constitutional system: constitutionalism and democracy are interrelated, constitutionalism serves best the needs of the operation of a democratic society. The constitution is the strongest source of legitimation for a modern democratic society.

Legitimacy is the acknowledgment of the validity of a social order. According to Max Weber, any activity in a social order is adjusted to pre-definable maxims; the existing order is regarded as valid in case these maxims are perceived by the people as obligatory in some way, or as a model to be followed. People's motives to follow suit may be quite diverse. Nevertheless the very circumstance that, whatever their personal motives, actors comply with the existing order increases the chances that actions, in general, will also adjust to the existing order.

Such legitimation might have internal, as well as external, guarantees. External guarantees are social conventions and the law. Social conventions enforce the order in such a manner that any divergence is generally and practically received with disapproval. As far as the law is concerned, a distinct group of people will apply physical and psychological force to coerce compliance with the law, or to sanction any violation of it.

To date, the general form of legitimation is legal legitimation; people consider an existing order as lawful, and comply with formally correct, customary or written rules. Even though law is a compulsory order, people's conception of legitimacy provides the grounds for compliance; ie, in their understanding, power, based on such external coercion, is legitimate.

The famous German lawyer, Gustav Radbruch once wrote that "democracy is certainly a priceless value; but a *Rechtsstaat* is like one's daily bread, the water one drinks, the air one breathes, and the greatest merit of democracy is that it alone is suited to ensure a *Rechtsstaat*" (Radbruch, 1963: 51). This is why every government these days is so eager to be acknowledged as one governed by the rule of law.

I am not as cynical as some, otherwise highly reputable, legal experts, who claim that the law is merely a means - appropriate, and applicable, for any purpose - and they, as technicians of the law, are able to formulate any legal arguments supporting whatever purpose. But neither do I consider myself a doctrinaire theoretician who believes that, by merely asserting abstract legal principles, he will find solutions for the acceptance of vital legal principles by the citizens, and for putting them into actual legal practise. There is no such abstract legal theoretical view which would not be connected to a specific problem within the existing legal system. Basic theoretical issues of the law are in fact legal responses to essential moral and, in large part, political issues.

During the last six to eight years of the Kádár regime in Hungary, legal practice was more liberal than the legal system, and increasingly more liberal than the written law. This is a highly unusual phenomenon, as legal practise generally lags behind written laws. During the enforcement of the law, there are several obstacles to overcome that do not seem to be obstacles in the written law.

A legitimate legal system is more than a formal system of rules. A legitimate legal system builds on legal security, justice and efficiency. A legal positivist regards efficiency as the criterion for validity, and derives the other two principles from efficiency. According to a natural lawyer, justice is the criterion for validity as well, based on Augustine's question: "And so if justice is left out, what are kingdoms except great robber bands?" (Augustine, 1963: 17). The foregoing three legal principles often conflict with one another, and in order to re-establish equilibrium, one or the other moves to the fore. Should, however, any of them suffer a permanent violation, legal order disintegrates, and the legitimating role of the law becomes questionable.

The reason why law can play a legitimating role is that, among its many functions, the protective role of the law in safeguarding citizens' rights *vis-a-vis* the state is of primary import. Without such protection, an order would merely be an external coercive one. In the past two centuries, and, increasingly in the last few decades, such protection of individual rights *vis-a-vis* state power has found expression in human rights. Human rights are elements of an international legal institution. In general, however, they become genuine rights provided that they are formulated as citizens' rights in the legal system of a state. There is no doubt of the merits of natural law in advertising and legalizing human rights. Natural law, influenced by the French Revolution, claims that people are created free and equal and, by virtue of birth, entitled to certain rights. According to Edmund Burke, by contrast, against the newly formed idea of human rights you must defend the rights of Englishmen protected by historical tradition and convention. In other words, you shall enjoy the enacted positive rights of any country. And however great the importance attributed to human rights on the basis of the natural law ideology, their enforceability has always been problematic, particularly because their realization has always been more difficult than enacting them, as citizens' rights, in the constitution of a given country. One usually reverted to human rights as the ultimate ideological or moral argument in favour of citizens who had already been deprived of their rights.

A legal order may not presume that people were born equal in every respect, even to achieve equality before the law. Similarly, it may not attempt to make them equal in every respect. Rather, in the formulation of constitutional rights, and in the constitutional protection of freedom, a minimal consensus should exist, namely that the differences between individuals may not serve as the basis for different treatment by the law, as such differences are irrelevant with respect to constitutional rights. The contrary is true as well, although it is a very strong statement, namely, that the constitution is not competent to set forth rights providing for relevant differences between individuals. The constitution is appropriate solely to guarantee the basic rights of citizens; rights that must not be violated by anyone, including the majority. In a constitutional democracy, no legitimate power shall have authority to override such rights.

In our modern world, the constitution is the foundation for a democratic system and society. In general, constitutions are the products of revolutions or wars. Hannah Arendt is perfectly right in saying that the purpose of revolutions is the attainment of freedom (Arendt, 1969), an act not identical to liberation or being liberated. If liberation is not followed by the enactment of freedom into the constitution, ie, the creation of legal guarantees for freedom, revolution will prove fruitless. A constitution may be the product of a revolution, and still fail to be novel or revolutionary in substance. A constitution can *only* guarantee that the government is limited by laws, and, in defence of the citizens' rights *vis-a-vis* the government and the state, provide constitutional guarantees - not in the form of uncontrollable promises, but as procedural safeguards. This is not a revolutionary act, albeit a revolutionary achievement.

Constitutionalism in Hungary

The fact that during the political transition Hungarian society opted for constitutional democracy was fundamentally the result not of rational considerations, but rather, and quite naturally, the consequence of a political decision. The importance of extremist and/or populist movements opposing constitutionalism was minimal. The political elite, together with the majority of the Hungarian society, deemed constitutionalism a worthy example to be followed as the only tool to maintain democratic law and order, and to prevent the recurrence of dictatorship. Therefore it is similarly understandable that, from among the ranks of the political elite, those who had a background in law came to the fore. Members of the legal profession had a theoretical, rather than practical, knowledge of the procedures and tools required for the creation of a democratic state based on the principles of constitutionalism. Thus, constitutionalism has become the strongest legitimizing force of political transition.

As one of the most important features of the constitutional paradigm, political decisions have to get a legally interpretable form in the constitution; a form that is not a manifesto, but something that offers procedural guarantees for the enforcement of the rights contained in the constitution. This, however, does not and should not be taken to imply that the law or even lawyers should decide between often conflicting moral and political values, and neither does it suggest that every political or moral consideration can be put in a legal form.

It is no coincidence, either, that politicians of the then governing coalition, by making references to constitutional legitimacy, always attempted to give constitutional backing to their decisions, which invariably required, or would have required, the amendment of the constitution. Legal experts, on the other hand, often used legal reasoning in order to obstruct political decisions that they found objectionable. This tension was not expressly counterproductive from a constitutional viewpoint. Often, as the result of the debates, compromises were made that created stronger constitutional foundations than any debate within the boundaries of the law or politics could have ever created. None of the significant political forces reverted, too often, to unconstitutional methods, and the legal experts were also keen not to understand law as the mere application of abstract principles. These facts, and the realization that law should, at least partially, be adjusted to the actual and real political and social conditions, are, without doubt, the greatest achievements of the Hungarian development.

In a society in transition, the development and perfection of constitutionalism takes a gradual course, ridden with compromise and strong political and moral battles. However, the historic moment when a paradigm of legal theory, with political and moral undertones, plays a dominant role in society is quite rare.

After the collapse of the communist regime, the Hungarian political community has been committed to constitutional democracy. For different reasons however, this commitment was laden with conflicts. In what follows I will attempt to analyse the general background of the conflicts and some hard cases in which the difficulties of realizing the constitutional principles are especially evident.

Hungarian constitutional history is an extremely short and simple story. Until 1946, Hungary had no Constitution in the modern sense, that is, as a basic law. However, in 1222, only seven years after the Magna Carta, a sort of feudal constitution, called the Golden Bull, was born in Hungary. This early development was, unfortunately, not followed by a continuous constitutional history. Up to the forties of this century, while the Golden Bull has always been referred to as the centuries-old Hungarian constitution (with special emphasis on the continuity principle), no real constitution was enacted. The first change took place when the parliament enacted a modern but provisional constitution in 1946. Three years later, in 1949, the new, already socialist parliament passed the new socialist constitution that was nothing but a copy of the Stalinist Soviet constitution (here the radical discontinuity principle was especially emphasized). This 1949 constitution was radically modified in 1989, and the modified version is the legal constitution in Hungary today. Modifications have, of course, been introduced even since that time. That is however, a political rather than a constitutional issue.

The political background of Hungarian constitutionalism is a longer and much more complicated problem. Hungarian legislation faced an unusual and exceptional situation, namely a transition of the social system. Before the new general elections - under the communist regime - Hungary, in comparison with other communist countries, was a relatively liberal state. Nevertheless, it was a very special kind of liberalism. The Hungarian legal practice was more liberal than the law itself. In the last decade, the communist party and its government very rarely enforced the then still valid antidemocratic and repressive laws. The so-called Constitution and all valid laws (including the criminal and civil codes) were, in many respects, tyrannical. During the last year of the old Parliament, legislation (both the Constitution and the codes) was changed and amended positively in many respects. However, the task of the new Parliament was to change basic legal principles in order to lay the foundations of a new, democratic system.

Hungary does not have a new Constitution. The old one is not completely old because it was last amended in 1989, under political pressure from the reform wing of the communist leadership and oppositional forces as well. This Constitution already contained guarantees of basic human and civil rights. In 1990, one-third of the text was modified and some articles were changed twice or even more frequently within one month. It is not a Stalinist Constitution any more but it has many controversial articles and is not respected by public opinion. It is a widely held opinion that the Constitution is easily changeable if practical political goals demand, though in fact this needs a two-thirds majority. There is no doubt that this Constitution is not a solid and widely respected basis for legislation. In the press and at different party meetings extreme right politicians have attacked the constitution as a Stalinist construction. The minister of justice in 1992, on the other hand, declared that it was impossible to introduce a new constitution and there was no need for it.

Let me mention two examples. Before the first session of the first new Parliament, the two biggest parties (Hungarian Democratic Forum, and Alliance of Free Democrats) made an agreement (the so-called Pact) but two important points of the agreement caused basic conflicts. First, the factual competencies and obligations of the President, who was a member of the AFD (then the biggest oppositional party), were not clearly defined. Secondly, the Free Democrats failed to agree on the most important economic issue, privatization, and consequently, the majority faction could make decisions alone about it (since this does not require a two-thirds vote). The Constitution (Article 9) states: "The economy of Hungary is a market economy where public and private ownership shall be equally respected and enjoy equal protection." This would be a standard article in any country where private property is dominant. In Hungary, where privatization is badly needed, this Article makes it possible for the government to exert its dominant influence on the economy. This seems increasingly to be taking place.

The role of the Constitutional Court proved to be decisive in strengthening the democratic development in Hungary. The Court was founded by an Act of 1989, but only half of the judges were elected by the old Parliament. Its foundation and existence proved to be the most dominant element in the development of a state of law in Hungary. The Court works under extraordinarily strong political pressure. Nevertheless, its judgments have mainly served the protection of constitutional and civil rights. It should not come as a surprise that the Court has sometimes been strongly attacked by government forces following certain judgments.

Beyond the scope of legislation, several other factors have also influenced constitutional problems:

1. The mass media and the press. The coalition parties and the government have had a pretty hostile attitude towards the press. Following the general elections, this bad relationship became even worse. Consequently, the press tried to exploit any information or unchecked gossip (much of which proved later to be true) attacking the legislative and executive power. As a result, in many instances the reaction of the public to certain bills preceded their actual enactment, thus exerting influence on the final text of the act. The influence of the press had a weak point. Most importantly, not all leading personalities of the press are respected by the public due to their role during the previous regime.

2. The indifference or apathy of the public to politics following the general elections and first sessions of legislation.

3. This apathy is connected to the present economic recession or even crisis situation in Hungary. It is well known that a capitalistic system and private ownership themselves do not guarantee a mocratic political system. It is also true that nowhere in countries without private ownership is there democracy at all. Democracy exists only in countries where there is private property and a capitalistic economy. It is fairly problematic whether it is possible to build up a democratic political and social system in a country where the economy the economy is in crisis. (In some Asian countries, the first steps towards democracy were taken after strong economic growth.) As a matter of fact, in Hungary the new democratic political structure was born but, with respect to constitutionalism, this is not the case. The shortcomings of constitutionalism are partly connected to poverty and the crisis situation in Hungary.

The four-year term of the first democratically elected Hungarian Parliament is over. However, the tendency to focus on the elimination of the heritage of the past regime, either in the form of retribution or restitution, has further continued. As a result, the establishment of a legal framework for a new economic structure and ownership relations has been put on hold. Because the foregoing tendency gained dominance, legislation has dealt with issues relating to basic civil rights and a democratic establishment. In short, contrary to the regular legislative practice of established democracies, in most cases constitutional issues are here debated.

Since I do not share the view that constitutional issues have a legal nature only, I perceive the situation as follows: serious political issues are transformed into merely legal ones since, due to the parliamentary dominance of the government coalition, the only means available for the opposition to challenge government policies is to route such issues via the standards of constitutionality. These are indeed borderline issues from the perspective of constitutionality. They may be understood as clearly legal ones, but if so, the public will have no understanding of the political and often moral implications lying behind these legal issues, and this is rather counterproductive for political democracy. Such issues involve the freedom of the mass media, the press and public opinion; retribution affecting civil rights and the general mood of the public; the relationship of the president to the government; and minority issues.

Due to its involvement in these issues, the Constitutional Court continues to be a key player in Hungary, and consequently, decisions on political issues - even if in rather abstract form - are often relegated to the Court. Whether one appreciates it or not, this is the only establishment body which continues to act without delay, and because the others fail to perform in this manner, its role at times proves to be politically overdominant. Due to this, the constitutional court is attacked from every side, but mostly by the government and the pro-government factions of the Parliament.

Some Hard Cases

Case 1: The 15/1991.(IV.13) judgment of the Constitutional Court. The collection and processing of personal data, without a strictly defined aim and for undefined future use is unconstitutional. It is unconstitutional to use a general and uniform personal identification symbol (personal identity number) that can be applied without limitation by any authorities. Effective as of December 31, 1991, all old regulations concerning the use of the personal identity number are repealed.

This decision of the Constitutional Court was widely challenged not only by the government but also by the public in general; what is more, even by many oppositional members of the Parliament. The opponents of this decision argued that the reconstruction of the new record keeping system would cause enormous costs, would threaten the public interest and lead to difficulties in keeping track of criminals, etc. Some opponents of the decision stated that it would have been more correct and fair if the Constitutional Court had left the decision within the competence of the Parliament or at least had conducted an opinion poll or public debate prior to the judgment, as is the case with the same issue in many European countries. The critics forgot only one thing: in West European countries opinion polls were conducted *prior to* the introduction of the personal identity number. In Hungary, however, the personal identity number was in use for a long period and the state, in principle, could collect data and information about every citizen. This resistance shows that the principles of constitutionalism are not deeply rooted in the awareness of the population, and the government and even the Parliament deems pragmatism more important than constitutionalism. This decision was one among the issues where the legal validity of its judgment was recognized but the competence of the Constitutional Court was contested.

Case 2: The opponents of the activity of the Court identify parliamentarism with the unlimited power of the Parliament. They consider the majority will to be a supreme value. But the Parliament also has constitutional limits. The rule of the law is the main safeguard of individual freedom, at least since the end of the seventeenth century. The realization of this freedom is easier in countries where consistent constitutional requirements have existed for centuries. In Hungary, where this is not the case, the Constitutional Court is sometimes forced to judge on the basis of such relatively open legal principles as human dignity or equality of citizens. This does not make these judgments political ones. For example, capital punishment is a constitutional issue and there does not need to be any abolitionist movement or consent of the parties and public opinion to decide about it. The issue of the use of the personal identity number is of a similar nature. The Constitutional Court is limited only by the Constitution. Only German positivism of the last century considers the laws and the constitution as a value in itself which lacks any substantive element. Sometimes the Court itself has limited its authority, for example, when it did not apply the preliminary (before a law has been enacted by the parliament) constitutional norm control, though the Constitution makes it possible.

The Parliament can exert influence over the Court in two ways: (i) by changing or modifying the act in the Constitutional Court. But if the modifications were too significant it would cause unease in foreign countries. (ii) by changing or modifying the Constitution itself. This would be regrettable and unfortunate because it would mean that the Constitution is no more solid than any other law requiring a two-thirds majority vote, which may be adjusted to everyday politics.

Case 3:   The amended Constitution of 1989 declared that "the Republic of Hungary is an independent, democratic constitutional state". In a constitutional sense, this signified political changes in Hungary. Constitutional statehood is a fact in part only, and in part it is a task to be accomplished. The whole legal structure has to be gradually harmonized with the constitution: not only regulations and the operations of state institutions have to be introduced to the society, but also the conceptual values of the constitution. Political changes in Hungary were carried out on the grounds of legality which also means that reflexive regulations of the legal structure must assert themselves. The amended constitution grew out of a formally impeccable compliance with the old legislative regulations, and as a product of them. Every regulation in force today has to be in full compliance with this constitution, regardless of the date when any given regulation was passed.

Two problems arise. What shall be done with the legal relationships arising out of the old - and by now unconstitutional - regulations? And can we consider the historical circumstances of the political changes when we pass judgments about whether the new regulations applying to unconstitutional provisions of the past regime are constitutional?

If we try to answer these questions on the grounds of constitutional statehood, the requirement of legal security is of greatest importance. Legal security is especially important if unconstitutional regulations are repealed, but it is even more important when the repeal affects legal relationships arising from such regulations. Otherwise, every change of regulation would imply a revision of several legal relationships. Closed legal relationships may not be changed either by regulations or by the repeal of regulations in a constitutional manner. The only exception is when another constitutional principle competing with the principle of legal security makes such change unavoidable. Even then change can only be justified where it does not cause disproportionately huge harm compared to the given aim. Such an exception may be the revision of a validly closed criminal proceeding for the benefit of the convicted person, if the proceeding was conducted on the basis of a - later so-defined - unconstitutional regulation. The reverse situation does not constitute an exception, ie, it is no argument in itself against legal security merely that the result of the legal relationships is unjust.

The answer to the second problem is that basic guarantees of a constitutional state may not be set aside by quoting historical necessities or the requirements of justice. No constitutional aims may be realized against a constitutional state. According to the Constitutional Court, legal security, relying on the material and formal principles of legal security, takes priority over partial and subjective justice.

Consequently, an act reviving prosecutability after the limitation period has expired violates the limits of the state's penal powers, because it affects such guaranteed rights, the restriction of which is not allowed by the Constitution even if other basic rights may be suspended or restricted. The basic institutions of criminal law must not be made relative, because the guarantees of criminal law are the results of a prior constitutional deliberation, namely, that the risk of unsuccessful prosecution shall be borne by the state. When the limitation period expires owing to the state's inability, the unprosecutability so acquired is absolute, and it may not be subsequently reduced or revived. Historical circumstances or justice may not be quoted in this context. Should this not be the case, it would involve an obvious omission of the guarantees of criminal law, which is absolutely antithetical to the principles of constitutional statehood. Law and order in a constitutional state may not deprive anyone of the guarantees of a constitutional state, because, as basic rights, they are available to everyone. Justice and morality might justify punishment; however, the legal foundation for such punishment is conceivable on the grounds of constitutionalism only.

According to the interpretation of the Constitutional Court, legal security requires from the state and legislation that the entire law, its divisions and regulations shall be clear, obvious, predictable and foreseeable with respect to their effect. In criminal law, a ban on retroactive effect, the prohibition especially of *ex post facto* provisions, and a ban on the application of analogy are directly deducible from predictability and foreseeability. The principle of legal security requires procedural guarantees, as well. The statute of limitation in criminal law restricts in time the state's ability to exercise its criminal powers. A failure shall fall on the state. In a constitutional state, the state has not and cannot have unlimited powers. The executive power itself is not unlimited, either. The executive power may interfere with individuals' rights and freedoms only pursuant to constitutional mandate and justification.

The criminal law system of a democratic state handles the principles of *nullum crimen* and *nulla poena sine* as a constitutional obligation of the state which means that the state has to codify in law, in advance, the conditions for its exercise of the criminal powers. It is not only that the state forbids crimes and threatens punishment by law, but, further, that the individual is entitled to be sentenced in a lawful manner, and his penalty shall be meted out lawfully as well. In a constitutional state, criminal law is not only a means, but also a protection of values, and is itself entrusted with values. Namely, constitutional criminal law principles and guarantees. Criminal law protects interests; nevertheless, it can not serve as a means for moral purification respecting the protection of moral values. This is why the Constitutional Court declares that any perpetrator can be sentenced and punished only on the basis of laws effective at the time of the perpetration of the crime. (Except, however, if the new law permits a lighter punishment.)

All this is applicable to the expiration of prosecutability. Expiry is a fact, but the facts determining it are legal facts. It shall be the court alone that validly determines whether the prosecutability of a crime has expired or not. Legislators have one single constitutional means only for having a say in the matter of expiry; namely, if they pass regulations more favourable or for the benefit of the accused.

The revival by law of prosecutability for an already expired crime is unconstitutional. With expiry, prosecutability irreversibly ceases because the causes stopping prosecutability set a limit on the state's criminal powers. These causes may not change the qualification of an act, since a crime remains a crime. When expiry ensues, however, it is the personal right of the perpetrator not to be punished. The principle of confidence in law requires that once a cause for stopping prosecutability has materialized, the prosecutability of crime shall not be revived by law. Expiration stops prosecutability regardless of why the perpetrator has not been prosecuted. The failure of the state does not fall on him.

The extension by law of prosecutability of as yet unexpired crimes is also unconstitutional. During the limitation period, expiry is meant primarily for law enforcement authorities, and according to the act, the authority may, by nullifying, tolling, revive the serving of full term without notification of the convict. The limitation period will also be extended if the authority suspends the proceedings, by indicating the duration of suspension. This is called the stopping of expiration. This means, however, that the institution of expiration provides insufficient guarantees for the anticipated stopping of prosecutability. It also assures that the rules for the calculation of the limitation period during the limitation period shall not change to the harm of the perpetrator. At the time of deliberation, the state's criminal powers are subject to the same restrictions as at the time of perpetration.

Should the limitation period be extended by a retroactive act, however, its unconstitutional nature may not be legitimized with the explanation that expiration was suspended. If expiration was indeed suspended at the time of the perpetration pursuant to then effective laws, then no new act is required to announce it. If however at the time of the perpetration expiration was not suspended, then the adjudication of expiration is the responsibility of law enforcement authorities only, and eventually that of the courts. Subsequently, legislators have no say in this matter.

It is completely unconstitutional that, pursuant to the law, expiration shall be revived if the state has failed to apply its "criminal code" due to political considerations. This however may mean many different things: proceedings did not commence, proceedings were stopped without legal reasons, the case was closed pursuant to unlawfully light measures, etc. It is even more difficult to define clearly what qualify as political reasons, since the time frame of the act is so long that it has failed to consider the multiple political changes. The criminal policy of an era may subsequently be termed unconstitutional, but it is not possible subsequently to deem non-existent the entire activities of criminal powers that functioned in contradiction with the principles of constitutional statehood, and conclude from the foregoing that expiry with respect to the indicated matters could not have commenced.

Both the act and the decision of the Constitutional Court touch upon the basics of the establishment of constitutional statehood. The question at stake here was not whether the real felons of the communist regime would be punished or not, but rather, whether the rule of law which affects the future of a democratic state shall be subordinated to the emotional needs of a segment of the population. Let me add that, due to certain political considerations, the needs of the constitutional state coincide with those of a reasonable decision. The political situation is rather simple. The political system in Hungary changed without revolution. The change, in part, is the result of compromise: they did not fire shots, we do not take revenge. The communist system was indeed inert, but one must admit, they could have fired guns.

Case 4: The freedom of the press and the electronic mass media became a constitutional problem in Hungary. A real fight or war has developed over the question of how the media can be independent from the state power. Both the government and the opposition wished to have control over the media. The ultimate point at issue is not only to do with the role of the media and free speech in a democratic regime but also with the fact that these problems most transparently manifest the vulnerable parts of the present constitution.

The fairly complicated issue may be summarised as follows. According to the government, a significant part of the media, especially radio and television, is biased and one-sidedly anti-governmental (obviously, the oppositional parties claim the same too, though in reverse). Therefore the government needs to exert a more direct and greater influence upon the media, first of all, with a personal appointment policy which is actually allowed by a governmental decree. The government has the political responsibility for public media. The right of the President of the Republic to appoint is just formal.

The Constitutional Court ruled the following in its two resolutions, one majority and one in dissent. (Personally, I believe that in both of them the Court has indulged in politics. This would be so even if the decisions were interpreted in favour of and for both parties. It was no wonder that instead of a deeper analysis the competence of the Constitutional Court came into the spotlight, being criticized by both parties (and also by the court). What is certain, though, is that the Court has expressed its opinion - with abstract constitutional interpretation - on obviously political dilemmas which, due to the lack of relevant provisions, may not be solved by the present constitution. Besides, if provisions had existed, the clarification of its blurred wordings would have required constitutional amendment.)

The resolution of the Constitutional Court (36/1992) argues that the Constitution permitted the President to act independently of the Government and Parliament in exceptional circumstances.

Three justices (Geza Kilenyi, Peter Schmidt and Imre Voros) submitted a parallel opinion. Geza Kilenyi argues that both the president and the prime minister are politically accountable, but their types of accountability are different. The prime minister's is direct, whereas the president's one is more broad, ie, it is not a question of superior or inferior responsibilities. Schmidt derives the competence and sphere of the president's power from the characteristics of the separation of powers. Therefore he holds the Court incompetent to resolve problems which should be elaborated by constitutional amendment. Imre Voros claims that the

Court extends its earlier interpretation on the competence of the president to political issues, and deals with questions on which the Constitution is tacit.

It is obvious that the Court has been standing under a strong governmental pressure for a long time. Many of its earlier decisions have already drawn the loathing of the governing parties. Nevertheless its legally often untenable decisions are full of politically consequential elements which do weaken the reputation of this highly esteemed democratic institution. However, it is more than certain that further political pressure is going to be applied to them. Actually, there was such a case recently, in which the Prime Minister demanded that rather than doing abstract constitutional interpretations the Constitutional Court should judge whether it was constitutional or not that the President of the Republic did not appoint the leaders of TV and broadcasting companies. (According to the Constitution the president can refuse the recommendation of the prime minister only if it is dangerous for the whole democratic system or formally illegal. Substantively the president does not have the right to judge the appointment). Nonetheless if the Court is willing - under the pretext of interpretation - to read into the constitution things on which the constitution was tacit, it should not be surprised by such expanding legal interpretative exactions. This is also the consequences of the claim of Laszlo Solyom, president of the Constitutional Court, that throughout the cases the Court writes the so far invisible future constitution of the country too.

Closing Remarks

Neither before the 1990 general elections nor thereafter, has any Hungarian political force been in favour of making a new constitution. According to one possible scenario, the drafting of a new constitution could have commenced, provided, however, that there had been agreement, by and among the parties, prior to the elections. In other words, a constitutional convention should have been held. According to another possible scenario, parties should have come to a consensual agreement regarding *every* constitutional issue, followed by a gradual amending process of the constitution, thus making way for the adoption of a new constitution. This would have required compromises on both sides. Even prior to the general elections, the relationship between the different parties had deteriorated to such an extent that no mutual accord was feasible with respect even to issues of commonly shared principle. This is why the two major parties of the time opted for a third possibility: a pact between the Democratic Forum and the Free Democrats. This act, however, postponed the drafting of a new constitution for many years to come. Such basic issues as, eg, the constitution, might necessitate compromises, but not for tactical, political considerations. Giving preference to tactics may result in unexpected consequences when, due to their unpredictability, anticipated benefits might just as well get reversed. Instead of symmetrical benefits, one sees the birth of asymmetrical drawbacks.

The current amendment practice of the constitution may eliminate insignificant inconsistencies. However, it will always depend on short-term political bargaining, and will not boost respect for the constitution. The initially frequent amendments brought about practically new constitutions, and were, therefore, under constant attack. Constitution-making is not identical to legislation, even legislation that requires a two thirds majority to pass, as legislators would, in line with the actual political set-up, draft the constitution for their own purposes, even when compromises are reached. If the Constitutional Court drafted its own "Invisible Constitution", that would not be desirable either, as this body, however respectable, is not the embodiment of national sovereignty.

The coalition programme of the government formed in 1994 called for the drafting and adoption of a new constitution. Only the ruling coalition, having a two-thirds majority, would have had enough power to do it. A new constitution, however, is not a matter of who has greater strength. A national consensus is required. Otherwise, in four years' time, a new and differently composed government might again re-draft the constitution. To date, there has been no consensus regarding either the substantive or procedural issues of constitution-making. Nevertheless, some progress between the government and the opposition has been made; it has been agreed that there will be no unconsensual constitution-making. The constitution, however, should immediately be amended in two respects. It should be stipulated that any amendment of the constitution shall be subject to the adoption of the new constitution. And similarly, that the change contained therein shall enter into force subject to approval by the successor parliament. Effective immediately, it should also be stipulated that the election law may be amended only during the first two years of the term of the government in order to prevent any tactical abuse of the law.

Bibliography

Arendt, H. (1969), *On Revolution,* New York, Viking Press.
Augustine, *City of God Against the Pagans,* vol. II, Book IV, chapter iv, translated by Green, W.M. (1963), Cambridge, Mass, Harvard University Press.
Kuhn, T. (1962), *The Structure of Scientific Revolutions,* Chicago, University of Chicago Press.
Radbruch, G. (1963), *Aphorismen zur Rechtsweisheit,* edited by Arthur Kaufmann, Göttingen, Vandenhoeck & Ruprecht.

7 Paradigm Lost?

The Constitutional Process in
Poland and the Hope of a
"Grass Roots Constitutionalism"

GRAŻYNA SKĄPSKA

Must a society have a constitution? What does it mean to have a constitution? These are not easily answered questions. Still, modern societies regard constitutions as important steps in their political development. Hence a constitution, in its different understandings - as a basic law of society, an ideological manifesto, the existing government's attempt to legitimize itself, or a nation's "birth certificate" - first and foremost creates a political obligation of official accountability, a rule of law, respect for citizens' rights, and due process, on the part of government. As the chairman of the Polish Constitutional Tribunal states, in the rule of law system - or rather in the European tradition, in the *Rechtsstaat* system - political power is based on the constitutional principle of the rule of law, and political competences result from the constitution (Zoll, 1996).

In the broader, sociological meaning, to have a constitution means to agree on the basic rights and basic principles of social and political order, it means to reach a fundamental "overlapping consensus" (Rawls, 1987) and to form a "constitution of society on which social cohesion depends (Shils,

I am very grateful for comments on a draft of this paper from colleagues from the Section on the Sociology of Law, Polish Sociological Association and formerly, the Chair of the Sociology of Law at Warsaw University, especially Anna Turska, Wiesław Staśkiewicz and Jerzy Kwaśniewski. I owe special thanks to Mirosław Wyrzykowski and Ulrich Preuss, who so strongly opposed some of the ideas presented here. The final form this paper has taken owes much to the exceptionally friendly conditions in Collegium Budapest, Institute for Advanced Studies.

1982). Consequently, what the written constitution means here, is the last stage of institutionalization and formalization of the process of forming a social constitution: a fundamental political consensus, rooted in the "spirit of constitutionalism" described as an expectation and a norm, according to which the government will recognize limitations put on it by law (Elster, 1993).

Questions concerning liberal constitutions are of profound importance in Central and Eastern Europe after the collapse of communism. They are debated with regard to the political development in which millions took part in an effort to democratize and liberalize a huge part of the European continent. The so-called peaceful revolutions of 1989 are compared to the great European and American revolutions of the seventeenth and eighteenth centuries since they moved whole nations and brought about a hoped-for freedom and democracy in the unliberal and undemocratic part of Europe. With regard to those peaceful and lawful political processes of profound change, it is even more important to debate their "jurisgenerative force" and their impact on the formation of new constitutions (Ackerman, 1996).

The events of 1989 were characterized by anti-authoritarianism and the declarations of their main actors that they would constrain political power by means of the law and principles of the *Rechtsstaat*, as the most important principles which govern state-society relations and which protect citizens against abuses of political power. In accordance with such efforts, constitution-making in Central and Eastern Europe began shortly after the first democratic elections, and new constitutions were duly proclaimed in Russia, Ukraine, Czechoslovakia, Romania, Bulgaria, and other so called "new democracies", with two exceptions: the Hungarian constitution was adopted just before the democratic changes, and the new constitution is still in the making; and Poland, after the first, semi-democratic elections in 1989, considerably amended her old constitution of 1952, known as the "Stalinist constitution", and only in 1997 proclaimed a new constitution.

The new constitutions institutionalized democracy and the rule of law, and outlined the fundamental principles for further reform: introduction of a free market, protection of civil rights and liberties, division of power, and also a vast range of social and economic rights.

However, after already eight years, questions about the "jurisgenerative force" of the events of 1989 appear anew. In 1997, some of the new democracies do not have new constitutions, in some of them a praxis of an "invisible constitution" has developed, which consists of the formation of constitutional principles by constitutional courts (Sajó, 1995), and some constitutions infringe upon the most fundamental liberal rights such as rights of ethnic minorities. More important, however, the new constitutions are accused of syncretism and incompatibility with challenges brought about by the transformation, first and foremost by liberalization of the economy and reform of the dysfunctional welfare system (Sunstein, 1993; Sajó, 1996; Ciemniewski, 1996). They are described as presenting a mixture of incoherent ideas, of a curious "neo-liberal-social- (or even socialistic) democracy", which are often treated as mere "documents" with no real-world consequences (Calda and Gillis, 1995). Without disputing claims as to the incompatibility of the new constitutions with the needs of economic and welfare reforms, one has to emphasize that the new constitutions reflect states of minds and habits of the hearts of their framers, and of broader constituencies for whom the economic reform was rather unexpected, and welfare reform threatened some vested interests (Kurczewski, 1992).

A specifically troublesome case is presented here by Poland, as a nation which has one of the world's longest constitutional traditions, reaching back to 1791, and which played a leading role in the events preceding the democratization of East and Central Europe.

After seven years of functioning under the old - albeit considerably amended "Stalinist" constitution of 1952. Poland finally has a new Constitution. In February-April 1997 the Constitutional Committee - composed of two majority parties in the National Assembly, the post-communist Democratic Left Alliance and the Polish Peasant Party, and such parties as the Freedom Union and the Labour Union - accelerated its work on the project of the new Constitution, faced by the coming election of September and threatened with the accusation that it had wasted three years of work (in the then-present parliament: altogether it was seven years). The opposition, not represented in the Parliament, argued that the amendments it had proposed were mostly rejected. Eventually, after discussions and important amendments actually imposed in the Constitutional Committee by the Polish Peasant Party (above all, the constitutional protection of the small and ineffective "family farms" and abandonment of administrative reform), the final version of the new Constitution was accepted by the National Assembly, signed by the President and accepted in a national referendum on May 25, 1997. In this referendum, 42.86 per cent of Polish citizens took part, and the Constitution was accepted by a slight majority - 51.71 per cent - of them. This means that it was accepted by about 23 per cent of Polish citizens. This does not seem to make a good starting point for the future of constitutionalism in Poland. The opposition parties immediately announced their intention to change the Constitution, and it does indeed have some serious shortcomings, though not necessarily those pointed to by the opposition parties which concentrated primarily on ideological questions. Above all, protection of property rights is not quite clear and the decisions of the Constitutional Court for the next two years can still be overruled by a qualified parliamentary majority.

Indeed, until 1997 one might even have spoken of an astounding "constitutional paralysis" which was already suggested by the abundance of constitutional projects (at least ten had been proposed: by the Upper House of the Polish Parliament, by the President, and by the *Solidarność* Union. The "constitutional paralysis" was visible in the battle between drafts of constitutions proposed by the Parliamentary Commission and by the non-parliamentary opposition. It was also characterized by conflicts concerning the fundamental concepts of the rights and basic principles of social self-organization, among which views on abortion, on Church-State relations, on the administrative division of government, and on decisions of the Constitutional Tribunal were, and still are, among the most controversial. In view of the growing controversies, two opposite views were presented in the constitutional debate in Poland: according to the first, which eventually succeeded, the parliamentary Constitutional Commission should present a finished draft, even if it did not fulfil public expectations, and even if it was unsatisfactory from the point of view of legal standards, and submit it to public referendum as soon as possible. According to the adverse view, there was no need to draft a new constitution at all.

This chapter presents, then, an invitation to the debate on the leading paradigm for the changes of 1989 in Central and Eastern Europe, on its institutional consequences, and on the cultural and cognitive foundations of constitutionalism in the broader context of liberalism, democratization, and post-communism. The debate will be concentrated on the idea of the "round table", on the institutional consequences of a very specific "legalism" or "constitutionalism" presented by the participants at the "round table", on political and social processes accompanying the prolonged process of constitution-making in a society which simultaneously is undergoing a process of liberalization and democratization, and is faced by the challenges brought about by a broader institutional and axiological crisis.

Arguments and Hypotheses

Considering all this, in this paper I will try to throw some light on and to form some hypotheses about the process of constitution-formation under the conditions created by the collapse of communism at the end of the twentieth century. According to my fundamental argument, the initial paradigm of the transformation processes, the paradigm of consensus and a "round table" is losing its legitimizing potential, and processes of liberalization and democratization of society and of differentiation of interests and fragmentation of values characteristic of liberalization and democratization, made the constitutional processes all the more difficult, the longer it took to form the constitution. The more time that passes after the *constitutional moment*, a moment of psychological and valuative unification of social souls and minds and of society's support for new political actors on which the new constitutional order could rest, the harder it is to bring the process to its conclusion. The concept of *constitutional moment* refers to the special position of political elites who participated in the "round tables" and were legitimized by a unifying principle, be it the principle of national independence, of political freedom, or of anti-communism, and who could impose a new constitutional order from above, and in this way consciously construct a new, in the best case liberal and democratic, order.

The phenomenon of the *constitutional moment* seems to stay in close relation to social and political time, to the division between old and new, and between the old regime and the new order. What we are observing is the loss of that special time which results in a loss of authority by the political elites. This is accompanied by exhaustion of the unifying, anti-communist principle which dominated social minds before the collapse of the old regime. Instead of unifying anti-communism, the liberalization of society and its democratization, but above all, modernization of its culture, disparities, clashes and conflicts appear and make the process of constitution-formation all the more difficult. In other words, the process of constitution formation stays in close reciprocal relationship with the transformation to a democratic and liberal society; it reflects the characteristic features not only of political processes in democratic society, but also of social processes and the actors engaged in them. Therefore, from the point of view of a "sociology of constitutionalism", it is particularly interesting to ponder the question of factors important for constitution formation when understood as a complex process of the formation of fundamental principles, laws and obligations incumbent on citizens and on the state. According to my argument, then, to debate the prospects of liberal constitutionalism in East Central Europe, one must reach "beyond the heads of lawyers" into the political process on the one side, and life-worlds of society on the other, to ponder the principles of political and social organization from below.

My argument is also backed by a very simple and, upon brief consideration, obvious observation. It shows that the process of constitution formation, understood as the formation of a social constitution that may be completed in the shape of a formal document, takes place under very specific circumstances. Firstly, it occurs after the collapse of a system, colloquially called the collapse of communism, in an effort to crush the political monopoly of one party, one ideology, and an all-penetrating authoritarian concept of social and political organization imposed on the society. Secondly, however, it is also taking place at the end of the period called modernity which roughly began at the time of the first wave of democratization, and accompanied the emergence of the first liberal constitutions, ie, roughly at the time of the French Revolution.

In the already vast literature on the subject, two of its different features are observed: the political and socio-cultural. Above all, changes in political organization are observed, specifically those which concern the concept of the nation-state and of people's sovereignty, vis-a-vis the growing importance of supra-national organizations such as, for instance, the European Union and international corporations (Bellamy, Buffacchi and Castiglione, 1996). Both of these processes contribute to the difficulties encountered by new democracies in their efforts to frame a liberal, modern constitution. With regard to socio-cultural changes, it is maintained that what we are witnessing is the emergence of a new phase in social and political development which is characterized by the "end of clarity" (Bauman, 1991), in which all aspects of social and political organizations are questioned, nothing is certain, and "anything goes" (Gellner, 1995). More specifically, and more relevantly to these remarks, the end of the period of modernization, it is claimed, is bringing about a profound crisis of political institutions, of law, and of the concepts of polity and politics (Giddens, 1994; Beck, Giddens and Lash 1994). These processes are not the specific subject of this paper, but one has to note that they overlap with the outcomes of the collapse, or exhaustion, of the communist regime. Instead of the certainties characteristic of the period of modernization, new forms of political organization and of law are postulated: more flexible, less authoritarian, no longer imposed from above by enlightened leaders, and more dependent on the actions of social actors (especially on civic social organizations). In that respect, reflections on modernity coincide with quite different, and characteristically opposing ideas accompanying the peaceful revolutions in Central Europe: the ideas directly expressed, for instance, by Vaclav Havel, for whom those revolutions represented a rebellion of real existing social actors against a "system" (Havel, 1985), and such ideas, which stress an alleged mass infantilization of societies, or even their "idiotization", as a legacy of the former regime (Sunley, 1996; Zięba, 1996; Nodia, 1996).

However, just to sketch the path of a counter-argument, one has to ask whether social actors do not need some certainty in their lives, some well protected rights, some well established and protected principles on which the social organization rests, as well as principles governing their dealings with political organizations, parties, governments, or police forces which, even if otherwise undergoing profound changes, not only still exist, but have at their disposal ever more sophisticated means for surveillance of society and protection of their vested interests. Hence, the question concerning constitutions after the collapse of communism does not lose its importance.

The main argument will be developed in the form of a theoretical test of the main hypothesis. According to it, among the different concepts ascribed to the contracts and negotiations metaphorically called "round tables", the concept of "political bargain" or a "deal" between elites has the strongest explanatory potential, but precisely the fact that it was a "bargain" poses the strongest obstacle to constitution formation. That hypothesis will be elaborated upon an analysis of the theoretical models related to the metaphor of the "round table", and the political and social contexts of the constitutional formation processes after the collapse of communism, the context of the political legitimacy of law and the characteristics of the "silent actor" or the "third party", ie, the social and political processes taking place in the society. As a consequence of this analysis, the possibility of "grass roots constitutionalism", and the formation of a "grass roots polity" will be outlined.

In order to illustrate my fundamental argument, in the following sections I will investigate social theories relevant to the interpretation of the process of constitution formation after the collapse of communism. The empirical reference for these theoretical considerations will be the example of Poland, but I believe that some of my conclusions are general enough to be applicable in any other society undergoing a process of democratic and liberal constitution formation.

Considering the process of constitution formation from that perspective, there are some concepts and theories which have special importance for such an analysis. Firstly, there are those which consider the *modi operandi* of the constitution-making process in a given time and space: Poland in the nineties. Secondly, there are concepts and theories which seem especially adequate for an analysis of law-making processes, ie, their political legitimation. Thirdly, there are concepts and theories which analyse the constitution-making dynamics after the collapse of communism, then predominantly concepts relevant for the formation of a democratic and liberal society.

The "Leading Paradigm": its Explanatory and Normative Potentials

Considering the peacefulness of the constitution-making processes, and also their contents (the already mentioned socialistic-socio-democratic-liberal syncretism), the "round table" poses here a metaphor and *modus operandi* of the constitution-making process, and the key concept for explanation of it.

Indeed, as has been emphasized:

> In recent times, few "images" have made as much (world) history, aroused so many hopes and achieved so much for freedom and democracy as the "round table". Invented by and in Wałęsa's Poland, it may, from the point of view of history and mankind, go back to King Arthur's "Knights of the Round Table" (Haberle, 1992: 66; see also Kis, 1995: 33).

The concept of a "round table", the heralded metaphor of the peaceful revolutions, is, however, an open concept with many meanings. It is linked to many doctrines and theories, but above all it remains closely connected to the concept of the social contract as a basis of constitutional and, in the broader sense, legal order. In Poland, the document fundamental for the further democratic changes took the form of a social contract between society and the communist party representatives, known as the "Gdańsk Agreement" of 1981.[1] Also the written results of the "Round Table Talks" of 1989 are colloquially referred to as a contract. On the whole, contractual and negotiated forms of law-making play an important role for the formation of law after 1989, in particular with regard to transformation of the economy, in the domain of labour law and individual and collective rights to participate in the privatization processes (Skąpska, 1991a).

The concept of the social contract, however, is related to at least three theoretical traditions, and three types of theories of the rational formation of a liberal social and political order, and of law. These traditions will be used here for an ideal-typical reconstruction of three theoretical models of social contract, and for an analysis of their consequences. Needless to say that in the social reality of the new order in formation after the collapse of the communist regime, these models overlap.

The first of those models is represented by the classical theories of liberalism of Locke or Hobbes, and it takes on its most advanced form in the thought of Immanuel Kant. It is also closest to the lawyer's concept of contract, as a result of free bargaining but conducted and concluded within the framework posed by the existing law. The second, most discussed and highly evaluated model, is based on the theory of the ethics of discursive procedures, and the concept of public discourse. The third is based on utilitarian doctrines, and currently is represented in the form of economic neo-institutional theories.

There are two sets of theoretical consequences of the classical doctrines of the social contract. Both of them are also related to the concept of *Rechtsstaat*. The first of them, in the form of legal positivism, has its roots in the doctrine of Thomas Hobbes, and is presented in the Kelsenian concept of constitutionalism. The second one takes the form of a natural law doctrine. To make a complex matter simple, both of those theoretical consequences of the classical doctrine are highly ambiguous when analysed in light of the post-communist changes, not to mention the broader perspective of the processes characteristic of the changes of modern society. From the point of view of this paper, there are two important types of arguments which question the classical doctrine of the social contract: one, doctrinal and the other, sociological.

In light of the Hobbesian doctrine, positive law poses the most important tool in constraining political authority and brings peace and order into society; it prevents abuse of accepted freedoms and liberties, but at the same time it prevents civil, fratricidal wars. Not surprisingly then, the classical doctrine has been very popular in this time of "peaceful" or "velvet" revolutions, which have also been called "lawful" (Skąpska, 1991b; on the Hungarian "lawful revolution" see Kis, 1995; Kidaly, 1995) but, above all, "self-limiting". Arguments based on the principles of classical doctrine emphasize the peacefulness and "lawfulness" of the changes, their orderly character, and the reciprocal constraints imposed by the existing law: constraints imposed on the still-communist authorities, but also on the democratic opposition. In that respect the observation of an Hungarian author, that in Hungary the inherited legal order was not suspended for a moment, would also be valid to a great extent also with regard to Poland.[2] So, in the reality of the post-communist society, legal positivism justifies the validity of law inherited from the old regime, unless it is changed according to the procedures also set out by the inherited, binding law, unless they are changed. This law, then, delineates paths of transformation. As a consequence, the peacefulness and orderliness of changes does not necessarily contribute to the establishment of a liberal state governed by the law, but brings about a danger of prolongation of the old institutional structures, protection of the old privileges, and the impossibility of punishment of the members of the Stalinist secret police. It contributes to the popular disenchantment with transformation, perceived as prolongation of the "old", and to a growing feeling of deception on the part of society. Furthermore, legal positivism contributes to its self-negation in the form of the above-mentioned emerging "invisible constitutions" - the growing role of constitutional review and law application in the law-making processes - as an answer to the necessities of transformation for which the old, but still binding, law has no answer.

This is quite in contrast to the continental European version of legal positivism and the concept of division of powers. One can remark, then, that, paradoxically, strict adherence to the philosophy of legal positivism in the changing reality of post-communist society opens the way to anti-positivistic, innovative practices contradicting the basic positivistic principles, and also, as it is sometimes claimed, limiting the law-making powers of democratic representation.

Analysed in the broader perspective, not restricted to the questions specific only to those societies which are undergoing accelerated democratization, the classical, liberal doctrine is exposed to criticism because of its "complacency" (Sciulli, 1992, quoted after Frankford, 1994), ie, lack of any other justification for obedience to law, apart from its formal rationality. Another important line of criticism of classical doctrine focusses on the inadequacy of legal concepts and institutions - such as, among other things, individual responsibility, formalized procedures of adjudication, and of law-making in representative democracies - to the risks and uncertainties of modern society, and alternative forms of organization characteristic of that society (Beck, 1994).

There is, however, also a third type of argument concerning classical doctrine, somewhat contrary to those already presented. It maintains that legal positivism requires also a specific type of legalistic culture, consisting in the high prestige of existing law, and subordination to it of political interests. I have already written elsewhere about the legacy of anti-legalism which characterizes post-communist transformation (Skąpska, 1994). This legacy of anti-legal culture was visible also at the time of the initial contract, the "Round Table Agreement" of 1989, whose partners in several cases broke the constitutional principles regarding free elections, contrary to their declared observance of the constitutional principles of the valid, albeit old, constitution (Jackiewicz, 1995).

In light of the second consequence of the classical doctrine, positive law is justified in a higher normative order which reflects principles of reason. Therefore a constitution, written or unwritten, should reflect natural, transcendental rights and liberties, which, by means of enlightened reason, are discovered and institutionalized. It is not the goal of this chapter to criticize the natural law doctrine as a basis of a social contract and of constitution. Moreover, examples of constitutions based on the concepts of natural and transcendental rights and constitutional principles rooted in them, such as, for instance, the principle of the dignity of a human person, illustrate their normative potential. However, the great difficulty with the institutionalization of natural law in a modern, democratic society, and especially in the context of the anti-authoritarian revolutions of 1989, is posed by the problem of determining the contents of natural rights which are, by their very nature, open-ended. In that respect, the incommensurability and incompatibility of basic rights and liberties is stressed. This raises the question of whether there might be an enlightened authority which, by means of reason, would establish the content of transcendental rights, would itself have a right to the moral interpretation of rights; a question especially acute in societies undergoing processes of democratization and liberalization. So, to emphasize the sociological argument, it is simply the question of why one man ought to obey the dictates of another, why the society ought to obey the authoritative translation of natural law principles into a constitution, especially if the authority which had supposedly to do it, lost its *constitutional moment*, missed the time of social support. That question is even more relevant for societies which once fought against authoritarianism, and which, because of their democratization, are suspicious of traditional authorities (like, for instance, in Poland the authority of the Catholic Church or of the intellectual elites, in Eastern Europe known as the *intelligentsia*).

Thus, the classical doctrine does not stand up to examination of its applicability for the explanation of constitution formation after the collapse of communism. Its legal positivistic version does not pass the test based on its own premises. Even if it had bound the parties to the actual negotiation and limited the space of their manoeuvres, which is an open question, it does not prohibit formation of such anti-positivistic institutions as "invisible constitutions" or law making by high courts. The concept of a contract based on the natural law doctrine does not pass the political and sociological test, since it is not clear why society should accept one concept of natural law principle and not another, imposed by some self-appointed authority, no longer perceived as such by the society.

The next two models of the *modus operandi* of the constitution making process are the model based on the theory of discourse ethics and that based on the economic neo-institutional theory.

Haberle states:

> The success of the "round table" is no coincidence. It can be justified from the point of view of constitutional theory, is culturally compatible and can be legitimized by the *ethics of discourse and* consensus [my emphasis, G.S.]. (...) it is the best visual and symbolic interpretation of the non-discriminating "live and let live" characteristic of the negotiation of pluralist constitutions that follows the collapse of a totalitarian system. The circle and the (round) table - these metaphors might be seen as a kind of "cultural gene" of humanity. (Haberle, 1992: 66, 67)

In light of those statements, application of the key concepts of peaceful revolutions - discourse ethics and consensus - needs closer consideration. It must be underlined, however, that those concepts relate to a theory concerned above all with the ideal of open and permanent public discourse, a discourse free from constraint, which anybody may enter and exit at any time, in which any argument may be presented and any conclusion reached, and in which any argument could be subjected to critical evaluation, as a foundation of democratic order. It is a theory concerned with the functioning of the public sphere, which encompasses the broadest social circles, and which potentially leaves nobody outside it (Habermas, 1982).

The concept of discourse ethics consists in fulfilment of the claims of truth, sincerity, and fairness as foundations for communicative actions and conditions of consensus.

Analysis of, and application of, this concept to the processes of constitution formation after the collapse of communism indicates two possible ways of thinking, and accordingly, two possible modes of its evaluation. Firstly, one may consider the explanatory and simultaneously critical potential of the theoretical concept. Secondly, one may assume the ethical and simultaneously universal justification of the political order whenever it is based on horizontal communication and consensus. In the first case, the concept of discourse ethics reveals its explanatory and critical normative potential in the investigation of real social processes when it is applied as a specific measure or a point of reference in order to indicate the distance between the ideal of discursive ethics and the real bargaining at the round table. As a tool of theoretical analysis, the concept of discourse ethics also has a normative potential. According to its author, the concept of the ethics of discourse is used to reveal and immanently to criticize the political order of modern society, of the operations of the complex "system" of modern democracies, and of formally rational law, deprived of their institutional, cultural roots (Habermas, 1982, 1993). It is used to reveal the sources of the political passivity of modern society that, as it is assumed, is not only more critical of unquestionable, transcendental order, but also more sceptical of the instrumental rationality and technical efficiency which reduces law to a great machinery consisting of routinized, calculable and quantifiable units. The concept of discourse ethics is then used to analyse the world of Max Weber's rationalistic "iron cage", incorporated in the form of modern law, devoid of any meaningful purpose and justice, in order to reveal normative possibilities of communication based on the ethics of discourse. These function as preconditions for the political order of a non-authoritarian society in which social coordination and the possibility of freedom are contingent. This theory, then, represents the universal postulate of procedural justice on which the order of the modern, pluralist, and open society should be based, and the universal postulate of modern constitutionalism founded on procedures of horizontal communication (Habermas, 1993).

As has been observed, however, normative theory based on the concept of discourse ethics, in order to be valid, must be empirically grounded; it must be posited within a cultural, but also within a political framework which it explains and criticizes, and whose normative potentials it reveals (Frankford, 1994: 1089).

In other words, the jurisgenerative force of the "round table" paradigm must be confronted with the political reality which it should justify, and which may corroborate or invalidate assumptions about the normative potentials of the political, initial consensus, and of the constitution formation processes initiated by it.

In this short chapter I restrict this empirical test to one, albeit important, problem, ie, the problem of the publicness of the proceedings and the scope of the public sphere it encompasses, in other words, to the role played by society in the process of concluding the initial contract, and in further processes of constitution formation.

To begin from the end, the metaphor of a "round table" does not pass such an empirical test, as far as the ongoing process of constitution formation in Poland is concerned. Above all, the initial contract known as the "Round Table Agreement" was concluded by representatives of the ruling communist party, under the leadership of the then-Minister of the Interior, and that part of the democratic opposition which was ready to compromise. Some of its important proceedings were not public at all, and these were not subjected to sustained, public critical evaluation.[3] What is even more important, as a result of the procedures set down during the initial contract, the first semi-democratically chosen Parliament was in its overwhelming majority composed of representatives designated by the communists: the initial contract granted them sixty five per cent of the seats in the Lower House. One has to underline the fact that, according to valid procedures for the preparing and enacting of a constitution, it was from the representatives of the Lower House that the members of the first Parliamentary Commission preparing a draft of constitution were drawn. These problems will be more thoroughly dealt with in the next section. One already has to observe here, however, that as a result of the electoral law, and the great fragmentation of the electorate, even at the time of the framing of the 1997 Constitution, in the Parliament chosen fully democratically, about two-thirds of the electorate was not represented in Parliament since, in the elections conducted in 1993, only fifty six per cent of the whole electorate participated, and thirty per cent of all votes were lost, due to the fact they were cast for parties which did not reach the electoral thresholds. Consequently, two-thirds of Poles had no representatives, and no possibility of democratic participation in the parliamentary constitutional discourse.

As far as the publicness of discourse and the functioning of the broad public sphere is concerned, the model of the "round table", based on the theory of discourse ethics and public discourse as fundamental for constitution formation, does not provide a model justifying those processes which are now taking place in Poland. Obviously, however, such a model fulfils its role as a model of critical analysis of the constitution formation process.

The analysis of the *modi operandi* of constitution formation leads us to an analysis of such situations where the initial contract is concluded by two parties, but its effects are important for a third. This model is used by representatives of the economic neo-institutional theory who assess the utility of a contract as a result of bargaining between parties, according to transaction costs and the utility of the concluded bargain. In light of this pragmatic and utilitarian theory, however, there is a great difference between economic and political bargaining. In the first case, the principles of free market operations constitute an intervening variable, which, even if only in the long run, influences the vested interests of the engaged parties.

For instance, the long run perspective may make parties restrict their too close cooperation at the costs of the third party, if in the long run the costs of such cooperation could be too high, and the gains too small. Therefore, calculations of costs in the long run make the parties choose the best solution. In the case of political bargaining, it has been argued, the result of bargaining does not provide the best solution, but a compromise between conflicting interests on which the third party has no influence, and the calculation of costs in the long run is very problematic. The next, and even more important conclusion, and a lesson one can learn from the neo-institutional economic theory, concerns the results of political transactions for the third party, and in our case, for that part of society which is not represented in the bargaining process. In light of this theory, there is then an even more profound difference between economic transactions between parties which do not affect the third party, and such transactions in which engaged parties represent power that may affect the third party adversely, that is, may spill over the external costs onto individuals outside the contractual relationship. In that case, as authors of this theory observe, the "trade" or "deal" is a subject of suspicion and moral evaluation, and, as they argue,

> [b]reakdowns and failures in the operation of the system are attributed to the "bad" men, not to the rules that constrain them. (Buchanan and Tullock, 1962: 281)

Therefore, paradoxically, the economic theory of rational bargaining turns our attention not only to the rationality of collective decision-making, but to the potential vulnerability of the bargaining process and its participants, to ethical evaluations expressed by the "third party" affected by the outcomes of the bargain. In other words, it indicates the possible sources of delegitimation of political elites, as well as the growing disappointment with the constitutional process on the part of society.

The Arithmetic of Failure

Let us go back for a while to the concept of the *constitutional moment*, mentioned earlier in this chapter, and let's explore more deeply the rationality of choices made by lawmakers. The concept of the *constitutional moment* could have a strong and a weak sense. In the strong sense, it is a moment of moral and intellectual concentration which consists of a social will to order the way into society's future and, consequently, to frame a constitution. In the weak sense, the term "constitutional moment" relates simply to favourable parliamentary conditions, to calculations of the feasible parliamentary conditions for constitution making.

Understood in either of these meanings, there have been two constitutional moments in the current process of creating a new constitution in Poland: after the first parliamentary elections which led to the formation of the new government under the leadership of prominent members of the democratic opposition, and after the 1993 elections which resulted in a seemingly coherent majority in the Polish Parliament. After 1989 social support for changes was exceptionally high, even though the reforms, especially the economic transformation, were not favourable to the majority of society. Moreover, had the new constitution been ready by 1991, it would have gained a tremendously significant symbolic legitimation, linking the democratic present with the heroic past, as the first Polish constitution had been proclaimed in 1791 in a great national effort of reform which was not only political and economic, but also moral.

Yet, strikingly enough, neither of those constitutional moments led in Poland to the formation of a new constitution.

Trying to answer the question why Poles missed their constitutional moments, one has to ponder firstly the political and institutional framework of the constitution-making processes and the characteristic features of the political actors. Contrary to the theory of discourse ethics, on which the metaphor of the round table is based, but also going beyond economic neo-institutionalism, the political interests of the actors, as well as the consequences of the already existing institutional frameworks, cannot be overlooked in an analysis of the constitution-making processes.

As Putnam observes, institutions have their "inertia and robustness" (Putnam, 1993: 4). They influence the processes of new institution creation; they exclude some possibilities and impose others. One has to stress that an important part of the institution is constituted by values and principles on which its functioning rests, the informal rules of the game which contribute to institutional performance, and the institutional culture, ie, the legal and constitutional culture of their performers. In Poland, the old constitution of 1952 proved to be an important factor in the process of the new constitution-making, but it should be hastily added that, as was stressed above, from the very beginning some of its provisions were broken by its very proponents.

One has to stress, above all, that no Constitutional Assembly - a body functioning "above political space and time", not involved in a fight for political interests, and not itself interested in the fulfilment of actual claims of electorates (Preuss, 1993) - has been formed, since one had not been envisioned by the still valid, old constitution of 1952.

Instead, according to procedures set for constitutional changes in the binding Constitution of 1952, the constitution has to be framed by Parliament: firstly by a commission composed of members from the Lower House, then, according to the Constitutional Act of 23rd April 1992 on the procedure for preparing and enacting a Constitution for the Republic of Poland, by a Constitutional Commission representing both Houses, the whole National Assembly (Art 4 of the Constitutional Act of 23rd April, 1992). Therefore, the constitution-making processes were, from the very beginning, directly involved not only in the fight for political interests of parties represented in Parliament, but they were also vulnerable to claims and wishes of electorates, for whose support the parties fight.[4]

The next important institution for the formation of a new constitution is the laws on political election. As has been observed, the electoral law in 1989 deliberately limited the possibilities of society to decide, according to the above mentioned bargain concluded at the "round table".

The next electoral law was fully democratic and resulted in the great fragmentation of Parliament, especially its right wing. Nevertheless, such a differentiated Parliament enacted several important constitutional laws: the provisional "Small Constitution" which regulated mainly the separation of powers, and the Constitutional Act of 23rd April 1992 on the procedure for preparing and enacting a Constitution for the Republic of Poland.

The third electoral law of 1993, in order to avoid over-fragmentation of Parliament and to enable the formation of a clear parliamentary majority, introduced a five per cent threshold for individual parties and an eight per cent threshold for coalitions, and a weighted electoral system that promoted parties which won the majority of votes. Those thresholds could be suspended only with regard to parties representing national minorities.

The thresholds introduced, as has been stressed, actually protected the strongest parties with stabilized electorates, effective organization on the national level, and with human and financial resources at their disposal, ie, the strong and well organized Social Democratic Party, as the former communist ("workers'") party renamed itself, together with its allies, predominantly the labour unions faithful to the old regime, and the equally well organized overwhelmingly post-communist peasant party which represents the strong electorate of numerous Polish peasants of very clear indeed, class interests. Those thresholds had a limiting effect on the decision-making of the democratic electorate for the second time in the most recent history of democracy in Poland, and on the representation of that electorate in the Parliament. As a result of the thresholds, and of the principle of proportionality and of bonus rules, as already noted, the majority of Poles was not represented in Parliament.[5]

Consequently, and independently of the stability of government, the second constitutional moment in the short post-1989 history of Poland also seems to be fading out, not only because of the stressed lack of democratic legitimation of the Parliament and its Constitutional Commission, but also because of the involvement of the parties represented in Parliament and in its Constitutional Commission, in a fight for interests, which are the more acute, the closer the next elections are. Constitution formation is therefore involved in processes of tactical alliances concluded by political parties, which results in sometimes unexpected changes of the constitutional provisions which were already accepted by the Commission, or unexpected postulates submitted by the President. The whole process of constitution formation is based then on unclear, non-transparent, rules of the game.

Therefore, chances that the formal document, a new constitution, once accepted and proclaimed would constitute a liberal polity were ever smaller, and so are the chances that the formally binding document will be transformed into a "social constitution", a result of society's judgment and self-reflection. Here the difference between a "normal Parliament" and a Constitutional Assembly should be accentuated once more, as a difference between a normal Parliamentary practice of law making, and a special moment in a society's history, a moment in which decisions on a society's fundamental institutional structures are made. As a Polish constitutionalist observes, electoral thresholds are introduced in order to create a parliamentary majority which would support a stable cabinet. A Constitutional Assembly, by contrast, should be "as representative as possible" for its purpose is not the support of a cabinet, but the crafting of a constitution which not only would be acceptable to all parties, but which, one may add, would reflect a "social constitution", a basis for the society's further development. Therefore, one has to agree that:

> The faltering of institutional reform in Poland suggests that rules which work well for governing may nevertheless impede constitution making. (Osiatyński, 1994: 32)

Therefore, as has been demonstrated, the institutional economic approach to constitution-making processes has its weak points. On the one hand, decision-making processes do not take place in a vacuum, but in a space already structured by existing institutions. Furthermore, the real processes of constitution-making occur in a situation of high risk because of their far-reaching consequences and the multiplicity of factors which influence their outcomes.

Stressing the current Constitutional Commission's crippled legitimacy, as well as the underlying differences of opinions concerning the values and fundamental rights regarding, for instance, the right to life of unborn children, and the right to unrestricted freedom of choice, and, consequently, to abortion; traditions - the predominantly Christian tradition of the Polish society; the model of the future state, its organization and conflict-solving procedures; the role of labour unions within it; the concept of land property and protection of peasants; the non-parliamentary opposition prepared its own proposal for the future constitution. On the basis of Art 2a of the Constitutional Act of 23rd April on the procedure for preparing and enacting a Constitution for the Republic of Poland, a draft Constitution was prepared, entitled the "Civic Constitution Project", and predominantly supported by the "Solidarność" Labor Union. Before the referendum, a battle over the proposed constitutions took place in Poland. This fight did not take place in Parliament, since the "civic project" was prepared by the opposition which was not represented in Parliament. This is even more crucial from the point of view of the decreasing importance of the "round table" paradigm. However, one may also question the legitimacy of the "civic project" unless it is subjected to sustained public debate and eventually accepted by the chosen representatives of the majority of society.

Grass Roots Constitutionalism in a Post-Communist Society

Are there any chances for a constitution in Poland? Has the "round table" paradigm of constitution-making lost any importance at all, any normative potential? In light of my argument, to tackle those questions one has to consider social processes accompanying constitution-making, the emerging principles of social and political organization, and therefore ponder the question of a "grass roots constitutionalism". It is not my intention to analyse thoroughly such great problems in a relatively short chapter. Therefore, I will reconsider the constitution formation process taking place in Poland in light of theories concerning some specific problems of societies after communism, and theories stressing the general problems of the overlap of post-communism and late modernization, in order to form some further hypotheses and to put forth some further questions.

By "grass roots constitutionalism" I understand a process of slow formation of constitutional principles "from below", in the every-day experience of citizens participating in local governments, non-governmental organizations, associations, and ethics commissions whose members participate in the decision-making processes or in conflict resolution, and construct their by-laws.   An empirical example of such a constitution formation process could be given by the tripartite commission functioning in Poland which deals with industrial conflicts and is composed of representatives of the government, of all labour unions, and of representatives of employers' organizations.

This question, then, concerns some forms of organic development "from below", formation of a "social constitution" by a society in its every-day practice (Kurczewski, 1990). This question also relates to the eventual legal form of such a constitution, as well as its validity and binding force. However, this is primarily important, if one considers the specific problems with constitution-making in a post-communist society. Considering the legacy of the communist system, one should then stress the political experience of a society that constituted a source of deterioration of a constitutional culture and the primary constitutional principles and concepts. Firstly, one has to stress the specific constitutional legacy of a society for which the formal, written constitution meant very little, since its very prescriptions were not binding at all, especially those which regulated liberal rights and liberties, and declared democracy. Hence, there is a lack of social trust in a formal declaration of democracy which, in light of experience, has no binding force at all. Secondly, one has to point to the destruction of the public sphere, destruction of public discourse that was of no interest to a society which functioned as an agglomerate of subjects deprived of private property, not making a profit, not paying taxes, and totally taken care of by the state. This gave rise to the already mentioned infantilization of the society, which had no actual, economically bounded and hence accountable interest in controlling the authorities and binding them by law. Indeed, according to present day sociological research, the rights most attractive to post-communist societies are still the social, economic rights (Kurczewski, 1992; Skąpska, 1996). Consequently, one has to point to the obvious deterioration of the concept of citizenship, civic virtues, and civic responsibilities. Considering such empirical arguments, one may then postulate the development of "grass roots constitutionalism" because one assumes it would foster the recovery of the meaning of the binding force of law, of the democratic principle, citizenship, public sphere, and so on.

Such empirically based observations and postulates are supplemented by sociological theories of modernization and democratization, as well as political theories of changing democracies in the modern world. Generally, those theories corroborate the proposition of organic development of a "grass roots" constitutionalism. Sociology and theory of law also complement such a standpoint and add here their own comment on the legal form of such a reverse development of constitutionalism. However, such a reasoning is not without loopholes, especially when applied to a society undergoing transformation after the collapse of a totalitarian system - a society which, at the same time, finds itself in a novel and uncertain environment, and is undergoing processes of liberalization which means firstly the awakening consciousness of specific interests, and efforts directed at their protection.

In the remainder of this chapter I will, then, explore the pros and cons of the hypothesis on the organic development of constitutionalism "from below", as a form of social contract constantly negotiated on the different levels of social organization.

As Beck emphazises, in western and in eastern Europe:

> The socially most astonishing and surprising (...) phenomenon of the 1980s was the unexpected renaissance of a political subjectivity, outside and inside the institutions (...) the themes of the future, which are now on everyone's lips, have not originated from the farsightedness of the rulers or from the struggle in parliament - and certainly not from the cathedrals of power in business, science and the state. They have been put on the social agenda against the concentrated resistance of this institutional ignorance by entangled, moralizing groups and splinter groups fighting each other over the proper way, split and plagued by doubts. (Beck, 1994: 21)

Political scientists point to the emergence of a new constitutional subject: the informed and responsible citizen's initiative in the form of groupings and associations that make a civil society. As the authors of such a proposition stress, parliament and political parties are no longer viewed as the only, or as adequate, organized expressions of the will of the people. This new tendency is already called "post-liberal" constitutionalism (Bellamy, Buffacchi and Castiglione, 1995: XI). Those authors, together with representatives of public law, proclaim the approaching end of classical liberal constitutionalism in view of the processes of European unification, and the weakening of the principles of "people's sovereignty" and majoritarian democracy, as well as the weakening of the sovereignty of the state. They postulate a multi-leveled, multi-layered legal order (MacCormick, 1996).

Finally, with regard to the sociology and theory of law, it is maintained that a broad and grass roots politicization implies a decrease of the central rule approach. Instead, cross-boundary, negotiated, "inter-systemic" mediating institutions are postulated, making possible ambivalences and transcending borders. The stress is put on the consensus building co-operation among industry, politics, science and the populace, together with informalization of jurisdiction (Beck, 1994). In this context, the model of a "round-table" is once more invoked, this time however not in the form of a contract between elites, but as a model of negotiation involving the directly interested parties, motivated by their local concerns, a model of negotiation between state agencies and interested citizens, and also a model of decision-making processes in local governments.

The normative concept of grass roots constitutionalism seems to be very attractive, especially in light of the deadlock in which the constitution formation process has found itself in Poland. It also has a special cultural appeal, considering the experiences and traditions of a society which has lived out its modern history mostly under a hostile state, and which has great experience in self-organization from below, self-defence and self-help, in that way protecting and cultivating its own identity.

All of those arguments, however attractive, leave some unanswered questions. One must then analyse the possibility of "grass roots constitutionalism" in a society which lacks a liberal tradition, in which protection of individual rights does not belong to the cultural heritage. There is no guarantee that those rights will not be abused, and that the collective goods of some groupings or associations, local communities, or labour unions, will not be put above individual rights. One has also to consider the processes of social liberalization, understood here in a different way than in the mainstream sociological literature, ie, as the growing consciousness of particular interests accompanied by efforts to protect them on the part of differentiated social groups, by the efforts to gain power, to have an impact on the decision-making processes in order to protect those interests. Such a meaning of liberalization is also very important in the context of a society which has lived for half a century in a state of imposed unity in which any social conflicts were suppressed, as impossible in a socialist society. Again, there appears a question, whether grass roots constitutionalism would protect those who are too weak, who have not enough power, and whose interests may consequently be abused in "multi-levelled" negotiations.

These are only a few questions and doubts concerning grass roots constitutionalism as still another form of a "round table" model of constitution formation, more attractive than the model of a "deal" but still leaving unanswered questions. This chapter has, then, no "happy-end". It points to a probably long process of constitution-formation, and establishment of the rule of law, or *Rechtsstaat* principles in Poland, embedded in the form of overlapping consensus, changing and flexible, and expressing the democratic will of the society "from below". Still, the liberal living constitution, embedded in developed democratic values, belongs to the sphere of far-reaching plans, not to political reality. One can only hope that constitution-making "from above" would meet the "grass roots" social processes of civic maturation, and that those processes will be reviewed as to their conformity with the protected individual rights of citizens.

Notes

1 That contract could also be called a social constitution: a document reflecting the dominant principles of social self-organization (in the form of freedom of labour unions), power relations (at that time acceptance of the dominant role of the Communist Party), and, most important, concepts of rights and liberties, accepted in the talks between the Communist Party, workers and their intellectual advisers in Gdańsk in 1981. The appraisal of the Gdańsk Agreement as a social constitution, to some extent still valid, was expressed by Wiesław Staśkiewicz after my presentation of an earlier version of this paper at the University of Warsaw, during the meeting of the Sociology of Law Section of the Polish Sociological Association, in November 1996.

2 This opinion is even more strongly expressed by the Hungarian lawyer, Janos Kis, who, on the basis of Kelsen's concept of transitional rules, insists upon the stability and continuity of the legal order in Hungary (Kis, 1995).

3 A highly instructive book on the talks of 1988 and 1989 (the first talk took place on November 28, 1988), in Poland known as the "Magdalenka talks", between representatives of the reform oriented communists under General Kiszczak, the then Minister of the Interior and one of the main figures responsible for the introduction of martial law in Poland, and representatives of the then still delegalized "Solidarność" Union, under Lech Wałęsa, presents the internal history of the Round Table Agreement, concluded in Poland in 1989. The ostensible rationale of the "Magdalenka talks" was to prepare the proceedings of the official Round Table, its procedures, timetable and contents. Yet it is clear that there were other aims. The book presents shorthand records of all talks conducted between November 1988 and February 1989. The author of that book, a collaborator of General Kiszczak, was secretary of the "Magdalenka talks". A reader of that book is astonished by the efficiency with which the communists obtained their aims, reaching far beyond the elections of 1989. Those aims were presented during the first meeting on 28 November 1988. They were

only partially free and democratic Parliamentary elections in 1989 in which candidates processed by communists would have a guaranteed sixty five per cent of the seats in the lower house of Parliament, the Sejm, creation of the President office whose first occupant would be General Jaruzelski, creation of the second house of Parliament, the Senate, and guarantee of the existing "constitutional order" (Dubiński, 1992: 11). During all those talks, which were conducted either in the village of Magdalenka near Warsaw, or in the building of the Ministry of the Interior, and in which only very few of the most prominent representatives of the reform oriented communists and members of the "Solidarność" Union took part, references to the "constitutional order" on the part of communists, and promises to observe the "constitutional order", ie, the order determined by the Stalinist Constitution of 1952, on the part of the members of "Solidarność", are very often repeated (Dubiński, 1990). As has been observed, as a result of the initial bargain, General Jaruzelski was to become a senior statesman and a guarantor of the concluded compromise *vis-a-vis* the Soviet Union (Rapaczyński, 1992: 31).

4   For a more thorough analysis of the constitution formation processes in the Polish Parliament see Rapaczyński (1992), Brzezinski (1993), Osiatyński (1994).

5   In the September 23, 1993 elections, the Union of the Democratic Left - composed predominantly of the postcommunist groups - above all the aforementioned Social Democratic Party of the Polish Republic and the labour unions closely linked to it received 20.5 per cent of the vote in the election, in which 56 per cent of eligible Poles participated. Because of the weighted electoral system, however, the Union of the Democratic Left obtained 37.2 per cent of the seats in the Sejm. The Polish Peasant Movement, which basically also represented a transformed former satellite of the communists, similarly won 15.4 per cent of the vote and received 28.7 per cent of the seats in the Sejm. The smaller centrist and right-of-center parties had been virtually eliminated from the Parliament, even though, as it had been observed, they received close to one-third of the total vote (Osiatyński, 1994: 31). The Solidarity Union itself fell 0.1% short of the threshold. The remaining 30% was subsequently redistributed among the represented parties. After that election, both victorious parties formed a coalition that came close to controlling two-thirds of Parliament, and, therefore, to controlling the law-making processes, and forming a new constitution.

Bibliography

Ackerman, B. (Polish edn.) (1996), *Przyszłość rewolucji liberalnej*, Oficyna Naukowa, Warszawa.
Bauman, Z. (1991), *Modernity and Ambivalence*, Polity Press, Cambridge.

Beck, U. (1994), "The Reinvention of Politics: Towards a Theory of Reflexive Modernization", in Beck, Giddens and Lash, *Reflexive Modernization, infra,* 3-55.

Beck, U., Giddens, A. and Lash, C. (1994), *Reflexive Modernization. Politics, Tradition and Aesthetics in the Modern Social Order,* Polity Press, Cambridge.

Bellamy, R., Buffacchi, V.and Castiglione, D. (1996), "Introduction: The Making of Democratic Europe", in the same authors (eds), *Democracy and Constitutional Culture in the Union of Europe,* Lothian Foundation Press, London.

Buchanan, J.M. and Tullock, G. (1962), *The Calculus of Consent. Logical Foundations of Constitutional Democracy,* The University of Michigan Press.

Brzezinski, M.F. (Winter, 1993), "Constitutionalism Within Limits", *East European Constitutional Review,* 38-45.

Calda, M. and Gillis, M. (1995), "Czech Republic", *East European Consitutional Review,* Spring, 68-70.

Ciemniewski, J. (1996), "Sejm i Senat w projekcie konstytucji RP", in J. Krukoski (ed.), *Ocena projektu Konstytucji RP,* Lublin, Towarzystwo Naukowe Katolickiego Uniwersytetu Lubelskiego, 37-48.

Dahrendorf, R. (1992), *Reflections on the Revolution in Europe,* Random House, New York.

Dubinski, K. (1990), *Magdalenka. Transakcja epoki,* (Magdalenka. Epochal transaction), Sylwa, Warszawa.

Elster, J. (1993), "Constitutional Bootstrapping in Philadelphia and Paris", *Cardozo Law Review,* 14.

Frankford, D.M. (1994), "The Critical Potential of the Common Law Tradition", *Columbia Law Review,* 94: 1076, 1076-1103.

Gellner, E. (1995), "Anything goes. The carnival of cheap relativism which threatens to swamp the coming *fin de millenaire*", *The Times Literary Supplement,* June 16.

Giddens, A. (1994), *Beyond Left and Right: The Future of Radical Politics,* Polity Press, Cambridge.

Haberle, P. (1992), "Constitutional Developments in Eastern Europen from the Point of View of Jurisprudence and Constitutional Theory", *Law and State,* 46, Tubingen.

Habermas, J. (1982), *Theorie des kommunikativen Handelns,* Suhrkamp, Frankfurt am Main.

———. (1993), *Faktizitat und Geltung,* Suhrkamp, Frankfurt am Main.

Havel, V. (1985), *The Power of the Powerless: Citizens versus the State in Central-Eastern Europe,* Hutchinson, London.

Jackiewicz, Z. (1995), "Wpływ prawodawcy na wynik wyborów", (Impact of law-maker on the results of elections), *Państwo i Prawo,* No 3, 44-51.

Kidaly, B.K. (1995), "Dictatorship, Lawful Revolution, and the Socialist Return to Power", in *Lawful Revolutions in Hungary 1989-94,* (ed.) Bela K. Kidaly, (ass. ed.), Andras Bozoki, Atlantic Research and Publications Inc, Boulder, Colorado.

Kis, J. (1995), "Between Reform and Revolution: Three Hypotheses About the Nature of the Regime Change" in *Lawful Revolution in Hungary 1989-94.*

Kurczewski, J. (1992), "Na przełomie ustrojów. Prawa i obowiązki obywateli" (Breakthrough in the Social Order: Polish Public Opinion on Civic Rights and Duties) in A. Kojder and J. Kwaśniewski (eds) *Między autonomią a kontrolą*; (Between Autonomy and Social Control) Warszawa, 215-232.

_____ (1990), "Konstytucja żywa", (Living constitution) *Res Publica*, 12, 2.

MacCormick, N. (1996), "Liberalism, Nationalism and the Post-Sovereign State", in Richard Bellamy and Dario Castiglione, (eds), *Constitutionalism in Transformation. European and Theoretical Perspectives, Political Studies*, Vol. XLIV, Special Issue.

Nodia, G. (1996), "How Different Are Postcommunist Trasitions?", *Journal of Democracy*, 15-29.

Osiatyński, W. (1994), "Poland's Constitutional Ordeal", *Eastern European Constitutional Review*, 29-38.

Preuss, U.K. (1993), "Constitutional Powermaking for the New Polity: Some Deliberations on the Relations Between Constituent Power and the Constitution", *Cardozo Law Review*.

Putnam, R.D. (1993), *Making Democracy Work: Civic Traditions in Modern Italy*, Princeton University Press.

Rapaczyński, A. (1992), "Constitutional Politics in Poland: A Report on the Constitutional Committee of the Polish Parliament", in A.E. Dick Howard (ed.), *Constitution Making in Eastern Europe*, The Woodrow Wilson Center Press, Washington.

Rawls, J. (1987), "The Idea of an Overlapping Consensus", *Oxford Journal of Legal Studies*, 7(1), 1-25.

Sajó, A. (1995), "Reading the Invisible Constitution: Judicial Review in Hungary", *Oxford Journal of Legal Studies*, 15, 253-67.

_____(1996), "How the Rule of Law Killed the Hungarian Welfare Reform", *East European Constitutional Review*, 5(1), 31-41.

Sciulli, D. (1992), "Theory of Societal Constitutionalism: Foundations of a Non-Marxist Critical Theory", quoted after David M. Frankford, "The Critical Potential of the Common Law Tradition", (1994) *Columbia Law Review*, 94, 1076-1123.

Shils, E. (1982), *The Constitution of Society*, The University of Chicago Press, Chicago and London.

Skąpska, G. (1991a), *Prawo i dynamika społecznych przemian*, (Law and the Dynamics of Social Change), Jagiellonian University Press, Kraków.

_____. (1991b), "Rule of Law from the East Central European Perspective", in *Law and Social Inquiry*, 4.

_____. (1994), "The Legacy of Anti-Legalism", in M. Krygier (ed.) *Marxism and Communism. Posthumous Reflections on Politics, Society and Law*, Rodopi, Amsterdam and Atlanta.

_____. (1996), "From Rights to Myths. Transformation in Post-Communist Europe", in A. Sajó (ed) *Western Rights? Post-Communist Application*, Kluwer, The Hague, London and Boston.

Sunley, J. (1966), "Post-communism: An Infantile Disorder", *The National Interest*, 44, 3-15.

Sunstein, Cass R. (1993), *Against Positive Rights, East European Constitutional Review*, 2(1), 35-37.

Sunstein, Cass R. (1993), *Against Positive Rights, East European Constitutional Review*, 2(1), 35-37.

Zięba, M. (1996), *OP, Po szkodzie? Przed szkodą? O Polsce, kapitalitalizmie i kontemplacji*, (After Damage? Before Damage? About Poland, Capitalism and Contemplation), Wydawnictwo Znak, Kraków.

Zoll, A. (1996), "Czy Polsce potrzebna jest konstytucja?" (Does Poland need a constitution?), *Tygodnik Powszechny*, 48, 1 December.

8 Rights and Freedoms under the new Polish Constitution[1]

WOJCIECH SADURSKI

Introduction

The long saga of producing the first Polish post-communist constitution is over. The Constitution of April 1997 replaced the package consisting of the Constitution of 1952 (riddled with amendments) and the so-called Small Constitution of 1992. These two constitutional documents did not have a satisfactory bill of rights. To be sure, Chapter 8 (articles 67-93) of the 1952 Constitution contained a very "generous" catalogue of rights and freedoms, as well as a list of citizens' duties, but it was a typical example of a purely declaratory, and ultimately meaningless approach to constitutional rights, from which any effective restraints upon state powers were absent.[2] The interim Small Constitution deliberately left the issue of rights and freedoms outside its scope.[3]

Quite understandably, a large part of the political, legal and intellectual controversies surrounding constitution-making focussed on the constitutionalization of rights and freedoms. While issues concerning the powers of the President, the government and parliament affected vested interests of various political parties and political actors to a higher degree than the proposed catalogue of constitutional rights, the latter issue more clearly mirrored the philosophical and ideological disagreements in Polish society. There was controversy as to the scope of religious freedom and the relationship between the Roman Catholic Church and the State, the rights of minorities, the right to life (with a possible extension to a prohibition on abortion and/or the death penalty), and the place of socio-economic rights in the Constitution. These are just a few examples of the areas in which debates about a constitutional charter of rights illustrated the wide range of views among the principal political actors in Poland, and among the community at large.

These differences were reflected in the constitutional drafts which preceded the new Constitution. By mid-1993, the constitutional menu in Poland consisted of seven "official" drafts submitted to the Constitutional Committee.[4] The drafts constituted the basis of the Committee's work aimed at producing a uniform text. The draft submitted by President Lech Wałęsa in December 1992, which contained a Charter of Rights and Freedoms,[5] is of notable importance when discussing constitutional rights.[6] This Charter, drafted by the Helsinki Foundation for Human Rights in Warsaw, was an exemplary document: coherent, well thought out, clear, and strongly protective of individual rights.[7]

Unfortunately, this cannot be said about the treatment of rights and liberties in the Constitution of April 2, 1997. While it does contain a long and impressive list of rights and freedoms, the philosophical conception of rights which emerges from the final product leaves much to be desired. Its defects may be largely due to the pedigree of the Constitution; the ostensible purpose of the exercise in which the Constitutional Committee engaged over the past three years before the final adoption of the constitution was to come up with a synthesis of previously submitted constitutional drafts and proposals. While the current Constitution is a new text, it carries weaknesses and liabilities indicative of a document produced as a compromise between divergent, and often mutually opposed, constitutional conceptions.

The eclectic nature of the Constitution reveals the impact, in various proportions, of three main conceptions which have competed in the process of drafting the Constitution. This divergence results from the uneven representation of the three conceptions in the Constitutional Committee. The three conceptions cannot be precisely characterized along party lines because they represent three distinct intellectual traditions rather than three political groupings (see Winczorek, 1996: 78-79). The socialist approach focussed mainly on socio-economic rights, associating them to a large extent with the social and economic tasks of the government. The Christian and nationalistic view focussed on the protection of traditional values such as family and religion, with a generally sympathetic approach to welfare and the protection of labour. The liberal strand emphasized the role of the Constitution as a restraint on legislative and executive action, focussing on civil and political rights and freedoms, while relegating prescriptions for social and economic policy to the political domain, rather than to the constitutional arena.

This chapter subjects the treatment of rights in the 1997 Constitution to a critical scrutiny from a liberal perspective. This is *not* the prevailing perspective among legal scholars in Poland, and even less so in Polish society as a whole. Concluding from a number of recent surveys, a Polish sociologist of law notes that Poles "affirm first of all a constitution as a social charter, and attach much less importance to traditional liberal political liberties and civil rights ..." (Staśkiewicz, 1996: 10). But it should be emphasized that the standpoint adopted in this article is not reducible to a simple assertion of the paramount importance of civil and political liberties, compared to socio-economic rights. This standard controversy does not fully reflect the differences between liberal and non-liberal approaches. I will assume that the purpose of constitutional rights (as compared to rights and entitlements specified by statutes and other sources of law) is intrinsically tied to the main function of a constitution in general, which is to define and restrict, in a fashion that cannot be easily changed, the scope and rationales for legislative and executive actions. Constitutional rights impose limits upon majoritarian decisions in the political process. A liberal approach views the constitutionalization of rights as a restraining device, increasing the costs of future political (including legislative) action disfavoured by the constitution-makers.

Statutory Restrictions of Constitutional Rights

The main precept of the general liberal understanding of rights is that a constitution serves as a safeguard of the broadest scope of individual liberties possible. This implies that a constitution should avoid conferring broad discretion upon the legislature in defining, elucidating, restricting and qualifying constitutional rights.[8]   If the constitutional authorization of legislative action regarding constitutional rights is very extensive, then these constitutional rights no longer effectively limit legislative action. Unfortunately, this is the model of constitutional rights that can be found in the 1997 Constitution of Poland.

Article 31(3) lists the following grounds for permissible statutory restrictions of rights: state security or public order, protection of the natural environment, health or public morals, and "the freedoms and rights of other persons," with the additional proviso that rights can be restricted on any of these grounds "when necessary in a democratic state" and that the restrictions must not "violate the essence of freedom and rights".[9] This is a rather extensive list of grounds for permissible restrictions. In addition, the Constitution explicitly allows certain rights to be restricted, eg, the right to travel inside and outside the country,[10] freedom of peaceful assembly,[11] and the right to strike.[12]   It is uncertain whether rights can be statutorily restricted on the grounds listed in the article 31(3) *only* when the Constitution expressly delegates this authority to the legislature in an article concerning a specific right, or whether the general grounds for permissible restrictions apply to all the rights (regardless of an explicit constitutional mandate for a statutory restriction of a particular right).

If the latter were the case, it is obvious that the value of entrenching constitutional rights becomes largely illusory, creating merely a set of general guidelines, subject to a legislative elaboration based on the legislature's views concerning the requirements of national security, public order, protection of the natural environment, health and public morals, as well as its views about the necessities of a democratic state and the substance of particular rights. Unfortunately, it seems that this interpretation is most likely to prevail, regardless of the specific intentions of the drafters. This is for two reasons. First, article 31(3) (a catalogue of the grounds for statutory restrictions of rights) is included in a subchapter called "General Principles", which suggests that its provisions apply to all the rights subsequently listed in Chapter 2 of the Constitution (that is, the chapter on "The Freedoms, Rights and Obligations" of citizens). Second, the framers could have used the model which was available to them in the form of Wałęsa's Charter of Rights, which explicitly stated: "The rights and liberties guaranteed by this Charter may be restricted only by statute and only when such a restriction is envisaged by this Charter".[13]   The fact that the authors of the new Constitution have not incorporated this wording may suggest that they had a different construction in mind. Namely, the authorization for the legislature to restrict *all* rights. If this is the case, then the value of constitutional rights is questionable.

There are at least two alternative models that were available to the drafters to avoid the erosion of rights. One was to confine statutory limitations explicitly to those rights which are described in the Constitution in a way which explicitly authorizes the legislature to restrict them (as in the Wałęsa draft). Another, perhaps better, solution would have been to abstain from including a general list of rights-restrictions and then list possible grounds for restrictions only in those particular articles proclaiming specific rights. The latter model has the advantage of flexibility; the grounds of possible statutory restrictions can be tailored to the substance of a particular right. This model has, for example, been adopted in the German Basic Law, where the list of permissible grounds for statutory restrictions varies from right to right.[14]   However, the model chosen by the Polish constitutional drafters displays the worst of both constitutional worlds by combining inflexibility with restrictiveness.

This becomes even more apparent when one considers "public morals" as a possible ground for statutory limitations of rights and freedoms.[15]   A blanket authorization limiting rights on the basis of public morals evokes the familiar dangers of majoritarian tyranny, by rendering individual freedom contingent upon the approval of others. In certain human rights documents, where the grounds for restrictions of rights vary depending on the particular right in question, the "public morals" exception has been used sparingly as a basis for statutory limitations. For example, in the European Convention on Human Rights "protection of morals" is cited *inter alia* in article 10, dealing with the right of expression, but not in many other rights provisions. In the German Basic Law, "morality" is cited in article 2, dealing with the right to free development of one's personality, but not, for example, in the context of freedom of expression (art.5), freedom of assembly (art.8), or privacy (art.10).

Rights and Policy Guidelines

One important inference from the conception of constitutional rights as effective restraints on the exercise of legislative power is that the rights should have a reasonably determinate content. This suggests that "rights" (in this sense) should be kept clearly separate from affirmative guidelines about the legitimate tasks of the legislative and executive authorities. Whether such policy guidelines properly belong in a constitution is another matter, which is beyond the scope of this chapter (though an argument can be made that policy guidelines are a matter for the ordinary legislative and political process, to be guided by a majority rule, within the limits imposed by the constitution).[16]   However, what *is* relevant to our discussion is the argument that such guidelines should be clearly separated from a list of rights because they play a different role in the constitutional text.

It is unfortunate that the 1997 Constitution blends constitutional rights(socio-economic and civil) with policy guidelines that have no determinate content to restrain the exercise of power. For example, in the sub-chapter on "Economic, Social, and Cultural Freedoms and Rights" the Constitution proclaims, *inter alia*, that "[p]ublic authorities shall pursue policies aiming at full, productive employment ...", (art.65 (5)) that "[p]ublic authorities shall support the development of physical culture ...", (art. 68 (5)), that authorities "shall pursue policies ensuring the ecological security of current and future generations" (art. 74 (1)).[17] To be sure, the sub-chapter devoted to the methods of protection of rights excludes these "rights" from a general system of protection and enforcement, and provides that they "may be asserted subject to limitations ons specified by statute" (art. 81). However, to include these policy goals alongside other rights, and to characterize them as "rights," as article 81 does explicitly, is to conflate rights in a strong constitutional sense with the declarations of goals which impose no determinate limit upon state power, and which cannot serve as tests of the constitutionality of state actions.

A leading Polish proponent of the view that the constitutional announcement of tasks for the state in the area of housing, work, etc does not contradict the essence of rights is Professor Tadeusz Zieliński, who distinguishes between "claim rights" and "programmatic rights," the latter "defin[ing] the tasks of public authorities in the area of welfare rights of citizens". In addition, "[a] right to work means only that a citizen has the right to assistance in finding a job by the public authorities. A right to lodging means only that a citizen is provided the opportunity to make use of policies leading to satisfying citizens' needs for lodging"[18] (Zieliński, 1996). But if *all* there is to a right is an opportunity to benefit from whatever the state policy is in operation, then it is redundant to call it a "right". It is just another way of enjoining the government to have *a* policy in this field.

In Polish constitutional discussions, the question of the socio-economic responsibilities of the state, masquerading as rights, was brought into the controversy regarding the self-executing powers of the Constitution. In another article Zieliński asserted that it was a mistake to pronounce a general principle of "direct applicability" with respect to the constitutional provisions,[19] because social welfare rights cannot be directly enforced without the intermediation of further statutory rules[20] (Zieliński, 1996). In response, Professor Ewa Łętowska suggests that the examples of constitutional provisions provided by Zieliński in actuality do not disprove the direct applicability of the Constitution[21] (Łętowska, 1996). Even if these provisions cannot, without legislative implementation, constitute the bases for judicial (or other) decisions, courts "apply" them nevertheless. This occurs because courts are compelled to use the Constitution as a source of "interpretive inspiration" in construing statutory laws. Even if a constitutional provision cannot serve as a basis for invalidating a statutory rule, it operates directly upon the judges by playing the role of "a constructive and axiological coherence-producing device of a legal system".[22] But such a defence of the idea of direct applicability of the provisions, which are too indeterminate to serve as a basis for invalidation of a statute, is possible only by broadening the definition of "direct applicability" to the point of rendering it virtually useless. If a Constitution "operates directly" merely by providing a "reading code" for interpreting statutes, then it is hard to see what constitutional provisions can ever be seen as *not* directly applicable, or not self-executing. With such a loose sense of operability, any constitutional pronouncement, however vague and indeterminate, may be seen to have some weight. But this "direct applicability", achieved through definitional fiat, is of dubious value when it comes to the most important function of constitutional rights, restraining the exercise of power.

The danger of a conflation of socio-economic rights with state policies is clear; the effect is the watering down of the effectiveness of *other* rights, including those that have a determinate meaning as limits on state action.[23] In this regard, I do not agree with Professor Herman Schwartz who emphatically rejects this "devaluation of rights" argument: "This notion that if some rights turn out not to be effective, others will be in some way degraded in value, is utterly complete nonsense"[24] (Schwartz, 1995). Schwartz's view may be justified in systems where the values of constitutionalism, rule of law, and the protection of rights are securely established, and where disagreements about rights pertain to the margins, rather than to their core meanings. However, in a system where a nihilist tradition of treating a constitution as a purely decorative instrument is strongly embedded, and where the fundamental notions of constitutionalism and rule of law have a weak place in the collective consciousness, everything that undermines a strict construction of constitutional limits upon discretionary governmental action is to be regarded with concern.

The constitutional drafters had before them a remarkable example of a document drawing a precise and clear distinction between the policy guidelines and constitutional rights. The Wałęsa draft Charter of Rights and Freedoms[25] clearly distinguished "Social and Economic Rights and Freedoms" (such as the right to education,[26] freedom of employment,[27] a right to safe working conditions,[28] a right to health care[29] and a right to social security[30]) from "Economic, Social and Cultural Tasks of Public Authorities". This was a logical and clear construction, amplified by an explicit statement that the latter "tasks" are fulfilled by the public authorities "depending upon their economic resources". In this way, the idea that socio-economic tasks apply to governmental actions and aspirations, rather than to determinate results, was constitutionally endorsed, but no pretence was made that these tasks and aspirations described a range of constitutional "rights".

One reason why the drafters of the new Constitution may have decided not to imitate this model is simply that they tried to distinguish themselves, for reasons of political convenience, from the authors of the Wałęsa draft. However, there may be a deeper reason, related to the implicitly adopted philosophy of rights which rejects constitutional rights as prior, relatively inflexible, and determinate restraints upon the exercise of state power.

Rights and Duties

The lack of appreciation for such a conception of constitutional rights is also seen in the inclusion of a sub-chapter on citizens' obligations.[31] In contrast to rights (properly understood), "duties" do not imply any restrictions upon state actions, except in a trivial sense when a state's failure to enforce the discharge of citizens' duties is objectionable. The list of duties in the Constitutional text plays no clear function.[32] Duties such as payment of taxes,[33] military service,[34] and protection of the environment,[35] can be imposed by statutes, as long as they do not contravene any specific constitutional rights. This is clearly indicated by the circularity of article 84: "Everyone shall comply with his responsibilities and public duties, including the payment of taxes, as specified by statute." A constitutional duty to comply with statutory duties seems to be a redundant notion.

This redundancy has its costs. For one thing, it dilutes the libertarian flavour of and introduces a statist rhetoric into the Constitution. The message is that, while the state has some duties toward its citizens, the citizens have duties not just to each other but also to the state. This message emerges from article 82: "Loyalty to the Republic of Poland, as well as concern for the common good, shall be the duty of every Polish citizen." The duty thus described is largely indeterminate, but it adds a statist flavour to the text. Secondly, the inclusion of duties alongside rights may be seen as implying that the enjoyment of one's rights is conditional upon the performance of one's duties. Although this is not stated explicitly, it may be one way of interpreting the reason behind the inclusion of duties in the Constitution. But such an implication is of course anathema to any liberal theory of citizens' rights where no one surrenders their rights by reason of the failure to discharge their duties.[36] The opposite view may be seen as a residue of the old, Communist approach to constitutional law, which emphasized the so-called interdependence of "rights" and "duties". But, strictly understood, this connection of rights and duties implies only that one cannot effectively enjoy one's rights if others do not perform *their* correlative duties. This does not amount to a normative proposition to the effect that one must be denied the enjoyment of one's rights as a result of non performance of one's duties (including the duties to respect other people's rights).

This thoughtless maxim of "no rights without obligations" is implied also by a general provision of the chapter on freedoms, rights and obligations: "Everyone shall respect the freedoms and rights of others."[37] The status of this general clause is unclear but, in any event, the article is redundant at best, and harmful at worst. If the only function of the clause is to announce a general moral maxim that citizens should be mindful of other people's rights and freedoms, then the article is redundant; no legal consequences may follow from it, and the moralistic nature of the precept renders it inconsistent with the functions of a constitution. But if the article is or can be interpreted as implying some *legal* consequences, then the consequence may be the reduction of one's rights resulting from non performance of one's duties. As a general proposition, this is a very dangerous formula, especially since the clause is included in the article that further lists the grounds of possible statutory restrictions of rights.[38] The very possibility of such an interpretation of the Constitution, which would render the general enjoyment of rights contingent upon the performance of one's duties, is antithetical to the notion of legally protected liberty.

"Horizontal" Rights

Liberal constitutionalism implies that, as a rule, individual rights are correlated to the duties of *the public authorities* to act in a way required by a right, or to abstain from acting in a way that would be inconsistent with the right. An imposition, by a constitution, of rights-related duties *upon private individuals* is an exception, at best. Of course, a well-ordered system imposes on individuals a number of duties which make the enjoyment of their fellow citizens' rights meaningful. But no rationale can be found for the "horizontal" operation of rights established by a constitution, which serves mainly to limit the range and justifications for state actions.[39] Once a constitution goes beyond the regulation of public authorities, and regulates relations between private citizens and the authorities, the danger is that the constitution will be used as a device for controlling and manipulating civil society.

The 1997 Constitution neither excludes nor mandates such a horizontal dimension of constitutional rights. This is in direct contrast with the Wałęsa draft which explicitly provided that the rights included in the Charter concerned only the relations between public authorities and citizens.[40] The absence of such a clause may provide future interpreters with an opportunity to argue for an extension of constitutional rights upon relations between citizens.

This may or may not be innocuous. Consider the example of the anti-discrimination provision: "No one shall be discriminated against in political, social or economic life for any reason whatsoever."[41]   If the rights also apply in a horizontal fashion, how far can the government go in enforcing equal treatment of one individual by another? Note that article 30 bans discrimination "in political, *social* or economic life" (emphasis added), and in contrast to article 32(1) ("All persons shall be equal before the law. All persons shall have the right to equal treatment by public authorities...") it fails to identify public authorities as the bearers of the duties correlated with the right to non-discrimination. A ban on private discrimination, which imposes specific duties on citizens, would be better handled by routine legislative action rather than a constitutional mandate.

Freedom of the Press

In the earlier version of the constitutional draft, freedom of speech and freedom of the press were included in the same article in the chapter on rights, freedoms and duties. This was quite logical: freedom of the press appears to be a close relative of the concept of freedom of speech, and some general principles protecting the former would seem to apply to the latter. Such an extrapolation is facilitated by the inclusion of both freedoms in the same article, as is the case with the United States Constitution,[42] and also a number of other constitutional documents.[43]

For reasons which are not particularly clear, the location of the freedom of the press within the constitutional text was changed in the late stages of constitutional drafting. Freedom of the press now appears not in the chapter on rights and freedoms, alongside freedom of speech, but rather in the first chapter of the Constitution. Article 14 states: "The Republic of Poland shall ensure freedom of the press and other means of social communication."

Some may perhaps argue that such a transfer actually enhances the significance of the principle of freedom of the media which is now treated as one of the main principles of the constitutional order. However, such optimism would not be justified. By moving freedom of the press outside the scope of the catalogue of rights and freedoms, the drafters deprived this freedom of protections generally extended to all rights and freedoms. Consequently, the rules of constitutional interpretation specifically tailored to rights provisions became unavailable in the case of freedom of the press. Further, specific remedies for rights violations do not apply to violations of freedom of the press.

This conclusion assumes that freedom of the press, construed as a right rather than as a general principle, can do the work which cannot be done by a right to freedom of speech. This would not be the case if freedom of the press were seen merely as part of a broader notion of freedom of speech. However, it can be argued that freedom of the press is not merely a narrower branch of freedom of speech (in which case the adding of "freedom of the press" to "freedom of speech" would be redundant) but, rather, that freedom of the press is a right distinct from that of freedom of speech, and one which conveys a message that is absent from general notions of "freedom of speech" or "freedom of expression".[44]

As one example of such an additional implication of freedom of the press, which is not necessarily included in a more general freedom of speech, one can mention the controversial issue of the journalists' duty regarding disclosure of confidential sources of information. One would have to stretch the notion of "freedom of speech" to fantastic lengths to argue that freedom of speech protects the right of journalists to refuse such a disclosure. However, such a refusal seems to be implied by freedom of the press: if the press is to be free, it must have broad access to informants who can trust that the journalists will not be legally bound to disclose their identities.[45]

This is not to say that including freedom of the press in the constitutional chapter on rights necessarily dictates the conclusion that a legal duty of journalists to disclose their sources is always unconstitutional. After all, the First Amendment to the United States Constitution has not been interpreted in this way by the Supreme Court.[46] What is evident, however, is that it is much more difficult to argue about the constitutional status of such a duty if freedom of the press is not characterized as a constitutional right. Regardless of the substantive conclusions, the argument about the unconstitutionality of a duty to disclose is facilitated if such a duty is seen as a case of rights violation (with all the remedies available to the victims) rather than violation of a general constitutional principle.

This specific example is not an academic issue in Poland. The question of whether journalists should be compelled by prosecutors and courts to disclose the identity of their informers is a hotly discussed issue, and a number of journalists have already been faced with the dramatic dilemma of choosing between the legal duty of disclosure and the principles of journalistic ethics, which demand the observation of confidentiality.[47] Whether the law should recognize a strong privilege of journalistic confidentiality is a matter which can be better handled by characterizing freedom of the press as a right, rather than as a general principle.

Conclusions

There is much that can be applauded about the list of rights in the 1997 Polish Constitution: it is extensive, the wording of specific rights is expansive rather than restrictive, and the mechanisms for the protection of rights and freedoms are robust and realistic. These mechanisms include a general recourse to courts with claims alleging rights violations,[48] a universal right of a complaint to the Constitutional Tribunal about the unconstitutionality of a law (subject to an eminently reasonable rule of standing: the challenged law must be the basis of a rights violation alleged by the complainant),[49] and assistance in the protection of one's rights by the Commissioner for Citizens' Rights (the Ombudsman).[50]

One may hope that, since the new Constitution proclaims the principle of "impartiality" in matters of religious conviction,[51] the laws similar to the broadcasting law of December 1992, which prohibited all radio and TV stations from offending "Christian values",[52] will not pass constitutional muster. While "impartiality" seems to fall short of the requirement of "neutrality" (by having a more "activist" ring to it), much depends on constitutional interpretation and, in this regard, there is no doubt that the Constitution provides an opportunity for a liberty-enhancing, anti-restrictive interpretation.

The same can be said about a number of other robustly formulated rights which potentially could be interpreted by the Constitutional Tribunal in ways supportive of individual liberties: for example a long and good list of rights to a fair criminal trial and other rights related to the criminal process,[53] strong privacy rights,[54] a right of access to information,[55] an impressively worded right to freedom of expression,[56] an elaborate set of rights related to freedom of religion,[57] freedoms of assembly and association[58] and rights of national and ethnic minorities.

Nonetheless, the robustness of these particular rights and of the mechanisms for their protection is put in question by certain aspects of a non-liberal conception which emerge from a number of features of the constitutional text. These include the general clause authorizing the legislature to restrict constitutional rights even when the Constitution does not state this explicitly with respect to a particular right, a conflation of socio-economic rights with guidelines for governmental action in the socio-economic spheres, packaging the rights together with citizens' duties, implying that constitutional rights operate not only in the relations of citizens with public authorities but also among the citizens themselves, etc. The result is that much will depend on the goodwill of legislative majorities and on future interpretations of the Constitutional Tribunal.

Notes

1   This chapter appeared first as Sadurski (1997).
2   For good characterizations and critiques of this approach to constitutionalism see, for example Brzezinski,1991: 88-96; Brzezinski and Garlicki, 1995: 23-5; Klich, 1996; Ludwikowski, 1995: 87-90; Osiatyński,1994: 112-13; Sajó, 1996: 141-43; Sunstein, 1992: 18-19; Teitel, R. 1994: 168-69.
3   For Brzezinski and Garlicki, this absence of a charter of rights was one of the major shortcomings of the Small Constitution, (Brzezinski and Garlicki, 1995: 40).
4   See "Constitution Watch: Poland" Summer 1993.
5   The Polish text was published in *Rzeczpospolita* [*The Republic*] (May 19, 1994: 12-14. For an English translation, see Frankowski (1996)
6   See Brzezinski and Garlicki, 1995: 47-48; Frankowski; Osiatyński, W, Fall 1992; Rzepliński, Summer 1993.
7   Subsequently, Lech Wałęsa distanced himself from the draft (for reasons of political expediency), and in particular, from its Charter of Rights. However, for purposes of simplicity the draft will be referred to hereinafter as the "Wałęsa draft".
8   See Osiatyński, 1994: 153-56. See also Elster, 1993: 198 (noting that the protection of rights in some post-communist constitutions is undermined when the relevant constitutional clauses are circumscribed by, *inter alia*, references to further regulation by statute).
9   Polish Constitution art. 31(3).
10   *Id.* art. 52.
11   *Id.* art. 57.
12   *Id.* art. 59(3).

13 *Draft of the Charter of Rights and Freedoms,* , at art. 5(2).
14 *Cf. Basic Law of The Federal Republic of Germany,* art. 5(2) (freedom of expression can be subject to limitations by statutes "for the protection of youth" and for the protection of "personal honour") *with* article 10 (privacy of letters, posts and telecommunications may be restricted by statutes in order "to protect the free democratic order or the existence or security of the Federation") *and with* article 11 (freedom of movement may be restricted by statutes when necessary to protect the free democratic order, to combat the danger of epidemics, to deal with natural disasters or grave accidents, to protect young people or to prevent crime).
15 *Pol. Const.* art. 31(3).
16 This is because a decision about the constitutionalization of socio-economic tasks has major (and, many believe, unfortunate) significance for the division of powers, although not necessarily for the actual position of citizens with respect to social and economic matters. In other words, failure to *constitutionalize* socio-economic rights does not mean that the state renounces any responsibility for the socio-economic interests of its citizens. Important arguments have been made in constitutional debates in Poland that constitutionalization of socio-economic policy will imply an important transfer of budgetary decisions from the legislature to the judiciary, which will have to decide about budgetary spending in the process of enforcing citizens' rights. *See* Osiatyński 1996: 262-69; Rapaczynski, 1993: 93, 107-108. This, it was argued, would subvert the current pattern of separation of powers. See Ciemniewski, 1996: 41-42.
17 Other policy tasks determined by the Constitution include the establishment of occupational counseling and training (art. 65(5)), public works to combat unemployment (art. 65(5)); combating epidemic diseases and countering the effects of environmental degradation (art. 68(4)), creating and supporting of financial aid to students in order to provide equality of educational opportunities (art. 70(4)), special aid to families with many children (art. 71(1)); satisfaction of the housing needs of citizens (art. 75(1)); and consumer protection (art. 76).
18 Zieliński, 1996.
19 *Pol. Const.* art. 8(2).
20 Zieliński (1996).
21 Łętowska (1996).
22 *Id.*
23 See Elster, 1993, at 198.
24 Schwartz, 1995.
25 *Draft of the Charter of Rights and Freedoms,* at chapter 3.
26 *Id.* art. 29.
27 *Id.* art. 30.
28 *Id.* art. 31.
29 *Id.* art. 32.
30 Draft *of the Charter of Rights and Freedoms,* art. 33.
31 *Id.* Chapter 5.
32 *Id* art.48.

33.   This is not an unusal construction in contemporary constitutionalism. In the current Constitution of Spain (of 1978, amended 1992), "Guiding Principles of Economic and Social Policy" (chapter III of the Constitution) are distinguished from "Rights and Freedoms" (chapter II).

34   *Draft of the Charter of Rights and Freedoms*, at arts. 82-86.

35   See, Sunstein, Spring 1992: 19 (explaining why western constitutions fail to impose duties on citizens). But see Winczorek, P. 1995: 92-98 (suggesting that some constitutional duties may perform useful functions). For a useful discussion of citizens' duties in other post-communist constitutions, see Ludwikowski: Spring 1995, 159-60.

36   *Draft of the Charter of Rights and Freedoms, supra* note 4, at art. 84.

37   *Id.* art. 85.

38   *Id.* art. 86.

39   See Winczorek, 1995: 92-93.

40   *Pol. Const.* art. 31(2).

41   *Id.* art. 31(3).

42   For an opposite opinion, see Wiśniewski, 1996 (criticizing an earlier version of the constitutional draft for not making it clear that constitutional rights impose clear obligations on citizens as well, not only on public authorities).

43   *Draft of the Charter of Rights and Freedoms*,   Article 1 of the Wałęsa draft stated:

   "1.   This Chapter prescribes the relations between persons within the scope of operation of the law of the Republic of Poland, and public authorities understood as:

      (a)   the legislative, executive, and judicial authorities (state authorities);

      (b)   the local self-government; and

      (c)   organizations or persons performing public functions delegated to them by the authorities specified in points 1 and 2.

   2.   The rights and freedoms prescribed in this Chapter are directly binding on public authorities."

44   *Pol. Const.* art. 32(2).

45   US. Const. amend. I: "Congress shall make no law ... abridging the freedom of speech, or of the press ...."

46   See, e.g., *Canadian Charter of Rights and Freedoms* (1992), art. 2; *Const. of Greece*, art. 14; *Const. of Hungary*, art. 61; *Const. of Ireland*, art. 40 (6.1.I); *Const. of Italy*, art. 21; *Const. of Japan*, art. 21; *Const. of the Netherlands*, art. 7.

47   For an expression of this view in American literature about the First Amendment, see Nimmer, 1975.

48   See *Branzburg v. Hayes*, 408 U.S. 665, 725 (1972) (Stewart J., dissenting). See also, Axberger, 1993: 150, 164-65 (describing a system of strong protection of journalistic sources in Sweden); Berka, 1993: 22, 3 (describing a similar system in Austria).

49   See *Branzburg v. Hayes* (holding that journalists can be compelled to appear and testify before grand juries investigating criminal cases).

50 In January 1995, the Polish Supreme Court established that judges or prosecutors may require journalists to reveal the sources of their confidential information if this is necessary to produce witness evidence in a criminal case (Judgment I KZP 15/94 of Jan. 19, 1995, 1995 *Orzecznictwo Sądu Najwyszego, Izba Karna i Izba Wojskowa* [Decisions of the Supreme Court, Penal Chamber and Military Chamber] reprinted in *Rzeczpospolita* [The Republic]: 17 (Feb. 15, 1995)). This rule was announced after the editor of a Lublin regional edition of "Gazeta Wyborcza" daily refused to disclose the author of an article. This non-disclosure subsequently became a basis of a criminal indictment. The Supreme Court based its decision on the supremacy of the Code of Criminal Procedure over the Press Law. Article 163 of the Code of Criminal Procedure provides that the court or the prosecutor may impose a duty to disclose matters which constitute privileged information upon persons who otherwise have a privilege to keep confidentiality. This was found to prevail over article 15(2) of the Press Law which provides authors of press articles the right to keep their sources confidential. See *Ustawa z dnia 26 stycznia 1984 r. Prawo Prasowe [Press Law Act] Dziennik Ustaw [Journal of Laws]*, Issue No. 5, Item No. 24: 45 (1984); for an amended text see *Rzeczpospolita [The Republic]*: 7 (Aug. 5, 1991); for an English translation, see "Polish Law Governing the Press", 11 *Cardozo Arts & Ent. L.J.* 569 (1993). As a result, journalists refusing to comply with a valid request to disclose their informer's identity can be held in contempt of court and face a fine or a one-month prison term.

    In late 1996 and early 1997 the controversy was revived when a number of well-known Warsaw journalists (including Aleksander Chećko and Karol Małcużyżski, respectively Editor-In-Chief and Managing Editor of "Życie Warszawy" daily, and Jerzy Jachowicz of "Gazeta Wyborcza" daily) were threatened with criminal prosecutions for refusing to disclose the sources in articles related to the so-called "Oleksy affair". See "Dyskusja o ochronie źródeł informacji: Dziennikarzu, skąd to wiesz?" ["A Debate about the Protection of Sources of Information: A Journalist, How Do You Know It?"] *Rzeczpospolita [The Republic]*: 4 (Jan. 17, 1997); "Ujawnienie tajemnicy: Kolejny dziennikarz oskarʃony" ["Disclosure of a Secret; Another Journalist Indicted"], *Rzeczpospolita [The Republic]*: 1, 11 (Jan. 18, 1997).

51 *Pol. Const.* art. 77(2).

52 *Id.* art. 79.

53 *Id.* art. 80.

54 *Id.* art. 25(2).

55 "Ustawa z dnia 29 grudnia 1992 r. o radiofonii i telewizji" ["Law of Dec. 29, 1992, on Radio and Television"], *Dziennik Ustaw [Journal of Laws]*, Issue No. 7, Item No. 34: 62 (1993). This law was found constitutional by the Constitutional Tribunal in its decision of June 7, 1994 (Judgment K 17/93). For a critique of the law, see Grudzinska (1993: 51-53); (Summer 1993), Van der Jeught (1996: 90-91); for a critique of the Constitutional Tribunal's decision, see Sadurski, (1994). For a defence of the Tribunal's decision (though not of the 1992 Law) see Siemieński (1995: No. 3); for a

defence of the 1992 law and of the Tribunal's decision, see Gowin (1995: 162-66).
56   *Pol. Const.* arts. 41-42.
57   *Id.* arts. 47, 51(1)-(2).
58   *Id.* art. 51(3).
59   *Id.* art. 54.
60   *Id.* art. 53.
61   *Pol. Const.* arts. 57-58.

Bibliography

Axberger, H-G. (1993), "Freedom of the Press in Sweden", in *Press Law and Practice: A comparative study of press freedom in European and other democracies*, 150, 164-65 (Coliver, S. (ed.)).
Berka, W. (1993), "Press Law in Austria", in *Press Law and Practice: A comparative study of press freedom in European and other democracies* 22, 35 (Coliver, S. (ed.).
Brzezinski, M.F. (1991), "Constitutional Heritage and Renewal: The Case of Poland", 77, *Virginia Law Review*.
Brzezinski, M.F. and Garlicki,L. (1995), "Polish Constitutional Law" in *Legal Reform in Post-Communist Europe: The View From Within*, 21, (eds) Frankowski, S. and Stephan, P.B.
Ciemniewski, J. (1996), "Sejm i Senat w projekcie Konstytucji RP [The Sejm and the Senate in the Draft Constitution of the Republic of Poland]", in *Ocena projektu Konstytucji RP [An Evaluation of the Draft Constitution of the Republic of Poland]* 37 (Krukowski, J. (ed.)).
"Constitution Watch: Poland" (Summer 1993), 2 *East European Constitutional Review*, 13.
Elster, J. (1993), "Constitution-making in Eastern Europe: Rebuilding the Boat in the Open Sea", 71, *Public Administration*.
Frankowski, S., (1996), "Lech Wałęsa's Draft of the Charter of Rights and Freedoms: An Overview", *Saint Louis-Warsaw Transatlantic Law Journal*, 65.
Gowin, J. (1995), *Kościół po komunizmie [The Church After Communism]*, 162-66.
Grudzińska-Gross, I. (Summer 1993), "Third Way: The Politics of Christian Values", 2, *East European Constitutional Review*, 51.
Klich, A. (1996), "Human Rights in Poland: The Role of the Constitutional Tribunal and the Commissioner for Citizens' Rights", *Saint Louis-Warsaw Transatlantic Law Journal*.
Łętowska, E. (13 August, 1996), "Co to znaczy 'bezpośrednie stosowanie konstytucji'" ["What Is Meant by 'Direct Applicability of the Constitution'"], *Rzeczpospolita [The Republic]*: 5.
Ludwikowski, R.R. (Spring 1995), "Fundamental Constitutional Rights in the New Constitutions of Eastern and Central Europe", 3, *Cardozo Journal of International and Comparative Law*.

Nimmer, M.B. (1975), "Introduction - Is Freedom of the Press a Redundancy: What Does It Add to Freedom of Speech?", 26, *Hastings Law Journal*, 639.

Osiatyński, W. (Fall 1992), "A Bill of Rights for Poland", 1 *East European Constitutional Review*

_____, (1994), "Rights in New Constitutions of East Central Europe", 26, *Columbia Human Rights Law Review*.

_____, (1996), "Social and Economic Rights in a New Constitution for Poland", in *Western Rights? Post-Communist Application*, 233, 262-69 (Sajó A (ed.).

Rapaczynski, A. (1993), "Constitutional Politics in Poland: A Report on the Constitutional Committee of the Polish Parliament", in *Constitution-Making in Eastern Europe*, A. E. Dick Howard (ed.)

Rzepliński, A. (Summer 1993), "The Polish Bill of Rights and Freedoms: A Case Study of Constitution-Making in Poland", 2 *East European Constitutional Review*.

Sadurski, W. (25 August, 1994), "Trybunał i tolerancja" ["The Tribunal and Toleration"], *Rzeczpospolita [The Republic]*: 5.

_____, (1997), "Rights and Freedoms under the new Polish Constitution; Reflections of a Liberal", *Saint Louis - Warsaw Transnational Law Journal*, 91-105.

Sajó, A. (1996), "Rights in Post-Communism", in *Western Rights? Post-Communist Application*, Sajó, A. ed..

Schwartz, H. (1995). "Panel Discussion", in *Constitution in Service of Democracy*, 221 (Irena Grudzińska Gross (ed.)).

Siemieński, F. (1995), "W sprawie respektowania wartości chrzescijańskich" ["On Respect for Christian Values"], 50, *Państwo i Prawo [State and Law]* 93 (No. 3).

Staśkiewicz, W. (1996), *Jakiej konstytucji Polacy potrzebują? [What Constitution Do Poles Need?]*, 10 (unpublished manuscript, on file with the author).

Sunstein, C.R. (Spring 1992), "Something Old, Something New", 1, *East European Constitutional Review*.

Teitel, R. (1994), "Post-Communist Constitutionalism: A Transitional Perspective", 26, *Columbia Human Rights Law Review*.

Van der Jeught, S. (1996), "Constitutional Protection of Rights and Freedoms - A Comparative Analysis of the Situation in Poland, the Czech and Slovak Republics, and Hungary", 3, *Journal of Constitutional Law in East and Central Europe*, 75.

Winczorek, P., (1996), *Dyskusje Konstytucyjne [Constitutional Discussions]*.

_____, (1995), *Prawo i polityka w czasach przemian* [Law and Politics in the Time of Transformations].

Wiśniewski, L. (20 June, 1996), "Tor przeszkód projektu nowej konstytucji" ["Obstacles Ahead of the Draft of a New Constitution"], *Rzeczpospolita [The Republic]*: 4.

Zieliński, T. (27 August 1996), "Prawo do chleba, mieszkania i pracy" ["The Right to Bread, Housing and Work"], *Gazeta Wyborcza [Electoral Gazette]*: 12.

Part III

Dealing with the Past

9 Can we do Justice to the Past?

ADAM CZARNOTA and PIOTR HOFMAŃSKI[1]

The Idea of Rehabilitation and Compensation for Criminal Repression

A period of radical political change inevitably leads to a settling of scores with the departing system. This takes various forms, which essentially depend on whether the changes occur in revolutionary or evolutionary circumstances.

A revolution typically leads to total condemnation of the past and a complete break with it. The victors do not feel any responsibility for any forms of activity of the defeated regime and totally condemn those activities. As a result there occurs a break in the continuity of the state and the formation of a new one.[2]

On the other hand, when there is an evolutionary transformation of the political system, the state retains its continuity, and members of the new elites acknowledge the state's responsibility for evils which it has inflicted on its citizens, though they feel no personal responsibility for them. Typically they are less determined to bring the authors of these evils to justice.[3]

In both cases there are changes in visions of the past and future, which lie within the foundations of the law. The law is deeply tied not only to history but to such visions, which are articulated by the dominating groups in the framework of the nation state. The American legal theorist, Robert Cover, persuasively analysed these connections, in his article "Nomos and Narrative" (Cover, 1983). The vision of the past contained in the law lends normative sense to the currently functioning law. The dominating vision of the past is connected not only with a feeling of national pride but also with a functioning sense of justice. To varying degrees and in varying forms, visions of the past are embodied in existing legislation and case law. This is particularly evident in constitutional legislation of the countries of east

197

central Europe, after the collapse of communism (see Czarnota, 1995: 83-101). The dominating national vision of the past, and the sense of justice connected with it, also have an influence on the criminal legislation of the countries which have overcome communism.

The range and depth of the political transformations which have occurred in Poland since 1989 do not amount to a total destruction of the legitimacy of the former elites who were deposed as a result of the transformations. The state has preserved its continuity, and so the formations which came to power after 1989 represent a subject which remains the same in law, though of course its political character is different. A manifestation of this legal continuity is the sense of obligation to correct injuries inflicted on citizens by representatives of the former regime. The change of the political situation and the change in the political regime have resulted in changes in the vision of the past lying at the foundations of the law, including the criminal law.

In this situation, there is nothing surprising in the fact that, from the time of the political transformation in 1989, cases have occurred in which rehabilitation has been sought, and where people repressed by the Stalinist apparatus of oppression, through their legal representatives, have tried to challenge court judgments against them. It soon turned out, however, that the grounds on which Polish law allowed challenges to judgments which had stood for years, and the procedures within Polish law for making such challenges, were not sufficiently broad or elastic to allow for the satisfactory treatment of this sort of matter. For realistic chances to change judgments rendered years ago occurred only in relation to those judgments which violated the law in force at the moment when the judgments were reached and this - because of the narrow bases for loosening the force of law - could only occur in a very limited range of cases. The modes envisaged in Polish law for making claims for compensation for injuries and suffering also turned out to be fruitless for the thousands of people oppressed by the Stalinist system. They were now barred because of the passage of time (see Daszkiewicz, 1990: 3ff).

This situation alerted lawyers and politicians relatively quickly to the necessity for some sort of general statute, with the help of which this ever more complicated problem might be resolved on a general scale. It turned out that every attempt to satisfy the victims of the former regime conflicts with the need to respect the elementary requirements of the rule of law, such as, for example, the principle that law does not act retrospectively, and thus forced on decisionmakers a choice between formal and material justice. Consequently, the problem of a legal approach to the communist past deeply divided the new governing elites. The attempt to make a legal break with the past, as seen in the example of the award of compensation for damages inflicted by the Stalinist apparatus of repression, taken together with the simultaneous recognition of the continuity of the state, and with that the continuity of the system of law, amounts to an attempt to square a circle. The problem torments not only political and legal elites, but also the societies of the former communist countries.

Independent of these general questions, two serious problems at a much lower level of abstraction presented themselves immediately. Firstly, a choice had to be made between a solution that depended on a review of the merits of court decisions which were little less than fifty years old, and one that simply declared them invalid. The first solution would undoubtedly be better from the point of view of justice. How much more complete is rehabilitation that stems from a judgment of innocence than rehabilitation which depends upon declaration of the invalidity of a former judgment? Acceptance of this conception would nevertheless result in unimaginable difficulties of proof. For courts would be forced again to conduct criminal trials in situations where the records of matters conducted in the 1940s and 1950s were in part not preserved, where the majority of witnesses presumably had left the land of the living, and where traces in the memories of those who happily had survived had become blurred to such an extent that it would be impossible to reopen anything today. Were we to decide on this solution, we would be faced with another incredibly difficult problem: whether, in reopening a matter, we should apply the law in force when the act occurred, or the law in force today. Neither of these alternatives is acceptable. Application of Stalinist law by the courts of an independent and democratic Poland is, for obvious reasons, unthinkable, even though many wrongs committed then could be corrected, by means of different interpretations of that law. Application of current law, on the other hand, conflicts with the elementary principles of the rule of law, since it depends upon acceptance of the retroactive operation of law.

Awareness of the above difficulties led to acceptance of a more fitting conception of the invalidity of judgments, more precise than the conception of treating all judgments given under Stalinism as invalid. This increase in precision is not accidental. For it has to do with a conception of treating judgments as invalid *ex tunc* (from then) and not *ex nunc* (from now). That means that the judgments of the organs of Stalinist repression were acknowledged as having been invalid from the very beginning, and thus from the time that they issued. At first glance, acceptance of such a legal construction seems inconceivable, for it would seem to imply the necessity that such judgments simply fall out of the picture of presently binding law. This conception begins, however, to gain sense if we take into account the possibility of exploiting the conception of an offence, which is accepted in Polish law, according to which it is an act not merely forbidden by law, but also "socially dangerous".[4] It is thus enough to change the criteria of judging that social danger, to reach the conviction that for years it was applied wrongly.

There was a second problem connected with the choice of one of the two suggested possibilities. For either one declares by law that particular judgments given in a particular period and by particular organs are invalid, or one entrusts decisions about invalidity to the judgments made under the assumption of the conception of invalidity *ex tunc*. Each of these conceptions has its virtues and flaws (see Daszkiewicz, 1990: 27ff).

Let us start with the first alternative. The idea is not new. It was applied in the Czechoslovak law on judicial rehabilitation of 25 June 1968[5] which was passed in the wave of political reform in Czechoslovakia that occurred just before the invasion by the Warsaw Pact states. According to this law, the judgments of certain organs were recognized as invalid *ex lege* on procedural grounds, in particular to do with the manner in which they were conducted, that manner in itself having contravened elementary principles of the rule of law. Another example of a legal act partly based on this conception is the Hungarian law of 14 March 1990, declaring invalid judgments infringing the rule of law, which had been delivered in the years 1945-1963,[6] that is in the period of the greatest intensification of repression both before 1956 and after the period of Kádár's normalization. According to this law, moreover, several categories of sentences (the criterion was the legal basis of these sentences and thus had a material character) were declared invalid by the same law on rehabilitation, without the necessity of taking any further action.[7] An example of a law which accepted, to the fullest extent, the conception of declaring with the force of law the invalidity of judgments, is the Soviet decree of 1989 on recognition of certain judgments as invalid.[8] This law envisaged that individual applications for a declaration of invalidity could only occur as exceptions to the rule laid down.

In Poland it was suggested that the conception whereby Stalinist judgments would be regarded as invalid *ex lege* should be accepted in a limited domain, namely judgments delivered by the so-called Special Committee for Fighting Abuses and Economic Damage.[9] In fact, the judgments of this Commission were delivered in a manner consistent with the then binding law but nonetheless, taking into account its inquisitorial procedure and the absence of any sort of possibility of defence, it is difficult today to regard its judgments as having the force of law in a state which, in one of the first post-communist amendments to its constitution and again in the constitution of 1997, declared itself a rule of law state. Moreover, judgments were handed down by organs not mentioned in the then binding legal order - such as secret sections in the courts, in which participation was legally unauthorized and morally repugnant, and which delivered hundreds of judgments that were criminal in character and - more important - were executed by the state apparatus of repression.

Taking a sensible decision required taking into account Polish realities. It would be absurd to say that every judgment given by Polish courts in the forties and the beginning of the fifties was an example of Stalinist repression. The realization of such an idea in Polish conditions would automatically have involved regarding as invalid and illegal, not only judgments given against people fighting for Polish independence, but also for example sentences of Nazi criminals, not to mention sentences of concentration camp guards, murderers from the SS, and so on (see Daszkiewicz, 1990: 14-15). On the other hand, a virtue of a general resolution would be resignation from overloading the already overladen Polish courts with thousands of new and - both in fact and law - truly complicated matters. The force of the first of these arguments nevertheless had to prevail, and the second of the possible alternatives was favoured, and that to the fullest extent.

This solution too is not unique to Poland, and was in part (in relation to particular judgments) adopted in the Czechoslovak law mentioned above. As we have argued, this solution, which relies upon entrusting decisions about the invalidity of judgments from the Stalinist period to the courts, also has virtues and defects. They are the direct mirror image of the virtues and defects of the other alternative outlined above. This second solution gives the possibility of selecting among judgments handed down in the Stalinist period, but it involves very serious problems of overloading the courts with a new, extraordinarily wide-ranging category of cases. We should add, too, that the passing of time brings with it serious problems of evidence, which nevertheless do not appear on such a scale as we would have to deal with if we were to decide in favour of a substantive review of judgments. It is, after all, one thing to act with the aim of establishing a statutory criterion of invalidity, and quite another to decide on the substantive merit of an act of judgment which came into force over fifty years ago.

The Sphere of the Law and Criteria of Invalidity

The law on invalidation of judgments against persons repressed for activity in aid of the independent existence of the Polish State, was passed by the *Sejm* on 23 February 1991[10] and came into force on May 24, 1991. The basic conception on which the legislation was based was that of recognizing certain categories of court decisions as invalid *ex tunc*. Acknowledging the force of the argument that - unlike a judgment of innocence - simple recognition of judgments as invalid does not lead to a complete rehabilitation, the legislation introduced to article 2, cl 1, of the law, a note according to which acknowledgment of the invalidity of a judgment is deemed to be equivalent to a declaration of innocence. This specification depends upon two basic matters: the question of classifying the classes of judgments which must be invalidated and the question of the criterion of invalidation.

According to art 1, cl 1 of the law, judgments handed down by Polish organs of pursuit and justice or by extra-judicial organs in the period from the beginning of their activity on Polish territory, beginning in January 1, 1944 until 31 December 1956, were recognized as invalid. Thus the statute did not limit itself to "judicial" repressions in the strict sense, since notice had to be taken of the fact that various types of commissions and secret sections, which under no criteria could be regarded as courts, had been active on Polish territory and had issued verdicts which required execution and were executed. Since, as we have mentioned, the judgments of these organs were not declared invalid *ex lege*, which might have been possible given the character of the organs, the law had to expand the procedures whereby their judgments also could be invalidated.

Time limits were specified by taking into account the circumstance that before January 1, 1944, Polish organs did not have any jurisdiction on Polish territory, since that territory was under German occupation; while after 31 December 1956, the political realities in Poland had changed sufficiently that to treat the activities of the apparatus of justice according to the same criteria would be simply to misunderstand the situation. That does not mean that there is no possibility of correcting judgments which were delivered with the force of law after 1956. However, this must take place in the course of altering their legality on the basis of general principles, resulting in their potential overruling or change, *ex nunc*, and not *ex tunc*.

The basic criterion for regarding judgments as invalid is the claim that the condemned act or actor was linked with activity on behalf of the independence of the Polish State or that the judgment was handed down in connection with such activity. This criterion is interpreted broadly. In truth, the statutory formulation suggests that it is objective in character, but nonetheless, in keeping with the principle of subjectivization in the dominant Polish model of criminal responsibility, there is no way of excluding the situation where, only after analysis of the subjective side, and the motives and impulses of the actor, can one decide whether to declare a judgment invalid.[11] Judgments handed down for opposition to the collectivization of agriculture and compulsory delivery of produce are also treated as invalid.

This sort of criterion, and the entrusting to the courts of the responsibility for declaring judgments invalid, have led to enormous difficulties in practice. For after nearly fifty years from the time in which the judgments were handed down, Polish courts are required to discern the motives and impulses that lay behind acts committed then, or the real reasons for which those judgments were handed down. Practice has shown that there are occasions where the matter is truly beyond discussion and it is possible to make a judgment simply after reading the record of the case if it reveals quite abnormal action by the court. Among such cases are sentences for participation in a group, where we know that these groups were fighting for Polish independence against Soviet occupation.

More problematic are sentences for illegal possession of arms. Of course, in many circumstances it is justified to presume that the arms were hidden with the purpose of aiding underground organizations and identifiable partisan groups. Often, however, nothing specific emerges beyond the fact that the accused possessed arms, and did not make this known to the authorities. For this he was sentenced, for example, to five years hard labour, which in the conditions that prevailed meant that he really did suffer. We must remember that directly on passing the front, long after the end of the war, Polish territory was virtually covered with corpses and discharged weapons. Often today a citizen comes before the court and states that he was hiding weapons for organizations fighting for the independence of the Polish State. The court has the enormous problem of choosing what criteria of judgment to apply to this situation.

Another category of matters is connected with so-called *"szeptanka"* (private passing of rumours). A huge number of judgments was delivered for the telling of jokes about the then prominent communist political elites or about the new social system and political regime. The basis for the sentence was the "anti-state" character of the accused and the danger that "the spreading of false information" bore for the stability of the communist system. If someone suffered a term of many years in prison for a little story about Uncle Joe Stalin, about whom no more need be said, or about Joseph

Bierut, who was President of the Polish People's Republic until 1953, then there is no doubt that he was a victim of communist terror and suffered unjustifiably. Can we presume, on the other hand, that he was sentenced as a fighter for the independent existence of the Polish State or that he was sentenced as a result of activity to this end?[12]

Still other difficulties are called forth by sentences for "opposition to compulsory acquisition". In starving postwar Poland, peasants were required under threat of punishment to surrender all their agricultural produce, which then was distributed by central agencies. This was linked with the agricultural policy of the communists in Poland. Most frequently, peasants were sentenced for not providing food to towns simply because they themselves had nothing or very little. Can one assume today, that they represented the Polish struggle for independence and fought for its independent existence? Today, peasants often appear before courts and try to persuade them that they behaved as they did because they rejected the communist idea of central distribution of goods and the agricultural policy of the Polish communists, and that their opposition was part of the struggle for a free market and, through that, a sovereign Poland.

However, the most difficult problem is the assessment of those convicted of violent acts who today, after many years, try to prove that the robberies and attacks they committed were politically motivated. The most typical situation concerned the provisioning of partisans. Partisans who hid in forests generally benefited from the support of people in the towns. Nevertheless this support was limited, partly because a respectable proportion of the Polish population accepted the new political order, partly because support for the partisans led to severe repression by the Stalinist apparatus, and more than once to the pacification of the whole countryside. In this situation, maintaining the partisans required thieving attacks on warehouses storing foodstuffs in the towns and to the application of force against innocent peasants, who either did not want to help, or were frightened, or simply had nothing to share. More than a few people died in these attacks. Today the question occurs whether this kind of act can be treated as an element of the struggle for the independent existence of the Polish state.

In many cases of this sort, courts have given a positive response, taking advantage of the rules written directly into the law of February 1991. According to its article 1, cl 3, a judgment is not invalidated if the good sacrificed was disproportionately greater than the good which was achieved or was sought to be achieved, or if the way of acting or the means applied were incommensurable to the result intended or achieved. This rule of proportionality, known in the law for a very long time, is of little help, however, against the accumulation of evidential difficulties involved in the resolution of concrete matters.

We know that in the post-war years, not only partisan groups were prowling about in the forests and their neighbourhoods, but also simple bands of pickpockets, ordinary criminals, who, taking advantage of the postwar turmoil and instability, engaged in looting. If today people sentenced for theft demand that judgments against them be recognized as invalid, then decisions on the application of the law on rehabilitation will be taken after deliberations in which the judges, instead of supporting themselves with arguments about matters of fact, are put in a situation where the only thing on which they can rely is either empathy or the ability to read tea leaves.

The Problem of Damages

According to article 8 cl 1 of the law of 23 February 1991, on the basis of which the illegality of judgments is claimed, damages can be demanded from the State for injuries inflicted and reparation for harm suffered, on the basis of such a past judgment. In the case of the death of the person harmed, the right is transferred to his wife, children and relatives. Obviously, this applies not only to deaths inflicted as a result of Stalinist repression (for example death penalties, attacks on prisoners in Stalinist cells), but also to the situation where a sentenced person, after suffering imprisonment, died of natural causes.

It is necessary to undertake a second court hearing to deal with the matter of damages. This second case has a limited scope and is concerned solely with establishing the amount of damages, since the question whether there is a basis for damages has been decided by the existence of an earlier judgment - that which declares invalid the judgment complained of.

At this point let us make a small digression. During the discussions which preceded the passing of the statute on rehabilitation, the deep conviction was expressed that judgments awarding damages would be rare in practice. Basically it was a matter of creating the possibility of rehabilitating people who, as a result of Stalinist repressions, were stripped of their good name. In actual practice, matters are brought forward more prosaically. Often there turn up in the court room the children of a fighter for Polish independence who was tormented to death, and they seek the invalidation of the judgment which sentenced him, knowing nothing precisely about him or about the ideals for which he fought, sometimes not even knowing his Christian name. They know only this much, that if a court invalidates the judgment they will have a basis on which to claim damages. Consciousness of ways of capitalizing, even on misfortune, occurs in times of difficult economic reform and from an economic point of view the actions of beneficiaries, not very concerned about their image or good name but about money, are hard to classify as irrational. One might have a different view if one were to apply moral categories.

The practice of the courts, when it is a matter of the level of damages to be awarded, starts from the assumption that damages should cover real harm suffered by the person imprisoned, taken together with the potential benefits that he could have obtained had he not been repressed. That is why, in order to identify what level of damages to award, it is necessary to establish the real conditions in which the sentenced person lived, and particularly the potential means that he had at his disposal and which he lost as a result of the repression. The average level of damages is between a quarter and a third of the average monthly income at the moment of the judgment of rehabilitation. This amount, of course, has to be multiplied by the number of months of effective loss of freedom.

The second element of damages is reparation for wrong suffered which in practice is much higher than the original damage found in the judgment. In calculating the amount of reparations, the court takes into account the length of time in which the prisoner was unfree and the conditions in which he was held, his subjectively perceived degree of pain and suffering, to the extent that these circumstances can today be determined, and also the consequences of his loss of freedom.

A different situation occurs where the sentenced person died, as a result of the repression inflicted upon him. Here the courts have an enormous problem, since they are fully aware that it is impossible to calculate a human life in terms of money. They keep in mind that the reparations which in such circumstances are the main element of damages, are those owed to the repressed person himself, and only by way of inheritance do they fall to his wife and children.

The problem of investigating damages is not only a question of the legal title, which goes with the court's decision to recognize a judgment as invalid. For the law gives a basis for awarding damages in two circumstances in which a prior judgment is not invalidated.

Firstly, it acknowledges that there were persons equally deserving of damages, against whom there never had been a judgment, but who nevertheless spent years in Stalinist prisons awaiting a judgment which was never handed down, either because of lack of evidence, or because of the political crisis which occurred in 1956, or because the unfortunate prisoners never survived to receive a judgment but died after repeated interrogations varied - as they often were - with the smashing of teeth and breaking of fingers. That is why art 11, cl 1 of the statute also entitles people who would have had grounds to claim invalidity of a judgment, if the accused was found innocent or the accusation was frozen on the grounds that the offence was not committed and there were no legal damages or reparation, and the people were held in custody or temporarily arrested.[13]

Secondly, not only the victims of Polish judicial organs are entitled to damages, but also those of Soviet organs to which the Polish authorities - specifically the Polish Committee of National Liberation - by a special agreement in 1944 transferred jurisdiction in the field of military activities on Polish territory after the entry there of Soviet forces.[14] This does not, however, amount to invalidation of the judgments delivered by a foreign state, since that would involve departing from the area of cognition of the Polish judiciary.[15] But nothing stands in the way of victims of such repression receiving damages from the treasury of the Polish Republic, if the sentence was connected with the struggle for the independent existence of the Polish State (article 8, cl 2a of the law).[16]

Both of these supplementary clauses, particularly the first, involve very great difficulties in practice. Art 11, cl 1 of the statute makes a ground of every repression which took place in connection with a criminal process then taking place, even if the process did not end with a judgment. Such a criterion, however, is very fluid. In one case of this kind the court of first instance faced the problem of establishing damages for the death of the father of the complainant, who was simply shot by a functionary of the Security Service (*Urząd Bezpieczeństwa* or *UB*) in his own yard. The court held that this was not connected with any current criminal proceeding; the father of the complainant belonged to an independence organization and for this reason alone was exterminated with a bullet in the back of the head. It was only on appeal that it was possible to establish that the functionary of the UB arrived with an arrest warrant, and shot the victim because the would-be captive, seeking to avoid arrest, tried to escape. This new state of affairs gave a basis for accepting the presumption that the death of the father of the complainant occurred in connection with proceedings, in the course of which an arrest warrant had been issued.

Another case occurred in connection with a decision to pay damages where a member of an underground organization had been shot in an encounter with a division of the militia and security functionaries. In truth there was no doubt that some action was being directed against the man shot, because he was being searched for by the militia. Nevertheless there was a lack of evidence that this action was connected in any way with the shooting encounter, which had occurred during an attempt to clean out "anti-regime activists" from the forest. The court refused to award damages.

The Polish Supreme Court is aware of the difficulties which attend these and similar cases. The Court accepts a broad explanation of art 2 and says that the bases for damages are fulfilled when the death of a repressed person was connected with a then current proceeding or at least an equivalent, though not with an armed struggle carried on "outside criminal proceedings".[17] Nevertheless it does not appear that the announcement of this legal opinion has relieved the accumulation of doubts in practice.

A Provisional Assessment

The statute on rehabilitation came into force directly after a prolonged discussion. It then seemed that the criteria ultimately chosen would allow fair distinctions to be made between "just" and "unjust" sentences, that the law would allow those who had given up long years of freedom and on more than one occasion their own lives for the independence of Poland, to be compensated for the wrongs done to them. Practice has shown, however, that these hopes have in large measure proved sterile. We have learnt, on the contrary, that striving for the criteria set out in the statute more than once has led to results contrary to common moral intuitions. For it is virtually certain that a series of judgments have been declared invalid which were handed down in purely criminal matters. This applies particularly to matters dealing with thefts. At the same time, in many cases the court has refused to hold a judgment invalid because it had proved impossible to show a connection between the actual or alleged act and the struggle for Polish independence, even though in reality that connection did exist. A judgment of invalidity could not, however, be given, since it could not be based on mere opinion.

The distinction between repressions carried out in "the framework of legal proceedings" and those "outside legal proceedings" seems to be deeply unjust. Do not those who went to the forests to fight against the Soviet occupier deserve to be treated in exactly the same way as those who did exactly the same, but were caught and suffered in Stalinist prisons or gave their lives on the gallows?

The statute limits the scope of procedures of invalidation, and the scope of claims for compensation, to judicial repressions. From the technical-legal point of view this makes sense, but is it just? And do not those who suffered repressions in German prisons and concentration camps, for struggles against Hitler, also deserve our recognition and memory, not to mention compensation for harm done to them in the fight for Poland? And the families of officers of the Polish army, whose remains rest in Katyń, Charkow and Miednoje. Do they not also deserve similar compensation to that awarded those whose forefathers were caught for subversive activity only three years later by a Soviet bullet, when as glorious victors the Soviets yet again crossed the eastern borders of Poland?

These and thousands of other doubts lead us to assess the statute on rehabilitation with scepticism. Law is not a good medium for every social ill and in particular it is not a good means for smoothing over the past. Joining law with history has a role for the future, in articulating values and a normative vision which binds a given society. That does not mean that law is a good means for easing the wounds of the past. Legal ways of thinking are different from historical ways. In the statute we have been discussing, and particularly in the application of the law, we have a clear example of the difficulty of connecting formal and pragmatic legal thinking with historical thinking. The difficulties in linking these two types of social practice are just too apparent, with consequences for our ability to realize a sense of justice. Perhaps the road chosen in the Republic of South Africa - the Reconciliation and Truth Commission led by Bishop Desmond Tutu - the main goal of which is public revelation of the dark stains in the past and their moral condemnation, is a better route to social reconciliation with the past than legal action. Perhaps it would have been better to leave aside morality and history. Perhaps even it would have been better to lower one's head with humility, in honour of the suffering of thousands of Poles, who in the struggle for their fatherland gave so much of themselves. Perhaps we should simply say to them: your blood and tears did not fall in vain.

Notes

1   An earlier version of this article appeared as Czarnota and Hofmański, 1996.

2   This does not mean, however, that the elites of the new formation resign from criminal prosecution of the perpetrators of crimes committed under authority of the law of the former regime.

3   On the question of responsibility for Stalinist crimes in Poland, see Gardocki, 1992: 61ff.

4   This is, after all, a conception introduced into Polish law on the model of the Soviet conception of crime.

5   Sbirka zakonu Československie socialisticke republiky 1968, no 26, poz 82.

6   Magyar Kozlony 1990, no 29.

7   It does not change matters that interested persons may apply to the appropriate organs for a declaration of invalidity, and that they have a right to complain if their application is rejected.

8   Cited by W. Daszkiewicz, 1990: 14-15.

9   That Commission was established by decree, on 16 November 1945 (Dziennik Ustaw no 53, 1945, poz 302, uniform text Dziennik Ustaw no 41, 1950, poz 274).

10   Digest of Laws, no 34, 1991, poz, 149, amendments Digest of Laws, no 36, 1993, poz 159, I no 28, 1995, poz 143.

11   Decision of the Supreme Court of 20 November, 1991, sygn I KZP 25/91, Judgments of Polish Courts, Criminal and Military Division, 1992, no 3-4, poz 22.

12   In a decision of 3 July 1992, sygn II KRN 90/92, the Supreme Court accepted that not every act of a person, which is an exercise of rights and freedoms, at the same time is "activity in aid of the independent existence of the Polish State".

13   See the interpretation of this clause in the decision of the Supreme Court of 26 March 1992, sygn WZ 35/92, Judgments of the Supreme Court, Criminal and Military Division 1992, no 11-12, poz 80.

14   Agreeement of 26 July, 1945, between the Polish Committee of National Liberation (PKWN) and the government of the USSR on relations between the Soviet High Command, and the Polish administration after the entry of Soviet armies on Polish territory.

15   See the decision of the Supreme Court, of 18 September 1992, sygn II KRN 116/92.

16   As in the amendment of 20 February 1993, Dziennik Ustaw No 36 (1993), poz 159.

17   Decree of 3 March, 1994, sygn I KZP, no 3-4, poz 17.

Bibliography

Cover, R. (1983), "Foreward: 1982 Term, Nomos and Narrative", *Harvard Law Review*, 4.

Czarnota, A. (1995), "Constitutional Nationalism, Citizenship and Hope for Civil Society in Eastern Europe", in A. Pavkovic, H. Koscharsky, and A. Czarnota (eds), *Nationalism and Postcommunism. A Collection of Essays*.

Czarnota, A. and Hofmański, P. (1996) "Polish Law Deals with the Communist Past", 22, 5 *Review of Central and East European Law,* 521-34.

Daszkiewicz, W. (1990), "Problem rehabilitacji i odszkodowań za bezprawne represje karne", 2, *Państwo i Prawo.*

_____, (1990), "Postępowanie rehabilitacyjne - jego podstawy i usprawnienie przebiegu" (Acting to rehabilitate - foundations and efficiency of the process), 9, *Państwo i Prawo.*

Gardocki, L. (1992), "Zagadnienie odpowiedzialnośći karnej za zbrodnie stalinowskie" (Questions of criminal responsibility for Stalinist crimes), 6, *Przegląd Prawa Karnego (Review of Criminal Law).*

10 Lustration and Decommunisation:

Ethical and Theoretical Debates

ANDRZEJ KANIOWSKI

(Translated by Martin Krygier)

The intention of this chapter is to reconstruct some essential qualities of the moral thinking of advocates and opponents of what we might call "moral lustration". Moral ideas are certainly not without importance from the point of view of realizing the principles of the "rule of law". Some kinds of moral thinking will contribute to the realisation of this principle; others can act against it. Both can be found in contemporary Poland. The reconstruction of both kinds of moral thinking seems to be absolutely necessary if we consider the formation of a "post-communist"[1] legal order. The problem of lustration and decommunisation is important, not only because it reveals such moral presuppositions but also because it itself has great significance for the realisation of the rule of the law. For the question immediately arises whether such lustration-decommunisation undertakings are in any way consistent with an intention to introduce the rule of the law, and if so, in what circumstances and to what extent.

In the first part of this chapter, I explain my reasons for introducing the term "moral lustration", as well as the essential differences between its advocates' and opponents' perception of the Polish reality of "communist" times. In the second part, I survey the mode of reasoning, as well as some fundamental principles of moral thinking, expressed by the advocates of lustration and decommunisation. Some apparent paradoxes to which this kind of reasoning can lead will be demonstrated. The third part will develop theoretical frameworks within which the manner of thinking and the moral claims of the opponents of lustration-decommunisation can be reconstructed and systematized. Finally, some reflections will be presented, all of them connected with the problem of the extent to which lustration-decommunisation procedures are compatible with the principle of the rule of law, and also with the question of whether moral thinking is all-important for the making of an order based on the principle of "the rule of the law".[2]

I

The term "moral lustration" comprises two phenomena which are linked with each other. First, it concerns the settling of accounts with the post-war Polish past - both the so-called Stalinist period as well as the years of real socialism - which was undertaken from the mid-1980s onwards by writers, journalists, clergymen, and most prominently in that period, by politicians who participated in political journalism at the same time. Secondly, when talking about "moral lustration" we have in mind some particular proposals for lustration-decommunisation statutes submitted to the Polish *Sejm* (parliament) in 1993 by some groups on the right wing of the political scene (including proposals submitted by Solidarity, and by the Christian-National Union, clearly backed by the hierarchy of the Roman Catholic Church). Both phenomena to which the term "moral lustration" refers involve morally condemnatory analyses of (a) the behaviour of certain individuals or whole social groups, such as writers, scientists, artists, or - generally speaking - intellectuals; and of (b) some attitudes taken to be typical of the past reality, such as opportunist attitudes. They also, finally, involve (c) construction of some negatively charged models of personality types formed under "communism". An example of such a model can be found in the studies of Father Józef Tischner of the personality type denoted as *homo sovieticus*.[3]

The term "moral lustration" has been introduced in the present chapter for two reasons. Firstly, it helps point out the links between both proposals for lustration-decommunisation statutes (discussed in 1993) and other activities practised in the spirit of moral condemnation of the whole period of the Polish People's Republic (PRL), as well as the common practice of condemnation of particular individuals for their attitudes and behaviour in the previous epoch. Even Czesław Miłosz, and such outstanding and internationally acclaimed Polish dissidents as Jacek Kuroń, Adam Michnik or Leszek Kołakowski were not spared, nor were whole groups,[4] or social strata, including men of letters, scientists, or intellectuals. Such a link certainly lies in the fact that the "moral lustrators'" view of the past of those individuals or groups is motivated not so much by the intention to analyse past reality and its mechanisms, in order to assess the underlying attitudes manifested by the incriminated individuals or groups, but by the wish to find those aspects of their lives that would - in the lustrators' eyes - be grounds for charges against them. The main ground, though understood in different ways, is that the "accused" participated in the structures of the old system or took part in public life (not only political or economic, but also literary, scientific and artistic).

Secondly, in introducing the term "moral lustration", I wish to limit my sphere of investigation of the attitudes of advocates and opponents of the lustration-decommunisation activities to a consideration of the moral sphere alone. Thus pragmatic and socio-technical arguments such as the argument that members of a given group should be denied certain positions in the new reality, for fear lest they fall easy prey to blackmail[5] have been mentioned only in passing in the present study. A closer look at these kinds of arguments reveals that an important role is played there by moral reasons, though they are not always eagerly articulated. This link with moral imagination characterizes the attitudes of both the advocates as well as the opponents of lustration and decommunisation, though of course the content varies between them. The pragmatic-technical arguments put forward in the course of the debates are, in fact, of secondary importance here (this is true equally of the thesis - put forward by advocates of lustration and decommunisation - that, for the sake of the effective functioning of the new political order, it is necessary to limit the public rights of certain groups of people, as well as the arguments of its opponents, that it is technically impossible to execute reliable lustration, or identification of the members of the special service groups). As a matter of fact, both the advocates and the opponents of lustration-decommunisation activities rely at base on ideas, convictions and moral evaluations without which technical-pragmatic arguments would lose their weight.

In considering the discussions of lustration and decommunisation, one should first of all assess what the current debate really is about, assuming we view it as an argument between different moral notions. Looking at the whole range of matters subject to "moral lustration", we can differentiate - as has been pointed out above - different kinds of objects as liable for "moral lustration". Without doubt, at the centre are the so-called special services as well as their secret allies; then there is the administration of justice and the political apparatus of the previous system, that is the centralized mono-party which used to control the whole sphere of public life (ranging from economy to art), as well as the so-called *nomenklatura*, ie, the system of positions and offices controlled by the mono-party; furthermore the various professional groups and social circles of journalists, writers, scientists, teachers, artists. The advocates and the opponents of lustration-decommunisation activities agree with each other that the past reality was to a large extent deformed, and that the new system now in the making ought to develop on different foundations. The conflicting parties also agree in principle on still another aspect as well, namely the moral evaluation of the special services and their secret allies.[6] None of the opponents of the lustration-decommunisation procedures has ever made any statements or formulated judgments that would give moral justification to the functioning of such institutions or this kind of activity. It seems that both conflicting parties condemn anyone's engagement in those services and co-operation with them (at least in so far as the system was engaged in suppressing the political opposition and the Church, rather than detecting criminals in, say, the economy - by accumulating secret data on the behaviour and attitudes of the controlled groups and storing information that could be used in some way against individuals or groups under investigation. Perhaps the similarity of the attitudes of both parties in this respect results from the fact that both of them acknowledge the existence of a connection between the actually realized aims of these institutions (which they usually declare quite openly) and the aims of the individuals operating within them (together with the consequences of their activity): the aim is to persecute, repress and harm others.[7]

The debates connected with lustration - that is, the revelation (in full or in part) of the data accumulated in the special service archives - do not then follow from different moral evaluations of the activity of those services and their allies, but rather from different estimations of the possibilities and social legitimacy of undertaking this kind of operation. Moreover, opponents generally take into consideration the potential circumstances which caused individuals to become involved in these kinds of services;[8] also the validity of the data might be questioned, as well as the consequences of potential false charges. These reservations - no matter how applicable they are - have no influence upon the moral evaluation of the special service political institutions, their activities and the individuals co-operating with them.

Similar agreement of moral evaluations exists with regard to those judges and prosecutors in the services, who co-operated by passing sentences which broke even the formally existing laws (eg, the right to defence) in the period when unjust or even criminal sentences used to be a standard practice. This is, however, where the similarities end.

The main source of differences seems to lie in different views of the relationship between a given institution or a given sub-system and the subjects operating within them. For many of those passing judgments on the departed communist reality, the link between the negatively evaluated aim of a given institution and the aims and intentions of individuals connected with it has ceased to be so obvious. Such institutions or sub-systems as those of the law, the media, science and education, or even the institution of the mono-party as such, which was in control of those institutions (or tried to be), are viewed by a number of citizens and authors who seek to settle accounts with the past as, firstly, institutions which realized a number of aims that are, or rather were, socially acceptable; and secondly, institutions or sub-systems in which there is no such unequivocal connection between the malign aim or particular function of the institution and the actual activity (aims and functions) of the individuals operating within its structure. After all, even if the media under censorship were supposed, say, to conceal some messages and depoliticize social consciousness, this does not necessarily mean that subjects operating within those institutions must be condemned, since they used to realize different functions or social aims which were accepted, or at least not considered morally wrong.

Thus we have a vast spectrum of institutions, social sub-systems and milieux (eg, writers, actors, scientists, etc) as well as individuals operating within them - all of them potentially subject to moral appraisal. This was a central - though not the sole - reason for the split within the former anti-communist opposition and its resulting division into ardent supporters of lustration and decommunisation, on the one hand, and their equally fierce opponents, on the other. The first camp comprises a large number of politicians and the right-wing or "Catholic-national" parties, as well as some literary circles (eg, those connected with the Cracow magazine *Arka*), and even some prominent writers (eg, Zbigniew Herbert, one of the most distinguished Polish poets). The other camp includes the Freedom Union, the party most "saturated" with intellectuals, former "Solidarity" advisers and former "dissidents", often with some earlier allegiance to the mono-party (ie, the PZPR, the Polish United Workers Party). It also includes the leftist Unia Pracy (the Union of Labour).[9] The most outstanding figures of the camp are the well-known leaders of the former anti-communist opposition: Adam Michnik, Jacek Kuroń, as well as Father Tischner.

The spectrum of possible attitudes toward lustration and decommunisation is fairly broad and we can differentiate some intermediate positions between these two polar options. For example, one for lustration without decommunisation, ie, depriving certain groups of individuals of part of their public rights (for some time, or even forever); another that advocates decommunisation as an independent "self-cleansing" process whereby certain professional groups rid themselves of morally compromised members; or one in which decommunisation is understood as a change of the principles of the functioning of institutions and sub-systems, without any simultaneous, automatic moral stigmatization of the individuals operating within those institutions.

The different attitudes of the representatives of both polar camps within the former opposition can be described in the following way.

1. The camp of the followers of moral lustration (and decommunisation) alleges the existence of a far-reaching connection between the institutions and the individuals operating within them. Since these institutions are regarded from the start as realizers of negative values (anti-values) and supporters of the totalitarian order, so the individuals operating within their structures deserve at least moral rebuke. There remains the problem of how to draw a demarcation line between, on the one hand, actors together with active or passive collaborators, who contributed to making and establishing the totalitarian state and who are therefore viewed as guilty, and, on the other hand, those who had nothing to do with the system and its institutions, and therefore are innocent. Drawing the line is certainly not easy. Nevertheless, according to advocates of this approach, those who did not participate in the given institutions are certainly innocent (the institutions may be assessed differently according to the degree of their appraisers' radicalism in tracing the "level of communisation" of a given institution, life sphere or milieu) - and either supported the only institution which has never given itself up to the mono-party, resisting all attempts at its subjugation, ie, the Roman Catholic Church, or at least remained in the background. Through the prism of the negative evaluation of the system, or its sub-systems and institutions, people are morally evaluated with a focus on the problem of their "blame" and the possibility of fixing that blame for the existence of the given system upon particular individuals, groups, social strata or milieux. The act of decommunisation that this camp advocates is a form of settling accounts with the previous system and its institutions through evaluation of the individuals (ie, either by judging them morally or by morally sanctioned deprivation of a part of their public rights, as well as barring them from certain positions).

2. The representatives of the opposite camp within the former solidarity opposition view things from a completely different point of view, notwithstanding that they too regard the old system negatively, are aware of the non-sovereign character of the Polish state, and they are also aware that some institutions or sub-systems (such as the legal system or the mass media) used to perform negative functions as well. Nevertheless, evaluation

of the system by this party is not automatically carried over to the evaluation of people. Although the past system imposed some unavoidable boundaries to individuals' activity (boundaries which, at the most, one could try to extend, as frequently happened), the activity of individuals is nevertheless open to different estimations and to a whole range of possible evaluations, from condemnation of deeds and behaviour, or downright contempt, to regarding them as neutral, or decent, or praiseworthy. Thus the potential demarcation line is drawn differently each time. It is not a line separating those to be blamed for the past system, as well as their allies, from the pure and innocent, but a line separating blameworthy individuals and behaviours from those who acted decently or even in ways that should be praised. The line is not drawn automatically, according to the degree of closeness (or distance) of an individual from a given institution or milieu, from one of the two central and fundamental institutions that used to mark the two spheres of the past reality, two domains of public and social life, ie, the institutions of the mono-party and its polar counterpart, the institution of the Roman Catholic church. The line follows, in a way, the whole range of institutions and sub-systems and is marked by some particular attitudes and behaviours in the definite socio-historical conditions that then existed.

II

Advocates and executors of moral lustration made their position manifest already in the mid-1980s when speculations began about writers' and intellectuals' offences under the communist regime. This applied to anyone who had "collaborated" with the system in one way or another, for example, by accepting communist commissions. This kind of behaviour was given the name of "home disgrace"[10] and that meant that it became the subject of moral condemnation by those who either viewed themselves as free from any blame or otherwise excused themselves on the grounds of having been "lured by communism" only temporarily, or also freed themselves from guilt on the simple ground that they were not born in the Stalinist era or started their adult life only after the turning-point of August 1980.

The way of thinking that manifested itself in these years was reflected in the draft lustration-decommunisation acts, mentioned above. The two most radical versions stipulated that a ban on the performance of specified functions or occupation of particular positions - for a period of fifteen years or without any time limitations - be introduced for individuals who had worked for institutions connected to the apparatus of repression and direct violence, as well as individuals holding any posts whatsoever in two organizations: the PPR (the Polish Workers' Party - closely allied with Moscow) operating until 1949, and its follower, the PZPR (the Polish United Workers' Party which was founded after the fusion of the PPR and the old social democratic party PPS - the Polish Socialist Party).

It is characteristic that the period liable to lustration was extended from 1944 up to 1990, without any differentiation between the period of physical elimination of political opponents and the armed underground, the years of the Stalinist terror, and the period of the so-called "small stabilization" during the time of Gomułka. What reasoning and ethical-moral evaluation underlies this lustration project? It is worth looking at it through the prism of the implications of such an undertaking. For example, on the radical version of the proposal, in a lustrated Poland neither Leszek Kołakowski nor a considerable body of the members of the opposition KOR (Committee for Workers' Defence), nor an ordinary member of the PZPR at the level of a village community or a factory, would be allowed to become a dean or vice chancellor of a university or even a member of a local council. Also characteristic of this version of the proposal was the apparent amnesia about the activity of PAX, the institution which had helped to legitimize and establish the former system, particularly under the leadership of Bolesław Piasecki, when it declared itself an organization of Roman Catholics actively co-operating in the construction of socialism. It consistently and ruthlessly attacked the revolt of 1956, both within the party itself and on a national scale, as well as the revolt of students and intellectuals in March 1968. Moreover, it zealously undermined the position of the Church.

If we assume that the advocates of the lustration-decommunisation proposals consciously drew the demarcation line thus and not otherwise, between those thrown into infamy or social ostracism and those regarded as innocent or deserving forgiveness, we should consider what kind of arguments and moral schemata must have underlain such a division. We can assume the makers of the proposal did not mean to eliminate their political or ideological rivals from the hitherto united camp of the anti-communist opposition, but that the proposal has some deeper (moral) grounding.

Overall there are two lines of argument. According to the first, the PRL was not a sovereign state, but had been a Soviet occupation zone and therefore the security service, the military command and the whole structure of the PPR and PZPR, including its lowest level authorities (only excluding the rank and file, who never had any serious functions) constituted - over the whole post-war period - a Soviet agency that executed foreign violence using Polish hands. They are therefore guilty of high treason, and this justifies the imposition of moral and political infamy on those people who - by participating in these organizations - allowed this to occur. The axiological foundations of such a verdict are in part clear enough: national independence is a supreme value and therefore all those who ever violated the supreme value should be deprived of certain of their public rights. An interesting, though puzzling, aspect of the lustration proposal is, however, that it does not include the *Sejm* of the Polish People's Republic among the incriminated institutions, although it was made up of the representatives of the PZPR as well as members of the so-called allied parties, the Catholic political organizations (PAX in the first place) and non-party members. One might have thought that from the point of view of the betrayal of the supreme value, greater blame ought to attach to a former member of the facade *Sejm* who typically consented submissively to whatever regulations or moves the executive authorities made. Such a person might more properly be charged with treason and legitimization of foreign occupation than a party member holding a post in some provincial production enterprise.

These accumulating doubts can be partly clarified by the second line of reasoning which underlay the lustration proposal and constitutes, it seems, the necessary complement to the first argument. This reasoning starts from the claim that "Communism is a criminal system" (S. Niesiołowski, a leading member of the ZChN, the National-Christian Union), *ergo* whoever had ever enrolled in the institution had identified with the communist ideology and has or had a part in the crime (at least in a moral sense). Therefore each member of the former communist party, or its present-day heir, is covered in the same infamy. Communism is the quintessence of evil and some part of that evil sticks to anyone who had ever acceded to this ideology. It becomes his permanent flaw.

We shall not consider certain matters - seemingly insignificant from the point of view of the advocates of lustration and our present study - namely whether and when the PZPR had been a communist party at all, or the even more interesting suggestion that, instead of proposing lustration and decommunisation, the proposed law should be extended to prohibit the activity of communist parties, that is to say, those parties which, for example, do not accept parliamentary democracy, encourage the dissolution of the national state, proclaim the abolition of private property, or, say, tend in the direction of a military or some other authoritarian form of government, etc. A question that remains worthy of consideration, though, is the repeated denigration of Leszek Kołakowski (by recalling the communist episode in his biography), or the attempt to make Jacek Kuroń responsible for the Soviet camps and the Lubianka and Kolyma prisons (as implied in statements by Father Rydzyk, head of the ultra-Catholic "Radio Maria").

It does not seem a valid or adequate explanation of this constant harping on the past and throwing around of allegations, to suggest that it simply results from the intention to disqualify political and ideological opponents, or authorities representing a totally or partially different ideological option. Such behaviours have their source and justification in the sphere of moral ideas. These ideas are the following. Whoever has ever once stained himself by accepting communist ideology and has therefore betrayed the two values, his faith and his nation, expressed in the concise formula: "Polak-Katolik" (Pole-Catholic), has thus permanently lost a third value, namely "honour", and therefore cannot occupy any position of "authority" (certainly not moral authority, and perhaps also intellectual authority). For it is "honour" that distinguishes, and is therefore the ground for acknowledging, merit. At this point there appears the problem - interesting from an ethical point of view - of stating what is blameworthy and what is praiseworthy. Praiseworthy is faithfulness to the values mentioned above, blameworthy is staining oneself, even if temporarily, and even in good faith. This point of view is clearly illustrated, for example, by remarks in the magazine *Arka*, by the critic Bohdan Pociej. On the margin of his remarks about Jarosław Iwaszkiewicz (an outstanding writer but also, for many years under communism, the president of the official Polish Writers' Union) he poses two questions quite explicitly: "Are writers, artists who had once had the misfortune to participate in or experience communist rule in the Polish People's Republic, to be reproached for their not so very great faults? Would it not be better to forgive them in the Christian manner and let their past be forgotten? The answer to the second question" according to Pociej, "follows from the answer to the first. Every single, even the tiniest, part in the strengthening of the communist evil (...) by a public person - and every writer or artist is such a person - cannot be totally forgotten: it ought to be recalled and noted scrupulously in the historical records - for the sake of at least some moral satisfaction. Today perhaps their role can and maybe even should be forgiven. Forgiveness, however, is not in the least identical with forgetting" (Pociej, 1994: 137).[11] The motivation that led anyone to participate is irrelevant. In any event, according to the lustrators such people's motivations had been thoroughly low, mercenary or opportunist.[12] Nor does it matter what the accused actually *did* in the public sphere, nor what was the possible quality of what they used to do as artists or scientists, and therefore it does not matter whether they unmasked the "corrupt and lying" language of the official propaganda, to use the words of the poet, Zbigniew Herbert. It also does not matter what they might have done when they stopped taking part in "strengthening the communist evil". Both blameworthiness and praiseworthiness were quite radically separated: the basic criterion for blameworthiness was "opening oneself" to the "people's rule", while the criterion for praiseworthiness (understood in some indefinite way) was loyalty to the leading values.

Let us return to the question of the validity of the ethical ideas of the executors of moral lustration and the advocates of the radical proposal of legal lustration and decommunisation. At the basis of their reasoning there is some form of the ethics of values, which introduces a clear order and does not allow any relativization of values or any possible plurality of values of the same level of hierarchical importance (as is stipulated in, for example, the ethics of values of N. Hartmann). As a matter of fact the proposal does not involve gradations (which might be made according to the level of suffering experienced when defending one's manifested attachment to these values). The necessary condition for the estimation of one's attitude or one's moral merit is non-departure from two supreme values (united in the phrase "Polak-Katolik" (Pole-Catholic)). That is why, though a man who - even if only episodically - departed from them might be forgiven, he is not able to accumulate the merit that would allow him to be treated as a "moral authority". This kind of moral thinking, which puts in the first place the requirement of non-departure from the supreme values can, on the one hand, lead to some apparent moral paradoxes, and, on the other, force one to a particular interpretation of the past reality.

One such paradox is the fact that the requirement necessary for a holistic "moral attitude" and deserving of moral praise will be fulfilled by what Adam Michnik calls the "cautious-unblemished ones", and not by those who, for example, in March 1968 "incautiously" enough - risking repression and imprisonment - articulated their opposition to the system, to the limitation of freedom, even though they had earlier been burdened with the flaw.[13] This seems paradoxical only in the light of a different moral attitude - for example, that represented by Adam Michnik - but not according to the radical version of an ethics of virtue or an ethics of values;[14] it does not lead to any paradox on the basis of the moral ideas of the advocates of moral lustration. As virtually any ethical system would affirm, the praiseworthiness of such a posture, which warrants attribution of moral merit, cannot be assured simply by the level of risk, sacrifices or self-denial undertaken. Its measure is the value in the name of which the sacrifices or denials were made (though not every ethical system will endorse the same value). Revisionists (or the leaders of the Prague Spring or the Polish March of 1968) opposed the system in the name of reforming it and extending freedom within it, and not in the name of the abolition of communism (as the quintessence of evil),[15] nor in the name of national independence. Therefore, though their deeds and attitudes might warrant some more or less positive moral evaluation, still they would be regarded as more mediocre than deeds or attitudes in the service of the supreme values, and - as was done in Czechoslovakia - they ought to be subject to moral ostracism on the basis of a lustration law. Therefore deeds cannot wipe out the earlier "self-tarnishing". There is no need to consider - in terms of their moral value - the possible meaning of these deeds and activities for the possibility of realization - in the later period - of the supreme values themselves.

In order to eliminate possible accusations of incoherence in the moral thinking of advocates of moral lustration, we ought to correlate with it their image of the incriminated PRL reality and the events taking place in it, so that, firstly, the whole period would reveal itself as having one unchanging characteristic in all its phases, as a reality that is not subject to any significant evolution (and therefore an image must be created that would not introduce any differentiation between the period of mass terror and physical elimination of potential opponents, and the period of political repression, persecution and secret murders in the 1980s); secondly, a re-evaluation of the image of the past reality must take place, so that less historical significance is attributed to people and actions expressing opposition to the system, though not in the name of the supreme value. As a result of that re-evaluation, first place ought to be given to attitudes and activities directed to attaining the supreme values.

Such diversity in schemes of moral thinking will for long remain a source of different approaches to the history of the PRL. A major feature of the system of moral thinking analysed here is the estimation of subjects and actions, first of all through the prism of whether they realize the supreme values, or betray them, and thus realize some anti-values.[16] Of secondary significance are the actual activities and attitudes of the subjects, as revealed in their immediate relations with other people (of course, at issue here are behaviours and attitudes revealed in the course of being a "public figure", or also participating in various kinds of political decisions or conflicts). The basic point of reference for the moral subject is therefore the values and not the remaining moral co-subjects. Also characteristic is rejection of the possibility of a serious analysis of possible motives or of the ideological basis for the "departure" from the values regarded as supreme, or speaking directly, the proclamation of anti-values. In Poland, such analyses were made for the first time by Czesław Miłosz in his work *The Captive Mind*, where he wrote about the "Hegelian bite" when referring to the intellectuals' attraction to communism. Also ignored is the problem of the length of time during which a given community, organization or institution should bear responsibility for crimes of the past (eg, Jacek Kuroń for the Kolyma camp, Roman Catholics for the night of St Bartholomew, or Jews for the murder of Jesus Christ).

III

Let us now consider the opponents of moral lustration. In this case we shall also make the assumption that it is not their intention to cover up their own past (particularly since, among those who have reacted most intensely against this practice are people who were never members of the structures of the past system, and in the times of the first Solidarity were frequently the ideological leaders or spiritual patrons of that movement). From the point of view of the advocates of moral lustration, one could ask whether the moral consciousness of their opponents was not burdened with the cardinal defect of being unable to differentiate between good and evil. Is their moral thinking so radically latitudinarian or permissive that they are unable to recognize what deserves to be condemned? This would be most peculiar since they often use the same or analogous terms as their opponents, terms such as "honour" and "dignity", and they have never questioned such values as national independence or the Christian faith. Rejecting (or suspending) such suppositions, let us try to explain what kind of scheme of moral thinking is shared by a larger part of the opponents of moral lustration, or at least the opponents of the methods of its execution which have been suggested or realized. We shall also make an additional assumption, which can be confirmed in the statements of the critics of the lustration activities of interest for us, that they agree with their opponents (or sometimes vehement enemies) that the PRL had not been a sovereign state and that "communism was a criminal system". Despite this far-reaching similarity, the opponents of lustration take a totally different position when judging the praiseworthiness or blameworthiness of human undertakings; they draw the demarcation line differently between what is base and what is worthy of moral praise.

The moral thinking of the opponents of the lustrators' concepts and actions differs in several respects from the manner of thinking of the advocates of this kind of undertaking. One of the fundamental differences is probably that the former make the very *subjects* of moral actions the central point of moral evaluations, ranking the institutions and organizations as secondary. And behaviour and attitudes are evaluated, not directly in relationship to ultimate values, but first of all from the point of view of their immediate importance for others, as well as their meaning from the perspective of other positive values than the two enumerated as supreme by the advocates of lustration. Thus the moral thinking of the opponents of lustration does not dispense with values, but the system of values is not strictly hierarchical so as to differentiate one or two supreme values. Rather, it accepts a multiplicity of positive values (or high values), frequently of the same rank. Those two specific qualities of the moral thinking of the opponents - making the evaluation of the moral attitudes and behaviour of others the main point of reference,[17] and introduction of a variety of positive values (apart from, say, independence these will be, for example, freedom, justice, and probably also some other values) - carry certain important consequences along with them, when it comes to the possibility of differentiating between moral behaviours and, in the light of that, differentiating moral appraisals.

When looking for some suitable frameworks that existing ethical theories could offer, frameworks that would best allow us to characterize the ways of moral thinking of the opponents of moral lustration (at least in its hitherto proposed and realized forms), it is worth referring to two concepts. One of them is the concept of ontic duty formulated in the 1930s by Herbert Spielberg (Spielberg, 1989). The concept can be situated in the circle of the phenomenological ethics of values and can be regarded as a necessary theoretical basis for the concept of "metaphysical guilt", as presented by Jaspers in his famous post-war studies of the "problem of guilt". The other concept which allows us to reconstruct the mode of thought of the opponents of moral lustration is the concept of supererogatory acts (usually defined as acts beyond the call of duty), or more precisely, the classification of moral activities developed by this theory.

The following features of the theory of "ontic obligation" (*ontisches Sollen*) ought to be listed as valid from the point of view of the present study. The theory treats as primary, not duties[18] (Spielberg, 1935) or values, but "morally required [conditions or] states of affairs" (*Sollverhalt*, a shorter version of *Sollsachverhalt*), and therefore states of the world which ought to occur. Such a "morally required state of affairs" is, for example, a "situation in which peace prevails", "a situation in which there is no persecution", or a "situation in which there is freedom", or a "situation in which there are no concentration camps with gas chambers", or one in which "extermination camps do not exist". In introducing the notion of "ontic obligation" Spielberg departs from thinking in terms of the categories of commands and prescriptions, fulfilment or neglect of duties. The notion of ontic obligation contains therefore the possibility of thinking about obligations as existing even where - as is often the case - there is no particular addressee for whom that obligation would become a duty.[19] It is only through the prism of the conception of "ontic obligation" that it is possible to understand Jaspers' notion of "metaphysical guilt" (as distinct from - let us recall - "criminal", "political", and "moral" guilt).[20] On the one hand, the way of thinking about "ethical obligation" suggested by Spielberg (like Jaspers' notion of "metaphysical guilt") lifts from concrete individuals, as it were, the need to engage in this or any other moral act. On the other hand, it deprives each individual of an easy self-justification according to which the undertaking of some activity (this or another moral act) was not, after all, *my* duty and therefore my peace of mind can rest undisturbed.

The conception of "ontic obligation" introduces still other elements to moral thinking, which are essential from the point of view of the problem of moral lustration. First, the conception anticipates the simultaneous existence of a multiplicity of "ontic obligations". Thus, instead of two supreme values which "await" realization, we have a multiplicity of "morally required states of affairs", each of them with a varying degree of intensity, where one's activity in aid of one may collide with the possibility of undertaking action to realize another.[21] Secondly, the conception of "morally required states of affairs" introduces the notion of the "degree of intensity of the obligatoriness of the state of affairs". This means that the degree of obligation, so to speak, increases as the gap widens between the "ideally required condition" and the "real state". And so, for example, the greater the limitations to freedom, the more relevant a given ideal state becomes - for example, a "state of freedom of speech", contrasted with the real state of affairs. According to the above principle, in the period of the Stalinist terror the "morally required state of affairs", denoted as a "state in which one's political opponents are not sentenced to death or long term imprisonment" was a matter of much greater intensity than in the time of the "small stabilization" of Gomułka's rule, when the "morally required state of affairs", for example "the existence of freedom of speech," was a matter of greater intensity than, for example, in the times of Gierek, or in the post-martial law period.

Most important for the conception of "ontic obligation" is also the category of the "possibilities of realization of the 'required state of affairs'", as well as the category of the "immediate urgency of the 'required state of affairs'". The first of these categories probably does not require closer characterization. The impossibility of realization of a given "required state of affairs" does not take away its obligatory character, but it can decide about its immediacy. And so, for example, the accusation against the participants in the Prague Spring, or those taking part in the Polish protests of March 1968, that they fought merely for freedom of cultural activity and not national independence, seems to lose its impact in the light of the moral thinking proposed by Spielberg, for the impossibility of realizing the "required state of affairs" of national independence was clear to both the active participants in the protest movements and to those who were "untainted", the onlookers who kept waiting for that independence. The first nevertheless undertook some attempt to contribute to the realization of at least one of a number of "morally required states of affairs"; they did contribute to realizing it, however partially.

It seems to me that the sorts of categories and differentiations that are introduced by the conception of "ontic obligation" can be observed in the moral considerations of the past epoch led by the opponents of haphazard lustrations, and they are decisive about the way people's attitudes and behaviours should be evaluated.

In order to fully reconstruct the moral sensibility of the opponents of moral lustration, it is in my opinion necessary also to take into consideration the manner of classification of activities and evaluation of attitudes proposed by defenders of the conception of supererogatory acts (calls beyond duty). The problem of the call beyond duty has been discussed at least since the Reformation. The modern discussion, in secular ethics, of the rightness of distinguishing supererogation as a separate category of moral activities was originated by Urmson's paper "Saints and Heroes" (Urmson, 1958). Without entering the numerous debates on this conception and the subtleties of particular propositions, let us only point out two elements of the conception "supererogation". The basic consequence of introducing the notion of supererogation is a rejection of the threefold classification of moral activities, which distinguishes only between activities that are required, prohibited or morally neutral. The defenders of the conception of supererogation point out that this threefold classification does not accord with our actual way of classifying activities, since we speak, after all - for example in the case of heroic deeds or acts of saintliness - of acts of high moral value, which at the same time are not morally required and therefore exceed the scope of duty, but - as a matter of fact - do contribute to the realization of some "morally required state of affairs". Therefore there is a category of moral activities which it is morally praiseworthy to realize, yet not morally blameworthy not to (as it would be in the case of activities dictated by duty). The first significant aspect of the concept of supererogation - from the point of view of this study - is its rejection of the dichotomous scheme according to which an activity can be either good only or bad only, or at the most indifferent and therefore to be included as if beyond the spectrum of moral appraisal. The rejection of that scheme and the introduction of the category of acts of supererogation is possible owing to (a) breaking the good/ought-to-be tie up, that is, resignation from that mode of thought which directly derives duty from "the good" or "the good" from duty, and (b) introduction of an additional dimension of evaluation of activities in the categories of "praiseworthiness" and "blameworthiness".

The other element of the conception of supererogation, in the non-standard version as presented by Gregory Mellema (Mellema, 1991) which should be attended to in the context of discussions of "lustration", is the notion of quasi-supererogation and quasi-offence. Supererogation denotes an act which is, as we know, not the fulfilment of a duty, that is to say, nobody can demand the fulfilment of this act from anyone; yet it is morally correct, while its abandonment is not morally blameworthy (a classic example is that of a soldier throwing himself on a grenade in order to save his fellows). Let us add that its praiseworthiness follows from the fact that it realizes or contributes to the realization of a certain "morally required state". If we accept the validity of talking about supererogation, then, as Mellema suggests, it seems legitimate to differentiate the elements of the category "offence". A quasi-offence involves:

1. doing something that is not forbidden
2. yet is considered blameworthy, while
3. abstaining from it is not a glorious deed.

An important element of the concept is that it allows gradation of evaluations, in accordance with which transgressions of increasing degrees of blameworthiness pass over into the category of forbidden acts, while supererogation, though it becomes increasingly praiseworthy, does not become obligatory.

The moral thinking of opponents of lustration doubtless resembles the conception of "morally required states of affairs" and the gradation of evaluations allowed within the supererogation theory; from this follows opposition to haphazard, dichotomous judgments of guilt and moral purity. The second element which determines their moral thinking is the consideration, not of isolated acts but of whole series, a whole range of acts, as stipulated by the conception of the "disjunctive-act". Thus when linking this conception with the conception of "morally required states of affairs" we can say that if someone has never undertaken any activity towards realization of one of the "morally required states of affairs" - addressed to no one in particular (as for example, the "state of freedom of speech") - he is guilty of a certain omission, though this is not yet blameworthy in itself. However, the estimation of someone's posture can - in the eyes of the opponents of moral lustration - undergo some change if a person who has so far successfully practised the tactics of non-commitment in the realization of "morally required states of affairs" - at the same time eagerly taking advantage of controlled goods, eg, scholarships or research grants - then suddenly puts on the airs of a prosecutor or becomes a "guardian of values".

The above brief survey of the essential determinants of the manner of moral thinking of the opponents of moral lustration reveals that, apart from some praiseworthy and very praiseworthy deeds (contribution to, acts in aid of, realization of "morally required states of affairs"), we shall obviously be confronted with what we may call wickedness, ie, the activity of those who had actively contributed to the condemnation, "mud throwing", repressing of those who had endeavoured to realize "morally required states of affairs". These we have decided not to consider in our discussion. There is a point between those extreme positions which separates "offences" from "supererogation". That point is very dangerous, since around it oscillates what is given the name of "ordinary human decency" but also what is given the name of "pharisaism".[22] There is only one protection against pharisaism, as is argued in the writings of Father Tischner, Professor I. Lazari-Pawłowska, and Adam Michnik: Let us not fall into self-admiration simply on the grounds of our having been "decent", nor let us fall into it when we have just been decent in times when decency was difficult.

IV

In conclusion, let us consider two problems put forward at the beginning of our study. Firstly, which of the reconstructed ways of moral thinking more accords with the principle of the rule of the law? Secondly, let us consider some connotations of the idea of decommunisation to which its advocates refer as well as the arguments with which they seek to justify their endeavours. In the light of these considerations we should be able to answer the question whether the idea of decommunisation can be realized.

The following form of reasoning appears characteristic of opponents of lustration and decommunisation: there was a certain reality which justified speaking of limited freedom of choice and was to a certain extent objective, independent of the will of individuals, independent to a considerable degree even of the wills of those who stood at the head of the hierarchy, since dependence on the USSR was an objective fact, which for several decades was swathed in an almost complete taboo (and that so far-going, that even the greatest public institution which was not integrated into the system, the Catholic Church, did not try at that time either to unmask this dependence or to unmask the very perpetrators of this dependence, the USSR, as an "evil empire"). The fact of dependence was obvious to everyone and represented an objective limit to every sort of activity at various levels. That is why people and their acts must be judged - according to the opponents of lustration and decommunisation - according to what people and institutions actually did in concrete historical circumstances and according to whether they contributed to any "morally required state of affairs". The fact of acting in conditions of limited freedom is - on this view - a circumstance which must influence the assessment of acts and behaviour, a circumstance which limits the scope of what one can expect of individuals, even though, of course, it is not a circumstance which justifies any action or omission whatsoever. The subject of moral evaluation is, moreover, in the first place an individual, and not a group. It is also characteristic of the mode of reasoning of opponents of decommunisation to put a positive criterion in first place, which requires that in regard to the behaviour of individuals one should have primary regard to what they did in the framework of the social-political reality which was as a whole a reality which in large part rendered impossible the realization of the level of a "morally called-for state of affairs". Moral thought directs itself to seeking out what was positive in the acts and attitudes of concrete individuals.[23]

The moral thinking of representatives of lustration and decommunisation appears also to embody a certain sort of maximalism and moral perfectionism which is, perhaps, highly valuable in times when there is a need to awaken preparedness to undertake heroic tasks, and thus in so-called "extreme situations", but which does not much lend itself to consensual regulation of common life in a normal, pluralist reality.[24] This type of thought starts from the highest values, placing high moral demands on individuals and, it appears, not allowing the view (at least not allowing it to the degree that it contradicts this type of thinking) that, quite apart from the intentions and will of individuals, the state of the real world might constitute a justification for certain acts or omissions. That one finds oneself in the sphere of dependence on the USSR thus does not work to justify anyone's accepting that fact - by participating in the structures of the system - but is even an incriminating circumstance. The moral thinking of supporters of lustration and decommunisation, taking as a starting point values or virtues which make strong moral demands, focusses on what is negative, what does not manage to attain those standards, on what, according to those standards, deserves to be condemned, whether it is found in the reality itself, in the system, or in people's behaviour. The consequence of this moral position, its focus on detecting evil, first of all in the system and in the institutions and individuals connected with it, is in turn the hasty auto-glorification of the lustrators and decommunisers themselves - as those who deserve moral acclaim on the grounds, and perhaps only on the grounds, that in their self-consciousness, they never identified with that system (though it may well have been the case that in those times they gave no public sign of this).[25]

Prominent in the moral thinking of opponents of lustration and decommunisation is unwillingness to draw clear, unambiguous lines between what is morally to be condemned and what deserves moral praise. This unwillingness, in turn, prevents them from hastily demanding praise for the fact simply that, behaving also as "moral pawns", they did not betray their "sense of good taste"[26] by "taking part in" "that" reality. Reluctance to draw a sharp and clear line between that which deserves moral condemnation and that which deserves moral praise, by no means suggests complete resignation from the possibility of holding legally accountable persons guilty of illegal acts or atrocities (for example, against political opponents). Distaste for sharp and unambiguous line-drawing is not a sign of absence of a moral sense. It results, first of all, from the realization that the past reality was more complicated than those who think in terms of moral dichotomies (good - bad; worthy of praise - worthy of blame) acknowledge, that the moral evaluation of actors and extras must be more nuanced; and thirdly at last, it results from the consciousness of insecurity that accompanies the mixing of legal judgment with judgments from a moral point of view.

There is an essential difference between the moral thinking of the advocates of lustration and decommunisation, and that of their opponents.

The former betrays a tendency to extend the range of persons and institutions subject to moral censure and, as a result, liable to civil, political, or criminal responsibility, while the other party tries to limit the range to cases of evident breaches of the law, lawless acts or atrocities, in other words cases of infringement upon "protected goods". Is the above difference in moral thinking of any significance from the point of view of the idea of the rule of the law, or may it be that the types of moral thinking and forms of moral consciousness I have analysed are of no concern from the point of view of building an order based upon the principle of the rule of law? The suggestion ought to be rejected. The kind of moral thinking more in accord with the idea of the rule of law is that of the opponents of lustration and decommunisation. This follows from at least two qualities of this kind of thinking:

(a)　a clear commitment to the principle of legality and,

(b)　the tendency to separate clearly "legality" and "morality".

Thus, a feature of thinking in accordance with the principle of legality is putting limits to the sphere of responsibility, and this follows from the fact that, first, according to the idea of the rule of the law one can be held liable only for things envisaged as offences by that law; secondly, one can be held responsible only for one's deeds and not for one's attitude, even if the latter is met with moral disapproval; thirdly, only an individual, and not a group, can be held responsible, and then only if he or she has legally guaranteed rights of self-defence in a court of law.

However, a doubt may arise whether the principles of legality can be applied in the special circumstances of the transitional period from the communist reality to the post-communist reality? Is it therefore not justified to depart from strict legality and

(a)　carry out decommunisation on the model of denazification realized in post-war Germany, as some decommunisers favour, or

(b)　following some pragmatic (and not ideological-moral) options, to apply the principle of group responsibility in some limited sense and restrict the rights and privileges of a particular group of people?

Let us consider the first variant. For the authors of the above analogy, according to which "decommunisation" is to be a counterpart of "denazification", an easy and adequate solution seems to be the characterization of the communist mono-party as a criminal organization, following the model of the classification executed by the International Military Trial at Nuremberg against the NSDAP,[27] the next step would be the "purification" of the institutions and the political-administrative sphere, by excluding the individuals responsible for the existence, and aiding the functioning, of the past system. One could say that this sort of characterization of the mono-party, the central institution of the past system, would correspond to commonly held opinions, expressed by some part of the society.[28] On the other hand, on closer scrutiny of the analogy between decommunisation and denazification posed by the decommunisers, it becomes clear that the authors of this sort of analogy either lack the most elementary knowledge of the practical circumstances, qualities and legal-theoretical complications of the post-war trials of the Nazi system, or they are involved in conscious manipulation, counting - more or less legitimately - on a lack of adequate knowledge in their electorates and among the wider public, as well as on the persuasive force of the suggested analogy.

It is necessary to remember two things. First, denazification was inscribed in the broader context of sanctions against Nazi Germany and was in itself a complement - demanded by an International Tribunal, let us add - to charges of crimes against peace, war crimes, and crimes against humanity. Without that broader context, without legally justified charges of criminal activities on a scale unimaginable by world opinion and with an unimaginable level of premeditated cruelty, denazification could only have been treated as a move which was supposed to eliminate a politically and ideologically defeated enemy. Analogies between the postulated decommunisation and denazification of Nazi Germany are therefore in this respect imperfect, since an operation requiring the passing of a decommunisation law (which would eliminate a certain group of people from political life) would lack the necessary broader context, necessary for bringing to court the leaders of "criminal organizations", responsible for, say, "crimes against humanity". To the extent that the last leaders of the Eastern Bloc countries, eg, Jaruzelski, Gorbachev, Zhivkov or maybe even Honecker might be charged in this way, most probably the idea would not find any understanding in the world nor win public acclaim.[29]

Secondly, the advocates of decommunisation law, drawing analogies between nazism and communism and calling for similar measures after the fall of communism as had been undertaken after the fall of nazism, seem not to realize the fact (or maybe they dismiss it as a negligible matter) that the denazification campaign comprised the whole population of Germany. And so, for example, in the American zone all adult persons (over 18 years of age) were obliged to make a formal detailed declaration as to their career before the war as well as their activity during it. Every adult member of German society therefore found him or herself a potential suspect; besides, the regulations introduced stated, among other things, that "external signs are not adequate proof; membership in the NSDAP, but also lack of any membership, were not enough for consideration of each particular case. Some kind of 'evidence of innocence' had to be submitted" (Ryszka, 1982: 293). Thus if we draw any analogies between the Nazi system and the post-war reality in Poland, saying that both of these totalitarian systems were equally "criminal", we ought to agree in consequence to accept the position of co-partners in crime, potentially responsible for the functioning of the totalitarian system still liable to prove our innocence (unless we had "arrived on American tanks", to use Jacek Kuroń's words). Maybe decommunisation carried out in this way would find a certain number of followers, convinced of their own political-moral immaculateness; yet the degree of general negative estimation of this sort of enterprise would doubtless not be lower than that of the post-war German society against denazification. In a situation when there is no external occupation administration that could supervise the execution of this kind of procedure it is bound to be a total failure. When drawing some loose associations between denazification and decommunisation, let us remember that the Nuremberg Trials and denazification were, on the one hand, directed against the whole country, its core institutions and the whole population of Germany, and on the other hand, in the case of both procedures it was, despite everything, necessary to determine the personal responsibility of each accused individual and every single suspect, taking into consideration any of their deeds or activities liable to legal and moral condemnation. The only clear analogy between denazification and decommunisation activities depends on the fact that in both cases the advocates of the above undertakings were clearly motivated by their moral disapproval of the particular ideologies and the social-political realities established upon the basis of them.

A clear moral foundation can also be traced in the justification of decommunisation presented by Andrzej Zybertowicz, which it is necessary to mention, even though its author does not draw any clear analogies with the denazification campaign and stipulates that "the aim of lustration and decommunisation is not the reparation of moral wrongs or implementation of 'historical justice'" (Zybertowicz, 1993: 9). The argument he presents is intended as a pragmatic-socio-technical study, with the principle of reasons of state lying at the basis of lustration and decommunisation. The justification of legal prohibition of the holding of certain public posts by certain persons was to be the "justified suspicion that a given person, considering his biography, could be susceptible to blackmail or bribery by, or ideological sympathies with, enemies of the state" (*ibid*: 12). Let us pass over the associations with practices of the Stalinist and Gomułka periods, when the accusation of "ideological sympathies with enemies of the state" would lead to the elimination and/or persecution of suspected individuals or groups, or at least their prohibition from participation in the public sphere.[30] On the one hand, Zybertowicz's justification of lustration and decommunisation is not to be an expression of any "moral settling of accounts with the past", but is supposed to "create conditions for the future" (*ibid*: 150). On the other hand, Zybertowicz admits openly that his reasoning, rooted in the postulated decommunisation statutes, would "assume collective guilt" (*ibid*: 160). The moral motivation and the pragmatic premises are linked with each other in the suggested justification, and only when thus entwined do they lend persuasive force to Zybertowicz's argumentation. When considered separately, however, both aspects of the justification of decommunisation seem to be most unconvincing.

Let us first look at the pragmatic aspect. When speaking of decommunisation, the justification of which is supposed to be necessary to "create the social basis on which to build a democratic state of the rule of the law based upon principles of a modern market economy" (*ibid*: 150), Zybertowicz refers to historical-sociological studies on failures in the building of "healthy market economies in Third World countries" and then he draws an analogy between the situation of those countries and the present system of relationships in the post-communist reality. Students of Third World countries, Zybertowicz writes, "point out that one of the main obstacles [to the making of a healthy market economy] is the social tissue those countries have inherited from the pre-capitalist forms of social order. For example, traditional tribal ties hinder the development of a work ethic and respect for legal norms, which are a necessary context for any modern market. Ever-present corruption and nepotism paralyse a country's ability to guarantee the proper development of the rules of the market. Likewise, the post- *nomenklatura* system constitutes the residue of forms of social relationships that foster the development of lame, peripheral capitalism, dependent on foreign power centres" (*ibid*: 150-51). It follows from the above reasoning, which also refers to pragmatic arguments as well as to the analogy presented above, that in order to realize a particular socio-political goal in the Third World countries, ie, to create the basis for the development of a "healthy market economy", we would have to legally forbid individuals being dependent upon or moulded by "traditional tribal ties". Perhaps this idea would not be regarded as particularly wicked by the dictatorial, if progressively inclined (one might say enlightened) economic reformers of those backward economic systems, who do not particularly care for the "cultural achievement of universal significance" that - according to Martin Krygier - the rule of law represents.[31] The idea would, however, be regarded as a horrendous misunderstanding by a true advocate of the principle of the "rule of the law".

The concept of using a legal instrument that would put limits on the economic activity as well as the civil rights of given subjects, in order to create a basis for the "building of a healthy market economy" seems to be backed by the utopian belief that it is possible to create such conditions that would guarantee the making and development of a market economy without any morally disagreeable deformation, without corruption, fraud or injustice. The illusion that the above phenomena can be averted by not permitting "people with particular biographies" to conduct certain sorts of activity feeds on the assumption that it is their "background" or their *curriculum vitae* that influences the behaviour of the actors operating within a certain autonomous economic sub-system and not some imperatives inherent in that sub-system, such as the quest for profit, the element of competition, etc. The inactivity of these sorts of system imperatives may be, at the most, evidence that the sub-system never acquired adequate enough autonomy, and that it is excessively tied to the administrative and political sub-system. The necessary basis for building a "healthy market economy" seems rather to be created through the development of clear, precise and stable laws that regulate the autonomous functioning of the economic sub-system as well as its interactions with other sub-systems of a society, and not through establishing a "sieve" - in the form of a decommunisation law - that would ban from acting in the sub-system all those who have been formed, for example, through "the practice of functioning within a state in which respect for the law was a very distant consideration" (Zybertowicz, 1993: 156).

The deeper structure of the justification of decommunisation presented by Zybertowicz is, as the author concedes, mostly of a moral nature and refers the reader to the notion of "collective guilt". From the fact that certain persons functioned within certain institutions and structures of the past system - particularly those functioning within the so-called *nomenklatura* - one draws a particular moral evaluation of them, or, more precisely, a typological personality portrait of the "man of the *nomenklatura*": an "opportunist" personality with a "higher than average susceptibility to blackmail and a higher than average liability to illegal activity".

Even if the above negative *aretaic* judgment is in some respect sound psychologically and sociologically, an advocate of the idea of the rule of the law is still confronted with the total mystery of how it is possible - in the modern society we live in, since we do not happen to live in an ancient *polis* with an aristocratic system of rule - that the civil rights of a certain group of people could be limited on the grounds of the moral qualities attributed (or even determined "scientifically" on the basis of some detailed sociological and psychological research) to the typical representative of that group or milieu. According to the above concept, for example, all members of the Italian Christian Democratic party, after its many years of rule, would have to fall under a regulation prohibiting them from taking up particular positions, since the corruption of the leaders of that party, their opportunism and pursuit of private interests were a sociologically proven and widespread phenomenon. The idea of preventing individuals of dubious morals from taking up certain posts and performing certain functions is doubtless dear to all those who themselves try to follow high moral standards. However, the idea of translating moral concepts into legal codification and the introduction of the above prohibition in the form of law seems to be totally out of keeping with modern legal consciousness. It expresses an illusory nostalgia for a republic governed by the rule of virtue. Contrary to those illusions, we will probably have to resign ourselves to the fact that unless we want to pay the perhaps even higher price of trying to establish a "republic of virtue", crooks, opportunists, those liable to bribery and every other possible moral defect must be - *nolens volens* - admitted to public, political and economic spheres. Mere negative moral evaluation cannot be a sufficient ground for limiting civil rights.

It can be seen, then, that the postulate of decommunisation, which calls upon alleged analogies with the post-war denazification of Germany lacks the necessary broader context, ie, the legally grounded and proven accusation of apocalyptic crimes committed by the country and the institutions against which legal action is taken, while the argumentation on behalf of decommunisation that refers to some pragmatic premises or negative moral estimation of the typical representative of the *"nomenklatura"* does not meet the requirements of modern legal consciousness. On the basis of the reasoning so far, from the legal point of view it seems impossible to make a persuasive case for giving legal force to plans of decommunisation. However, it cannot be denied that in these plans there is an accurate intuition, namely that the past communist reality had numerous dark sides, deserving - at least - moral condemnation. However, the translation of that correct intuition into an accusation of moral and legal guilt and recommendation of concretely written-down responsibility for evil - in the sense accepted by the advocates of decommunisation - seems to be totally impossible and inconsistent with the principles of the rule of the law.

It also seems unlikely that a democratically elected Polish parliament will pass any extensive decommunisation acts that rest upon the justification presented by the advocates of this sort of idea. The fact that bills of this kind are not passed will doubtless be interpreted by the advocates of decommunisation as evidence of domination over the mass media, key economic institutions, and educational institutions by the representatives of the old *nomenklatura* and its allies, and thus as a proof of the correctness of their thesis that the post-*nomenklatura* is blocking change. For this reason, too, the advocates of the decommunisation bills might find themselves in a similar position to that once occupied by leftist intellectuals (for example, those from the circle of critical theory) who condemned the evil of the capitalist reality, perceived as stupefying minds and smothering with its mechanisms (among others, its mass culture) any potential criticism of that evil. One such mechanism turned out then to be the mechanisms of parliamentary democracy which, in the eyes of the critics, serve the preservation of the *status quo* and paralyse the ability to perceive evil and to identify its perpetrators and their collaborators. Democracy, the rule of the law and similar "civilizational achievements" thus appear as mechanisms to be blamed jointly for their inability to render "accounts of wrongs" to the public, as well as impediments to modernization. In this situation the investigators of moral and social evil have either to remain frustrated, or to resign themselves to the fact that evil cannot be completely eliminated; nor can harm inflicted be completely repaired - unless it escalates beyond a certain critical point, which provokes the turmoil of revolution. The only framework within which evil can be removed is, above all, that of the legality of a democratic state under the rule of law.

IV Postscript

Almost three years have passed since this chapter was first drafted. In the period of government by the coalition of ex-communists (SLD) and the Peasant Party (PSL), discussions on the theme of lustration and decommunisation ceased to be the focus of public opinion. It even seemed to me that the chapter had come merely to have historical value, that it had become mere documentation of certain distant quarrels. It is true that, on the initiative of one PSL representative and some from the opposition (from the Freedom Union and the Union of Labour), the former parliament began work on a lustration law, but this did not awaken any great emotion (perhaps outside the circle of parliamentarians and people keen to run for a position as senator or one of the highest departments of state). This lack of great emotions most probably resulted from the fact that the plan for this law - which the former *Sejm* passed at the end of its term (before the elections of 1997) - merely envisaged that candidates for either house of parliament would make a declaration stating whether they had or had not collaborated with the special services. Naturally enough, there were stormy debates among the parliamentarians about such concrete matters as the definition of conscious collaboration, the kinds of services collaboration with which should be exposed, and certain other - in sum, second rank - problems. These problems were second rank in the sense, first, that they only related to persons who wanted to make a political career, and secondly, that exposure of the fact of collaboration with the secret services of the PRL was in no way an obstacle to one's right to run as a member of the *Sejm* or Senate - the moral appraisal of that fact was left to the electors. From this point of view one can say that the lustration law was in no respect a means of "settling accounts", for it did not impose accountability on anyone nor was anyone threatened with suspension of basic civil rights. It was only intended to serve transparency in public life, that is, it allowed the exposure of facts by their nature secret, which naturally - and on this there was a far reaching consensus - should be known to electors.

The law also envisaged the calling of a special Lustration Court, which would be appointed by district judicial councils. Its task would be to verify the truth of the declarations made by candidates (sanctions were only applicable in the case of false declarations). Already before the elections, there were difficulties with the appointment of the twenty one judges who were to sit in the Lustration Court. It turned out that the judges were very reluctant to apply, but it also occurred that judges keen to accept the job (I might add that there were few of them) were not acceptable to their colleagues in the district gatherings of judges. Notwithstanding attempts to appoint judges to the Lustration Court, even after the deadline established by the law had elapsed, and notwithstanding clear pressure from the new governing team, appointment of the new organ was never achieved.

This fact was interpreted by the coalition of the right-wing, anticommunist, Solidarity Electoral Action (AWS) and the liberal-pragmatic group of *intelligentsia,* the Freedom Union (UW), as evidence of hostility to the new regime and testimony to the low moral standards of the judiciary.

AWS activists - including members of the government (specifically the Deputy Minister of Justice) - began an attack on the judiciary, without doubt aiming (as was openly stated by publicists of AWS) at creation of a particular atmosphere which would induce judges to "meet the needs of society". Such "meeting of the needs of society" should simply be understood as being at the disposal of the political leadership, acting in accordance with its political or ideological expectations.

On 17 December, 1997, a majority of the *Sejm* passed amedments to the law on the organization of courts of first instance. These amendments, whose fate is not yet determined, since it might be vetoed by the President, envisages removal from judicial work of those judges who in the years 1944-89 "handed down obviously unjust judgments, limited the rights of parties, unjustifiably closed proceedings to the public" (this concerns - in the opinion of the spokesman for this law and also the President of the Supreme Court, Adam Strzembosz - about 20 of around 6600 judges in Poland); on the basis of this law, earlier judges convicted of these named offences would also lose certain retirement benefits to which judges are entitled.

The above-mentioned changes have a twofold character. On the one hand, and on the basis of noble motives, it is a question of "coming to terms with the past" in the administration of justice. Equally important, on the other hand, and less nobly, but dictated by political interests, it is about subordinating the judiciary to the political leadership, *inter alia* by limiting "judicial self-government", as the unfortunate Deputy Minister of Justice has declared it his intention to do. Recently the judges themselves, shocked both by the offensive opinions the Deputy Minister had expressed about the whole judiciary and the lack of reaction about these pronouncements from the Minister (Hanna Suchocka from the UW) and the Prime Minister, responded with sharp criticism.

This aim of subordinating the judiciary is only, it appears, an element in the realisation of a more fundamental intention, that of the so-called moral conversion of the state and the society, which in consequence means the use of the state as an instrument for the realisation of the moral ideas of right-wing and national-Catholic groupings. The question of decommunisation has in a way now been put off until later. Decommunisation realised according to the original ambitions - for example, as prohibition of former members of the Party apparatus or of members of such earlier departments as censorship or counter-espionage, from performing specified state functions - would certainly fulfil the expectations of radically anti-communist groups or Catholic-nationalist formations. People who might have been affected by decommunisation in this sense have, however, either found themselves profitable engagements outside the sphere of positions which the state can affect (for example, in the private economy and in banks) or - like a proportion of members of the special services - are now among the loyal collaborators of right-wing groups, or are in the *Sejm* among that over thirty per cent representation won by the left in democratic elections (although this is certainly a rather small group, given the fairly young age of the SLD members).

Certainly, right-wing politicians still use the slogan of decommunisation, but today it has quite a different sense. For while five or six years ago, the promoters of decommunisation might still have been concerned about possible guilt and responsibililty for the former system, about depriving persons who had once performed certain functions of certain of their public rights, today decommunisation does not mean removal of *apparatchiks* from certain functions, but rather has to do with a struggle over a particular vision of the state, of law, of freedom and of individual rights. Under the slogan of decommunisation, which naturally is directed first of all against the present parliamentary opposion (against the SLD) a fight is being waged against a particular ideological option, namely the left-liberal option. As a way of distancing themselves from the former system, ever-younger representatives of the radical right put out the slogan of decommunisation and in their mouths it has a significance much more radical than what was formulated five or six years ago. Christian-nationalist groups suggest the delegalisation of the SLD, not even appealing to responsibility for the past but justifying such delegalisation on the basis that since this group fights with the Church and opposes the Church's postulates and demands in questions such as abortion, pornography, education and upbringing, it is simply "destroying the moral order ot the state". An extreme faction of the radical Right, the Republican League, also argues from the principle of "deduction from the concept": Communism was just as wicked as Nazism, and the SLD are post-communists, so one must treat them in the same way as the Nazis were treated in Germany after the Second World War.

The paradox lies in the fact, of which the ideologists of the radical right are certainly well aware, that the "post-communist" formation slated by them for delegalization - and certainly its parliamentary leadership - moved some time ago to a liberal position. In contemporary Polish conditions, liberal ways of thinking about the state, power, and thus about liberties, gain political support mainly - this perhaps sounds paradoxical - from the "post-communist" formation. Decommunisation is therefore basically a war with the "leftist, secular, liberal" option and the vision of the state represented by that option. Today there is a fundamental conflict precisely around the vision of the state, which not only will not weaken but will indeed strengthen (as several right-wing representatives state openly). The result of this conflict is not yet decided.

Of course, the proponents of decommunisation naturally intend to maintain the appearance of legality while realizing their desires. Thus the appearance of the "rule of law" would still be retained since the laws giving the state its new character are portrayed as conforming to it, for they have gained the acceptance of a democratically elected majority (though the "post-communist" president presents a poblem here, since by vetoing certain laws he might sometimes make it impossible to realize the wishes of the majority). Yet for the rule of law in contemporary conditions, something more is necessary and the "post-communists" at present in opposition are demanding that: what is needed is preservation of fundamental rights and freedoms. Will the desire to introduce a radical moral revolution by means of the measures available to the state not lead to violation of these rights and freedoms? It is hard to predict this unequivocally. Nevertheless it is without doubt worrying that spokesmen for decommunisation do not now speak of these basic rights and freedoms, even though they called precisely upon them when in their time they protested against the "communist" system.

One thing is certain. In an admittedly somewhat different form, in the form of conflicts over concrete laws of a structural-ideological character, we will continue to confront this same conflict, a conflict of two forms of moral consciousness, of which one is closer to the moral political conceptions of Aristotle and St Thomas Aquinas, the other to those of Kant and post-Kantians. These conceptions are very distant from each other and one should not count on a quick or easy bridging of the gap which separates them. Nevertheless, a state of permanent conflict is not foreordained. Because it is impossible to isolate ourselves from the European Union, in which a liberal democratic order is a certain standard, we can expect that notwithstanding strong designs to limit rights and freedoms "legally", these plans will fail.

Notes

1 This expression should appear in quotation marks. It refers to the period of Soviet domination, has little descriptive value and reveals little of the specific characters of the authoritarian political systems included under this name. Today it is of primary use to express moral-political disapproval of, or hostility to, the subject of the term, whether people, attitudes, institutions, social groups or simply a whole reality.

2 Parts II and III of this article were presented at the VIth Congress of Polish Philosophy, 4-9 October, 1995, Toruń, Poland.

3 Though Father Tischner is not himself a supporter of lustration or decommunisation. Father Tischner is a philosopher and a priest, one of the most distinguished Catholic intellectuals whose position has differed greatly from the mainstream doctrine of the Roman Catholic Church regarding such matters as the attitude to a democratic state under the rule of law, to liberalism, and to lustration and decommunisation. Clear evidence of Father Tischner's different attitude is his publicly displayed friendship with such figures as Leszek Kołakowski and Adam Michnik, who, in the eyes of a substantial number of Catholic clerics, are regarded, if not as enemies of the Church then certainly as intellectuals who exert a negative influence on the consciousness of Polish Catholic society.

4 These included, naturally, members of the former mono-party, through which over the last half century several million people certainly passed. From these, there emerged from time to time further groups - rather numerous by Eastern European standards - who without any doubt played roles as opinion leaders of the opposition. Today a significant part of them belong to the Freedom Union and another part to the left-wing Union of Labour.

5 The studies of Andrzej Zybertowicz rest upon this sort of argumentation. He is the author of perhaps the only extensive work defending the need and principle of "lustration and decommunisation" (Zybertowicz, 1993).

6 There is perhaps a similar agreement in evaluation of the institution of censorship which doubtless generated social harms, yet the harms it inflicted on particular individuals were of a different calibre.

7 Perhaps the morally negative evaluation of the "political special services" would not be endorsed by the radical advocates of the primacy of justice - understood in a specific way - over law-abidingness, since they believed the new order created in 1945 was a revolutionary order that would make up for all the past (real or imaginary) social wrongs; it was to fight all the (real or imaginary) enemies of the new, just order.

8 That is, whether the collaboration was freely given or whether the freedom of a given individual at the moment of undertaking collaboration with the special services was limited, and therefore he or she was, for example, acting under pressure.

9   I omit here the SLD (People's Democratic Party) camp, often regarded by its opponents as "post-communist", which displayed a negative attitude towards the lustration-decommunisation activities.

10   See Trznadel, J. (1990). The book is a collection of talks - analytic-accusatory in tone - with men of letters, on writers' "symbiosis" with the communist system.

11   It is worth signalling an important question at this point, important at least from the point of view of ethical theory, which was not formulated by Pociej, namely who is entitled to render the act of forgiveness in the case of guilt so understood? We can only assume it is not God or history, but some particular individuals who have been wronged - in this case by Jarosław Iwaszkiewicz as a public figure - if not actively, at least through his attitude or his literary output. The author of the quoted words either takes the position of an objective observer who points out to zealots that the culprit's guilt was not so great and therefore he ought to be forgiven, or he is himself wronged in some indirect way. For example when Jarosław Iwaszkiewicz published the author's books in regime publishing houses, the latter's output was liable to censorship while the blameworthy writer somehow justified the existence of the institution that persecuted the present accuser. Putting it briefly, if one says something can be forgiven it must be fairly clear what are the causal relationships, often quite complex, between the accuser and the accused. If, for example, Jacek Kuroń says he forgives his oppressors, who detained him in prison, interrogated him, slandered his name, intruded into his flat, etc., it seems quite clear who is rightly to be blamed and what for, and who is entitled to forgive and with what authority. Words of forgiveness expressed by a wronged man sound truly authentic and do not create the suspicion that their author's intention is not to forgive anyone but rather to elevate his own moral image.

12   Zbigniew Herbert formulated it thus in his answer to the question "why were some people lured by the red fly-paper": "(a) ...they acted from fear and in bad faith... (b) they were driven by conceit which, strangely enough was an outcome of fear... (c) they acted from low mercenary motivations" (Trznadel, 1990: 184).

13   This is what Adam Michnik wrote about those "cautious-unblemished ones": "they were simply absent for all those years from the world of political conflicts. They certainly loathed communism and did not believe in its value for a minute. They would keep themselves to themselves; they would not join the PZPR. However, they drew a conclusion from their anticommunism and their belief in the non-reformability of the system, namely that one ought to stay far away from the democratic opposition too. When others were sent to prison the 'cautious-unblemished ones' functioned quite safely in the official structures" (Michnik, 1993: 27-28).

14   I omit here some significant differences between these versions of ethics, since they are not significant from our point of view.

15   It constitutes the quintessence of evil because of - among other things, or maybe first of all - the atheism inscribed in it, or the fact that - using the words of Father Tischner - it is "one of the versions of European neo-

paganism", "Homo sovieticus", *Tygodnik Powszechny*, 25 (2130), 24 June 1990.

16 "Realizing anti-values" refers to support for the "forms of European neo-paganism" mentioned earlier, or allowing oneself to commit "betrayal of the nation". This could consist in the fact that - belonging to the second or third generation born in the PRL - one did not want to occupy a position lower than foreman in a factory, since the limits on places for the "clean and untainted" among the academic literary elite had been completely exhausted.

17 The problem is simply whether the given behaviour or activity causes direct harm to others, or whether they do some good for the others - naturally also recognized as such by those others.

18 Spielberg earlier wrote a work directed against what he called "ethical legalism", applying not only to Kantian ethics.

19 For example, it applies in the case where a whole group of soldiers dies from a hand-grenade, because not one of them moved and gave his own life to shield the others. The example does not come from Spielberg, but is taken from discussion on supererogatory acts, yet, in my opinion, it demonstrates well something Spielberg understood under the notion of "ontic necessity".

20 This is how Jaspers explains the concept: "There exists a solidarity between people as people, on the strength of which each is burdened with co-responsibility for every evil and injustice on earth, and in particular for crimes committed in his presence or knowledge. If I do not do all that I can to prevent it I am an accessory" (Jaspers, 1979).

21 For example, Adam Strzembosz (a representative of the right, and also President of the Supreme Court) recalled a certain judge from the Stalinist period, who never delivered a dishonest judgment, and thus contributed to the possibility that a "morally required state of affairs", in which "the accused are honestly judged", might be realized. He could not at the same time realize another "required state", such as "the nonexistence of a system based on repression and coercion", say, by underground armed struggle. One can similarly interpret the example, cited by the poet Zbigniew Herbert in discussion with J. Trznadel, of a German doctor from an extermination camp, who was acquitted in a trial in 1945, when it turned out that he helped prisoners. Contribution to the realization of the "required state of affairs" which is a "state in which the tormented are helped" at the same time excluded contribution to realization of another, say, the destruction of the morale of German soldiers from an emigre propaganda centre; a "morally required state", such as the "nonexistence of the totalitarian system" or "the nonexistence of criminal wars". We should understand the study of Jan Błoński on Poles' blame for the Holocaust in the same spirit. (Błoński, 1994).

22 See the chapter, "The Traps of Pure Thinking", which concludes the volume of Tischner, J. (1993).

23 This is why representatives of this point of view will, in the case of General Jaruzelski, rather take into account the fact that he was prepared to open dialogue with the opposition and facilitate the "Round Table" talks, and

secondly - as is even emphasized by some right-wing intellectuals who operate with different moral schemata than the national-christian option analysed here - that while holding the office of president in the difficult, opening period of the transformation of the political system, he fulfilled his functions unexceptionably. It might be worth noting in passing that the moral opponents of the "round table", even though they themselves fought for votes in the "contract parliament" which was its result (a parliament with free elections for the upper house but with 65% of places in the lower house reserved for the Party and groups from the old system), now morally disavow that earlier decision to enter into the "round table" negotiations; and after some time - when in completely free elections the representatives of this sort of thinking failed to attain a dominant position - they interpret that solution as a conspiracy between the *nomenklatura* and an anti-national fraction of the old (and for some even, only pseudo) opposition.

24   In a society without any differentiation of ideas, that perfectionism could even, perhaps, fulfil positive functions, as a catalyst stimulating individual excellence in the realization of values held in common in the society. In a pluralist society, this sort of moral thinking encourages conflict, since "conflicts develop precisely when people of stubborn character identify themselves so completely with some particular norm that they become blind to everything else" (Ricoeur, 1991: 45).

25   Those whom one might call "inspectors of moral matters" often forget that, as a matter of fact, they did function in some institutions of the old system, worked in teaching institutions, had academic positions, enjoyed certain social privileges which came the way of the groups to which they belonged, published their scientific works or poems in official publications. Only Jacek Kuroń has addressed himself to this issue, reminding the decommunisers that they "didn't come here [ie, to this country, to this reality - AMK] on American tanks".

26   As one might put it, in connection with the words of Zbigniew Herbert, for whom "nonparticipation" in the old reality was simply "a matter of taste".

27   For the sake of accuracy let us add that the act of accusation was directed first of all against the members of, in the first place, the government of the Third Reich, then the Political Corps of the Leaders of the NSDAP (Das Korps der politischen Leiter der NSDAP) and the SS, SD, Gestapo, etc.

28   Electoral decisions, revealing the degree of support for proponents of decommunisation might, it is true, be a certain indication of how large, or rather how small, a part of the society.

29   Moves which depend upon charging named leaders with crimes committed by, say, Pol Pot - to which it seems that the harshest decommunisers are prone - without doubt bear no analogies to the activities of the Nuremberg tribunal.

30   We can naturally make the distinction here that, after all, the former rulers followed false "reasons of state" and did not have any democratic legitimization. This sort of distinction, however, puts a duty upon the present advocates of decommunisation to honour the democratically proclaimed *status quo*, ie, to accept the fact that the "post-communist"

parliamentary majority which, after all, has the legitimacy which flows from free elections has the right today to interpret Polish "reasons of state".
31   See Krygier (1990) citing E.P. Thompson (1977). We might note in passing that Zybertowicz also refers to Krygier's essay, declaring his sympathy for "the model of a democratic law-governed state", *op.cit.*, 11.

Bibliography

Błoński, J. (1994), *Biedni Polacy patrzą na getto* (Poor Poles Look at the Ghetto), Cracow, English transl. in *My Brother's Keeper? Recent Polish Debates on the Holocaust*, ed. by Polonsky, A. (1990), London and New York.

Jaspers, K. (1979), "Problem winy" (The Problem of Guilt), *Etyka*, vol. 17.

Krygier, M. (1990), "Rządy prawa. Kulturowe osiągnęcie oznaczeniu uniwersalnym", 12, *Res Publica*, 50-53.

Mellema, G. (1991), *Beyond the Call of Duty. Supererogation, Obligation and Duty*, State University of New York Press, Albany.

Michnik, M. (1993), "Niewygodna rocznica" (An Uncomfortable Anniversary), *Gazeta Wyborcza*, 27-28, II.

Pociej, B. (1994), "Wokół muzyki" (4) (Around Music (4)), 50, *Arka*, 137.

Ricoeur, P. (1991), "Osoba: struktura etyczna i moralna" ("The person: ethical and moral structure") in *Zawierzycz czlowiekowi. Księdzu Józefowi Tischnerowi na szescdziesiąte urodziny, (To trust in persons: for Father Joseph Tischner on his sixtieth birthday)* Cracow, Wydawnictwo Znak, 45.

Ryszka, F. (1982), *Norymberga. Prehistoria i ciąg dalszy* (Nuremberg. Pre-History and Aftermath), Warsaw, 293.

Spielberg, H. (1989), (1935), *Gesetz und Sittengesetz. Strukturanalytische und historische Vorstudien zu einer gesetzesfreien Ethik*, Max Niehans Verlag, Zurich und Leipzig.

_____, *Sollen und Durfen. Philosophischen Grundlagen der ethischen Rechte und Pflichten*, bearbeitet und herausgegeben von Karl Schumann, Kluwer Academic Publishers, Dordrecht/Boston/London.

Thompson, E.P. (1977), *Whigs and Hunters,* Harmondsworth, 265.

Tischner, J. (1993), *Spowiedz rewolucjonisty (The Confessions of a Revolutionary)*, Cracow.

Trznadel, J. (1990), *Hanba domowa (Home Disgrace)*, first edition, Instytut Literacki, Paris 1986, new expanded edition, Test Press & Versus Printing House, Lublin.

Urmson, J.O. (1958), "Saints and Heroes", in A.I. Melden (ed.), *Essays in Moral Philosophy*, University of Washington Press, Seattle, 198-216.

Zybertowicz, A. (1993), *W uscisku tajnych sluzb. Upadek komunizmu I układ postnomenklaturowy.* (In the Grip of the Secret Services. The Fall of Communism and the Post Nomenklature System), Komorów, Antyk Pres.

11 Lustration or the Czech Way of Screening

JIŘINA ŠIKLOVÁ[1]

Written long before the Velvet Revolution, Vaclav Havel's play *Temptation* is a tragicomic farce about a scholar at an institute who is working "to counter the isolated but nevertheless alarming expressions of various irrational viewpoints". In the "interest of science" (as well as for personal profit), Dr. Foustka, a grotesque Czech name for Dr. Faust, signs a pact with a devil, that is, with a foolish man named Fistula, employed by the secret state security. In a departure from Goethe's Faust, Margarite is here portrayed as a good secretary who has many lovers and who survives everything. Ultimately, Foustka meets his end while attending a "revolutionary" trade union ball. There he catches fire and dies but no one pays attention to his tragedy, consumed as they are by their own affairs. Understandably, the play could not be performed in public before 1989, but many read and enjoyed it in *samizdat* form. After the lustration or screening law was passed in 1990 in Czechoslovakia, we all performed this play. But no one laughs now. Lustration in the Czech Republic is also a tragicomic farce.

The word lustration is derived from the Latin *lustratio*, which means purification by sacrifice or by purging. In other countries, words such as "debolshevization" or "decommunisation" are used. Lustration is the process of screening individuals in positions of political or economic influence in order to determine whether they once had ties to the former state security service (to the StB in the Czech case). Screening of current and future state officials and employees aims to determine the extent of their collaboration with the former secret police.

Informally, lustration had already appeared in Czechoslovakia before the first free election in June 1990. Wary of potential political scandals, all competing political parties screened their own candidates, even if their names did not appear in StB files. Political parties were not, however, required to withdraw candidates whose names turned up on the lists.

This process culminated on October 4, 1991, in what became known as the lustration law. A parallel event occurred in September 1990 when the "November 17 Commission" was created, first, to investigate the circumstances that led to the Velvet Revolution and second to focus on the lustration of Federal Assembly deputies. On March 22, 1991, the second commission revealed the identities of ten deputies whose names appeared in StB registers and who had nevertheless refused to step down.

In September 1991, the federal government proposed lustration on a person-by-person basis. The full list of those deputies accused of collaboration by the November 17 Commission can be found in an article by Jan Oberman (1991). This 1991 "debolshevization law" was partly shaped by the attempted coup d'etat in the USSR. Types of collaboration were divided into three categories: A, B, and C.

Category A collaborators were agents or informers or owners of conspiratorial apartments. Category B collaborators were classified as "conscious collaborators" who were registered as "trustees". Category C individuals were mere candidates for collaboration; this category was eliminated later, in November 1992. Jan Kavan was a category C collaborator because, while in London in 1969, he was in contact with an employee of the Czechoslovakian Embassy whom he knew to be a member of the secret police.[2] Though category C should never have been included in the law, being named in that category was sufficient to tarnish or even ruin a political career. The consequences for category A and B collaborators were clear, but there were lengthy deliberations concerning category C. The so-called "candidates for collaboration," were usually those who had been brought in for a "talk". Usually they were singled out for having had some contact with the West - they had relatives abroad or even sought permission to visit their relatives there. Finally, they were asked directly to collaborate with the secret police. These "talks" often sufficed for a person to be listed as a potential confidant.

President Havel opposed the lustration law because of its implicit presumption of guilt rather than of innocence. The underlying principle, moreover, was collective guilt. Havel stressed that proof of a clean record (that an individual was not an StB confidant) should have been defined explicitly as not having been employed in the special professions. But he signed this defective law anyway. Simultaneously, in February 1992, the Independent Appeals Commission was created. Its members were drawn from deputies of Parliament, the Ministry of Internal Affairs, the Ministry of Defence, and the Federal Security and Information Service (FSIS). The commission was created to judge whether "accused" persons were or were not conscious collaborators according to the criteria laid down in the "lustration law". The Independent Appeals Commission began its work but was quickly overwhelmed by individuals claiming to have been unjustly accused. Individuals from categories A and B were "quiet" and "silently withdrew" into other jobs to which "lustration" did not apply. Many of these individuals now sit in lucrative positions as entrepreneurs or lawyers, they belong to advisory committees, and they have "networks" that are impressive and useful for their present Western partners. I think that they are very satisfied. Some political parties (in the Czech Republic, the former communist party split into four different parties) do not advocate "lustration" in their programmes and their members in Parliament are not required to udergo screening. The StB register contains approximately 140,000 names of so-called StB collaborators. Half of these, 70,000, are registered as "candidates for collaboration". About 4,000 have requested that their cases be reviewed. This law applied only to those who occupied the top positions in Czechoslovak radio and television, in the state press agency, in colleges and universities, and to judges and prosecutors. The law states that "positively lustrated" individuals cannot be employed by the Ministry of Internal Affairs or the Federal Security and Information Services. Both the Minister of Internal Affairs and the Minister of Defence, however, may pardon staff members who are guilty of StB collaboration, but whose dismissal jeopardizes "an important security concern of the state."

Society was split into two groups. One side favored lustration, while the other opposed it. The lustration law became a burning political question partly due to the cause célèbre of Jan Kavan. Not only was it difficult to verify the information in the StB files, but how was it possible to prevent its misuse? Lustration supporters argued that those who were compromised by the files might be blackmailed, leaving them vulnerable to political manipulation. Others held that information in the files was incomplete, that at least ten percent of its registers were destroyed by the StB in the first days after the revolution, and that certain documents were still possibly in the hands of the former secret police.

Another conflict centered on whether or not the names in StB files should be published. This issue was finally resolved when the so-called Wild Lists were published in the journal *Rudé Krávo*[3] by an initiative of the Anticommunist Alliance. The Alliance was founded in the spring of 1992 (ie, it had not existed as an active opposition group under the communist regime) and led by Petr Cibulka, a former dissident and prisoner of conscience.

Alliance members got hold of the StB files illegally, created computer disk copies and made them available for publication. Disk copies were sold openly on the streets. Along with the Alliance-distributed disks, a second list was published in the newspapers *Telegraph* and *Metropolitan*, containing the names of 252 Czech and 114 Slovak journalists. Vaclav Havel criticized the publication of the "Wild List", describing it as "embarrassing and absurd". The International Helsinki Committee, for its part, protested the law, charging that the screening, which barred high-ranking officials of the Communist Party from holding elective positions for a five-year period, violated international human rights proclamations. The International Labor Organization (ILO) in Geneva claimed that the law violated Art. 111 of the ILO "Convention on Discrimination in the Workplace".

After the breakup of Czechoslovakia, Vladimir Meciar's government in Bratislava announced that it would repeal the lustration law in Slovakia, but this was never done. The Slovak Christian Democratic Movement suggested that the abolition of the law would send a negative signal to the rest of the world, while the Slovak Statistical Office conducted a survey finding that more than half of all Slovaks favoured retaining the law. Though not abolished, in Slovakia the law is currently considered "invalid" and lays dormant.

A third period of "debolshevization" began with the "Law on the Illegitimacy of, and Resistance to, the Communist Regime". Havel signed the law on July 22, 1993, after it was adopted by an overwhelming majority in the Czech Parliament on July 9, 1993. This law declares that the former Czechoslovak communist regime was "illegitimate" and "criminal" and that the Communist Party, its leadership, and its members are responsible for the manner in which the country was administered between 1948 and 1989. They are responsible for the systematic destruction of the traditional values of European civilization, for the intentional violation of human rights and freedoms, moral and economic decay accompanied by judicial crimes, and terror against those who held views in conflict with state orthodoxy. They are responsible for the replacement of a functioning market economy with a command economy and for the destruction of traditional principles of ownership. In the name of political and ideological goals, they abused education, science, and culture, and destroyed the environment. This 1993 law, however, is more of a proclamation than a piece of practical legislation. It is significant for its moral implications because, without the law, it would be difficult to deal with the communist past. This law morally justifies and honours all individuals and groups who, "on the basis of democratic, moral or religious conviction", resisted and fought against the former regime. It also extends the post-communist rehabilitation laws to those who were not rehabilitated on the basis of previous rehabilitation laws.

Negative reactions to the law came from the Communist Party of Bohemia and Moravia and from the Left Bloc, of which many former communists are members. These groups sent letters of protest to the Council of Europe, Amnesty International, and the Socialist International, arguing that the law is "discriminatory and based on the principle of collective guilt". It is paradoxical that such protests were raised by the Communist Party which, in all countries where it ruled, applied the principle of collective guilt in its ruling theories (eg, the class struggle, etc). For opportunistic reasons, it now invokes a democratic principle that it had previously denounced. According to Havel, the law in question is without strictly judicial flaws and does not contradict the Czech Charter of Fundamental Rights and Liberties. He asserted that "through this law, the freely elected Parliament is telling all victims of communism that society values them and that they deserve respect". But others argue that the law condemns the regime as illegitimate and makes no distinction between hardline Stalinists, guilty of judicial murders and the creation of concentration camps, and the Dubcekite reformists who attempted to democratize the regime and give it a human face.

The final chapter of the lustration saga began in autumn 1995. The law was due to expire at the close of 1996 but, on September 27, 1995, Parliament extended the screening period until the end of the year 2000. President Havel vetoed the extension on October 6, 1995 and returned it to Parliament, arguing that the law was only relevant for the "revolutionary phase", and that it was time to introduce normal rule-of-law conditions, which could permit no trace of collective guilt. But the Czech Parliament disagreed and, on October 18, the extension of the lustration law came into force.[4]

Personal Assessment

In his article "The End of Decommunization", Stephen Holmes (1994) asks why no "witch hunts" have occurred in post-communist countries, and why in two countries only, East Germany and the Czech Republic, screening laws of some sort had been adopted? Why is this issue not being dealt with, why is it of so little concern or interest to the people? I will attempt to answer these questions, giving as an example my own experience as a witness at the trial of *Jan Kavan versus Denní Telegraf* (*Daily Telegraph*), which took place in January 1996.

Equipped with British citizenship, Jan Kavan founded the so-called Palach Press in London after the August 1968 invasion of Czechoslovakia. He was a former Czech student leader and he knew and maintained contacts with many Czechoslovak citizens. Kavan was summoned to the Czechoslovak Embassy in London in 1969. While there, he spoke with Embassy officers, allegedly received money (the sum of 45 British pounds had been mentioned), and collaborated by making sure that Czech students who were at that time in Great Britain legalized their presence. Later he organized illegal shipments of books and magazines to the ČSSR. I myself maintained contacts with him from 1972 until my arrest in 1981, and I was never "let down" by him. But in 1990, Jan Kavan, as a member of the first Czech Parliament, "tested positive" in the screening process and was labeled an StB agent in the C category. He appealed the outcome of the screening and was cleared of the allegations after several hearings in January 1996. In March 1995, Vaclav Eminger published an article in *Denní Telegraf*, which stated that "all claims made by Kavan, that he had shipped eight thousand kilograms of books and sent 100 couriers in the course of years without any knowledge on the part of StB, are mere lies".

Jan Kavan filed libel charges against Eminger for this statement. On January 31, along with Jan Ruml, the Minister of Interior, and Petr Uhl, I testified in what was a civil case against the allegations made in Eminger's article. The judge showed no interest in the subject of the books and magazines, but wanted to know only how much the books weighed. Indeed, the judge seemed clueless about the underlying issues in the case. The Prague Municipal Court ruled in Kavan's favor and ordered that the journal publish an apology. So Kavan had won a five-year lustration battle. Little information appeared in the Czech press on this topic. Journalists seemed more interested in the expected birth of the son of the Minister of the Interior, who was also present as a witness in the trial, than in the trial itself.

My concern here is not Kavan, nor the weight of the books, but the approach. Once again we have witnessed, though at a much less tragic level, what Hannah Arendt wrote in *Eichmann in Jerusalem. A Report on the Banality of Evil* (1965). Arendt pointed out that evil could never exist without the small and "merely" obedient administrators of totalitarian regimes who did nothing else but play by "the rules of the game" of those in power. In Czechoslovakia, with some 15.5 million inhabitants, there were, before November 1989, 1.7 million members of the Communist Party, which come to about nine percent of the total population. Since the Party was clearly a ladder facilitating career mobility, many of its members were competent, ambitious, flexible, opportunistic, adaptable, and full of aspirations. That is why they became party members in the first place. Young people, not yet "invited", and people who would have liked to have joined but could not (perhaps because their sister had emigrated), were placed on a waiting list. Such people are among those who now take credit for never having been members of the Communist Party. Such people were among those who clamoured for the Screening Law's five-year extension. To prove their own moral superiority, these people write slanderous articles about those who were pressured to collaborate. I too could try to benefit from the fact that I took no part in the communist coup of February 1948 and that I was never a member of the People's Militia. In 1948, I was in the mountains and was far more interested in dirty scribblings in the hotel bathroom than in what "some" Klement Gottwald was proclaiming on the Old Town square in Prague. To present this as my moral strength or wisdom, however, seems less than moral. Unfortunately, many young journalists or politicians do not hesitate to do so.

I recall a letter by Jiří Gruša, a writer and the current Czech ambassador to Bonn, who emigrated in 1981. We debated moral issues across the border. Grusa put forward an interesting parallel:

> Two groups of young women sit in a Slavia café. One group is approached by a rich looking sheik with diamond rings who invites the girls to his hotel room. The other group condemns those who went 'to bed' with the man, conveniently forgetting that they themselves were not asked. Some young journalists and 'moralists' today try to take credit for the fact that they were never members of the Communist Party and never signed up with the StB (though they only received their education and their positions at the prominent Forecasting Institute). Today, they write in their brief biographies - following each article - that they used to attend illegal seminars held in private apartments. They forget to mention that they are among those 'girls' who were never invited by the rich sheik in the first place.

I recall that Arnošt Lustig, a writer and a Terezin survivor, and perhaps also of Auschwitz, once mentioned that an SS officer threatened that at the end of the war the SS would mix the cards so that fifty years later the Jews would still be hanging each other. This is what Hannah Arendt wrote about and what is now being dealt with in my country. I should point out that I personally opposed the screening law as early as January 1990. I am strongly against collective guilt, an inadmissible principle in the case of lustration today, just as it was in the case of the pre-war German population of our border areas (ie, the Sudeten Germans). I also oppose screening because the law affects only those who, for personal reasons, lack of understanding, naivete, or momentary weakness got involved with the StB. Those in whom the communist regime took scant interest are not obliged to reveal what they did to oppose the regime. The fact is, they were not even approached by the StB. A Czech proverb says "for a nettle, lightning is not dangerous". Today, these people, the nettles, take pleasure in patronizing those who had, in one way or another, taken part in political life. They have only one slogan exclusively for themselves - *Maul halten und weiter dienen*, shut up and go on serving. The screening-law debate is of interest to many journalists who in the past wrote for official media about the great achievements of the regime and who signed a conformity statement after Charter 77 (ie, the so called "Anti-Charter"). But many never signed up to collaborate with StB. Some even did so, but since they do not hold elected office, they are not subject to the screening law.

The screening law does not affect high-ranking Communist Party members, or StB officers for whom spying was a job description. They have become private entrepreneurs, do not aspire to elected posts or jobs as university rectors or department chairs and now "only" sit on boards of directors of various joint-stock companies. The screening law purportedly addresses the moral aspects of those who acted "immorally". But those who, as part of their profession, conducted interrogations, compromised people, and forced them to collaborate, are immune from the law. Only moral people can receive moral punishment. That is one more reason why I am against the screening law. I might mention that I personally have the "perfect alibi".

Lists of StB agents have appeared in a Czech newspaper, but only unofficially. Many people, who found themselves listed, literally collapsed when they saw their names. Others searched for their own name with trepidation and then, with perverse pleasure, for names of friends and family members. It was like the "shrieking" of the humiliated. Instead of hating those who caused these people to find themselves in such a situation (ie, the StB agents), they laughed at the moral failures of their colleagues. Many people on the lists were in absolute despair. I wrote a number of personal letters to such people, telling them how much I respected them regardless, and often received responses saying that such letters, including mine, kept them from suicide. Some of them did commit suicide. Others had to fight for their rehabilitation for many years. Zdena Salivarová, Josef Škvorecký's wife, collected and published some of the confessions in a book entitled *The Accused*, published in Toronto. Pavel Kohout wrote a novel, *I am Snowing*, about the games the StB played on people. I know that I did not contribute personally to the attempt to publicly examine StB activities. I am simply not ready to look for my "cops", considering it absurd that I, having wasted part of my life being chased by "cops", should now waste more of it by chasing them. But someone should. It is important that their mechanisms should be described precisely and brought to light.

Unfortunately, we are not the last generation living under fascist or other totalitarian regimes. I do not believe in KGB or Mossad conspiracies, but I myself am occasionally surprised that all of those who were sentenced (four people only) are now out of prison having been released on parole for good behavior after serving only half their terms. Alojz Lorenz, an StB General, was sentenced for abuse of power, but since he is Slovak he returned to Slovakia where the screening law is no longer in effect (although it was never legally scotched). If General Lorenz crosses the Czech border and someone takes notice, he could be instantly arrested. I am sure that he will be careful to collect mushrooms only near Vihorlat or Cop on the borders of Ukraine or Hungary. This same Alojz Lorenz, the last StB chief, testified in court that he had tried to reform the communist regime and that, according to him, the West believed "that the Communist Party's pragmatic reformers would be the vehicle of change". Having said this, he left for Slovakia and became an entrepreneur while former dissidents, the innocent, debate over his "heritage". Everything seems to follow the premeditated scenario to which Arnošt Lustig referred: former dissidents are clawing at one another while the former StB is no longer the focus of anyone's attention.

I understand why the collaboration of common people, friends, and acquaintances seemed more interesting to the November 17 Commission than the activities of the StB officers themselves. StB officials and communist party members were not equal partners with the investigators, while the collaboration of some of their friends hurt them. Why this proved so interesting to journalists and other "uninvited" girls from the Slavia Cafe, I have already explained.

In his article, Holmes asks why no "witch hunts" were held in the post-communist countries. My answer is that witch hunts are occurring, at least in the Czech Republic, but they are moral not legal. These *auto-da-fés* are smoke-free and therefore "environmentally friendly". They hurt only those capable of being injured by lost honour. My second answer to Stephen Holmes is that real witch hunts must be organized in the name of another, renewed but living ideology. But there are no ideologies in post-communist countries today.

At an international seminar titled "Is Socialism Coming Back?",[5] the Bulgarian President Zhelyu Zhelev said that all the East European revolutions resemble one another but that the restorations are dissimilar. According to him, Bulgaria is not endangered by a new communism but by a post-communist way of thinking. Communism in its classic form, defined by class struggle and nationalization, cannot be restored, but post-communist ways of thinking can profoundly jeopardize the new system.

We continue to live, work, have fun, make money, laugh. But we do not reflect and that is the heavy burden we carry with us. It is said that the old and blind Greek poet Homer died in a fit of anger when he could not solve a riddle posed to him by some children: "What is it?" they asked, "Those we can catch, we kill and throw away. Those we cannot, we carry with us." The answer: lice. In addition to being a children's riddle, the story has yet another dimension that could be applied to post-communist countries in their attempts to cope with the past. We can only cope with what we have grasped, identified and reflected upon. The unknown, that which we cannot grasp, we carry with us like lice and have no chance to shed until we grasp it. Too often, we simply forget that we carry this baggage, which nevertheless slows us down. We are like an obese person who forgets that he is loaded down with several dozen extra kilos and that these are an extra burden for his heart and ultimately shorten his life.

Notes

1   This chapter first appeared in *East European Constitutional Review,* vol.5, No.1, Winter 1996, 57-62.
2   For more on the *Kavan* case, see Lawrence Weschler (1992).
3   *Red Cow*, Nos. 32, 33, 34, 38, Vol. II, 1992 .
4   See *East European Constitutional Review*, Czech Republic Update, Vol. 4, No. 4, Fall 1995.
5   Organized in Prague by the Friedrich Neumann Foundation in September 1995.

Bibliograpy

Arendt, H. (1965), *Eichmann in Jerusalem. A Report on the Banality of Evil*, revised and enlarged edition, Viking Press, New York.

Holmes, S. (1994), "The End of Decommunization", *East European Constitutional Review*, Vol. 3. Nos. 3/4, Summer/Fall.

Oberman, J. (1991), "Laying the Ghosts of Past", *Report on Eastern Europe*, No. 24, 14, June.

Wechsler, L. (1992), "The Velvet Purge: The Trials of Jan Kavan", *The New Yorker*, October.

Part IV

Crime

12 Is Revolution a Solution?

State Crime in Communist and Post-Communist
Poland (1980-1995)

MARIA ŁOŚ and ANDRZEJ ZYBERTOWICZ

Introduction

There is a risk in focussing on the darker, hidden side of a process so noble
and inspiring as a peaceful transition from totalitarianism to democracy. We
hope that our chapter will be read with a full understanding that there is
much more to this process than the crimes, the treachery and the hypocrisy
we depict in these pages. But we also hope that the things we write about
will not be perceived as aberrant, marginal occurrences, unconnected to the
core of the macrostructural changes taking place in Poland in the 1990s. It
is our conviction that no serious sociological, politological or economic
analysis of the nature of these historical changes is conceivable without at
least some grasp of the historical roots, power relations, group interests,
habits, hidden technologies and material arrangements that produced
criminal underpinnings of the processes in question.

In the same vein, we maintain that all those who have tried to analyse
the "evolution" and eventual self-destruction of the communist system in
straight, "above-ground" terms of traditional sociology or economics miss a
vital part of the reality concerned; an oversight that renders impossible a
congruent and meaningful explanation of those developments (see Łoś,
1990b).

M. Łoś would like to thank Cezary Fudali for his help in collecting information
for this chapter the University of Ottawa for sponsoring his assistantship. We are
also grateful to Dr Jeffrey Ross and Konrad Turzyński for their comments on
earlier versions of this text.

The main purpose of our chapter is to search for answers to the key question of the efficacy of radical systemic change as a tool for eradicating state crime. A relatively extensive presentation of the nature of the criminal schemes in question is vital to a meaningful evaluation of the remedies employed. Both the unique nature of state crimes in the post-communist transition period and the availability of some hitherto secret material that throws new light on communist state crimes fully warrants, in our view, this approach.

We start by analysing "state crime" dynamics in the 1980s, focussing both on the criminal and criminogenic nature of the prevailing systemic arrangements as well as on crimes committed by, on behalf of, or with encouragement from the Communist Party (the Polish United Workers' Party - hereafter the Party), especially crimes committed by the security services.[1] We shall also look at specific legal measures, institutional arrangements and resistance strategies that were employed before 1989 to curtail some of the abuses or reduce their immediate impact.

Subsequently, we shall look at developments in the 1990s and attempt to trace the role and fortunes of the main players identified earlier - the communist system's power networks - in the period of dynamic transition towards market economy and democracy. We postulate that those old networks, partly legitimated and shielded by the new establishment, have become a vital infrastructure for new forms of organized/state crime. The documentation we provide lends support to our working hypothesis, according to which the peaceful "transfer of power" in 1989 was contingent on the unencumbered opportunities for advancement of the old regime's power-network interests (see Zybertowicz, 1993).

In the subsequent section of this part of our chapter, we scrutinize a variety of remedial actions that have been taken or still could be attempted and try to evaluate their actual and/or potential impact. The aim of this section is not to develop a full-blown programme of social and legal change, but rather to provide a check-list of rudimentary measures designed to ensure at least some accountability of new and old elites.

Our chapter testifies to the known problems of any pioneering effort. While we present some cautious and tentative conclusions, we also point to some unanswered questions, seemingly insurmountable barriers to information gathering, and not always unequivocal implications of the established "facts".

The 1980s

The Police State

Prior to 1989, Poland was a party-state where all sectors of life and government were subordinated to the Communist Party. Yet until the infamous 1976 amendments, nothing in the constitution (of 1952) could entrust the Party with a monopoly of power. In fact, the constitution did not mention the Party at all. Its rule had no basis in the law - it was founded on illegal usurpation and backed by a foreign power.

The 1976 constitutional amendments - introduced amidst many protests - added a vague section that stipulated that the Polish United Workers' Party (ie, Communist Party) was the leading political force in the construction of socialism. Nevertheless, the rules governing this leadership, the Party's legal status and its relations with the other institutions described in the constitution remained undefined.

Moreover, based on Lenin's doctrine of the unity of powers, there were no legal guarantees of judicial independence.[2] Supreme Court justices were appointed for five years only and could be recalled even before the expiration of their term; the renewal of their appointments depended on the political evaluation of their performance by the Party.

A key role within the criminal justice system was played by the Prosecutor General (*Prokuratura*), an extremely powerful body whose many tasks included criminal investigation, prosecution in criminal cases, supervision of prisons and oversight of the state administration (Strycharz, 1983: 67-70). It worked in tandem with the militia (the uniformed police) and secret services. Formally subordinate to the State Council, the *Prokuratura* was, in reality, directly controlled by the Administrative Department of the Party's Central Committee.

By far the most important tool of Party rule was the state security apparatus. The extent and depth of its penetration into both formal and informal structures of social life justifies the "police state" label often used in respect of communist societies. Yet this categorization has rarely been subjected to any systematic empirical test, and the implications of police state reality for the process of transition to democracy have attracted hardly any attention from social scientists. It is impossible to appreciate the ramifications of this without having at least some grasp of the role and status of the police organizations prior to 1989; one can then ask questions about their subsequent transformation and, in particular, about what has happened to the army of people they employed and the collective experience and expertise they embodied. Without this kind of information, it would be impossible to undertake any real discussion about post-1989 state crime and its prevention.

The organizational infrastructure of the Polish police state was composed of two ministries: the Ministry of Internal Affairs and the Ministry of Defence. Their structure and tasks were shrouded in complete secrecy.[3]

The *Ministry of Internal Affairs* (hereafter MSW, its Polish acronym)[4] has often been referred to as "a state within a state" (Pytlakowski, 1991). Its structure and functions were regulated by secret decree. It was charged with policing all aspects of the society, including the command economy. While the Party traditionally treated the ministry as its subordinate, in the 1980s, under General Czesław Kiszczak, its various divisions achieved relative autonomy, at least on the regional level (Ochocki, 1992: 11,128).

The services making up the ministry were largely independent of each other and carried out their own recruitment of informers, aiming at systematic penetration of all areas of life. Every single institution or work unit (a factory, school, newspaper, association, etc) was assigned a special "guardian angel" from one of the services. In some cases, for instance in factories producing military equipment, "angels" were based in the military counterintelligence of the Ministry of Defence. Their primary task was to recruit and cultivate a network of informers within the assigned unit and to gather inside information about the overt and covert dealings of the unit and its individual members, as well as their possible political and criminal deviations.

The MSW's *Intelligence* branch (Department I) had 600-700 regular employees (Kaszyński and Podgórski, 1994: 79). The service had its own recruitment officers operating in all major urban centres of Poland and probably a few hundred informers working for them within the country. Among its diverse activities, the service was expected to take care[5] of all major international financial and trade transactions conducted by Polish state institutions. Its Section XI was exclusively concerned with the infiltration of the elites of the Solidarity movement both inside the country and among the Polish *emigré* circles.

Department II, *Counterintelligence*, had divisions in every administrative district [*województwo*] and was in charge of operations involving communication networks, transportation, power stations and energy transfer units. It also covered foreigners (especially diplomats and journalists) and provided protection for the Soviet Army units stationed in Poland.

The *Security Service* (SB) employed around 25,000 people in 1989 (Widacki, 1992: 178). Its network of informers was about a hundred thousand strong in the late 1980s;[6] it is likely however, that not more than half of them were actually productive. Within the Security Service, Department III "covered" predominantly "white collar" institutions such as health care, banks, education, and state administration (including the justice system) and all kinds of social and political organizations.

The work of the SB Department IV was focussed entirely on organized religions and national minorities (Widacki, 1992: 75-94). About 90% of its resources were devoted to surveillance and infiltration of the Catholic Church. Its Disorganization ("D") Section and its local counterparts in several regions were involved in a whole range of insidious activities - mounting anonymous smear campaigns against clergy and other persons active in churches, generating conflict, publishing bogus memoirs and special periodicals clandestinely sponsored by the ministry, staging brutal assaults, destroying property, kidnapping, making illegal threats, and carrying out break-ins, arson and murder (Komisja, 1991: 219-220; also Albert, 1994: 847-8; Fredro-Boniecki, 1990; Widacki, 1992: 64-73; Zieleniewski, 1990).

Department V, also subsumed under the SB, was in charge of trade and industry, while Department VI was involved with agriculture and food processing. All SB departments used services of the Bureau of Observation, but the latter also ran its own informers, especially in public places - hotels, restaurants, etc - likely to be entered by persons tailed by the secret police. The departments and the bureau had branches in all of Poland's administrative districts.

The *Citizens' Militia* (the uniformed police) employed about 80,000 people in the late 1980s. Additionally, the Voluntary Reserve of the Citizens' Militia (ORMO) counted 350,000 members, but many of them were practically inactive. The ORMO was used as a pool from which the so-called Trusted Persons were drawn. They were not registered informers, but provided useful information nonetheless.

Both the SB and the militia were very heavily involved in prisons and gaols, where they routinely conducted their secret operations and interrogations (Alexander, 1984: 49-64). The real bosses of penal institutions, the special prison police (Protection Section), were only formally employed by the Ministry of Justice; their actual employer was the

Ministry of Internal Affairs (Alexander, 1984: 60-1; see also Moczydlowski, 1988: 323).

Yet another police organization within the MSW was the *Directorate for the Protection of Functionaries*, whose main function was to police the police. It recruited its own informers among the militia and the SB members. The number of the Directorate's operatives was slightly below 200 (Widacki, 1992: 152-3), while the number of secret informers is difficult to estimate.

Finally, the *Directorate for the Reconnaissance of the Border Guard* concentrated its recruitment of informers in those administrative districts that adjoined the state borders (21 districts out of the total number of 49) as well as in international airports. The number of functionaries was 600, and the estimated number of informers was in the range of 6,000;[7] the number of functionaries is hard to establish.

All the above-mentioned services of the Ministry of Internal Affairs were drawing heavily upon the resources provided by its Passport Office, which facilitated recruitment of secret informers from among those applying to travel abroad.

Every department of the ministry was assigned special Soviet advisors who were granted free access to operational files.[8] Moreover, a Unified System of Data on the Enemy, which had its headquarters in Moscow, began operating in Poland in 1978. It was a fortnightly updated computerized network that contained information on all the internal and external enemies of socialism covered by the secret services of the Soviet Bloc countries. Its Polish data are said to have been destroyed.

One possible indicator of personnel continuity following the post-1989 overhaul of the internal security system is the fact that two-thirds of the operatives of the present Office for the Protection of the State (UOP) had worked in the secret services under the old regime.

Any attempt to substantiate the "police state" claim must also include the role of the *Ministry of Defence*. Its special services were heavily involved in the invigilation and secret policing of the "internal enemy". While *Military Intelligence* carried out standard intelligence tasks, it also covered financial aspects of all Poland's military equipment exports (including transactions with the Arab oil-exporting states) and imports. It had about 3,200 functionaries in 1981 (Bereś and Skoczylas, 1991: 181) and an unknown number of agents.

The areas of interest of *Military Counterintelligence* included factories producing military equipment and economic transactions connected with military affairs. Its operatives numbered around 4,500 in the mid-1980s; its informers numbered about 25,000-30,000, of which approximately 20% were persons not employed by the ministry. In addition to the normal counterintelligence protection of the army, the service's tasks included sheltering the families of military staff from the "bad influence" of the Catholic Church, surveying "political moods" in the country and infiltrating opposition groups. Furthermore, the service had informers inside the two "satellite" parties that, together with the Communists, formed the ruling bloc. During the 1980s, both Military Intelligence and Counterintelligence were employed (according to some sources, almost routinely) by the Party's first secretary, General Wojciech Jaruzelski, to probe the work of the civilian secret services.

In principle, each of these services carried out its infiltration of different social circles quite independently. There existed, however, centrally coordinated cross-checking procedures to prevent multiple recruitment. As well, all services had access to central archives and centrally coordinated records of anyone who came under their particular sphere of interest. The "sphere of interest" consisted of two categories of people: the informers and the "enemies".

In the 1980s, the main mission of all the secret services within both ministries was to infiltrate, monitor, control, manipulate, and neutralize the political opposition. While the Intelligence services covered the opposition's contacts abroad, Counterintelligence focussed on its contacts with foreigners inside the country. Other tasks were treated as being of secondary importance. Despite the fact that by the late 1980s all these services had been bureaucratized and to some extent demoralized, they could still serve as a formidable instrument of possible social engineering. Yet students of the East European transformation, who routinely pay lip service to the standard characteristics of the communist system as a police regime, seem to find it unnecessary to include the role of the secret services in their explanatory models of the process of systemic transformation.

The long period of decadence and gradual disintegration of the regular state/party control system, following the military suppression of the Solidarity movement in December 1981, particularly contributed to the state's greater dependence on the secret police (Łoś, 1995). Contrary to what some commentators have been implying, the Communist Party did not abandon its reliance on terror in the post-Stalinist period. While it toned down the violence considerably, it had no choice but to continue to rule through fear and to preserve the paramount status of the Ministry of Internal Affairs. Despite a modicum of change, there was a basic continuity in the personnel and methods of the ministry throughout the communist period.[9]

Till the very end, the Party's exercise of power was based on the *"nomenklatura* principle", which meant the Party's exclusive right to recommend and approve people for all positions of authority in all areas of public life. The hierarchical *nomenklatura* class acted both as a transmission belt for the party line and as a unified, vertical system of control. The official hierarchy of command and subordination within the *nomenklatura* was, however, modified by personal relations of blood, friendship, hatred or mutual corruption, which in turn provided additional mechanisms of communication and decision making.

That the Party placed not only itself but also its members above the law was epitomized by the rule according to which any potential criminal charges against them had first to be considered by special party commissions and brought to the attention of the *Prokuratura* in exceptional cases only, following the expulsion of the suspect from the Party. Functionaries of legal agencies were reminded of the binding force of this unpublished (and illegal) rule during employees' meetings and conferences (Czabański, 1981; Holwiński, 1981).

Following this brief description of the formal status of the main organs of the state in communist Poland, it can be concluded that the actual principles of their functioning were not backed by law as they did not even correspond to the highest law of the land. Even after the 1976 amendments, the constitution did not justify the *de facto* absolute power of the Communist Party. Moreover, the secret status of the *nomenklatura* principle and the predominance of secret "laws" in the regulation of state organs makes it difficult to speak about the legality or otherwise of their functionaries' activities. When laws themselves appear to be unlawful, the very definition of "state crime" becomes problematic. But the sheer numbers of personnel involved directly in the "technologies of terror" and immersed in the subcultures of illegality, violence and peculiar solidarity must lead to questions about the uses they might have been put to in the post-communist reality. Before we address this question, however, we shall look at some examples of state-organized crime in communist Poland.

Martial Law, December 1981

The emergence in 1980 of a nine-million-strong movement under the banner of Solidarity posed an enormous threat to the totalitarian principles of the communist regime. The imposition of the "state of war" by the State

Council on 13 December 1981 was an illegal act. According to article 33, section 1 of the constitution, such a decision could be made only in the case of military aggression, and the competent body was the Diet. Only when the Diet was not in session could the decision be made by the State Council.

On 13 December 1981, the *Sejm* was still in session, and so the State Council's declaration of the state of war was unconstitutional. To compound the illegality of this process, the State Council acted formally on orders of General Jaruzelski's Military Council for National Salvation (WRON), an *ad hoc* body with no legal status at all (Albert, 1994: 826). Furthermore, while Solidarity was perceived by the communist leaders as a threat, it could not possibly be construed as an external military enemy. As well, although the relevant decree was not published until 14 December 1981, the State Council declared that it would come into effect immediately after its passage - that is, on 12 December at midnight. To ensure greater effectiveness, arrests began even earlier. As a result, scores of people were detained for actions that were absolutely legal up to 14 December, and were detained for months without charge or sentenced to long prison terms under laws that not only were passed illegally but were made known only through radio and television announcements and street posters.

Many Western commentators saw the introduction of martial law as a measure of last resort, taken only when Solidarity "went too far" in challenging the principles of the communist state. Yet secret work on some form of violent assault against the nation had begun soon after demands for free trade unions were first formulated by the striking workers at the Polish seacoast. An order (number 031/80, dated 16 August 1980) of the Minister of Internal Affairs established a special Commanding Team (*Sztab*) charged with preparations for a forceful solution, named "Operation Summer 80". The order delegated to the team powers normally reserved for the minister and placed the SB entirely at their disposal (*Komisja*, 1991: 13; Paczkowski, 1995). The minutes of the Politburo meetings of that period offer a chilling record of the cynicism and alienation of these powerful but frightened men plotting to outmanoeuvre "the enemy" (*Tajne dokumenty*, 1991; also *Polityka*, 1990: Dec. 1991a, b). Unsurprisingly, the labels "enemy" and "foe" (*przeciwnik*) were reserved for a peaceful movement at home, while "ally" (*sojusznik*), the other constantly used term, stood for the Soviet Communist Party leadership.[10]

The state-of-war decree and related regulations (for example, concerning internment of political activists) were prepared in secrecy by the MSW and the Ministry of Defence. Not even the all-powerful Politburo had access to the specific content of these legal preparations. None of the restrictions applied, however, to high KGB and Soviet Army officials, who were consulted and briefed on several occasions. The KGB assumed the responsibility for printing the relevant public announcements (Paczkowski, 1995: 14). The State Council went far beyond its legal mandate when it accepted the final decree submitted to it on 13 December 1981.

As early as 15 October 1980, a decision was made to prepare a list of people to be interned in the event of a serious crisis. By December 1980, it contained 12,900 names. A "shadow" Solidarity leadership was groomed to take over the union upon the arrest of its real leaders. A number of gross provocations were planned and executed by the MSW in order to escalate the conflict and justify the military clamp-down. The most active Party members were armed and formed into special fighting squads.

Based on a detailed analysis of the preserved archival materials, Polish historian Andrzej Paczkowski, an expert for the Parliamentary Commission on Constitutional Responsibility, concluded in 1995 that the introduction of a state of war amounted to an illegal coup and that the security apparatus was authorized by the highest party/state levels to use illegal means to implement it (Paczkowski, 1995: 15; see also Albert, 1994: 826). Yet the commission, which had pursued its investigation of the possible constitutional responsibility of the authors of the "state of war" since 1993, recommended in February 1996 that no legal action should be undertaken. The recommendation was subsequently accepted by the Parliament.

The mobilized forces included 80,000 soldiers, 49,000 reserve militia troops and 249,000 MSW functionaries (*Komisja*, 1991: 18). It was estimated that approximately sixty people died between December 1981 and December 1982 as a result of beatings, torture and the use of force against peaceful demonstrators. Many more deaths were indirectly caused by the war measures (*Committee in Support*, 1983b: 13). Around 10,000 people were interned without charges. In March 1983, the Minister of Internal Affairs stated that 2,580 persons had been sentenced since December 1981 for anti-state activities and 1,462 for offences under the state-of-war decree. Typical "crimes" involved the possession of leaflets, the display of Solidarity pins and other banned symbols, the organization of meetings or demonstrations, and the refusal to work in militarized enterprises. Many of these cases were tried in military courts, where accused persons were often deprived of their basic legal rights. Many judges were forced to sign a "loyalty oath" and a number of those who refused were dismissed (Łoś, 1983: 405-6; see also The Polish Helsinki Committee, 1984: 96). According to General Jaruzelski, the total number of people interned without charges was 10,554 (Jaruzelski, 1992: 420). Many thousands lost their jobs (Albert, 1994: 830).

One year after its introduction, the state of war was suspended by an illegal decree according to which most of the repressive measures of the "martial law" became codified into the existing legal statutes. All legal bills enacted during the state of war (including laws on trade unions, censorship, juvenile delinquency, and persons who avoid employment) retained their force (Łoś, 1983: 407-9). Thousands of men were conscripted into the army and sent to military penal camps (*Committee in Support*, 1983a: 1-9).

The 1989-91 Extraordinary Parliamentary Commission to Investigate MSW Activities conducted inquiries into several "pacification" operations in which the MSW forces were apparently authorized by their superiors to use live ammunition without strict instructions as to the circumstances justifying its use.[11] These operations included the 1981 pacification by special anti-riot police (ZOMO) of the striking coal mine "Wujek" (where nine miners were shot dead and dozens were wounded) and an assault on a peaceful demonstration in Lubin in 1982 (where three people were killed and more than a dozen wounded).

Despite binding regulations, issues of firearms and ammunition were never recorded, thus preventing any future identification of the functionaries involved. Nor were any attempts made to match returned firearms with their users or bullets removed from wounds and bodies with the arms from which they were fired. The evidence was destroyed or altered, scores of witnesses arrested and convicted on fabricated charges, and others threatened or coerced into giving false statements. All these activities were conducted deliberately and methodically under the Chief Military *Prokuratura* supervision. The Commission's findings illustrate the total impunity of the security forces in a situation where investigations of their abuses of power were bound to be conducted, in effect, by themselves. Yet this failure to prosecute seems to extend into the post-1989 period. While three police officers were brought to trial in 1995 in connection with the Lubin murders, none of them have been convicted (Ostrowski and Podemski, 1995). A protracted trial of those accused of the "Wujek" killings is equally unlikely to result in convictions. Those who masterminded the assaults remain untouchable.[12]

Murders by the Police

The 1989-91 Parliamentary Commission cited in the preceding section looked at 115 cases[13] of "unexplained" or unprosecuted deaths linked to Security Service (SB) activities in the 1981-89 period. It dropped an additional seven cases (including three deaths of priests) when the *Prokuratura* initiated its own inquiries. The commission concluded that there was sufficient evidence to recommend criminal investigation in 91 instances, where there was obvious MSW involvement.

This list included instances of individuals being shot by MSW functionaries, a number of alleged suicides in which the MSW was implicated, deaths caused by such "accidents" as "falling" out of police vehicles or windows, cases of people dying shortly after being severely beaten during arrest or interrogation, as well as seven alleged SB murders of Catholic priests (*Komisja*, 1991: 181-228). Predictably, any investigations undertaken by police or *Prokuratura* aimed at muddying rather than uncovering the facts. The material evidence was never secured, and in those rare cases where charges were laid, the trials were not concerned with finding the truth. In many cases, the *Prokuratura* investigations and internal MSW inquiries were guided by an *a priori* assumption that the police were not involved. Their main focus was on suppression (usually through repression) of any rumours or claims to the contrary (*Komisja*, 1991: 204-213).

The Extraordinary Parliamentary Commission to Investigate MSW Activities completed its report in 1991. Despite its recommendation to initiate or re-open investigation in 91 cases of probable MSW involvement in murder, the response of the post-communist *Prokuratura* and courts has been very slow and selective. Even in those cases where legal actions have been undertaken, they seem to be hesitant and rather contorted. By the end of 1995, criminal charges were brought against 49 persons, only four of whom were convicted and given prison sentences (Ostrowski and Podemski, 1995: 6-8). Moreover, a four-year-old criminal investigation of the activities of the SB anti-Church section ("D") has been plagued by incompetence and lack of will.[14] A prosecutor who reviewed the case in 1995 concluded that to date there have been so many prosecutorial errors that the investigation should start from scratch (*Rzeczpospolita*, 14 November, 1995, 11). The following case study illustrates our assertion that change in the system has not automatically led to prosecution of former state criminals.

CASE STUDY 1

On 12 May 1983, a nineteen-year-old high-school student, Grzegorz Przemyk, son of a dissident poet and activist, Barbara Sadowska, was detained and then beaten at a police station in Warsaw. Two days later, he died in hospital as a result of injuries sustained during the beating. His mother had also suffered injuries several days earlier when a gang of MSW functionaries attacked a convent in Warsaw, which housed the Primate's Aid Committee for Political Prisoners (Polish Helsinki Committee, 1984: 47, 50). Przemyk was detained when he refused to show his identity papers to the police, who had stopped him for disorderly behaviour.

The beating of Przemyk was witnessed by his schoolmate, who was also detained. Another friend heard his cries from the street (*Życie Warszawy*, 1984: 6). Once taken to the medical emergency station, Przemyk, apparently mistreated by two ambulance attendants, was examined by a psychiatrist, who ordered him hospitalized in a mental institution. However, upon his mother's intervention, Przemyk was released into her care. Although he had no visible injuries, a surgical intervention proved that his stomach was completely crushed and he was beyond saving. A medical autopsy showed that he had been severely beaten by professionals who could administer blows without leaving any outside marks.

The case was widely publicized by opposition circles and Przemyk's funeral was attended by at least several thousand people. School youths, university teachers and prominent writers sent petitions demanding a full explanation of his death. The expected visit of Pope John Paul II made the situation particularly embarrassing for the authorities.

Under the pressure of these developments, the Politburo decided, on 24 May 1983, to treat the Przemyk case as "extraordinary," and a special group chaired by Gen. Mirosław Milewski was established. Milewski, the chair of the Central Committee Commission on Law and Legality that oversaw the work of the MSW, was a Politburo member, a Central Committee secretary and a former minister of Internal Affairs[15] (Fredro-Boniecki, 1990: 11). A special team of three SB officers was set up at the Party Central Committee building to inspire the mass-media publications and coordinate them with the official version of events. A number of rank-and-file militiamen were given instructions as to how to answer questions from the *Prokuratura* office and what to say in court in order to avoid discrepancies in their testimonies (*Prawo i Życie*, 1995a: 36).

Within the MSW, the handling of the case was supervised by Minister Kiszczak himself and the Militia Chief. The ministry's operations were parallel to the investigation undertaken by the *Prokuratura*. Operational contacts and resources of the secret services were employed in order to compromise people belonging to the social circle of Sadowska and witnesses. These actions also targeted dissident *émigré* groups outside of Poland.[16] The SB located and "informally" interrogated 108 persons who might have known something about the events at the medical emergency station (Żurek, 1995: 37). The *Prokuratura* investigators were not informed and no official written record was made of these interrogations, although some of them were secretly tape recorded (KES, 1995: 3).

The victim's mother was placed under surveillance 24 hours a day. Her legal representative was arrested on trumped-up charges; his files on the case were unlawfully seized by functionaries of the MSW (Polish Helsinki Committee, 1984: 51-2); several prosecutors were invigilated, and a deputy head of the *Prokuratra* who did not show enough zeal in obeying Party orders pertaining to this case was fired (Ordyński, 1995: 1, 14). Following unsuccessful attempts to bribe the two young witnesses with prospects of study trips abroad and jobs in the MSW, they and their families were harassed and shadowed for months.[17]

Evidence was fabricated to back a claim that Przemyk's fatal injuries had been caused by the two ambulance attendants. They were threatened and framed into accusing each other (Polish Helsinki Committee, 1984: 52). Several incidents were staged in order to convince the public that it is common for medical personnel to beat and rob patients. In connection with one such operation, Dr Barbara Makowska-Witkowska was sentenced on a trumped-up charge of assault and spent over a year in prison[18] (Makowska-Witkowska, 1988: 137-188).

At the conclusion of the trial in July 1984, the two accused militiamen were declared not guilty and the ambulance attendants were found guilty only of criminal negligence (they were sentenced to two years and one and a half years in prison respectively). The doctors involved were found guilty of unintentional criminal negligence for failing to provide appropriate medical assistance to Przemyk; their sentences were waived on the basis of the July 1983 Amnesty Act. In August 1984, Kiszczak issued special financial awards to thirteen MSW functionaries for their handling of the investigation (Grochmalski and Szczepaniak, 1995: 2).

In April 1990, the files of the 1983-84 investigation were uncovered just in time to prevent their illegal destruction. On many documents there were hand-written remarks by Minister Kiszczak indicating the desired direction of the investigation. In July 1990, the case was reopened in the Warsaw District Court and the earlier trial was declared invalid. In April 1991 the list of the accused MSW functionaries was extended by the prosecutor in charge of the new investigation to include the former director of the Bureau of Inquiry and Investigation of the Militia Headquarters, one of those commended by General Kiszczak in 1984 (Sroka, 1991: 2). Among witnesses interrogated by the prosecution were: General Jaruzelski, General Kiszczak, the then deputy prime minister Rakowski and General Milewski. They all claimed to have very poor recollection of the case.

After one year and a half, in April 1993, the *Prokuratura* office finally sent the files to the court. Yet the trial did not start until May 1995, five years after the reopening of the investigation and almost six years after the collapse of the old system. In October 1995, the key witness told a journalist that a few days before the new trial was to begin, strange cars had appeared in the village he now lives in and stayed close to his house, strangers had tried to invite his children for ice cream and somebody had tampered with his father's car (Misiak, 1995).

This case study shows a comprehensive and massive cover-up operation. It involved at least a few hundred persons employed in state agencies, all of whom broke, disregarded or twisted the law that was valid at the time. The persons involved included officials at various levels of the Party, judges, prosecutors, militiamen, secret-service functionaries and journalists. It may seem rather puzzling that the supreme levels of the communist state became so deeply and directly engaged in this relatively minor case. It appears, however, that the Party was defending its apparatus of violence under circumstances in which it already felt threatened by society. It was a display of bunker mentality by an insecure tyranny.

It is worth noting here that neither the Party nor its secret services were able to control all elements of the case: some prosecutors, some judges, and some witnesses refused to act as puppets. The fact that it took five years to prepare a new trial strongly suggests, however, that the principle of "dirty togetherness"[19] remains in operation and the old power networks have not lost their vitality. That should explain why some witnesses and other persons involved in the case seem to feel insecure even today. It appears likely that a cover-up continues to protect certain more important figures who should have been charged in the case.

The Cover-up of the Security Service's Criminal Enrichment Schemes

Communist security services engaged in criminal economic ventures to supplement their already disproportionally large budget (Henzler, 1990b: 1, 5; Smoleński's interview with Kiszczak, 1991: 10). The clandestine nature of their operations made it easy for them to engage in schemes involving burglary, fraud, smuggling and other forms of organized crime of staggering proportions. In principle, criminal gains were used to finance the services' ideological mission: to combat class enemies at home and to support Marxist parties and movements abroad. Yet the rules were lax enough to allow massive private appropriation of the proceeds from those predatory, illegal ventures. This contributed to internal problems and antagonisms within the service and the whole Ministry of Internal Affairs. In rare instances, secret agents were convicted of criminal offences when they claimed too large a share of the stolen goods. Others, who threatened to speak up, were liquidated.

One MSW-directed crime ring, which operated in Western Europe in 1968-71 and managed to steal and smuggle into Poland huge quantities of gold, jewels, precious stones, and other valuables, was investigated by an internal ministerial commission in 1984. Apparently, most of the goods that had been deposited in the MSW vanished without a trace (Henzler, 1990b; Jurczenko and Kilijanek, 1991; Smoleński, 1991). Despite the commission's recommendation to pass its final report to the *Prokuratura* (Piecuch, 1992), the Politburo, headed by General Jaruzelski, decided against it and the matter was hushed up (*Życie Warszawy*, 1990: 1). In his 1991 interview,

Kiszczak justified the cover-up, claiming that an exposure of the operation would harm Poland's interests and credibility (Smoleński, 1991). In 1990, seven persons were charged with corruption in connection with this affair (*Życie Warszawy*, 1990: 1), but the charges were later dropped due to insufficient evidence that the accused men had gained personally from the crimes.

The Endowment of the "Nomenklatura"

The lack of any political or social control over the Party and its tight rule over the legal system led not only to the unchecked power of the party/police state, but also to a feeling of omnipotence and impunity among its officials.[20]   One of the attributes of communist rule in Poland (and in other Marxist states, see Łoś, 1990b) was mutual corruption networks of ruling cliques that aimed at organizing their relationships in such a way that every member of the clique had an opportunity to take advantage of the resources controlled by other members.[21]

In the 1970s, managing the country became for the Party elite synonymous with owning it, that is, having unhampered use of its wealth and institutions. In the 1980s, the Party introduced pseudo-market reforms that enabled a formal legitimation of the *nomenklatura*'s "informal property rights" of the earlier period (Łoś, 1992, 1994a, b). The new pro-entrepreneurial, pro-market rhetoric facilitated a conversion of the long-standing *nomenklatura* practices of illegal appropriation of state resources, corruption and organized crime into officially hailed schemes of privatization that turned the party "apparatchiks" into "entrepreneurchiks" (Tarkowski, 1990; also Łoś, 1992, 1994a, b). But the old mentality and habits persisted:

> all the wives of party secretaries, ministers' sons, and police colonels' brothers who open private firms rely not on low-cost production or product superiority in their quest for profit but on political linkages that assure them privileged access to scarce inputs from the state sector. The unchanged state sector, with its pseudomarkets, infects the private sector, and the distorted existence of the latter makes it a fertile ground for rent seeking by the ruling stratum. (Winiecki, 1990: 69)

A slew of new laws[22] led to a proliferation of officially registered joint-stock companies and partnerships founded on the basis of, and in parasitic symbiosis with, the state-economy units (similar schemes in

Hungary were dubbed "golden parachutes"; see Botos, 1990: 137). The main objective was to secure a "legal" transfer of state property into the hands of the party-class (Zybertowicz, 1993: 36). A Polish sociologist wrote about the new breed of communist capitalists thus:

> From his workplace he takes anything that can be used as capital to help launch a private enterprise: raw materials, machines, cars and so on... His main capital is not money but rather his privileged position of "access" to policymakers and bureaucrats... The Enfranchised *Nomenklatura* Man... flies a company plane, has his own sports club, and hunts with colleagues, retiring at night to the luxurious lodges built for high level officials in the 1970s. (Gliński, 1992: 150)

One of countless examples of the private appropriation of state-economy assets for a symbolic payment involved a joint-stock company, Igloopol, where:

> the stock-holders...including the director [of the parent state company] and former vice-minister of agriculture...in exchange for less than 9 billion złoty secured assets valued at about 200 billion złoty...provided by their parent enterprise, based on *contracts they signed with themselves [in their double capacity]*. (Tittenbrun, 1992: 147; emphasis added)

A 1989 investigation by the Highest Chamber of Control confirmed the parasitic pattern of the *"nomenklatura* companies". It issued a report which showed that they were created mainly to subvert tax and wage regulations, inflate prices, create monopolies, use state offices for private gain and channel state assets into private ventures (Baczyński, 1989: 1-4; Milewska, 1989: 1; Tittenbrun, 1992: 143). The first post-communist government, however, accepted this mechanism for the massive enrichment of the *nomenklatura* class, partly in the hope that it would have an "erosive effect" on that class. Yet it may be argued that instead of the anticipated weakening of the communist elite's cohesiveness in the wake of its ideological conversion and atomization through individualistic entrepreneurial pursuit, the well-entrenched informal mutual-corruption networks were strengthened by their new opportunities to capitalize on their crimes and to venture into new, more daring criminal schemes (Łoś, 1994b: 82-4; Zybertowicz, 1993: 32-45).

By the time of the first (semi) democratic elections in July 1989, there were already three thousand joint-stock companies. In 75 per cent of cases they had been created on the basis of the 1,700 largest state enterprises (Tittenbrun, 1992: 143). At the beginning of 1990, among the people occupying key positions in joint-stock companies, were 705 chief executives of state enterprises, 304 lower rank executives and chief accountants, 580 directors of state-controlled co-operatives, 80 party functionaries and activists, 57 municipal presidents, 9 heads of districts and their deputies, and 38 directors of district-government departments (Skarzynski, 1990: 4).

While in the 1970s the criminal enrichment schemes of the ruling groups within the economic and security sectors were probably relatively unconnected, the late 1980s were characterized by their relative merger. The new opportunities of direct property conversion, transfers of funds of substantial value, and creation of joint ventures with foreign capital, attracted keen interest from the Security Service members who did not want to be left out. As mentioned earlier, each workplace, organization or office had its own SB "guardian angel". This person ran a net of secret informers and was, as a rule, fully apprised of life under the formal façade of stern communist institutions (Zybertowicz, 1993: 32-45). Due to their inside knowledge, these agents were exceptionally well placed to pressure officials who were designing high-stake deals into inviting them as partners, paid protectors or providers of useful intelligence. Close links of SB and military agents with their often influential secret informers were also the basis for various profitable endeavours.

Moreover, security agents were always heavily involved in areas requiring extensive foreign contacts, such as diplomacy, foreign trade and sport, which presented them with unique opportunities for smuggling, hard-currency graft and speculation. In the 1980s and into the 1990s, they could finally invest their illegitimate foreign earnings by setting up sham joint ventures or so-called Polonia (*émigré*) companies. These types of companies were offered especially favourable tax terms in the name of attracting foreign investments (Zybertowicz, 1993: 39-43). Finally, the information obtained through technological espionage was a commodity that could acquire a high price on the black/free market (Żabicki, 1992).

In sum, the *nomenklatura* networks of the late 1980s appeared well prepared for the shift towards capitalism and determined to capitalize on their privileged position and connections. Moreover, they had been socialized to regard legal constraints as not applicable to themselves.

Policies Implemented in the 1980s

Responding to pressures from international bodies and a dissatisfied society at home, the Party and the Military Council of General Jaruzelski tried to build an image of Poland as a state ruled by law. Among the institutions introduced in the 1980s with the explicit aim of monitoring and enforcing the legality of the state and its representatives were the Superior Administrative Court (1980), Tribunal of State (1982), Constitutional Tribunal (1986), and the Ombudsman (1988). Moreover, a 1980 constitutional amendment removed the Highest Chamber of Control from the government's supervision and subordinated it to the Diet only (reversing a 1976 amendment; Mordwilko, 1994: 57-8).

The Superior Administrative Court opened a venue for citizens to lodge complaints about administrative decisions if they believed that the law had been violated.

The Tribunal of State was to adjudicate in cases of alleged constitutional or criminal responsibility of the highest state dignitaries in connection with the performance of their official duties. Yet the real rulers, the Party leadership, were excluded from the Tribunal's jurisdiction as their posts did not have constitutional bases.

The Constitutional Tribunal was to rule on the constitutionality of laws that were passed after March 1982 (thus excluding laws based on the 1981 Martial Law decrees and other enactments of that exceptionally repressive period). The Tribunal was not empowered to examine laws from the perspective of international law (Łętowska, 1994: 32). Moreover, its decisions could be overruled by the Diet. The right to submit laws for review was restricted to certain state bodies and organizations (Łętowska, 1994: 16).

The Ombudsman, or Commissioner for Civil Rights Protection, was charged with the task of intervening when citizens' civil rights were infringed by the authorities.

The Highest Chamber of Control controlled the legality, efficiency and rationality of economic, financial and administrative activities of the state administration and economic organizations, co-operatives, local councils and other agencies (Lang, 1994: 40).

All the above institutions were potentially useful instruments of the rule of law, but their primary function in Poland during the 1980s was to try to provide legitimacy to a system that was not based on law. While the Ombudsman's office and the Superior Administrative Court could claim some achievements, they could not alter the overall political context or the vagueness of the constitution. The first ombudsman, Ewa Łętowska, asked later about her role in improving the plight of prisoners, acknowledged the narrow limits of her mandate:

Of course, I was critical about the repressive law of May 1985 that filled up prisons beyond capacity and was marked by Draconian severity, but my role was to check on living conditions like the cleanliness of bathrooms and latrines, the taste of the prison soup, etc., not to change the law. (Łętowska, 1992: 124)

The usefulness of the State Tribunal was purely symbolic as the Party and its leaders could not be touched, and rare attempts to hold former state dignitaries accountable for their actions were undermined by the nature of the system itself and the close ties of criminal "togetherness" within the ruling stratum.

CASE STUDY 2

In 1982, the Diet Commission for Constitutional Responsibility undertook an investigation of the activities of several top governmental officials from the 1970-80 period. Two years later, the commission concluded that there was enough evidence to charge two of them, the prime minister, Piotr Jaroszewicz, and his deputy, Tadeusz Wrzaszczyk, with gross violation of the constitution, wilful mismanagement of the economy, and withholding from society information about foreign debt and the depth of the economic catastrophe (Kowalik, 1990: 193-6). The commission cross-examined 46 witnesses and looked at 2,299 documents; its work is recorded in more than 100 volumes, and the final justification for submission of the two cases to the Tribunal of the State numbered 107 pages. Several months later, an amnesty was introduced that abolished responsibility for any crimes committed before July 1984 for "political reasons" (Kowalik, 1990). Thus, any crimes that might have been committed by Jaroszewicz, Wrzaszczyk, Gierek and many others responsible for the rampant corruption and pillage of the national economy in the 1970s were forgiven and forgotten by their successors.

This "case study" is but one example of a general rule that no institution of constitutional control can be effective where there is no political will and where the ruling party places itself above the law. It is also worth noting that in communist Poland the very concept of "constitutional responsibility" of state officials was a legal fiction, given that many governing bodies, including such seats of power as the Party and the Central Planning Commission, had no constitutional basis and government operation was regulated mostly by decree rather than proper legislation (Kowalik, 1990: 203-4).

In the case of Poland and other Soviet Bloc countries, the only way to try and stop some of the state crimes was to abolish the communist state itself. In the second part of this chapter we look at the efficacy of this radical solution.

The 1990s

The Police State in Transition

Near the end of the 1980s, when the communist economy virtually collapsed and Polish people were bitterly angry about unbearable levels of repression, humiliation and deprivation, the Ministry of Internal Affairs (MSW) initiated a "dialogue" with the informal opposition, which culminated in the Round Table talks in the spring of 1989. According to an account by the then Minister of Internal Affairs, Czesław Kiszczak, his ministry envisaged the need for some form of power sharing and endeavoured, by means of secret infiltration, to effect and exploit the opposition's division into two camps: the "constructive opposition" and the "radicals":

> In the period between...the waves of strikes in 1988, the confidential dialogue with the opposition intensified.... As the head of the Ministry of Internal Affairs, I had *a fully up-to-date picture of the situation in opposition circles* and easy contact with its representatives.... In January 1989, the Xth Plenum [of the Party]...finally cleared the way for a dialogue with the sector of the opposition which we then called *"constructive"*. (Kiszczak, 1990:11, emphasis added; see also Bereś and Skoczylas, 1991)

With Poland being the first country in the Soviet Bloc to abolish the communist monopoly, the opposition forces had to be careful not to provoke a violent reaction from either the Soviet Union or the domestic apparatus of coercion. According to Edward Wende, a renowned defender in political trials under communism and a senator in the 1989-93 period, the Round Table talks were underwritten by a secret agreement. He claimed that the

Party put forward the following conditions: "We will give up political power, you will give us a free hand in economic matters... We will give you the power, you will not search our pockets" (Wende, 1994: 3). While we have no way of verifying whether such an agreement was explicitly negotiated and achieved, it is evident that the whole process of systemic transition unfolded as if such an agreement were indeed in force.

The Solidarity forces were not treated as equal partners at the Round Table talks, which were held on the Communists' terms and constituted a form of compromise between the strong opposition and a considerably weakened, but well-entrenched, establishment. Its mounting problems notwithstanding, the Party still had the backing of the Soviet Union, whose reaction could not be easily predicted. What followed were semi-free parliamentary elections (in June 1989) whereby 65% of the seats in the lower house were reserved for Communists and their allies. The Party's first secretary, General Jaruzelski, became president and the opposition candidate, Tadeusz Mazowiecki, became the first non-communist prime minister. The two key ministries - Internal Affairs and National Defence - remained under communist leadership until July 1990. According to Polish historian Wojciech Roszkowski:[23]

> President Jaruzelski did not interfere with a gradual dismantling of communist rule and even to some extent contributed to the mollification of the former ruling class's resistance. At the same time, however, he shielded the conversion of its members into legitimate entrepreneurs. [In the same period], a large part of the documentation of the communist regime's lawlessness was either destroyed or hidden. For instance, based on an unwritten decision by E. Bula, the chief of the Military Counterintelligence Service, that service's archives were destroyed. Jaruzelski himself ordered the destruction of the minutes of the 1982-89 Politburo meetings. (Albert, 1994: 899)

Apart from the Supreme Court, the new government did not conduct any review of the judiciary inherited from the communist era. Its "verification" of prosecutors did not include a security screening. In 1990, the Ministry of Internal Affairs was reorganized, the Security Service (SB) was dissolved, and the State Protection Agency (UOP) was created. Many former SBs took advantage of early retirement provisions. Of the 24,000 former SB functionaries, 14,000 decided to undergo a "verification" procedure carried out by the newly created Qualification Commission, whose mandate was to exclude applicants who had previously violated the law or basic human rights. Ten thousand applicants were positively verified, although not all of them became UOP employees. Central and district

Qualification Commissions consisted of senators, members of the lower house of Parliament (including many former communists), lawyers, representatives from Police Headquarters, as well as members of the Solidarity Union. It has been alleged that many commission members feared secret revenge from the disqualified SBs (Henzler, 1990a: 1) and some were secret informers themselves (Widacki, 1992: 118). Some of those screened out by the commissions were later allowed to join the UOP quietly; many others found employment in the regular police force (which was not subject to "verification") and various private security agencies. The military secret services were exempt from any form of screening.

The move towards democracy has released into the newly forming market a sizable army of specialists in covert operations. They had been professionally trained in infiltration, networking, dirty-money laundering, setting up front organizations, interception of information, bribing, and so forth. They have retained access to various resources related to their former career and through personal links have remained connected to all levels of power within the post-communist state. These developments have triggered a process of replacement of state violence/crime (practised by the secret services) by professional organized violence/crime (practised through powerful informal networks as well as private security agencies and other for-hire services).

A partial privatization of the communist security apparatus - through the creation of private security and detective companies - was legally possible thanks to the 1988 Economic Activity Act. In 1994 such companies employed more than 100,000 people, while the state police employed 98,000 (Czapska, 1994; Hugo-Bader and Wiernikowska, 1994: 6). Although this new industry provides needed protection for persons, property and private businesses, security companies are also engaged in illegal debt collection, deal enforcement and various other tasks that may involve use of undercover methods, blackmail, threats and physical force. They often employ people with criminal records, and subcontract work informally. Some of these companies are also used as fronts for well-developed criminal schemes and are strategically placed to exploit and protect major illegal economic ventures as well as foreign intelligence operations (Hugo-Bader and Wiernikowska, 1994: 7-9).

The "Power Conversion" Process

When the Party dissolved itself in January 1990, one of its factions constituted itself as the Social-Democratic Party of Poland (SdRP) and took over the Party's material wealth, including its foreign bank accounts (for details, see Janecki, 1996, a and b). In the period between the 1993 parliamentary elections and the 1995 presidential elections until the 1997 parliamentary elections, the group came close to monopolizing power in Poland. Its members' political careers were shaped in the 1980s - a period in which the Party grew relatively weaker and the influence of the special services increased.

One of the most striking features of the 1989 revolution was the so-called "conversion of power" phenomenon (Staniszkis, 1991). This concept refers to a situation where a group, which holds a privileged position under one political system through its control of resources of certain kinds, is able to preserve its privileged status under a new system by shifting its control to resources of a different kind.

Empirical research (Szelenyi and Szelenyi, 1995; Wasilewski, 1995; Wasilewski and Wnuk-Lipiński, 1995) confirmed that one of the features of the post-1989 transformation was a conversion of political assets into economic ones (ie, capitalist property). The bulk of the *nomenklatura* class has succeeded in retaining its ruling position by exerting control over the spontaneous and formal privatization processes, capital formation, and creation of new economic and financial institutions. A smaller, but still significant, segment of the *nomenklatura* (one quarter) managed to hold to their senior decision-making posts in various domains of public life (Wasilewski, 1995: 118). The former elite's access to political power rapidly expanded, however, in the wake of their electoral victories of 1993 and 1995. In short, they appear to have traded their political capital for economic capital and then used the latter to regain political power. It is beyond the scope of this chapter to dwell on the issue of possible conspiracies as a moving factor behind the post-communist transformation. Our focus is on the impact of the power conversion process on the effectiveness of law enforcement and prevention in the area of state crime.

Once the communist structural context that constrained the shift in property rights was left behind, it became critically important to the *nomenklatura* class to build a new context capable of sustaining their newly acquired property rights. Jadwiga Staniszkis conceptualizes their strategy with reference to what she calls the "politics of institutionalization". That is to say, the informal power networks that evolved in Poland could not officially institutionalize their power position and, therefore, used various techniques to anarchize the state as a method of quasi-institutionalizing their control over crucial economic and political processes. Staniszkis argues that although this kind of politics remains outside the realm of traditional political institutions (such as parliaments and political parties), the politicians themselves (parliamentarians, cabinet ministers) play an active part in it. Their role, however, is not to exercise public control over the political process, but rather "to oil the wheels of a process which they hope will bring personal gain or party political advantage" (Staniszkis, 1995: 47). This leads to the *depoliticization and technocratization* of fundamentally important decisions that are "being hijacked from the political structures of the state" and to the *privatization of certain components of the state* that are "being diverted to the promotion of group interests rather than the public interest" *(ibid)*. According to Staniszkis, these political strategies of institutionalization "do not demolish the facade of democracy - they just ignore it" *(ibid)*.

The power conversion process was made possible by a number of conditions deeply rooted in the communist past:

1. The Mafia-like operation of communist networks of power. This is epitomized by the phenomenon of "dirty togetherness", which has - according to Podgórecki - created "'perverse' forms of loyalty based on a matrix of different, more or less connected, partnerships aiming at making use of all formal and official structures in order to take them over for private goals, taking advantage of their administrative potential and formal power" (Podgórecki, 1993: 99). Since "the pool of official positive decisions is limited...the dirty partnership uses its private connections to take over part of this pool for itself. Hence, less is left for official procedures. Sometimes dirty togetherness takes over the entire pool" (Podgórecki, 1994: 115).

2. The omnipresent "police state" networks.

3. The top-down character of liberalization and the elitist character of the Round Table contract (Zybertowicz, 1995/96).

4. The massive and illegal destruction/theft of files of the communist secret services.

5. Effective obstruction of all attempts at lustration (ie, vetting for possible collaboration with the secret services) and decommunization (see for example, Łoś, 1995).

We are going to elaborate on just one of these factors: the deliberate destruction and theft of secret files performed in the 1989-90 period by the top officials within the Internal Affairs and National Defence ministries (Jurczenko, 1991; Jachowicz, 1990). This operation has prevented representatives of the new order from having access to documents that are crucial to any attempt to win disclosure of the scale of the former system's lawlessness or to bringing the culprits to account. Furthermore, the incineration of large quantities of files provided a convenient smokescreen for an even more dangerous operation that consisted in the "privatization" of the most sensitive files or parts of them. There are at least two reasons why, once in private hands, this material becomes a source of power:

1. The documentation of crimes committed by various communist functionaries can be used to blackmail and, therefore, influence or "discipline" them;

2. The secret files, which provide information on the Secret Services' infiltration of all types of social groups, including former opposition circles, can be used to blackmail and discredit those members of new political elites who acted as secret informers.

Two separate *Prokuratura* investigations of file-destruction operations were launched in 1991. One of them targeted a group of generals and colonels in charge of Military Counterintelligence, the other focussed on the top leadership of the MSW. It took four years for these investigations to result in trials. Yet one of the two criminal trials that were initiated has been discontinued, the other proceeds very slowly and no one has been convicted so far. Given that there has never been any "lustration" of judges and prosecutors, there is always a possibility that those who prepare indictments and sit in judgment may include past informers.

Law Enforcement and Impunity

Seven years after the collapse of communism in Poland, the vast majority of the enormous number of state crimes committed under the former system remain unpunished. There has been only one trial of persons responsible for

Stalinist crimes against the Polish nation. It lasted three and a half years and resulted eventually in convictions of all twelve defendants. Eleven of them were sentenced in March 1996 to prison sentences ranging from four to nine years, while one received a suspended sentence. All of them appealed their sentences and remain at large. No other actions are pending (Ostrowski and Podemski, 1995). In a number of cases all necessary conditions are met: crimes are well documented, culprits identified and relevant legal regulations are in place. Moreover, Poland's courts are now, at least in principle, independent.

Even in those rare cases when a legal action is initiated against individuals suspected of state crimes committed during the communist period, the police, the *Prokuratura*, and the judiciary move extremely slowly, bureaucratic obstacles appear again and again, and an impressive array of legal chicanery is employed to prolong or stall the proceedings. Among the cases plagued by endless legal haggling are: the 1970 Gdańsk massacre that resulted in at least several dozen deaths; the shooting deaths of the nine "Wujek" miners in 1981; the 1982 assault on the crowd in Lubin; the 1983 murder of Przemyk, and the 1984 murder of Father Popiełuszko; the murderous actions of MSW department IV, Group "D"; and the illegal destruction of secret files and documents in 1989-90.

In a brief case study, we explore and illustrate the justice system's impotence and vulnerability in dealing with the machinery of the former SB crimes.

CASE STUDY 3

In August 1994, a criminal trial that lasted two years ended in an acquittal of the two defendants: General Ciastoń, a former deputy minister of Internal Affairs and head of the SB, and Zenon Płatek, former director of the ministry's Department IV.[24] They were charged with using one of their subordinates as an intermediary in the murder of an outspoken patriotic priest, Father Popiełuszko. In the explanation of the verdict, the presiding judge expressed his frustration:

> The real problem lies in the weakness of the *Prokuratura* and the whole justice system... We do not know the truth... Outside the courtroom, some of the witnesses - former MSW functionaries -

were telling judges that ever since they were called as witnesses in this case, they and their families had experienced many strange, inexplicable things. Fear is the feeling that many of the witnesses shared.... The trial has made it clear that the prosecutor has no chance [to uncover the truth]. (Góral, 1994a: 10-11)

Later, the judge elaborated on this point, when he responded to an interviewer's queries about problems with the *Prokuratura*'s evidence: "They stemmed from the power of the MSW and the weakness of the Justice ministry. The MSW was - and according to some still is - a ministry that no one is able to control" (Góral, 1994b: 11). Subsequently, the Supreme Court president, Professor Strzembosz, informed the press about various odd and alarming incidents that had happened to Judge Góral and to some other persons who cooperated with the court. The tyres of Góral's car were punctured, windows smashed, his apartment broken into and his case files searched. He was repeatedly pointed at by the same group of strange-looking characters who appeared near him in various places. (The judge's application to carry a gun took a year to process.) Another person involved in the trial, an auxiliary judge, received a bogus phone call summoning him to the court - during his absence his apartment was set on fire, killing his mother-in-law. He was also approached by strangers who made threats and reminded him that "the case was not over". Another auxiliary judge was beaten up twice by unknown assailants. Despite these and many other strange incidents, no formal investigation was launched to identify the perpetrators (Januszewski, 1995: 10-11).

Another area of impunity involves state crimes that have occurred in the post-1989 period. In none of the large-scale criminal economic scandals involving state officials that have been uncovered during the past seven years has convincing legal action been taken. The largest economic schemes include such notorious cases as FOZZ (see the case study below); the Art-B company;[25] numerous spectacular banking frauds;[26] gigantic criminal affairs involving import/export manipulations and tax/tariff evasion related to roubles, alcohol and potatoes; and the Kmetko's credit operations. A close look at one of them will illustrate the scope of these criminal ventures and the problems they pose for the justice system.

CASE STUDY 4

The Fund for External Debt Management (FOZZ) was established in early 1989 by the communist government led by Prime Minister Mieczysław Rakowski. It was designed for surreptitious buying out of the Polish foreign debt on the secondary market (ie, at much lower prices than its face value). While Poland was not the first country to engage in such transactions, it was clearly an illegal practice in the light of international regulations.

The fund soon became involved in various ramified, national and international operations, the bulk of which had nothing to do with its formally, though unofficially, defined tasks. These activities continued after the collapse of the communist regime. Despite several well researched publications on FOZZ (for example, Bikont, 1991; Dakowski and Przystawa, 1992), the full scope and consequences of the fund's operations have yet to be determined. Two points of particular relevance to our chapter can safely be made, however.

Firstly, the deliberate misuse of funds in the range of one billion USD, much of it apparently transferred to private accounts abroad. A large part of the resources the FOZZ managers controlled was used for providing lavish credits at interest rates much below current inflation levels. Needless to say, these credits were extended only to those closely connected with the communist power networks. Secondly, the fund's main operations were executed with the full involvement of, and under direct control by, the communist Secret Services (both military and civilian).

Eventually, in 1992, a revealing secret report prepared for the then prime minister, Jan Olszewski, was leaked to the press. It alleged that the FOZZ director and several of his close associates were long-time secret informers of the communist Military Intelligence. According to the report, the chairman of the fund's board of trustees (the then deputy-minister of Finance) had also been for some time a secret informer and eventually an undercover employee of

Intelligence (Raport, 1992). Another credible source claims that the FOZZ director was for many years involved in the arms trade with Iraq and Libya on behalf of the Military Intelligence Service (Bikont, 1991). Names of some other members of the FOZZ board of trustees can be found on the list of alleged informers of the Polish communist Secret Services that was prepared by the then Minister of Internal Affairs, Antoni Maciarewicz, in June 1992 (*Gazeta Polska*, 1993: 3).

The FOZZ operated outside any statutory control and had no unified accounting system. Although in a space of a few months, it performed a number of multinational banking and business operations using several international intermediaries, it took years of investigation to trace the operations effected.[27] In March 1993, after a criminal investigation was completed and the case sent to court, the prosecutor in charge of the investigation, Janusz Kalwas, was asked by a journalist whether it was "relevant for this case that a group within the FOZZ management had collaborated with various secret services". He responded: *"We were not interested in that"* (Kalwas, 1993: 8; emphasis added). So far, no single trial has originated from the *Prokuratura* investigation, and all suspects enjoy freedom. Some of them are very active in the business of privatizing the economy.

In many large-scale economic schemes there is evidence of corruption among high-level officials, and at least in some cases, involvement of persons either employed by or associated with the former and/or present secret services is quite well documented.[28] In some instances, entire police units are involved in shady business ventures (for example, the Poznań district police headquarters corruption scandal); in other cases, police officers are actively involved in criminal rings (for instance, automobile-theft operations - see Góralski and Jachowicz, 1993; Pacewicz *et al*, 1994). Faced with state/organized crime, the justice system seems unable or unwilling to comply with its mandate.

Countless charges of crime against state banks have been laid and then dropped (see Doliniak, 1995, for details), and in some of those cases, prosecutors involved in investigations were subsequently hired by the banks involved (Urbanek, 1995: 7). State banks have extended credit liberally to "deserving" customers who had no intention of paying them back. According to the head of the Highest Chamber of Control, Lech Kaczyński, the names of those who obtained such endowments can be found on the list of the hundred wealthiest Poles (Kaczyński, 1995b: 8). He also conceded in a press interview that "in our social life, there are zones that neither the Chamber nor...the Ministry of Justice is able to penetrate. There are networks that no one can touch" (Kaczyński, 1995a: 12).

It appears that the entire process of private-capital creation - the basis of the systemic change in Poland - relies in considerable measure on criminal economic schemes related to the privatization of the state economy, international financial operations, money laundering, and so forth. Andrzej Mościskier suggested, at a conference in Poland, that during the transition period, informal power networks operate on the basis of a three-step strategy:

1. They ensure that suitable legal loopholes and organizational conditions exist to enable massive, semi-legal property-rights shifts - from public to private sectors.

2. They effect property rights shifts and multiply the capital thus appropriated by means of operations that provide high returns at a low risk (made possible by inside information about pending changes in, for instance, currency value, interest rates or customs regulations, and by the exploitation of hybrid - state/private - forms of ownership).

3. When the illegality of their operations is exposed, they take concerted action to frustrate the due process of law and they employ diverse methods to spread disinformation and manipulate information markets.

In our view, it is unlikely - although not impossible - that the post-*nomenklatura* network is directed by one central "mastermind". Rather than a well-orchestrated conspiracy of power-seeking individuals motivated by a coherent set of principles or goals and coordinated from a single centre, there appears to be a set of ramified, self-regulating and overlapping networks operating on the basis of roughly drawn rules and tacit agreements. Nevertheless, there is enough evidence to assert that the state/organized/economic crime operations are much less chaotic and ephemeral than is officially acknowledged.

Policies for the 1990s

Very little in the way of anti-state-crime policies has been implemented in the post-revolutionary period, the official stand being that of denial rather than openness. It is difficult to compare the volume of state crime prior to and following the 1989 Round Table Agreements. Marketization of the economy and its opening to the West have raised the monetary stakes involved in economic crimes. The privatization of large parts of the formidable security apparatus has shifted violence from state agencies to their private clones, manned often by the same people, but now subordinated to the logic of economics rather than politics. The departure of the Soviet Army divisions, the symbol of coercive subjugation of Poland to its powerful neighbour, left the country awash with arms and military equipment, diverted by Soviet army personnel into open-air markets and trafficked throughout the land. Does the responsibility for the failure of the 1989 revolution to curb state crime in Poland lie in the specific nature of the Polish revolution (negotiated, "controlled", "top-down", piecemeal) or in the intrinsic inability of revolutionary changes to pluck out the informal roots of the well-entrenched police state? Or is it an inevitable part of the early stages of capitalism? While all these factors are pertinent, we feel that their criminogenic potential has been vastly underestimated in Poland.

Below, we enumerate what we consider to be potentially useful policies and indicate to what extent they have been tried in the period of systemic transition in Poland (1989-95).

1. Responsive Revolution

The elitist nature of the process of change and the alienation of both the anti-communist and ex-communist elites from the grassroots have thwarted the sense of shared responsibility among ordinary citizens and blocked avenues for social control of the state. The emphasis on formal institutional democratization and abstract notions of the rule of law was not accompanied in Poland by any measures that would truly empower individuals and give them a renewed sense of citizenship.

2.   Constitution

The overthrow of the old regime should have been followed by the passage of a new constitution. The preservation in post-communist Poland of the inherited constitution, albeit in an amended form, prevented an explicit divorce from the well-established communist tradition of double-faced law, whose "facade" and "shadow" sides might be poles apart (Podgórecki, 1991: 172-3). The failure to enact a new constitution until 1997[29] has facilitated the creation of legal loopholes and inconsistencies and placed the emphasis on legal continuity rather than a radical break.

3.   Constitutional Review

The role of the Constitutional Tribunal, created in 1982, has been limited by several factors: the absence of a fully legitimate new constitution; the fact that the tribunal's decisions are not final and may be overruled by Parliament; the absence of a mandate to apply the precepts of international law; and the statutory deadlines that prevent re-examination of laws inherited from the previous system unless they have been amended (Commissioner, 1993: 60-81; *Nowa Europa*, 1995: 2). Its considerable contribution to the protection of civil rights in Poland notwithstanding (Rzecznik, 1994: 5-21), the tribunal has been unable to address and correct the process of creation of legal loopholes and inconsistent laws and statutes that appear designed to increase rather than decrease the opportunities for corruption and unfair enrichment by well-informed, well-organized networks.

4.   "Lustration" or Security Screening

(Special legislation that would bar former secret-service agents and collaborators from public office for a specified period of time.) The failure to implement any "lustration" or security screening procedures within the top echelons of the state administration (including the justice system and the state financial sector)[30] resulted in a situation where many influential state positions are occupied by persons who for many years were accustomed to a double life and the ethos of treason. They are likely to have developed a high degree of moral callousness and are obvious targets for blackmail.

5. *"Decommunisation"*

(A procedure based on legislation that would bar former Communist Party officials and those who held top *nomenklatura* posts from occupying important public offices for a certain period of time.) The failure to make any formal judgement about the legality of the Soviet-imposed communist system and the role of the Party and its leadership has enabled the former *nomenklatura* class to close ranks with former agents in the massive project of the "privatization"[31] of the state. A well-defined procedure equipped with due legal safeguards could probably have helped to prevent the type of collusion between the economic and political elites that occurs in contemporary Poland.[32]

6. *Adequate Funding of the Court System*

The relatively low salaries of Polish judges and prosecutors serve to increase their susceptibility to corruption and cause a constant outflow of the best-qualified lawyers to other, much more profitable, lines of legal work. A more adequate remuneration of judicial and prosecutorial personnel would go a long way towards improving the justice system's quality and prestige.

7. *Conflict of Interest Laws*

Legal regulation of the status of civil servants. Legal regulation of lobbying. The first post-communist prime minister barred civil servants and government officials from holding any remunerated appointments outside their employment. His successor repealed this order and made it possible for civil servants and state officials to combine their poorly paid jobs with lucrative positions on boards of trustees and supervisory councils of joint-stock companies formed by the State Treasury. An anti-corruption law of June 1992 has legitimated cross-appointments of those government officials who are authorized by their supervisors to do so. The regulations are not fully clear, however, because of the existence of earlier, more stringent statutes that have never been repealed. Multiple appointments and involvement in private economic ventures by state functionaries open many opportunities for corruption, abuse of office and conflict of interest. Moreover, the absence of any legal regulation of lobbying practices has contributed to a dangerous symbiosis between business and parliamentarians as well as other politicians. Finally, the failure to introduce clear legal definition of the status of the civil service legitimizes patronage and opportunistic politicization of the state administration.

8.   *Parliamentary Supervision of Secret Services*

A Parliamentary Commission for Special Services has been established in Poland only since October 1995. The commission is empowered to deal with complaints against the civilian and military secret services, to review nominations for directors and vice-directors of these services, and to give an opinion on relevant legislative initiatives. The commission's first challenge came in December 1995, when the Office for State Protection[33] alleged that Prime Minister Józef Oleksy, a former communist official, had been spying, first, for the KGB and, later, for the Russian Intelligence (from at least 1983 and until 1995).[34]   Under pressure from the opposition, a special commission has been formed on the basis of the Parliamentary Commission. It has been broadened to include members of all opposition parties and granted investigative rights. While its mandate does not entitle it to study the substance of the allegations - they were investigated by the Military *Prokuratura* and promptly dropped - the commission has undertaken an assessment of the legality of the evidence-gathering methods employed. Despite fears of undue pressure by ex-communists on the commission's proceedings, its preliminary report found no fault with the secret services' work. The partisan division within the commission - with the majority of its members representing the ruling (ex-communist) coalition - did, however, find expression in the final report. The report's conclusion, endorsed by coalition members' votes exclusively, implied that the officials and agents involved might have violated the law. Contrary minority conclusions were attached to the report.

Although it was created too late to halt the abuses and misuses of power prevalent within the Secret Services during the earlier transition years, the Parliamentary Commission has proved its potential, albeit limited, usefulness in its handling of the Oleksy affair. The extraordinary nature of this case, however, makes it impossible to assess the commission's ability to monitor and guide the operation of these services.

To create minimum conditions for its effectiveness, the commission should be granted permanent investigative powers and its mandate should be broadened to include a greater impact on the type of operations undertaken and the methods employed. Furthermore, it is crucially important that the chairperson and at least half of the members come from opposition parties.

9. Judicial Control and Civilian Observation of the Police

Complaints against the uniformed police in Poland are handled internally by the police. Despite the lack of judicial control and external supervision of their work, police forces (including secret services) were granted new powers by Parliament in 1995. Rules related to the use of arms were relaxed and the allowance of almost unlimited use of surreptitious methods of evidence-gathering, such as electronic surveillance and mail inspection, is based on administrative rather than judicial authorizations.

Furthermore, the new law has empowered the police to employ such methods of entrapment as provocation and police-controlled illegal transactions. Many critics see the new police law as a first step towards the return of the police state. The broadening of police powers - especially in the absence of any attempt to provide for proper judicial control and civilian monitoring - is unlikely to contribute to better state-crime control and opens new avenues for abuse of state power by the ruling elite. It adds to the confusion about the status and role of the post-communist police force and considerably increases opportunities for corruption and direct police involvement in political trickery.

10. Extension of the Statute of Limitations for Prosecuting Major State Crimes Committed Under the Totalitarian Regime

Given that state crimes could not be effectively prosecuted under the previous system, the statute of limitations should be counted from the moment systemic change began. In Poland, a law to this effect was finally passed in 1995, six years after the collapse of communism.

11. Replacement of the Old Criminal Code Sections Related to Economic Crimes with a Coherent Set of New Norms Relevant to the New, Radically Different Economic Order

A 1994 Law on Protection of Economic Circulation was passed too late to curb the wave of rampant economic crime in the transition years, during which evidently obsolete communist criminal law applied. Moreover, the new bill has many obvious shortcomings and it is not integrated with the rest of the criminal law that still awaits a major overhaul (Monkiewicz and Nizińska, 1993: 8-13).

The new law addresses problems related to money laundering, obtaining credits on false pretences, concealing assets from creditors, insurance fraud, major customs offences, violations of fair bidding procedures, computer crime, and so forth. The lack of relevant criminal norms in these areas facilitated the rampant plundering of the state economy and private exploitation of the state banking sector. By the time the new law was passed, the major players had already accumulated huge capital and Poland became "the European money laundering centre" (Kapuściński, 1994: 18-19).

12. Levelling the Field of Political Competition

The assets of the former ruling party should have been nationalized. Political parties and their election campaigns should be financed by membership fees and grants from the state budget - the only controllable sources of funds. Strict accounting and reporting regulations, backed by sanctions, should apply.

The Social-Democratic Party of Poland (SdRP) took over most of the wealth of the Communist Party, while refusing to pay the Party's and its own debts. The SdRP also received special seed money (partly repaid in November 1990) from the KGB to organize its founding congress, launch a newspaper and invest in profitable ventures (Janecki, 1996a; Parchimowicz, 1991). The investigation into this affair was discontinued due to "the minimal public harm involved"[35] (Janecki, 1996a).

It was evident in both the 1993 parliamentary election campaign and in the 1995 presidential election campaign that the SdRP had huge funds at its disposal and was the only party that could afford an "American-style" campaign, assisted by Western media and image consultants (Ash, 1996: 10). Its sheer financial power and lavishness of style played an important role in the SdRP's successful domination of the political scene. Other parties, unable to compete with SdRP financially, have been pushed into its shadow. It is noteworthy that despite election campaign spending limits per candidate, there are no sanctions for their infringement or for failure to submit a financial report.

13. Free Press

Given the lack of political will and the reluctance of the *Prokuratura* and other control agencies to expose the crimes committed by the stalwart power networks, the role of the free media becomes pivotal. Formally, there is no longer censorship in Poland, and diverse political groups can reach the public through a variety of private media and/or public television. Nevertheless, several factors limit the potential role of the mass media as a forum for the successful exposure of state crimes. Firstly, many of the old, well-established print media were "privatized" by their former communist editors and managers. Secondly, the communist journalistic training and experience have neither equipped journalists with investigative skills nor instilled in them a sense of social or professional responsibility. Thirdly, the proportion of secret service informers and collaborators was exceptionally high among journalists under the communist system. Fourthly, intimidation and threats are sometimes used to prevent publication of potentially damaging information. Fifthly, the absence of an enforceable defamation law contributes to the proliferation of totally irresponsible, often politically motivated, accusations. Deluged with an incessant flow of sensational rumours and denunciations, the public is no longer able to distinguish between potentially important disclosures and sheer fabrications. This provides a protective shield to those whose crimes are exposed by diligent journalists. The vast dimensions of these crimes actually increase the likelihood of their being treated with incredulity.

Epilogue

The above analysis of concrete processes of systemic transformation in Poland suggests that change introduced through negotiated agreement between the old regime's elite and the opposition elite creates a fertile ground for proliferation of "crime at the top". A revolution based on "a gentlemen's agreement and a handshake" has lulled vigilance and disarmed the opposition forces. It has led to a wilful underestimation of the formidable apparatus of the totalitarian police state and its potential forms of disintegration and survival.

Most of the policies listed at the end of our chapter seem to be prudent measures to take in a situation where change in systemic rules and laws widens the opportunities for corruption and private exploitation of public resources. These measures are neither radical nor guaranteed to work, but they appear as logical responses to the normative vacuum created by the collapse of the old order. As policies they are designed to set some minimal bureaucratic and legal safeguards compatible with democratic society. The fact that they were not introduced at all or instituted only after several years suggests that there was no political will to counter the "nomenklaturization" of the processes of privatization of the state economy and transformation of the state.

Given the specific focus of our chapter, we have deliberately left out of our analysis fundamental issues of the nature of post-communist changes and their broader political and economic context. Our paper should be read as a warning and a reminder that the well-entrenched and profoundly corrupt power networks fostered by Soviet-style totalitarianism have a life of their own and are more likely to subvert the rules of democracy than to play by them. In our view, institutional changes in Poland went only so far as was compatible with the interests and aspirations of those who have become their principal beneficiaries. By letting the communist ruling class strengthen its power bases and take over the process of transition, the anti-totalitarian forces have helped to prolong a hybrid formation that continues to subsidize the former *nomenklatura* at the expense of the rest of society.

As with any pioneering effort, our inquiry into the oblique territory of post-communist state crime should be treated as exploratory and open-ended. All the more so since the subject under study - the posthumous life of a police state - is intricate and precarious. We can only say that the material we have presented has passed many stringent tests of credibility. We have taken a cautious path, choosing to underestimate the extent and depth of state crime in contemporary Poland rather than rely on unverified sources. Still, due to the very nature of the research, any diagnosis must remain tentative.

Notes

1   We use the term "secret services" as an umbrella category that encompasses intelligence, counter-intelligence, political police and special forces.
2   See Rzepliński's book on the Polish judiciary (1989) for full documentation of this point.
3   It is worth noting that General Wojciech Jaruzelski, who was the Party's first secretary in the 1980s and the president of Poland in 1989-1990, had earlier been a Vice-Minister and Minister of Defence for 21 years (1962-

83). In 1981, he nominated General Czesław Kiszczak, his long-term comrade and former chief of Military Intelligence and Counterintelligence, as the minister of Internal Affairs. (He remained in that office until July 1990).

4   Much of the information on the MSW's structure and functions comes from Dominiczak, 1994. The author is a former high-level functionary of that ministry.

5   "Taking care" involved the provision of intelligence and counterintelligence vetting/surveillance of all persons participating in important trade negotiations, inclusion in official delegations of secret collaborators or undercover agents employed in relevant trade agencies, protection and control of document circulation, attempts to infiltrate foreign parties involved, etc.

6   The population of Poland was around 38 million.

7   Our assessment, based on various sources.

8   The claim by former communists that Intelligence was excluded from this penetration is difficult to verify.

9   Among its employees in active-duty positions, some 75% belonged to the Party, and the percentage was even higher in the Security Service. The overall share of Party cardholders in the adult population was 8% in 1988 (12.2% in 1979; Sułek, 1992, 250-4).

10   According to various archival sources, General Jaruzelski and his Minister of Defence, General Florian Siwicki, asked Soviet leaders for assurances that military assistance would be extended in the event that the Communist Party was unable to hold to power or that martial law resulted in anarchy (Kersten, 1995).

11   The then Minister of Internal Affairs, Czesław Kiszczak, issued a coded order on 13 December 1981, which authorized district police chiefs to make decisions about the use of firearms against those who resisted the martial law. Charged in the 1990s with endangering the lives and health of miners in two coal mines, he was acquitted in July 1996, after a lengthy trial (Jachowicz, 1996a, b; Ordyński, 1996).

12   According to the commission, the criminal cover-up involved the highest leadership of the party/state, including General Jaruzelski (*Komisja*, 1991: 13-119).

13   They included also victims of the "Wujek" mine pacification and the Lubin massacre.

14   Inquiries into these crimes have been made particularly difficult as almost the entire contents of the MSW archives relating to the Church (including individual files kept on every priest) were destroyed in 1988 (probably after secret copies were made; Grocki, 1993: 25).

15   Milewski personified the Security Service, which he joined in 1944 when he was only sixteen years old (Mołdawa, 1991: 396). He also had strong links to the Kremlin and played a key role in the preparation and implementation of the "state of war" (Albert, 1994: 792, 811-830).

16   See the document of 16 June 1983 issued by Colonel Józef M. of the Militia Headquarters, *Prawo i Życie*, 28 Nov. 1995: 34.

17   This information is based on the witnesses' statements during the interrogation and the new trial in the 1990s.
18   She was fully rehabilitated after the collapse of communism.
19   Adam Podgórecki's notion; see, for example, 1993: 21, 99; 1994: 115.
20   For documentation and analysis, see Łoś 1984.
21   For a detailed analysis and bibliographical information see, Łoś, 1984, 1988, 1990a, b; Tarkowski, 1983, 1990).
22   Relevant legal developments include: the gradual rehabilitation of the pre-war Code of Commerce of 1934, especially its rules on joint-stock companies; the passage, in December 1988, of the Law on New Economic Activities; and the enactment, in February 1989, of the Law on Selected Conditions of Consolidation of the National Economy, which granted state enterprises the right to sell, let or lease their capital assets and facilities.
23   Writing under the pen name Andrzej Albert.
24   This verdict was quashed in March 1996 by the Court of Appeal, which ruled that the justification of the acquittal was biased and arbitrary in its treatment of the evidence tried.
25   In connection with this scandal, several directors and employees of state banks have been sentenced to prison terms of between 2.5 and 4.5 years. Moreover, one of the two principal figures - both of whom fled to Israel - has been extradited to Poland in 1986 (from Switzerland, where he was visiting).
26   At least 4 billion USD were lost between mid-1989 and mid-1995 through reckless allocation of credits and loans by state banks (Zybala, 1995: 50). As a basis for comparison: the total value of Polish exports in 1995 was 16 billion USD.
27   On the political context of the FOZZ operations and their cover-up, see Dakowski and Przystawa, 1992.
28   See Łoś for example, Kwaśniewski *et al*, 1994, on the Kmetko affair; Kraśkowski, 1994, on InterAms; and Raport, 1992, on Art-B.
29   The Constitutional Act of 17 October 1992, the so-called Small Constitution, was a thoroughly inadequate temporary bridge between the old communist constitution and a long-expected democratic one.
30   See Łoś, 1995, for a discussion of an aborted attempt at lustration in 1992 and an analysis of the ongoing lustration debate in Poland.
31   This terms refers to subordination of both state asets and state functions to private interests.
32   The Czech experience with the 1991 lustration/decommunization law seems to confirm the potential usefulness of such a measure in preventing the deliberate subversion of state functions and limiting the new state's susceptibility to crime.
33   Subordinated to the then president, Lech Wałęsa.
34   Prime Minister Oleksy resigned from his post in January 1996, but was promptly elected leader of the key party within the ruling coalition, the ex-communist Social Democracy.
35   While investigation into this matter had been opened twice, each time it was promptly discontinued. In both cases, the Ministers of Justice were

former Communists: Włodzimierz Cimoszewicz in 1993 and Jerzy Jaskiernia in 1995.

Bibliography

Albert, A. (1994), *Najnowsza Historia Polski: 1914-1993*, Vol. 2, London, Puls Publications.
Alexander, W.M. (1984), *Agentura. Państwo Policyjne*, Berlin, Pogląd.
Ash, T.G. (January 1996), "'Neo-Pagan' Poland", *New York Review of Books*, 11.
Baczyński, J. (December 1989), "Nadużycia pod szyldem przedsiębiorczośći", *Polityka*, 16.
Bereś, W. and Skoczylas, J. (1991), *General Kiszczak mowi... prawie wszystko*, Warszawa, BGW.
Bikont, A. (November 1991), "W poszukiwaniu zaginionych milionów", *Gazeta Wyborcza*, 16.
Botos, B. (1990), "The Agony of Transition", *Most Economic Journal on Soviet Union and Eastern Europe*, l(l).
Commissioner for Civil Rights (1993) *Annual Report*, Warsaw, RPO.
Committee in Support of Solidarity Reports (10 March 1983a), no. 12, ("Internment in Military Penal Camps").
Committee in Support of Solidarity Reports (13 April 1983b), no. 13, ("Victims of War").
Czabański, K. (20 November 1981), "Przywileje", *Solidarność*.
Czapska, J. (1994), "Growing Privatization of Penal Justice and the Personal Security Feelings in Poland", Paper presented at the World Congress of Sociology, Bielefeld.
Dakowski, M. and Przystawa, J. (1992), *Via Bank i FOZZ*, Komorow, Wyd, Antyk.
Doliniak, K. (1 September 1995), "Przekręt w banku", *Cash*.
Dominiczak, H. (1994), *Historia Służby Bezpieczeństwa PRL (1944-1990)*, unpublished manuscript.
Fredro-Boniecki, T. (1990), *Zwycięstwo Księdza Jerzego*, Warszawa, Niezależna Oficyna Wydawnicza.
Gazeta Polska (1993), no. 4, ("Lista Konfidentów").
Gliński, P. (1992), "Acapulco Near Konstancin", in Janine R. Wedel (ed.), *The Unplanned Society. Poland During and After Communism*, New York: Columbia University Press.
Góral, J. (24 August 1994a), "Nie znamy prawdy", *Gazeta Wyborcza*.
———— (24 August 1994b), "Interview", *Gazeta Wyborcza*.
Góralski, R. and Jachowicz, J. (7 January 1993), "Policjanci i złodzieje", *Gazeta Wyborcza*.
Grochmalski, P. and Szczepaniak, J. (14-15 October 1995), "Taśmy prawdy", *Tygodnik Ilustrowany Poznaniak*.
Grocki, M. (1993), *Konfidenci są wśród nas*, Warszawa, Editions Spotkania.
Henzler, M. (18 August 1990a), "Przeswietlanie SB", *Polityka*.

_____ (20 October 1990b), "Złote puzzle" *Polityka*.
Hołwinski, J. (29 May 1981), "0 legalnym bezprawiu", *Solidarność*.
Hugo-Bader, J. and Wiernikowska, M. (24 June 1994), "Ochraniarze", *Gazeta Wyborcza. Magazyn*.
Jachowicz, J. (24 July 1990), "WSW zaciera ślady: zniszczono 40,000 teczek", *Gazeta Wyborcza*.
_____.(24 July 1996a), "Proces ważny i trudny", *Gazeta Wyborcza*.
_____.(30 July 1996b), "Uniewinniony", *Gazeta Wyborcza*.
Janecki, S. (1996a), "Wielka gra", *Wprost*, 21 January.
_____ (1996b), "Związki towaryzskie", *Wprost*, 28 January.
Januszewski, R. (4 February 1995), "Śmierć na telefon", *Prawo i Życie*, no 5.
Jaruzelski, W. (1992), *Stan Wojenny: DLACZEGO....*, Warszawa, BGW.
Jurczenko, I. (9 March 1991), "Kto niszczył akta SB?", *Prawo i Życie*, no 10.
Jurczenko, I. and Kikijanek, K. (1991), *Ludzie z "Żelaza". Największa afera w polskim wywiadzie*, Warszawa, BGW.
Kaczyński, L. (5 May 1995a), "Interview", *Życie Warszawy*.
_____ (10-11 June 1995b), "Interview", *Superexpress*.
Kaszyński, K. and Podgórski, J. (1994), *Szpiedzy, czyli tajemnice polskiego wywiadu*, Warszawa, Ikar.
Kalwas, J. (6 March 1993), "Interview", *Prawo i Życie*.
Kapuściński, P. (12 June 1994), "Pranie na sucho", *Życie Gospodarcze*, no. 24.
Kersten, K. (1995), "Czym grozili starcy z Kremla? ", *Polityka*, 16 December, 71-74.
KES (27 September 1995), "Rozmowy z oficerami MSW", *Gazeta Wyborcza*.
Kiszczak, C. (8 September 1990), "Tajemnice Magdalenki" (An interview), *Polityka*.
Komisja Nadzwyczajna do Zbadania Działalnosci MSW. Sejm RP, (1991), "Sprawozdanie z działalności w okresie X kadencji Sejmu RP (1989-91)", Warszawa.
Kowalik, H. (1990), *Mali ludzie Gierka*, Koscian, "Omnibus".
Kraśkowski, L. (17 November 1994), "Czy Waldemar Pawlak jest skorumpowany", *Życie Warszawy*.
Kwasniewski, P. *et al* (29-9 May 1994), "Kmetko story", *Gazeta Wyborcza*.
Lang, J. (1994), "Ocena porównawcza rozwiązań proponowanych w projekcie ustawy o NIK", *Biuletyn. Ekspertyzy i Opinie Prawne*, 3(13), Warszawa, Wydawnictwo Sejmowe.
Łętowska, E. (1992), *Baba na Swieczniku*, Warszawa, BGW.
_____(1994), *Po co ludziom Konstytucja*, Warszawa, Helsinska Fundacja Praw Człowieka.
Łoś, M. (1983), "Law and Order in Contemporary Poland", *Canadian Slavonic Papers*, 25(3).
_____ (1984), "Corruption in a Communist Country: A Case Study of Poland", *International Annals of Criminology*, 22(1-2).
_____ (1988), *Communist Ideology, Law and Crime*, London, Macmillan Press; New York, St. Martin's Press.
_____ (1990a), "Dynamic Relationships of the First and Second Econonmies in Old and New Marxist States" in M. Łoś (ed.), *The Second Economy in Marxist States*, London, Macmillan Press.

_____ (ed.) (1990b), *The Second Economy in Marxist States*, London: Macmillan Press; New York, St.Martin's Press.

_____ (1992), "From Underground to Legitimacy: the Normative Dilemmas of Postcommunist Marketization" in Bruno Dallago *et al* (eds), *Privatization and Entrepreneurship in Post-Socialist Countries*, London, Macmillan Press; New York, St.Martin's Press.

_____ (1994a), "Property Rights, Market and Historical Justice: Legislative Discourses in Poland", *International Journal of the Sociology of Law*, 22.

_____ (1994b), "The Retrospective Revolution in East-Central Europe", *International Journal of Contemporary Sociology*, 31(1).

_____ (1995), "Lustration and Truth Claims: Unfinished Revolutions in Central Europe", *Law and Social Inquiry*, 20(1).

Makowska-Witkowska, B. (1988), *Wezwanie*, Warszawa, Iskry.

Milewska, K. (29 August 1989), "Uwłaszczanie nomenklatury", *Życie Warszawy*.

Misiak, E. (10 October 1995), "Zastraszony świadek", *SuperExpress*.

Moczydlowski, P. (1988), *Drugie życie w instytucji totalnej.*, Warszawa, Uniwersytet Warszawski, IPSiR.

Mołdawa, T. (1991), *Ludzie Wladzy: 1944-1991*, Warszawa, PWN.

Monkiewicz, Z. and Nizińska Z. (December 1993), "Wybrane problemy regulacji prawnej przestępczosci gospodarczej", *Raport Biura Studiów i Ekspertyz*, no. 54, Warszawa, Sejm RP.

Mordwilko, J. (1994), "Informacja charakteryzująca główne kierunki zmian w Konstytucji od 1952r do 1994r", *Biuletyn. Ekspertyzy I Opinie Prawne*, 4(14), Warszawa, Wydawnictwo Sejmowe.

Nowa Europa (19 July 1995), ("W Polsce pogarsza się stan bezpieczeństwa prawnego").

Ochocki, M. (1992), *Byłem człowiekiem Kiszczaka. General Marek Ochocki w rozmowie z Krzysztofem Spychalskim*, Łódz, Wyd,"ATHOS".

Ordyński, J. (19 May 1995), "Rozpoczyna się nowy proces", *Rzeczpospolita*, 19.

_____ (24 July 1996), "Próbował obalić przemocą ustrój", *Rzeczpospolita*.

Ostrowski, M. and Podemski, S. (6-8 December 1995), "Pamięc nieprzedawniona", *Polityka*.

Pacewicz, P., Jachowicz, J. and Talko, L. (16 March 1994), "Gang wraca do Otwocka", *Gazeta Wyborcza*.

Paczkowski, A. (29-30 July 1995), "Odpowiedzialność za stan wojenny", *Rzeczpospolita*.

Parchimowicz, I. (23 November 1991), "Gra w dokumenty", *Polityka*.

Piecuch, H. (1992), *Wojciech Jaruzelski Tego Nigdy Nie Powie. Rozmowy zGeneralem Pozogą*. Warszawa, Wyd, Reporter.

Pietrzyk, L. (31 October-1 November 1995), "Interview", *Życie Warszawy*.

Podgórecki, A. (1991), *A Sociological Theory of Law*, Milano, Dott, A. Giuffre Editore.

_____ (1993), *Social Oppression*, Westport, Con, London, Greenwood Press.

_____ (1994), *Polish Society*, Westport, Con, London, Praeger.

The Polish Helsinki Committee (1984), *1984 Violations of Human Rights in Poland*, London, Lira Books.

Polityka (25 August 1990), ("Z tajnych archiwów").

Polityka (30 November 1991a), ("Z tajnych archiwów").

Polityka (7 December 1991b), ("Z tajnych archiwów sprzed 10 lat").
Prawo i Życie (7 October 1995a).
Prawo i Życie (28 November 1995b).
Pytlakowski, P. (1991), *Republika MSW*, Chicago-Toronto-Warszawa: Andy GraFik.
"Raport Wydziału Studiów gabinetu ministra SW" (3 July 1992), *Tygodnik Solidarność*.
Rzecznik Praw Obywatelskich (1994), *Biuletyn*, no. 24 (Warsaw).
Rzeczpospolita, 14 November, 1995
Rzeplinski, A. (1989), *Sądownictwo w Polsce Ludowej*, Warszawa, Oficyna "Pokolenie".
Skarzyński, E. (1990), "Uwikłani w spólki", *Tygodnik Demokratyczny*, no. 26.
Smoleński, P. (30 March, 1991), "Polityka i złoto. Opowiada Czesław Kiszczak", *Gazeta Wyborcza*.
Sroka, L. J. (28 April 1991), "Kulisy sprawy Przemyka", *Gazeta Policyjna*.
Staniszkis, J. (1991), "Patterns of Change in Eastern Europe", in P.R.Weilemenn *et al.*, *Upheaval Against the Plan*, New York, Berg.
Staniszkis, J. (1994-95), "The Politics of Post-Communist Institutionalization in Historical Perspective", Working Paper Series, no. 1, University of Michigan, International Institute.
Strycharz, S. (1983, "Problemy organizacji i funkcjonowania organów ochrony prawnej w systemie profilaktyki i resocjalizacji", in Adam Krukowski (ed.), *Prawne Podstawy Resocjalizacji i Zapobiegania Przestępczosci*, Warszawa: PWN.
Sułek, A. (1992), "Farewell to the Party", in Janine R. Wedel (ed), *The Unplanned Society*, New York, Columbia University Press.
Szelenyi, I. and Szelenyi, S. (1995), "Circulation or reproduction of elites during the postcommunist transformation of Eastern Europe: Introduction", *Theory and Society*, vol. 24.
Szymanowski, T. (1987), "Stan aktualny i postulowane kierunki rozwoju systemu penitencjarnego w Polsce", in Teodor Szymanowski and Andrzej Rzepliński (eds), *Doświadczenia i perspektywy systemu penitencjarniego w Polsce*, Warszawa, Uniwersytet Warszawski, IPSIR.
Tajne dokumenty Biura Politycznego PZPR a "Solidarność" 1980-1981, (1991),London, Aneks.
Tarkowski, A. (1990), "Endowment of Nomenklatura, or Apparatchiks Turned into Entrepreneurchiks, or from Communist Ranks to Capitalist Riches", *Innovation*, 4(l).
Tarkowski, J. (1983), "Patronage in a Centralized Socialist System: The Case of Poland", *International Political Science Review*, vol. 4, no.4.
Tittenbrun, J. (1992,) *Upadek Socjalizmu Realnego w Polsce*, Poznań, Dom Wydawniczy Rebis.
Urbanek, M. (12 August 1995), "Prokurator - swój człowiek", *Polityka*, 12.
Wasilewski, J. (1995), "The Forming of the New Elite: How Much Nomenklatura is Left?", *Polish Sociological Review*, no. 2.
Wasilewski, J. and Wnuk-Lipiński, E. (1995), "Poland: Winding road from the Communist to the post-Solidarity elite", *Theory and Society*, vol. 24.

Wende, E. (24 December 1994) Interviewed by Radosław Januszewski, *Prawo i życie,* no. 52/53.

Wesołowska, M. (1981), "Korzenie zła", *Polityka,* 2 May.

Widacki, J. (1992), *Czego nie powiedział generał Kiszczak,* Warszawa, BGW.

Winiecki, J. (1990), "Obstacles to Economic Reform of Socialism: A Property-Rights Approach", *The Annals of the American Academy of Political and Social Science.*

Zabicki, T. (23 June 1992), "Co chce ukryć Milczanowski?", *Nowy Swiat.*

Zieleniewski, M. (1990), *Rozkaz zabić,* Oficyna Wydawnicza, Angraf.

Zurek, E. (7 October 1995), "W pamięci tylko krzyk", *Prawo i Życie.*

Zybala, A. (17 November 1995), "Teraz wojna", *Wprost.*

Zybertowicz, A. (1993), *W uscisku tajnych służb,* Komorow, Wydawnictwo Antyk.

_____(1995/96), "A Neglected Dimension of Contemporary Social Movements Dynamics: Secret Services in the Field of Constraints and Facilitations for Social Movements", Working Paper Series, no. 15, University of Michigan, International Institute.

Życie Warszawy (June 6, 1984), ("W swietle zeznań swiadków").

Życie Warszawy (11 October 1990), ("Dalsze szczegóły sprawy Milewskiego, Wywiad zajmował się rabunkami").

13 Social Transformation and Crime: A Crisis of Deregulation

SUSANNE KARSTEDT

The "New Great Transformation"?

For contemporaries, the sweeping break-down of the socialist states was a unique event that revealed a new quality of extremely rapid social change. Social scientists saw in the break-down of the former social order and the introduction of free markets and democracy the opportunity of a nation-wide "labouratory experiment" (Giesen and Leggewie, 1991) that would yield fresh theoretical insights. Obviously, these views were caused by the exaggerated expectations about the introduction of a market economy and the emergence of "civil society". Since these expectations have failed, it is now *continuity* and resistance to change that attract the attention of social scientists. When continuity is addressed, historical comparisons as well as comparative approaches to the variety of existing market economies and democracies in the western world, that have each taken a different approach to solve the problem of balance between economic liberalism and social protection, are the analytical tools of choice for "sociological realism" (as contrasted to "economic utopianism", Bryant, 1994: 58-77).

It is in this context, that Polanyi's (1978) analysis of the "Great Transformation" from feudal-agrarian to industrial society at the end of the eighteenth and beginning of the nineteenth century provides a backdrop for the "New Great Transformation" as the "revolution" in the East European states has been recently renamed (Bryant and Mokrzycki, 1994; Glasman, 1994: 191-217). Polanyi centered on the "ensemble" of cultural values, regulations of labour and commodity markets, and the provisions for social welfare in the emergence of free markets and a liberal state. He showed in which way inconsistencies, structural discontinuities and the break-down of the traditional social regulatory order resulted in a wave of pauperism and social disorganization in the first half of the nineteenth century. His focus was on the collision between continuities and change, between the normative regulation of economic life and the demands of a developing (industrial) economy.

This comprehensive view of socio-economic change that gives equal weight to its cultural, socio-structural and economic dimension, and relates markets and production to the normative structure of a society, has made Polanyi's analysis an outstanding example for those who want to apply "sociological realism" (Bryant, 1994: 59-77) to the transformation of East European societies. He can be also named as a forerunner - and the frequent references to his work show that scholars are quite aware of this fact - of the "theory of regulation" that has emerged during the last decade (Mahnkopf, 1988; Hübner and Mahnkopf, 1988: 7-28; Aglietta, 1979; Boyer, 1988: 67-94; Lipietz, 1986: 16-40). The crucial concept of this theory is the "mode of regulation". This refers to the basic rules and regulations of markets, consumption, the relation between work force and management, as well as to an accompanying system of social welfare and education (see Lipietz especially for education). By this, the specific historical institutional framework and the national differences between industrialized capitalistic countries (ie, countries with more or less free markets) are stressed in contrast to a unifying concept of "capitalism".

Though there are many different facets in Polanyi's work, it seems that one specific feature is somewhat neglected. The "Great Transformation" is an account of the transformation of one "mode of regulation" to another, and it started first with the *deregulation* of markets - in the very technical sense this concept has nowadays (Rose-Ackerman, 1992; Ayres and Braithwaite, 1992) - and swept to the system of social welfare (Speenhamland system). Regulation restarted in the second half of the nineteenth century, now adapting to the meanwhile more developed industrial societies and market mechanisms.

This process of deregulation and re-regulation obviously was related to social disorganization and especially to deviant behavior and crime. It induced a pauperization of the population (Polanyi, 1978: 125), and a wave of crime, in the streets as well as in the emerging markets of capital and commodities and in business administration (Rudé, 1985; Hall, 1975: 87-106; Hughes, 1988). The eighteenth and nineteenth century witnessed fraud, and corporate and white-collar crime, on a hitherto unknown scale because the new markets and business practices mostly lacked regulation.[1] Here again, Polanyi's analysis provides a backdrop for diachronic as well as synchronic comparisons. Thus deregulation in the United States is directly linked to white-collar crimes in the savings-and-loan industries (Calavita and Pontell, 1990: 309-341) and in the bond markets (Stein, 1992), and the process of transformation in the former socialist countries seems to be accompanied by an increase of crimes, especially of white-collar crime and organized crime (Ewald, 1993a: 28-32; 1993b: 106-109; von der Heide, 1993: 19-21; Bienkowska, 1991: 43-54; Kury, 1992; Boers *et al.*, 1994).

In this paper the impact of deregulation and delegitimation of the "institutional forms" (Boyer, 1988: 70-5) that encapsulate economic activities, on deviant behavior and crime will be analysed. Its purpose is to identify those structural conditions during the "new great transformation" that create social disorganization and its related phenomena, and the proposition is advanced that processes of deregulation affect "crimes in the suites *and* crimes in the streets", "crimes of greed" as well as "crimes of need" (Braithwaite, 1991: 40-58; 1993: 215-31). I start by discussing the basic principles of the theory of regulation and I develop a typology of "regulatory" crises that are combined in the social transformation of East Central Europe. In a next step, the impact on different types of criminality - white-collar crime, crimes of elites and juvenile delinquency - will be analysed.

Abolishing the (Im)moral Economy: Transformation and Deregulation

Basic Concepts: Modes of Regulation

The "new great transformation" in East Europe has confronted politicians and scholars with the fact that free markets need an "institutional framework" of norms, habits, laws and regulating networks. This has raised anew the interest of social scientists in the "moral dimension" of the economy (Etzioni, 1988; Hirschman, 1988: 90). This institutional framework ensures the approximate consistency of individual behavior and decentralized decisions with the economic processes of production and consumption for day-to-day operations and in the long run. The "institutional forms" (Boyer, 1988: 67-94) determine the rules of reasonable economic conduct and define the norms that draw the line between legal and illegal economic decision-making. They constitute the "moral economy" (Thompson, 1980: 66-129) by determining what is to be expected as a just and fair share for the different social groups. "This body of interiorized rules and social processes is called the *mode of regulation*" (Lipietz, 1986: 19). It is especially its moral dimension that is crucial for the relationship between the process of transformation and crime.

Boyer (1988: 73-5) identifies four institutional forms that are important in this context:

1. *Monetary and credit relationships* define the mode of interaction between separate economic units. They determine the *time horizon* for decision-making on investments and revenues. The rules and norms give guidelines as to what gains can be *reasonably* expected in a given economic situation, and in this way, they help us distinguish between gains from legal and those from illegal activities.[2]

2. The *"wage-labour-nexus"* combines those institutions that are related to work organization and the standard of living. It includes the technical and social divisions of labour and its implications for skilling and deskilling, and the determinants of direct and social wages. As such, it relates the institutions of education and training on the one hand, and the state welfare services on the other hand to the labour market (Boyer, 1988: 72). The framework of social values and norms that is established within and around these institutions mainly governs expectations and perceptions of "fairness" of the share that a person is entitled to with regard to skills, work duration and in the case of not being in the labour force. Within this regulatory network the values of investments in cultural and social capital are determined (Bourdieu, 1983), as well as the standards of living for the various groups and classes in the society.

    In advanced capitalistic societies, "democratization of consumption" (Hirschman, 1988: 76) seems to have abolished the stricter norms and rules of "legitimate" consumption of former times, but still there are "subtle differences" (Bourdieu 1992), that point to the fact that these norms still have a considerable impact. In contrast, in socialist societies consumption was highly regulated by a distributive bureaucracy and directly related to privilege, power and stratification.

3. *"Competition"* is the third crucial institutional form. Competition is a destructive social force and relationship (in contrast, for example, to cooperation) and has to be constrained and "encapsulated" by social norms and a suitable regulatory network (Etzioni, 1988: 199-216). Even the most competitive market economies rule out certain kinds of deviant or illegal forms of competition (eg, killing one's competitor).[3] The main function of regulations on competition is the maintenance and restoration of a contractual equilibrium by protecting or limiting bargaining powers (eg, by Anti-Trust Laws). Legal institutions and norms step in when the "weak ties" (Granovetter, 1973: 1360-80) of professional and business relations break down in the competitive atmosphere of markets.

4. Finally, *state interventions* establish an institutional form that operates differently from market relationships. In modern advanced economies, interventions are typically based on laws, coercion as well as incentives (or a mixture of both types, see Ayres and Braithwaite, 1992). Especially the institutions of the welfare state have mainly intervened where markets fail, ie, in the wage-labour-nexus. The scope, extent and intensity of state interventions depend on the power and influence of different groups to demand interventions in their interest. A diversity of powerful groups (business, labour, other "autonomous elites" (see Etzioni-Halevey, 1990: 317-50)) will create a broad, extensive and diversified institutional framework of intervention, while if one powerful group "captures" the state, interventions in the economy will be more far-reaching and intense.

The combined institutional network is built from values and norms, social bonds and governmental intervention. The system of values, norms and rules defines "a rationale that guides the decisions of those concerned" and "defines and *justifies* mutual expectations (Smouts, 1993: 447). The laws of regulation are often less coercive and repressive (as, for example, in the penal laws) but comprise statutory instruments, administrative orders *et al.*, and rely and adapt to a considerable extent to existing practices and social relationships. Now, what happens when this regulatory order and institutional framework is dismantled and transformed mainly by means of "deregulation"?

Types of Regulatory Crises

Polanyi's analysis of the "Great Transformation" and Thompson's description of the "moral economy" (1980) of eighteenth century Britain provide vivid examples of the processes of deregulation that were driving the "Great Transformation" to industrial society. The deregulation of the corn-markets abolished the paternalistic system of distribution and consumption that had fulfilled basic needs of the poor and the working classes. It gave way to the evolution of a more complex retail-system that destroyed the local markets. The retailer, who had not only been of bad reputation but was even outlawed in some regions, became a necessary "institution" in the developing markets and could slowly gain legitimation. The crisis of transformation and deregulation that both authors describe was caused by several steps of de- and re-regulation: the *deregulation* of the corn-markets and the labour-market by the abolition of the workman's statutes made a re-regulation of wage floors and of provisions for social welfare necessary. The establishment of the so-called Speenhamland system that was intended to serve both functions had detrimental effects on the labour-markets. After its abolition in 1834 it left the English poor to the mechanisms of the labour market without the minimal provisions of welfare and without the local bonds of community, neighborhood and family (Polanyi, 1978: 121). The resulting pauperization of large parts of the population were witnessed with horror by contemporaries, and during the 1830s and early 1840s deportation of men and women to Australia for even minor crimes reached its peak (Hughes, 1988).

Within this web of deregulation and regulation processes that shaped the Great Transformation, three types of regulatory crisis can be identified:

(a) A *crisis of inconsistency* occurs when there is a discrepancy between social bonds, values and norms on the one hand and the economic (market) practices and structures on the other hand. Such a crisis induces illegitimate but not necessarily illegal behavior (as, for example, the various complaints about trade practices in the corn-markets showed).[4]

(b) Institutional forms and especially legal regulations depend on their legitimation and their enforcement. A *crisis of enforcement* will change the behaviour of target groups in industries and markets, and reactions of the general public by diminishing the moral condemnation of the respective actions (Erickson *et al.*, 1977: 305-17). Non-enforcement devalues the specific rules of regulation, but its impact might easily spread to other parts of the regulatory system (Marx, 1981: 221-46; McCormick, 1977: 30-39). If suitable agencies of enforcement are not created or existing ones are dismantled,[5] or widespread covert facilitation of norm violations by high-ranking individuals or members of powerful groups occurs, enforcement of legal regulations and the supporting institutions is undermined.

(c) Polanyi based his analysis mainly on what can be defined as a *crisis of imbalance*. While social welfare and wage floors were highly regulated by the Speenhamland system, emerging industrial production and markets lacked regulation; this created an imbalance between labour and other markets with detrimental effects especially for the labour market. Imbalances between deregulated and regulated areas in the same market produce unintended consequences, and create opportunities for illegal behavior.[6]

All three types of regulatory crises are combined in the "New Great Transformation" of East Central Europe. The socialist societies were highly regulated - or "overregulated" - societies (organizational societies: Meier, 1990: 3-14, feudal societies: Pollack, 1990, both for the GDR; Yanowitch, 1977, Lambert, 1984: 366-85 both for the USSR). The balance between norms, social bonds and formal, governmental regulation was disturbed by an overwhelming proportion of formal, legal regulation, often by penal laws. Consequently informal norms and social bonds became the foundations of the second or "shadow economy", that operated mainly illegally, though it was used and legitimized by everybody (see Łoś, 1988; Rosner, 1986; Thaa *et al.*, 1992).

The transformation started with an *enforcement crisis*, since the non-enforcement of rule-breaking, mainly by elites, the at least irregular prosecution of economic crimes, and corruption, had nourished delegitimation and devaluation of the institutional framework on a large scale. A crisis of *inconsistency* developed, when the institutional framework and formal regulation did not fit the informal norms and social bonds that were essential to fulfill even basic needs of the economy and the population. These inconsistencies developed along the line between formal institutions and the informal, partially illegal "institutional forms" like the use of privileges, direct exchange of goods and other practices that ensured the functioning of the economy and a modest standard of living (Thaa *et al.*, 1992 for the GDR; Jowitt, 1983: 275-97 for the USSR; Matthews, 1978; Clark, 1993). This crisis continued after the introduction of a market economy, though in a different form. The new market economy could neither be based on a functioning *formal* mode of regulation nor on social bonds and a system of norms that enabled legal *and* legitimate economic transactions. It had to rely mainly on the informal and partially illegal institutional forms, and especially on the tightly knit networks of privilege and control by handing out favours, that the bureaucratic elites had established and that constituted the core of the informal economy.

The crisis of *imbalance* in the regulatory system was mainly caused by dismantling the system of social security that hit - as in the "Great Transformation" to industrial society[7] - mostly the institutions of the wage-labour-nexus. The emergence of markets and especially a "free" labour market - combined with sweeping industrial deconstruction - has destroyed the links that connected educational institutions and the acquisition of skills with the organization of work and the hierarchy of status. This has produced new social inequalities (see Szydlik, 1992: 292-314, for the GDR; Duch, 1993: 590-608 for the USSR; Jurczynska, 1993: 59-84 for Poland), and since former legitimate expectations of income and consumption are gone, a new normative structure to cope with these inequalities has not yet been established. Surveys show that the introduction of free market economies is widely welcomed and accepted by the population, but the emergence of the new inequalities is equally rejected (see Häder, 1991 for the GDR; Jurczynska, 1993: 59-84 for Poland; Duch, 1993: 590-608 for the USSR).

Both the crisis of enforcement and the crisis of imbalance have produced a typical pattern of attitudes in the populations of the former socialist states: they profoundly distrust the state, which is expressed in a delegitimation and devaluation of its institutions (the police, the justice system), while at the same time there is a strong dependency on the state for social security.

Deregulation, Anomie and Crime

The prevailing explanation of the increase of crime during the transition period is centered on the theory of anomie and social disorganization. Both apply to crimes "in the suites" and "crime in the streets" (Braithwaite, 1991: 40-58). The original version of this hypothesis has been phrased by Sutherland (1983 (1949): 255-57). He identifies two forms of social disorganization: the "anomie form" of social disorganization is related to a change in regulatory systems, and especially to a gap between the value system of the general public (including business) and the practices of business. Interestingly, he identifies the change from a lesser to a more regulated economy and the opposite direction both as anomic, since in both cases values, norms and actual practices differ to a large extent. As has been shown, the deregulation crisis of the transformation causes a severe disintegration of values, norms and the institutional framework from actual economic practises. The transformation creates such imbalances in the mode of regulation of the wage-labour-nexus, that connections between legitimate expectations, the social and cultural capital to attain such aspirations and its structural conditions are abolished. These crises of regulation cause social disorganization in its anomic forms for different groups at different levels of society: elites are as much affected as the middle and lower classes.[8]

(a)   Deregulation, Crimes of the Elites and White-Collar Crime

The bureaucratic, centralized and profound regulation of the economy in the socialist societies of East Central Europe produced a criminogenic economic structure (Lambert, 1984: 366-85; Łoś, 1988; Rosner, 1986; Clark, 1993): White-collar crimes - from theft at the working place, exchange of rare goods, bribery to corruption - were rather widespread at all levels of the hierarchy of industrial organization and the administration, the party and the government. Within this system of illicit transactions the elites had a prominent place. They controlled the "formal economy" by administering production and *distribution* of basic and luxury goods (eg, apartments, holidays, cars, etc.) and the informal economy by the privileges that they had and could grant to others. Since the formal regulation failed to make decentralized economic decisions compatible, corruption served as means of "compensation for a lack of consensus on private goals" (Huntington, 1968: 64). The elites were in the most powerful position on either side of the economy.

The transformation to free markets (and a democracy) and the accompanying deregulation of the economy should have erased the opportunities for such crimes. In contrast, all available data point to a significant increase of white-collar crimes and especially crimes by the former (and new) elites (Karstedt, 1995), which falls in line with the argument of this chapter, that it is deregulation that causes crime. The regulatory crises of the transformation affect the crime rates of elites (and white-collar crime) by two processes:

1. As for the general public, the introduction of free markets and the dismantling of the state bureaucracy has destroyed the link between the elites' skills, their cultural and especially social capital in the form of social bonds and networks, and their status and income expectations. In addition to their formal power they are losing their privileges and the power, which these provided within the informal economy (mainly by granting access to positions and valuable goods) while they see a new elite emerging from the markets. This form of anomie and the crime it initiates may be illustrated by the following incident: A Russian general, who had done private business with military equipment (a private airline), gave as a justification for his actions, that his income did not correspond to his (former) status, and he confronted the court with the question: "Why do I, a general, get only 30,000 roubles per month, while businessmen make millions?" (Schmidt-Häuer, 1993: 22).

2. While deregulation of the economy has spread during the transformation and was quite extensive, new regulations take a longer time to be established, to be integrated into the mode of regulation and to be accepted by the population (Sutherland, 1983 (1949): 256). In this situation, the social bonds and norms of the former illicit economy provide the crucial institutional forms and modes of regulation of the basic socio-economic relationships. The members of the planning bureaucracies, the new elites of the market economy and the "winners" from the "second economy" revive old and constitute new networks. They exploit their informational lead and use their illegal gains to get a share in the privatization of the economy and to start from there with legal business (Beckherrn, 1991: 33). Combined with "regulation" in the illegal economy deregulation has created a situation of *lacking* as well as contradictory standards, that has caused corruption and white-collar crime by former and new elites on a large scale (Schmidt-Häuer, 1993).

It would be wrong to identify crimes by the elites with white-collar crime in general (Weisburd *et al.*, 1991; Braithwaite, 1985: 1-25), though the regulatory crisis may have caused a higher proportion of white-collar and other crimes that are committed by the elites, than in West European countries or the United States. An increase in general white-collar crime (especially fraud of all kinds) will be mainly caused by a lack of (legal) regulation in consumer markets and a lack of normative "encapsulation" of rewards and gains as well as competition. Consumers are in the weakest position in the new markets, since they have to cope with new sales strategies, and consumer organizations have not yet been established (see Thompson, 1980: 66-129, and Polanyi, 1978 for similar processes in the eighteenth and nineteenth centuries; Boers, 1994: 21-74; Kury, 1992 and 1994 for Germany). Though the population trusts the police more than many other institutions, they shy away from reports to the police and seem to have less trust in courts (Boers, 1994: 21-74; Korfes, 1994: 215-250; Häder, 1991; Bienkowska, 1994; Kury, 1994: 165-198; Jurczynska, 1993: 59-84). Especially those with anomic, alienated attitudes and attitudes of powerlessness - most prominent in the youngest (under 21 years) and the oldest age groups (over 50 years) and in the groups of unemployed - have significantly less trust in the justice system (Korfes, 1994: 226-230).

Though privatization has legalized gains from economic activities of all kinds, many markets (eg, stockmarkets) are still not efficiently regulated in correspondence with economic practices. Obviously like the situation in the United States at the beginning of the nineteenth century (see note 4), there are no standards that define legitimate revenues from business. Neither businessmen nor the public are capable of deciding what kind of gains from what kind of business are legitimate or not, and consequently, legal and illegal activities can easily be mixed. In an analogous way competition is structured by violence, by racketeering and corruption, which severely impedes the development of the economy; this has added to a demoralization of the entrepreneurial middle class and might as well endanger the process of democratization (*International Herald Tribune*, 1994a: 4; 1994b: 1, 6).

(b) Deregulation, Inequality and Crime

All data resources available - official crime statistics, self-reports and victimization surveys (Boers *et al.*, 1994: 21-74) - show an increase in crime rates since the start of the transformation process during the late 1980s. This has been (especially with regard to property crimes and juvenile delinquency) mainly attributed to the process of (catching-up) modernization (Boers, 1995: 16-21). The rise in private consumption of households and new retail strategies have simply increased the opportunities of crime for theft and burglary to the level of West European countries (Kury, 1994: 165-98). As in these states, a positive correlation between crime rates and private consumption was observed, indicating a process that was driven by the increase of opportunities, and not by an increase in relative or absolute deprivation (Field, 1990; Bennett and Basiotis, 1991: 262-87).

Meanwhile this situation has changed, as more recent data from 1994 show:[9] though the rates of simple property crimes do not exceed those of the former FRG, burglary and robbery rates are significantly higher for the younger age groups (less than 30 years old) than in West Germany. Victimization surveys show that assaults have increased since the transformation, and rates are higher than in the former FRG (Boers, 1994: 21-74; Ewald *et al.*, 1994: 75-170). These are crimes that are mainly related to social inequality (Blau and Blau, 1982: 114-29).

It has been argued in the previous section that the "crisis of imbalance" has mainly affected the wage-labour-nexus and thus produced social inequality to an extent hitherto unknown in socialist societies. Several processes are combined in this result: The deregulation and deconstruction of industries has abolished employment opportunities and status expectations by extensive deskilling. The cultural and social capital that has been accumulated by education and professional training (cultural capital), and by establishing social bonds and networks (social capital), has lost its value; consequently legitimate expectations of status and income, that were based on this capital, cannot be fulfilled. The gap between consumption opportunities and attainable living standards has widened (for *circa* 50% of the population of the former GDR; Gutsche, 1994: 192). The new social and economic differences are not supported by a majority of the population who adhere to egalitarian values and demand supporting policies from the government (Duch, 1993: 597 for European Russia; Jurczynska, 1993 for Poland; Häder, 1991 for the GDR). Success within the emerging system of social differences is attributed to chance or supporting networks, and therefore the population is especially resentful of former officials who have managed to stay in their high positions (Boers, 1994: 46).

Anomie and feelings of powerlessness are highest within the younger and the older age brackets; the younger are mostly hit by the devaluation of their cultural capital (ie, educational achievements and professional skills), while for the older age groups the abolition of social security seems to be crucial. Crime will mainly be found to be the prominent anomic reaction mainly in the younger age group, while an increase in suicides or alcoholism is more probable for the older groups.[10] The most recent statistics show that higher crime rates in the East can mainly be attributed to all age groups under 30 years.   This is especially so of burglary and robbery (Criminological Research Institute, 1995).

The connection between anomie and delinquency was confirmed in a comparison of juveniles in East and West Berlin (Hagan *et al.*, 1995: 1028-52): Youths in East Berlin have higher anomic aspirations, that are for both groups related to school delinquency (vandalism and violence).[11] Data from a crime survey in 1991 show that those who perceive a gap between economic supply and economic opportunities have significantly more often committed shoplifting; again, these attitudes prevail in the youngest age group under 21 years (Korfes, 1994: 192). On the other hand, Hagan *et al.* found that the impact of anomic aspirations on youths from East Berlin is suppressed by their better integration into the family and in schools. Schools were more egalitarian and less competitive than in the West and families provided tighter networks of social (and economic) support, which were essential under the conditions of a socialist economy. Thus, the structural continuity has until now preserved this kind of social capital that is embedded within these networks, and it acts as a countervailing force to situations of anomie for juveniles in East Berlin more than for those in the Western parts of the city.

The "New Great Transformation" and the Durkheimian Principle

The analysis presented in this paper indicates that the "New Great Transformation" can be conceptualized in terms of a break-down and deregulation of crucial modes of regulation of the former socialist societies. Three types of regulatory crises were identified that each contribute to the increase of specific forms of crime. It was argued that white-collar crimes and crimes of the elites will have a disproportionate share during the transformation, due to a lack and/or conflict of standards. The deregulation of the wage-labour-nexus, the subsequent increase in inequality, and the devaluation of cultural and social capital produce anomic situations, that result for the younger age groups in aggressive property crimes. The connection between deregulation - anomie - crime holds for "crimes in the suites" as well as for "crimes in the streets", though for each an impact of different processes of deregulation and a different type of crisis can be identified. Most interesting is the fact that social bonds and networks (as social capital) provide a contervailing force against crime in the younger age groups and possibly in the lower classes of society (Karstedt, 1995), while networks of former and new elites provide opportunities for, and further, crime.[12] This points to the structural continuities that preserve vital social networks amid the process of transformation. Nonetheless, the functions of these networks change and consequently so too does the key role which they have in relation to criminal activities of different groups.

Again looking back to the first "Great Transformation" might help to put rising crime rates in perspective. Crime rates - and especially violent crimes - decreased later in the nineteenth century, though the great transformation obviously had increased them. The Durkheimian principle that every society produces its specific rates of deviant behaviour is equally valid for a specific historical situation, and for the types of crime, that are prevalent during this situation. Though public opinion (Boers, 1994: 21-74; Ewald *et al.*, 1994: 75-170) and the institutions of social control focus on the "crimes in the streets", the crimes of elites and white-collar crime may be more dangerous for the transformation: they may prolong the deregulation-crisis that has produced them.

Notes

1   Famous examples are the John Law Scandal in France, which according to Soboul (1973) had its share in the dissolution of the Ancien Regime, or the Tulip Scandal in the Netherlands as well as other emerging types of white-collar crime (Hall, 1975).

2   For example, an investment by the First Lady in the US, Hillary Clinton, that yielded a 1000% revenue within a year, immediately raised suspicions, because such gains seemed to be out of range.

3   Illegal markets like drug markets consequently allow for *all* forms of competition and especially violent forms (see, for the mafia, Catanzaro 1994).

4   Such a crisis of inconsistency developed in the US at the beginning of the century, when large-scale operations in industry and markets started. In 1907, in a complaint about the bad standards of "business honour" the president of the American Economic Association named three types of inconsistencies: the lack of social bonds ("no personal contact with his workingmen, his customers"), the lack of contractual equilibria ("trusteeship for thousands of stockholders") and the lack of norms defining legitimate revenues ("large profits from monopolies that are legal but sometimes economically and social unjustifiable") (Jenkins, 1907:3).

5   The deregulation of the savings and loan industry was accompanied by cutting budgets and personnel in the supervising agencies, and the later "scandal" can be attributed to the incapability of supervising the industry; in a similar way, the deregulation of air traffic was not accompanied by a suitable increase of controlling the traffic that had expanded as a result of increased competition (Rose-Ackerman, 1992).

6   In the United States, the fact that the governmental insurance system was not changed and adapted, while the savings-and-loan industry was deregulated, was the starting point for fraud on a large scale (Calavita and Pontell, 1990; Stein, 1992: Rose-Ackerman, 1992).

7   See Glassman (1994) though with a different emphasis.

8   Sutherland (1983 (1949): 257) notes that his theory starts from the *description* of the conflicts of standards, not from the *causes* of social disorganization. As such a cause, processes of deregulation are introduced here.

9   Prof. Christian Pfeiffer from the Criminological Research Institute of Lower Saxony kindly provided the data from the 1994 crime statistics.

10   Suicide data show an increase for the GDR after reunification (Gutsche, 1994: 197).

11   Anomic aspirations are equally related to right-wing extremism, for which an additional direct effect of living in East Berlin was observed.

12   The impact of the delegitimation of the institutions of social control is not considered in this paper (see, for crimes of elites, Karstedt, 1995; in general Korfes, 1994).

Bibliography

Aglietta, M. (1979), *A Theory of Capitalist Regulation. The US Experience*, NLB, London.

Ayres, I. and Braithwaite J. (1992), *Responsive Regulation. Transcending the Deregulation Debate*, Oxford University Press, Oxford.

Beckherrn, F. (1991), *Tal der Wende. Wohin steuert Osteuropa?*, Knaur, München.

Bennett, R.R. and Basiotis, P.P. (1991), "Structural Correlates of Juvenile Property Crime: A Cross-National, Time-Series Analysis", *Journal of Research in Crime and Delinquency*, 28.

Bienkowska, E. (1991), "Crime in Eastern Europe", in Heidensohn, F. and Farrell, M. (eds), *Crimes in Europe*, Routledge, London.

———— (1994), "Die wichtigsten Aspekte der Kriminalitätsentwicklung im heutigen Polen: die letzte Dekade", in Boers, K., Ewald, U., Kerner, H.-J. et al. (eds), *Sozialer Umbruch und Kriminalität*, vol. 1, Forum-Verlag, Bonn.

Blau, J.R., Blau, P.M. (1982) "The Cost of Inequality: Metropolitan Structure and Violent Crime", *American Sociological Review*, 47.

Boers, K. (1994), "Kriminalitätseinstellungen in den neuen Bundesländern", in: Boers, K., Ewald, U., Kerner, H.-J. et al. (eds), *Sozialer Umbruch und Kriminalität*, vol. 2, Forum-Verlag, Bonn.

———— (1995), "Ravensburg ist nicht Washington. Einige Anmerkungen zu Thomas Feltes und Heike Gramckows 'Bürgernahe Polizei und kommunale Kriminalprävention - Reizworte oder demokratische Notwendigkeiten?'", *Neue Kriminalpolitik*, 7, no. 1.

Boers, K., Ewald, U., Kerner, H.-J. et al. (eds) (1994), *Sozialer Umbruch und Kriminalität*, vol. 1 and 2, Forum-Verlag, Bonn.

Bourdieu, P. (1983), "Ökonomisches Kapital, kulturelles Kapital, soziales Kapital", in Kreckel, R. (ed.), *Soziale Ungleichheiten. Soziale Welt*, Sonderband 2, Schwartz, Göttingen.

———— (1992), *Die feinen Unterschiede,* 5th edition, Suhrkamp, Frankfurt a.M.

Boyer, R. (1988), "Technical Change and the Theory of Regulation", in Dosi, G., Freeman, Ch., Nelson, R. et al. (eds), *Technical Change and Economic Theory*, Pinter, London.

Braithwaite, J. (1985), "White-Collar Crime", *Annual Review of Sociology*, 11, 1-25.

———— (1991), "Poverty, Power, White-Collar Crime and the Paradoxes of Criminological Theory", *Australian and New Zealand Journal of Criminology*, 24.

———— (1993), "Crime and the Average American", *Law and Society Review*, 27.

Bryant, C.G. (1994), "Economic Utopianism and Sociological Realism: Strategies for Transformation in East-Central Europe, in Bryant, C.G. and Mokrzycki, E. (eds), *The New Great Transformation? Change and Continuity in East-Central Europe*, Routledge, London.

Bryant, C.G. and Mokrzycki, E. (eds) (1994), *The New Great Transformation? Change and Continuity in East-Central Europe*, Routledge, London.

Calavita, K. and Pontell, H.N. (1990), "'Heads I win, tails you lose': Deregulation, Crime and Crisis in the Savings and Loan Industry", *Criminology*, 36.

Catanzaro, R. (1994), "Violent Social Regulation: Organized Crime in the Italian South", *Social & Legal Studies*, 3.

Clark, W.A. (1993), *Crime and Punishment in Soviet Officialdom. Combating Corruption in the Political Elite 1965-1990*, Sharpe, London.

Criminological Research Institute of Lower Saxony (1995), *unpublished Data from the Crime Statistics 1994*, Hannover.

Duch, R.M. (1993), "Tolerating Economic Reform: Popular Support for Transition to a Free Market in the Former Soviet Union", *American Political Science Review*, 87.

Erickson, M.L., Gibbs, J.P. and Jensen, G.F. (1977), "The Deterrence Doctrine and the Perceived Certainty of Legal Punishment", *American Sociological Review*, 42.

Etzioni, A. (1988), *The Moral Dimension. Toward a New Economics*, Free Press, New York.

Etzioni-Halevy, E. (1990), "Democratic-Elite Theory. Stabilization Versus Breakdown of Democracy", *Archives Europeennes de Sociologie*, 31.

Ewald, U. (1993a), "Die große Einheit oder: Das "Horror-Szenario"?" *Neue Kriminalpolitik*, 5, no. 1.

_____ (1993b), "Kriminalität nach der Wende - Bild und Wirklichkeit in den neuen Bundesländern", *Neue Justiz*, 3.

Ewald, U., Hennig, C. and Lautsch, E. (1994), "Opferleben in den neuen Bundesländern", in Boers, K., Ewald, U., Kerner, H.-J. et al. (eds), *Sozialer Umbruch und Kriminalität*, vol. 2, Forum-Verlag, Bonn.

Field, S. (1990), *Trends in Crime and their Interpretation*. HMSO Research Study no. 119, HMSO, London.

Giesen, B. and Leggewie, C. (eds) (1991), *Experiment Vereinigung. Ein sozialer Großversuch*, Rotbuch, Berlin.

Glasman, M. (1994), "The Great Deformation: Polanyi, Poland and the Terrors of Planned Spontaneity", in: Bryant C.G. Mokrzycki, E. (eds), *The New Great Transformation? Change and Continuity in East-Central Europe*, Routledge, London.

Granovetter, M. (1973), "The Strength of Weak Ties", *American Journal of Sociology*, 78.

Gutsche, G. (1994), "Der gesellschaftliche Transformationsprozeß in Ostdeutschland aus der Sicht der kriminologischen Forschung - Gedanken zu einem Forschungsdesign", in Boers, K., Ewald, U., Kerner, H.-J. et al. (eds), *Sozialer Umbruch und Kriminalität*, vol. 2, Forum-Verlag, Bonn.

Hagan, J., Merkens, H. and Boehnke, K. (1995), "Delinquency and Disdain: Social Capital and the Control of Right-Wing Extremism among East and West Berlin Youth", *American Journal of Sociology*, 100.

Häder, M. (ed.) (1991), *Denken und Handeln in der Krise*, Akademie-Verlag, Berlin.

Hall, J. (1975), "Diebstahl, Recht und Gesellschaft. Die ökonomischen Verhältnisse und ihr Einfluß auf das Recht", in Lüderssen, K.and Sack, F. (eds), *Abweichendes Verhalten II. Die gesellschaftliche Reaktion auf Kriminalität*, Suhrkamp, Frankfurt a.M.

von der Heide, F. (1993), "Zur Kriminalstatistik 1991 für die neuen Bundesländer", *Neue Justiz*, 47, 1.

Hirschman, A.O. (1988), *Entwicklung, Markt und Moral. Abweichende Betrachtungen*, Fischer, Frankfurt a.M.

Hübner, K. and Mahnkopf, B. (1988), "Einleitung", in Mahnkopf, B. (ed.), *Der gewendete Kapitalismus. Kritische Beiträge zur Theorie der Regulation*, Westfälisches Dampfboot, Münster.

Hughes, R. (1988), *The Fatal Shore. A History of the Transportation of Convicts to Australia 1787-1868*, Pan Books, Reading.

Huntington, S.P. (1968), *Political Order in Changing Societies*, Yale University Press, New Haven.

International Herald Tribune (1994a), "Corruption Threatens to Spill Russia's Economic Brew", 14. 11. 1994.

———— (1994b), "Extraction Squeezes Russia's Middle Class", 23 Nov. 1994.

Jenkins, J.W. (1907), "The Modern Standard of Business Honor", *Publications of the American Economic Association*, 8.

Jowitt, K. (1983), "Soviet Neotraditionalism: The Political Corruption of a Leninist Regime", *Soviet Studies*, 35.

Jurczynska, E. (1993), "Changing Cultural Patterns in Polish Society", in Coenen-Huther, J. and Synak, B. (eds), *Post-Communist Poland. From Totalitariarism to Democracy*, Nova Science Publication, New York.

Karstedt, S. (1995), "Macht und Moral: Zur Rolle gesellschaftlicher Eliten in Prozessen der Normerosion", Forthcoming in Gessner, V. and Frommel, M. eds), *Normerosion*, Nomos, Baden-Baden.

Korfes, G. (1994), "Einstellungen der Bürger in den neuen Bundesländern zu den Instanzen der Strafverfolgung", in Boers, K., Ewald, U. and Kerner, H.-J. et al. (eds), *Sozialer Umbruch und Kriminalität*, vol. 2, Forum-Verlag, Bonn.

Kury, H. (ed.) (1992), *Gesellschaftliche Umwälzung. Kriminalitätserfahrungen, Straffälligkeit und soziale Kontrolle*, Max-Planck-Institut für ausländisches und internationales Strafrecht, Freiburg i.Br.

———— (1994), "Kriminalität und Viktimisierung in Deutschland - Ergebnisse einer Opferstudie", in Boers, K., Ewald, U. and Kerner, H.-J. et al. (eds.), *Sozialer Umbruch und Kriminalität*, vol. 1, Forum-Verlag, Bonn.

Lambert, N. (1984), "Law and Order in the USSR: The Case of Economic and Official Crime", *Soviet Studies*, 36.

Lipietz, A. (1986), "New Tendencies in the International Division of Labour: Regimes of Accumulation and Modes of Regulation", in Scott, A.J. and Storper, M. (eds), *Production, Work, Territory: The Geographical Anatomy of Industrial Capitalism*, Allen & Unwin, Boston.

Łoś, M. (1988), *Communist Ideology, Law and Crime*, St. Martin's Press, New York.

Mahnkopf, B. (ed.) (1988), *Der gewendete Kapitalismus. Kritische Beiträge zur Theorie der Regulation*, Westfälisches Dampfboot, Münster.

Marx, G.T. (1981), "Ironies of Social Control: Authorities as Contributors to Deviance through Escalation, Nonenforcement and Covert Facilitation", *Social Problems*, 28.

Matthews, M. (1978), *Privilege in the Soviet Union. A Study of Elite Life-Styles under Communism*, Allen & Unwin, London.

McCormick, A.E. (1977), "Rule Enforcement and Moral Indignation: Some Observations on the Effects of Criminal Antitrust Convictions upon Societal Reaction Processes", *Social Problems*, 25.

Meier, A. (1990), "Abschied von der sozialistischen Ständegesellschaft", *Politik und Zeitgeschichte*, vol.16/17.

Polanyi, K. (1978), *The Great Transformation. Politische und ökonomische Ursprünge von Gesellschaften und Wirtschaftssystemen*, Suhrkamp, Frankfurt a.M.

Pollack, D. (1990), "Das Ende der Organisationsgesellschaft. Systemtheoretische Überlegungen zum gesellschaftlichen Umbruch in der DDR", *Zeitschrift für Soziologie*, 19.

Rose-Ackerman, S. (1992), *Rethinking the Progressive Agenda. The Reform of the American Regulatory State*, Free Press, New York.

Rosner, L.S. (1986), *The Soviet Way of Crime. Beating the System in the Soviet Union and the U.S.A.*, Bergin & Garvey, Massachusetts.

Rudé, G. (1985), *Criminal and Victim: Crime and Society in Early Nineteenth-Century England*, Clarendon Press, Oxford.

Schmidt-Häuer, Ch. (1993), *Rußland im Aufruhr. Innenansichten aus einem rechtlosen Reich*, Pieper, München.

Smouts, M.-C. (1993), "Some Thoughts on International Organizations and Theories of Regulation", *International Social Science Journal*, No. 138.

Soboul, A. (1988) (1973), *Die große Französische Revolution*, 5th rev. ed. 1988, Athenäum, Frankfurt a. M.

Stein, B.J. (1992), *A Licence to Steal. The Untold Story of Michael Milken and the Conspiration to Bilk the Nation*, Simon & Schuster, New York.

Sutherland, E.H. (1983) (1949), *White-Collar Crime: The Uncut Version*, Yale University Press, New Haven.

Szydlik, M. (1992), "Arbeitseinkommen in der DDR und der BRD", *Kölner Zeitschrift für Soziologie und Sozialpsychologie*, 44.

Thaa, W., Häuser, J. and Schenkel M. et al. (1992), *Gesellschaftliche Differenzierung und Legitimitätsverfall des DDR-Sozialismus. Das Ende des anderen Wegs in die Moderne*, Francke, Tübingen.

Thompson, E. (1980), "Die moralische Ökonomie der Unterschichten im 18. Jahrhundert", in *Plebeische Kultur und moralische Ökonomie. Aufsätze zur englischen Sozialgeschichte des 18. und 19. Jahrhunderts*; selected and introduced by D. Groh, Ullstein, Frankfurt a.M.

Weisburd, D., Wheeler, St., Waring, E. and Bode, N. (1991), *Crimes of the Middle Classes: White Collar Offenders in the Federal Courts*, Yale University Press, New Haven.

Yanowitch, M. (1977), *Social and Economic Inequality in the Soviet Union*, Robertson, London.

Part V

The International Dimension

14 The Collapse of Totalitarian Regimes in Eastern Europe and the International Rule of Law

DENCHO GEORGIEV

One of the most important aspects of the perception of the idea of rule of law in Eastern Europe, preceding and during the historic changes which took place at the end of the 1980s and at the beginning of the 1990s, was that of its *external* or its *international* dimension. Society, it was felt, had to be based on the idea of law - not any law, but one conforming to certain principles, requirements and standards, which existed *outside* that particular society in the international sphere, in countries perceived as "normal", as models of the *Rechtsstaat.*

The importance of the international dimension of the idea of the rule of law can be understood only if one is aware of the general mood in Eastern Europe at that time. There was a wish not only to get rid of totalitarian rule in one's own country but also to become part of an international community of states adhering to democratic values, including that of the rule of law. Every step in the course of the "velvet revolutions" was undertaken with a view also to the outside world. It was of paramount importance for the population in Eastern Europe how the changes in their countries were perceived in other democratic countries. Often at demonstrations one could even see slogans written in English or some other Western language. The processes of democratization and reforms were aimed in particular at taking these countries on the "road to Europe". The "reintegration into European and international structures", membership in European organizations such as the Council of Europe, association with and prospective membership in the European Union became parts of an obsession with Europe which is indicative of the central place of the "external" dimension of the social changes and the underlying perceptions which led to the fall of totalitarian regimes in European Europe. In a country like Bulgaria future membership in the European Union became not only the single most important priority of its foreign policy, one of the very few issues undisputed by any of the domestic political forces, but also a strategic goal seen by ordinary citizens as the key to their own better futures.

In Eastern Europe the adoption of "external" democratic standards and the idea of rule of law were in fact different aspects of the same effort directed against totalitarian rule. Democratic standards were regarded as constituting part of the idea of the rule of law and the rule of law itself was seen as an "external" standard.

The rule of law, however, was not only a political slogan, not just a set of characteristic features to be copied from the constitutional practice of other states but, moreover, an ideal which had serious implications for the prevailing opinions in society in general about the social role of law, its essence and functions, and also for the thinking of lawyers and their views about law and legal theory.

An implication directly following from the "external" dimension of the idea of rule of law concerned the role and nature of international law. If democratic standards were to be found "outside" one's own country, the most natural place to look for them was, of course, international law. Such international legal instruments as the United Nations Universal Declaration on Human Rights, the two Covenants - on Civil and Political Rights and on Economic, Social and Cultural Rights - and the European Convention on Human Rights, all played a highly prominent role in the domestic political discourse.

A logical consequence of the belief that democratic standards exist on the international level and have to be taken over and implemented domestically in the course of the democratic transformation of society was the feeling that international law must be given a special place in the national legal system. It is quite indicative of this approach to the rule of law that in the new Bulgarian Constitution of 1991 (the most definite one in Eastern Europe in that respect), alongside the provision declaring the rule of law within the country - Article 4 says that "the Republic of Bulgaria is a *Rechtsstaat*" - the principle of primacy and direct effect of international law was introduced. Paragraph 4 of Article 5 of the Constitution provides that "[i]nternational treaties, duly ratified, published and entered into force for the Republic of Bulgaria, are part of the domestic law of the country. They take precedence over those provisions of domestic legislation that contradict them". In addition the Constitutional Court examines the compatibility of domestic legislative acts with generally recognized rules of international law (Article 149, paragraph 1.4).

The adoption of the constitutional principle of the primacy of international law over domestic legislation which - as I am trying to demonstrate - followed from the specific perceptions about the rule of law in Eastern Europe during the collapse of totalitarian regimes, constituted a major change of attitude to international law. Before that the official legal doctrine in Eastern Europe was built upon the principle of sovereignty and the dualist approach to the nature of the relationship between international and domestic law. International and domestic law were regarded as two separate legal spheres regulating different social relationships, and therefore the rules of international law could not have direct effect in the national legal order without first having been "transformed" into rules of the domestic legal system by the sovereign state itself. Although it was claimed that this dualist approach was Marxist-Leninist, in fact it was not very different from the Western positivist approach dominating international legal theory, especially at the end of the nineteenth and at the beginning of the twentieth centuries, which seems still to be an influence on the thinking of many Western lawyers and scholars. This approach to the relationship between international and domestic law was combined with a special emphasis on the principle of sovereignty as the supremacy of the state in its territory and its external independence in international relations. The stress on sovereignty was of course absolutely essential for maintaining the power relationships within totalitarian societies and the possibility of direct effect of international rules and "external" standards, such as those concerning human rights, was ideologically unacceptable.

Alongside the link between the rule of law and the supremacy of international law, which was outlined above and which is political and derives from popular perceptions, there is yet another, deeper, conceptual link between the idea of the rule of law in Eastern Europe, and the supremacy and direct effect of rules of international law in the domestic legal order. This link has to do with the supremacy and direct effect of "higher" legal rules in general.

Although, under the totalitarian regime, theoretically at the top of the hierarchy of domestic law there was the constitution with its fundamental rights and liberties, in reality these constitutional principles were never invoked in courts and never directly applied by them. In fact, they could - at best - be considered as precepts for the legislator whose acts were not subject to judicial constitutional review. This led to the phenomenon, characteristic of totalitarian society, of a "reverse" hierarchy in the legal system whereby lower ranking norms were sometimes more important than the higher ones and extra-legal political - often unwritten - rules of behaviour and individual instructions by the administrative or political authorities could have a greater actual force than legal norms. Most importantly, the will of political authorities could hardly be challenged on the basis of legal rules or principles.

Thus the supremacy of the political over the legal in the totalitarian societies and, hence, the absence of rule of law consisted not in the lack of law or order - on the contrary, there was more than enough law and order - but in the absence of conformity of the norms of law with general principles, ie, with "higher" legal rules. Although such "higher" legal rules existed and featured in the constitutions, they were not enforced and therefore one could not speak of a society of law and of a rule of law.

Moreover, this state of affairs had also its theoretical and doctrinal justification in the very concept of law which was adopted. Law was defined as the will of the state which in its turn was considered to express the will of the ruling class. If law was merely an expression of the political will of the ruling class and its state, then the very concept of *Rechtsstaat* sounded like a tautology because everything which was ordered by the state was law and consequently every state was a *Rechtsstaat.*

The new democratic society, on the contrary, was seen as subjecting the arbitrariness of political authority to "higher" legal rules, which had both to have supremacy over lower ranking norms and be directly applicable. One of the key features of the "Rechtsstaat" was to become the direct applicability of constitutional norms and judicial review of legislative acts by the Constitutional Court. Article 5, paragraph 2 of the new Bulgarian Constitution states that the provisions of the Constitution have direct effect.

From this perspective the supremacy of international law and its direct applicability in the domestic legal system were an extension of the very essence of the *Rechtsstaat* further, into the international sphere: not only constitutional provisions, but also rules of international law were to be accorded the status of those "higher" norms which would serve as standards for assessing the validity and legitimacy of other, lower ranking legal rules.

It is not difficult to see that the doctrinal justification of the legal system of totalitarian society was in essence identical with the theory of legal positivism. The concept of law as "the will of the state" is not different from John Austin's definition of law as the "command of the sovereign". It is not surprising, therefore, that the rejection of the legal system of totalitarian society was accompanied by anti-positivist moods in legal theory. There was a revival of the interest in theories of natural law which were hitherto considered ideologically unacceptable (see Boichev, 1994: 19-23, 38, 62-68, 91, 106-119 ff). Legal theoreticians, even before the collapse of the totalitarian regime, started speaking of the difference between "the law" and "the statute" - a difference which did not fit well in official rigid positivist canons which did not conceive of any law beyond the statute (Boichev, 1994). This difference can, again, be seen as expressive of the same quest for standards, embodied in the "law", its unwritten principles included, and "external" to the arbitrariness of political power which takes the form of written legislation. Thus the anti-totalitarian ideal of a *Rechtsstaat* shares the quest for external standards with the naturalist legal doctrine.

On the other hand, however, it should be noted that the very concept of *Rechtsstaat* does not necessarily imply the doctrine of natural law as its theoretical background. The correspondence with the "law" means indeed a correspondence with higher ranking rules of law and also with legal principles; it can also be understood to require judicial review as a procedural method to bring about that correspondence. It does not necessarily mean a correspondence with principles of natural law not recognized by positive, written law.

Although positivist in essence, the official legal theory in Eastern European totalitarian societies did not - unlike John Austin's theory - regard international law as a non-legal normative system ("positive morality"). Nevertheless, official doctrine could not overcome the intrinsic limitations of the dualist positivist approach to international law. So it was only after the collapse of the totalitarian regime that it became possible to give international law a much higher status, which corresponded to the new, anti-totalitarian and essentially non-positivist, effort to set up a *Rechtsstaat*.

Given the essential role of the "external" or international dimension for the perception of the rule of law during the times of change in Eastern Europe, it would be logical to ask the question whether the "external" sphere itself, and international law in particular, corresponds to the requirements deriving from the concept of rule of law. Is the concept of rule of law applicable to the sphere of international law at all? As we have seen, it is an implicit assumption of the notion of rule of law as it developed in Eastern Europe that the "international" sphere was a "source" of the rule of law, that in some sense it even "contained" the rule of law. This is particularly obvious in the case of Bulgaria which has the most clear-cut constitutional provisions on the rule of law and on the supremacy and direct effect of international law. If this implicit assumption is erroneous then it may turn out that Bulgaria, which introduced the supremacy of international law *because* of the idea of the rule of law, would find out afterwards that there is no rule of law, in the international sphere.

Such a discrepancy, if it exists, may have a twofold effect. It might be the starting point of an erosion of some of the values which lay behind the revolutions in Eastern Europe and then it would be a source of disillusionment with democracy. Or it could be perceived as a challenge and an inspiration to examine international relations and the system of international law in the light of these values which are inherent in the concept of rule of law and underlay East European aspirations to democracy, and then try to transform that system in the spirit of the transformations of Eastern Europe. In the latter hypothetical case it could paradoxically turn out that Eastern Europe has started its changes referring to "international" models, only to become itself a model for international change.

I will not attempt here to assess international law in terms of all possible aspects of the idea of the rule of law but only from what appears to have been its most important aspects in the times of democratic change in Eastern Europe.

A key aspect, as we have seen, was the supremacy of the legal over the political which is most clearly embodied in the respect for and enforcement of "higher" rules and principles, including, for example, judicial review as a procedural method to achieve the correspondence with such "higher" rules and principles. Looking at international law and international relations in terms of this aspect of the concept of rule of law, different, diverging tendencies can be discerned.

On the one hand, the system of international law contains rules, principles and procedures in which the idea of correspondence with higher-ranking rules is embodied. The most significant instance is that of the peremptory norms of international law: the so-called rules *jus cogens*. According to Article 53 of the Vienna Convention on the Law of Treaties, an international treaty is null and void if at the time of its conclusion it contradicts a peremptory norm of general international law. Under the Convention a peremptory norm of general international law is a norm which is accepted and recognized by the international community as a whole, as a norm from which no derogation is permitted and which can be changed only by a subsequent norm of general international law of the same character. Article 64 of the Vienna Convention provides that if a new peremptory norm of general international law emerges, any existing treaty that contradicts such a norm becomes null and void and is terminated.

If a participant in a treaty challenges the validity of that treaty on the basis of the provisions of the Vienna Convention on *jus cogens*, there is a procedure envisaged by Article 66 that to some extent resembles domestic procedures of judicial review in cases of contradiction between legislative and constitutional norms. Under this procedure a party to a dispute over the application or interpretation of Articles 53 and 64 can submit the dispute to the International Court of Justice, if other ways to resolve the dispute have failed.

These provisions of the Vienna Convention on the Law of Treaties can however hardly be considered sufficient to justify a conclusion about the existence of an international rule of law. They have never been applied and could be seen as similar in status to constitutional principles in the totalitarian societies. Their impact is limited owing to various reasons, both of a technical and of a more general nature. Technically the possibilities of judicial review are very limited because it is only the parties to a treaty who are entitled to challenge their validity.

Even more important is the fact that there is no clarity as to the substantive contents of *jus cogens*. During the discussions in the International Law Commission, consideration was given to whether to give at least examples of some specific rules of *jus cogens*. However, it was decided not to include any example because this might lead to misunderstanding as to its position with regard to other cases which were not mentioned. The examples suggested included treaties contemplating unlawful use of force and other acts criminal under international law, such as trade in slaves, piracy and genocide. Treaties violating human rights, the equality of States and the principle of self-determination were also mentioned as possible examples (see *Yearbook,* 1966: 169, 247-9). More significant than these technical limitations of the applicability of the rules of *jus cogens*, however, is the fundamental and general supremacy in the sphere of international relations of the political over the legal - and not vice versa - which manifests itself in a number of ways. This makes it difficult, if not impossible, to speak of an international rule of law.

From this perspective, international law seems to share the deficiencies of totalitarian societies: there is no rule of international law because, although there are legal rules and principles - just as there were in the totalitarian societies in Eastern Europe - there are no effective mechanisms ensuring their enforcement. More specifically, there are no mechanisms ensuring the correspondence of "ordinary" rules with "higher"-ranking general principles.

The supremacy of the political over the legal in international relations has not only been described but also widely advocated, especially by the school of "political realism". Hans Morgenthau, the classic representative of the school, sees international law as "a primitive type of law primarily because it is completely decentralized...". Although he does not deny the *existence* of international law, he does not consider it "effective in regulating and restraining the struggle for power on the international scene" (Morgenthau, 1948: 211).

His scepticism concerns not only the efficacy of the basic principles of international law but also their validity. He explicitly describes such a basic international instrument as the Charter of the United Nations, which contains the most fundamental international legal principles without which an international rule of law is unthinkable, as being of "doubtful efficacy" and "doubtful validity" (Morgenthau, 1948: 211).

Generations of postwar diplomats and politicians were brought up on the postulates of political realism, directed against what was named a "legalistic-moralistic" approach to foreign policy. Morgenthau describes the "legalistic approach" as "a logical development from the utopian, non-political conception" (Morgenthau, 1951: 101) and the "intoxication with moral abstractions" as one of the "great sources of weakness and failure" (Morgenthau, 1951: 4).

If one is to identify the reasons for the absence of rule of law in the international sphere, however, it is not any inherent "ineffectiveness" or the "primitive character" ascribed to international law which are at the roots and constitute the direct source of the supremacy of the political over the legal and, hence, of the impossibility of the rule of law in international relations. On the contrary, the allegations about the "ineffectiveness" and "primitive character" of international law serve only to justify the disregard of law in favour of considerations of power. In fact the basic principles of international law are disregarded not because they are ineffective, but vice versa: these principles are ineffective because they are *thought* to be insignificant, unimportant, irrelevant.

The perception of the subordinated role of international law and its principles during the Cold War and under the conditions of ideological confrontation was deeply rooted and followed from the nature of totalitarian regimes and from the construction of international society at that time. Law tended to be regarded merely as a mimicry of power.

A very explicit example of the supremacy of the political over the legal in Soviet political thinking was the so-called Brezhnev doctrine, formulated on the occasion of the intervention of the Warsaw Pact countries in

Czechoslovakia in 1968. An article in *Pravda* which is considered to have formulated that doctrine states *inter alia*: "The socialist countries respect the democratic norms of international law... In the Marxist understanding, however, the norms of law, including the norms of the relations between socialist countries, cannot be interpreted in a narrow formal way, outside the general context of class struggle in the contemporary world... Those who speak of the 'illegality' of the action of the allied socialist countries in Czechoslovakia forget that in class society there is, and can be, no non-class law. The rules and norms of law are subordinated to the laws of class struggle, to the laws of the development of society. These laws are clearly formulated in the teaching of Marxism-Leninism and the documents jointly adopted by the communist and workers' parties. One should not lose sight of the class approach because of formal legal reasoning. Those who do this, losing the only true class criterion for the evaluation of legal norms, begin to apply to events the measures of bourgeois law" (*Pravda*, 26 September, 1968: 4).

The subordination of international law to political considerations of power during the Cold War can also be demonstrated in Western political thinking. Referring to the Cuban missile crisis, Dean Acheson, former US Secretary of State, said:

> I must conclude that the propriety of the Cuban quarantine is not a legal issue. The power, position and prestige of the United States had been challenged by another state; and law simply does not deal with such questions of ultimate power - power that comes close to the sources of sovereignty ... No law can destroy the state creating the law. The survival of states is not a matter of law. (Acheson, 1963: 13-15)

During the period of the Cold War, the kind of thinking that privileged the political over the legal was inevitable. It was inconceivable for the official political ideology of the totalitarian societies of the Soviet bloc, which regarded law as the product of the will - and hence of the political power - of the governing class, to subordinate that power to norms of law not created by itself, since this meant to subordinate it to external, and therefore hostile, antagonistic, class forces.

The Cold War is now over, and with the collapse of totalitarian regimes in Eastern Europe, ideological confrontation has disappeared, while liberal democratic thinking seems to enjoy a global and unchallenged triumph. This does not mean, however, that the legal thinking and the political thinking about law, which constituted the background for the deficit of rule of law in international relations, have also disappeared completely. They may not take the same forms, since the official doctrine of East European socialist societies does not exist any longer, but there are no clear signs that the subordination of the legal to the political has also gone into history.

One reason for this is that both official socialist ideology and Western "political realism" borrowed from the established legal doctrine of positivism the understanding of law as the product of power. Thus the Cold War, the ideological confrontation, and official Marxism, merely strengthened an already existing concept of law and their disappearance does not automatically lead to the disappearance of this concept. If a new kind of political thinking is needed for an international rule of law, this new thinking has to be based on a concept of law different from that of classical legal positivism.

It is quite obvious that the criticism of international law by "political realism" implies a concept of law identical with that of positivism. Hans Morgenthau criticized international law as a "primitive type of law" because of its decentralized character: "decentralized with regard to the three basic functions which any legal system must fulfil: legislation, adjudication and enforcement" (Morgenthau, 1948: 211). The complaint about the decentralization of international law is in fact a complaint that there is not enough power behind international law. It coincides with John Austin's characterization of international law as "positive morality", that is, not *real* law which should be based on the command of a sovereign. The implicit assumption of the thinking based on such a concept of law is that the only way to a better international order would be through more centralized power and, ultimately, through a world government based on the model of existing states and on the model of domestic, national law.

This, however, is the exact opposite of the ideal of rule of law and, also, of recent East European approaches to this notion. The idea of rule of law aims not at more power and even less at a more centralized power but, on the contrary, at legal normative restraints on the arbitrary use of power.

A concept of law which could serve the ideal of rule of law, and of an international rule of law in particular, would regard law not as the product of power and as the command of a sovereign but as a product of society and the result of a decision-making process democratically recognized by society, which would contain binding rules for the exercise of power and principles with which all lower-ranking norms would have to conform. The decentralized nature of international law is, on this view, not an argument against but, on the contrary, in favour of the validity of the norms of international law. Indeed, why should the decentralized nature of legislation be an argument against the validity of international legal rules? If international obligations can be assumed only with the consent of the state concerned, this should be seen as enhancing, not diminishing, the validity of that obligation.

Although, as has been pointed out, the collapse of totalitarian regimes has not led automatically to a change in legal and political thinking about law, which would facilitate the rule of law in international relations, the end of the Cold War and of ideological confrontation have nevertheless created new *opportunities* for such a change in legal and political doctrine and for the introduction of rules and procedures guaranteeing the international rule of law. Although there seems to be some awareness of these opportunities, both among statesmen and the public at large, there have been no serious efforts in that respect: no far reaching proposals for institutional and legal innovations which would adequately meet the challenges and problems facing the world of today.

Paradoxically, ideas about "world government" and "world law" were discussed by scholars after the Second World War when the cooperation between the great powers was quickly replaced by confrontation, and the impetus given through the creation of the United Nations Organization was lost. It is only *now* that these ideas, inadequate during the period of the Cold War, have real opportunities and should be given more attention.

After the end of the Cold War, an international rule of law not only seems possible, it is also becoming increasingly necessary. Increased interdependence, the dangers from technological development for the environment and for the security of mankind, the dangers of terrorism, religious fundamentalism and nationalist extremism, the need for structured co-operation in a multitude of fields, require more international order. The world has become smaller and continues to shrink and is much more in need of order than ever before.

One way of ordering society is, indeed, through power. The utopia of a world government reflects this possibility. Another way of ordering international society is through rules: rules of law which have to be enforced and which should be consistent with each other and with certain basic principles. The choice is first between anarchy and order and then between power and law as the fundamental principle of order.

Order through the rule of law is less utopian and in fact more "realistic" than the "realist" approach of power. The mere balance of power - the proposed "realist" solution - is *per se* no guarantee against political arbitrariness and can be no substitute for the rule of law. Conceptually within this solution, abuses of power are possible and admissible both at the decentralized level and at the international level if they do not affect the power of the other participants in the balance. The mere balance of power, unless combined with legal mechanisms and institutions, that is with elements of the rule of law, can be no stable solution for world order.

A world government, the other radical solution through power, is of course unrealistic and utopian because it requires a dramatic loss of sovereignty on the part of existing states. It does not solve the problems raised by the need for an international rule of law: conceptually it does not provide guarantees against abuses of power and political arbitrariness at the new hypothetical central level. So it cannot be a substitute for the rule of law either. Even if we could have a world government, the rule of law would be necessary in order to construct that government in a democratically acceptable way. The rule of law, on the other hand, is possible and necessary even without a world government: this is a minimalist approach which, far from precluding, can *facilitate* more ambitious projects for systemic change.

What is the International Rule of Law and What is Needed for its Establishment?

The international rule of law is a way of ordering international relations through rules and mechanisms for their enforcement. It is not a world order in itself, neither is it a substantive solution to the problems facing the world. It is only an approach of ordering through rules of law rather than through power. The international rule of law is neutral with regard to the *substance* of the order it institutes: it can only be based on rules such as they have been made. They can be good or bad, just or unjust. Law, and the rule of law, are artefacts, man-made constructions and they can be as imperfect as human creations can be (Georgiev, 1993: 14).

The international rule of law is international law in action, it is enforced international law. The existence of international legal norms alone is not a sufficient condition for the existence of the international rule of law. In order for these norms to function in practice, there should be legal and institutional mechanisms for their enforcement, including sanctions in case of violations. Contrary to what legal positivism and political realism suggest, the absence of mechanisms for the enforcement of norms of international law does not influence their validity, however. The absence of international rule of law does not necessarily mean absence of international legal rules.

These two aspects - existence of valid legal rules and general legal principles, on the one hand, and existence of legal and institutional mechanisms for their enforcement, including the enforcement of the correspondence of legal rules with general principles, on the other hand - constitute the criteria for the existence of an international rule of law. These criteria are verifiable and on their basis one could conclude whether or not the international rule of law exists in a certain field of international relations.

The international rule of law can exist in some spheres of international relations while not existing in others - either because no legal rules have been adopted or because the mechanisms for their enforcement are lacking or deficient.

The answer to the question whether there is a global rule of law for the entire area of international relations, would depend on whether valid global and fundamental principles and norms of internal law exist and whether they are actually enforced. The role of such global fundamental principles and norms could be played by the basic principles of international law and the norms of *jus cogens*.

The fact that the international rule of law can exist in some spheres of international relations and not in others means that it can serve as a practical step by step approach to the ordering of international society. Unlike the "all or nothing approach" necessary for the institution of a world government, which would require one single, politically dramatic and decisive constitutive act, the approach of ordering international society through an international rule of law resembles and is related to the functionalist approach to international organization. Following functionalist ideas one can conceive of the international rule of law in separate areas in which, then, it has to be real and effective. The success in such areas is capable of generating an impulse for spill-over effects to other areas. The functionalist approach which has been so successful in European integration is becoming important after the Cold War at a global level as well.

What Could be Done to Make Use of the New Opportunities which have Emerged at the End of the Twentieth Century for the Promotion of the International Rule of Law?

The adequate background for the international rule of law would be, as I have tried to point out, the formulation of an alternative way of political and doctrinal thinking about the essence and role of international law. The formulation of such alternative approaches to international law cannot change, of course, or at least cannot change immediately, the now prevailing attitudes to international law. It would facilitate such change, however, and, ultimately, the establishment of different elements and aspects of the rule of law in international relations.

Moreover, political theory and legal doctrine *by themselves* can hardly lead to really significant political change or institutional innovation; it was not political theory and even less legal doctrine that led to the changes in Eastern Europe. Actually, it is practical political action that can give a strong impetus for changes in theory and doctrine. As was mentioned, the establishment of the United Nations gave such an impetus which could be felt in theoretical debates even after conditions had become inadequate.

Organized public pressure can be one form of such practical political action. The efforts of the European federalist movement after the Second World War led to the establishment of the Council of Europe which was influenced by federalist ideas, and, later on, though indirectly, to the establishment of the European Community.

More important is governmental action in certain fields of international co-operation through which international legal regimes with elements of the rule of law can be introduced. The success in such limited fields could spread to other fields of international co-operation.

One of the most obvious examples of a successful international regime is European regional integration. The functioning of the European Community is based on law and on the possibility to enforce legal rules adopted by Community institutions. Moreover, it is a community based on law and not on power because, among other things, its judicial institution, the European Court of Justice, has actively contributed to the development and implementation of a legal doctrine of integration that has become the theoretical foundation of European Community law.

Another, more recent example, of an international regime, based on law, is the system of the World Trade Organization. In its framework, detailed binding international rules for world trade were adopted and a new effective dispute settlement mechanism will ensure the enforcement of these rules. Thus, it seems that with the results of the Uruguay Round of multilateral trade negotiations and the establishment of the WTO a decisive step towards introducing the rule of law into the world trading system has been undertaken.

Introducing the rule of law into separate spheres of international relations can no doubt promote and enhance the rule of law in international relations. To speak of *the* international rule of law *globally*, however, means that the whole *system* of international relations and of international law should conform to the requirements for the existence of the rule of law: there should be valid binding rules, there should be general rules (principles) with which ordinary rules have to conform, and there should be an effective mechanism of enforcement both of rules and of their conformity with the general principles.

As regards the first of these elements, there can be no doubt about the existence of international law as a normative system of valid legally binding rules (see Georgiev, 1993).

As for the general rules and principles of international law, from the point of view of an international rule of law there are deficiencies, both in respect of their contents and in respect of their status.

As pointed out, it is not clear which exactly are the rules of *jus cogens*. The "general principles of law recognized by civilized nations", which are regarded as sources of international law (Article 38 of the International Court of Justice), also have the potential to serve as "higher" rules, conformity with which is necessary for the rule of the law. But there is no clarity about their contents either.

In 1970 the United Nations General Assembly unanimously adopted the "Declaration of Principles of International Law Relating to Friendly Relations and Co-operation among States" which contains an enumeration and elaboration of several basic principles of international law and has thus brought considerable clarity as to their contents. What remains unclear, however, is the status of these principles and, hence, their ability to serve as "higher" norms of law, necessary for the rule of international law. Ironically, it was the Soviet doctrine of international law that regarded these principles as rules of *jus cogens*, whereas the United States and the United Kingdom denied them such a character (Henkin, 1980: 648).

The international rule of law would require much more clarity with regard both to the contents of the principles of international law and to their status as "higher" norms to which ordinary rules have to conform if these principles are to be a guarantee against political arbitrariness, and to ensure the primacy of the legal over the political and thus a minimum of international order.

From the point of view of the rule of international law, some of the basic principles of international law have systemically a special and particularly important place. It would be difficult to speak of the primacy of the legal over the political, of law over power if, for example, the principle of non-use of force is unclear or if it is not enforced and not observed. Then, even if the other elements of the rule of law were present in the international system, we could not speak of *the* international rule of law.

The other basic element of the international rule of law, enforcement, is probably its weakest point. The acceptance of the compulsory jurisdiction of the International Court of Justice and the enforcement of the rules and principles of international law have to undergo qualitative developments if we want to introduce the rule of international law.

The collapse of totalitarian regimes in Eastern Europe and, as a result, the disappearance of global ideological confrontation with the end of the Cold War, have opened new opportunities for the establishment of the rule of law in the international sphere. The challenge to take advantage of these new possibilities should be faced by governments and statesmen, but also by lawyers - both judges and scholars. Many instruments for the establishment of the rule of international law are present, albeit in a latent and, in some cases, embryonic state, in the international legal system. It is a matter of interpretation and requires the active role of international tribunals, similar to the role the European Court of Justice has played for European integration, to activate and develop these instruments.

The international rule of law is now a real possibility through which the most essential elements of a world order, necessary for the survival and future progress of mankind, could be introduced.

Bibliography

Acheson, D. (1963), 57, *American Society of International Law Proceedings.*
Boichev, D. (1994), *Pravova Darzhava*, Sofia, Jurispres.
Georgiev, D. (1993), "Politics or Rule of Law: Deconstruction and Legitimacy in International Law" 4, *European Journal of International Law.*
Henkin, L. et al (1980), *International Law. Cases and Materials*, St Paul, West Publishing Co.
Morgenthau, Hans J. (1948), *Politics Among Nations. The Struggle for Power and Peace*, New York.
_____ (1951), *In Defense of the National Interest: A Critical Examination of American Foreign Trade*, New York.
Pravda, 26 September, 1968, 4.
Yearbook of the International Law Commission, 1966.

For Product Safety Concerns and Information please contact our EU representative GPSR@taylorandfrancis.com Taylor & Francis Verlag GmbH, Kaufingerstraße 24, 80331 München, Germany

Batch number: 08153774

Printed by Printforce, the Netherlands